THE MYTH OF ISLAMIC BARBARISM AND ITS AIMS

The same French soldier (on the book cover) has just shot the Algerian

S.E Al Djazairi

MSBN BOOKS

S.E. Al-Djazairi: *The Myth of Islamic Barbarism and its Aims*; MSBN Books 2020 edition.

ISBN: 9781973250012

Website: msbnbooks.co.uk
Email: info@msbnbooks.co.uk

© S.E. Zaimeche Al-Djazairi

No resale, reproduction, or downloading of this work on the internet is allowed.
Use of extracts from it is permitted as long as such extracts do not exceed what is necessary to make an argument.

Design and Artwork: N. Kern

Cover: French soldier about to shoot Algerian civilian walking away

S.E Al-Djazairi lectured and researched at the University of Constantine in Algeria. He also tutored at the Department of Geography of the University of Manchester, and worked as a research assistant at UMIST (Manchester) in the field of History of Science. His publications include papers on environmental degradation and desertification, issues of economic and social development, as well as politics and change in North Africa. He also contributed historical entries to various encyclopaedias.

Website: msbnbooks.co.uk
Email: info@msbnbooks.co.uk

Recently Published works by the same author:
Islam in China, 3 vols.
Our Civilisation (5 vols).
The Destruction of the Environment in/of the Muslim World.

CONTENTS

THIS WORK	1
TEN CENTURIES IN THE MANUFACTURE OF AN IMAGE	13
TEN CENTURIES OF PRACTICE IN RESHAPING THE TRUTH	39
SCHOLARSHIP AND PEOPLE OF LETTERS' ROLE	55
THE MEDIEVAL MODELS: THE CRUSADES AND MUSLIMS OF SICILY	74
THE RENAISSANCE, THE OTTOMAN 'THREAT' AND THE MOORS QUESTION	87
THE CONQUEST OF 'BARBARIANS' AND THEIR MASS CLEARING	104
WOMEN	115
CAPTIVES, SLAVES AND RACISTS	130
'TURKISH BARBARISM' AND ITS EFFECTS	163
THE CIVILISING MISSION IN THE LANDS OF ISLAM	175
FROM BOSNIA TO IRAQ	192
THE LATEST: THE 2016 COUP IN TURKEY	208
CONCLUDING WORDS/QUOTES	225
BIBLIOGRAPHY	229

THIS WORK

'The Sword of Islam', 'The Islamic Threat,' 'The Roots of Muslim Rage,' 'The Green Peril,' Islam's New Battle-Cry': in a veritable flood of publications with these and similar titles, various authors seek to explain Islam to us,' says Lueg,[1] who adds:

> Simplified and undifferentiated descriptions of Islam in the media fan the flames of vague fears of a supposed threat to Western culture, and create a hostile image of Islam.
>
> For a long time the Islamic Middle East was seen as the polar opposite of the West and the enemy of Christianity.... Hardly anything on the Middle East, or on historical clashes, or points of contact between the East and the West, is learned in schools. Instead of knowledge or at least an unbiased examination of Islamic societies, we have clichés and stereotypes, which apparently make it easier to deal with the phenomenon of Islam. The Western image of Islam is characterised by ideas of aggression and brutality, fanaticism, irrationality, medieval backwardness and antipathy towards women.[2]

This image, besides its genesis, implications, usages and outcomes, all date centuries back, ten precisely (as shown in Chapters 1-2-3-4). Vitkus writes:

> The demonisation of the Islamic East is a long and deeply-rooted tradition in the West - spanning the centuries, from the early medieval period to the end of the 20th century. It harks back to ancient representation of Eastern empires and invading hordes that predate Islam, including the Assyrians and the Persians of the Ancient World. The Classical and Biblical stereotypes that were established in the collective consciousness of the West were further sharpened and solidified later by the historical experience of 'Holy War' that began with the rise of Islam, continued during the period of the crusades, and endured during the Spanish Reconquista and Ottoman imperialism. In Western Europe, a long history of military aggression and cultural competition (taking place primarily, but not entirely, in the Mediterranean Basin) served as the basis for the prevailing conception of the Islamic 'Orient' during the 16th and 17th centuries.[3]

After the 17th century, as the Ottoman realm began to enter its long phase of decline (18th-19th centuries), whoever Christian took whatever weapon was around and rid himself of the Turks, whilst elsewhere, the Muslim land, just as other lands, were

---

[1] A. Lueg: The Perception of Islam in Western Debate; in *The Next Threat*; edited by J. Hippler and A. Lueg; (Pluto Press;
[2] Ibid.
[3] D.J. Vitkus: Early Modern Orientalism: Representations of Islam in 16th and 17th century Europe; In *Western Views of Islam in Medieval and Early Modern Europe*; D.R. Blanks, and M. Frassetto ed.; (St Martin's Press; New York; 1999); pp. 207-30; at pp. 208-9.

carved up between the now vigorous and triumphant Europeans.[4] France and Britain, the most vigorous and triumphant of the lot, gleaned the most, and other Europeans got the rest. Often the sharing out got a bit out of hands, and led to squabble over the choicest bits (India and Egypt, for instance), and when Morocco's turn to be gobbled came (in 1912,) the case went to the First World War Court (just as squabble over former Ottoman territory in the wake of the Balkan wars (1912-1913) led to more conflict, which eventually fuelled the rancour and ferocity of the First World War. The turn of Turkey herself arrived at some point (1918-19), ready to be carved up, in fact not just Turkey, but also China and even Russia (after the 1917 Bolshevik Revolution),[5] but these three countries got away with it; not the moribund Arab world, though, which was sliced according to lines drawn by Sykes and Picot.[6]

As Muslims by now lay vanquished, under firm Western Control, they served as canon fodder in more than one place (First and Second World Wars, Spanish Civil War (1936-1939) Vietnam (1945-1954)...) whilst their lands were being systematically looted. Now, the centuries old Islam and Muslim savagery, backwardness, etc, had no reason d'etre and so were pushed back.
In the second half of the 20th century, the Cold War raged between the ex Soviet Union and the West, and Muslims served the anti Bolshevik cause, doing a lot of the dying in places such as Vietnam, Afghanistan, Korea, even. Consequently, their usual barbarism and threat were relegated to the background. During that time, it was left wingers, the world over, especially in Central and Southern America, who were the focus of the ire of the civilised world, being liquidated in their hundreds of thousands. The CIA led the task, assisted by the Church here, thugs there, International Aid Agencies elsewhere, and the media everywhere. Then, suddenly, as the Soviet Union began to unravel, throughout much of the 1980s (in large measure thanks to fickle Muslims), the West rediscovered the centuries old foe again. Takeyh and Gvosdev sum up this new phase for us:

> Having triumphed over Communism, the Western system of free-market economics and liberal pluralist democracy was now seemingly under threat from a new rival, for "with the death of communism, Islam is the global alternative," energized into a mass movement following the Gulf War. Samuel

---

[4] T. Gordon, *History of the Greek Revolution*, 2 vols; Edinburgh, William Blackwood, 1832. J. McCarthy: *Death and Exile: The Ethnic Cleansing of Ottoman Muslims, 1821-1922* (Princeton, NJ: Darwin Press, 1995. S.J. Shaw and E.K. Shaw: *History of the Ottoman Empire and Modern Turkey*, Cambridge University Press, 2 vols; 1976.
F. McCullagh: *Italy's War for a Desert;* Herbert and Daniel; London; 1912.
[5] For some details see: Li Ung Bing: *Outlines of Chinese History*, edited by J. Whiteside, Shanghai, Commercial Press, 1914, pp. 594-595. For sources, see our Islam in China vol 3. Appropriate chapters or extracts; but best to consult the work by Hosea Ballou Morse: *The International Relations of the Chinese Empire*, vol 3, the Period of subjection, 1894-1911; Paragon Book Gallery; 1918, especially chapter 5, pp. 101 fwd. For Russia see: F.B. Reeves: Russia Then and Now, 1892-1917; G.P. Putnam's Son, 1917, pp. 3-39. RUSSIA. No. 1 (1919). A Collection of Reports o Bolshevism in Russia, Presented to Parliament by Command of His Majesty. April 1919. London, Published by His Majesty's Stationary Office, 1919; George Stewart: *The White Armies, a Chronicle of Counter Revolution and Allied Intervention, New York*, The MacMillan Company; 1933. F. McCullagh: *A Prisoner of the Reds, The Story of a British Officer Captured in Siberia*, John Murray, London, 1921.
[6] E. Mead: *The Baghdad Railway; A Study in Imperialism*; MacMillan; New York; 1924.

P. Huntington warned his audience that 'the Islamic Resurgence has manifested itself in every Muslim country; in almost all it has become a major social, cultural, and intellectual movement, and in most it has had a deep impact on politics." Hassan al-Turabi of Sudan confidently predicted, 'Objectively, the future is ours," and Western scholars began to echo his assessment by predicting that 'the future of the Muslim world lies with the Islamic political alternative." The emergence of an international radical Muslim network, epitomized by Al-Qaeda, an outgrowth of the guerilla struggle waged against the Soviet Union in Afghanistan during the 1980s, seemed to presage a new chapter in the struggle of militant Islam against the West.[7]

According to many Western commentators [Esposito noted just when the war on Islam began in 1992]

> Islam and the West are on a collision course. Islam is a triple threat: political, demographic, and socio-religious. For some, the nature of the Islamic threat is intensified by the linkage of the political and the demographic.[8]

Patrick Buchanan could write that while

> Negotiating for hostages with Shiite radicals who hate and detest us, ... their Muslim brothers are populating Western countries. The Muslim threat is global in nature as Muslims in Europe, the Soviet Union, and America proliferate and prosper.[9]

> Other observers, such as Charles Krauthammer, in the midst of the un-ravelling of the Soviet Union, spoke of a global Islamic uprising, a vision of Muslims in the heartland and on the periphery of the Muslim world rising up in revolt: a 'new "arc of crisis"... another great movement is going on as well, unnoticed but just as portentous: a global intifada.'[10]

Hippler and Lueg, writing in the mid 1990s, also noted how:

> In almost all forms of the media, 'experts' seek to enlighten us on the new dangers from the East: holy wars, fanatical masses, the revenge of the Middle Ages on modernity and of religion on the Enlightenment. Islam is sometimes a challenge, sometimes a threat. The conquest of Vienna by the Turks is apparently once again imminent. With Khomeini, Gaddafi, Saddam Hussein, Arafat and the Algerian fundamentalists, the anti-Western wave is rolling on, at any rate splashing across popular magazines and television screens. The threat might be a spiritual one, an Oriental counter-model to Western civilisation; it might result in stopping the flow of oil, or in a cultural invasion by immigrants from Turkey to the Maghreb. It might lie in the Islamic atom bomb, in terrorism or in a threatened Islamic fundamentalist world revolution in the Iranian mould. Simple minds might even see it as a battle of

---

[7] R. Takeyh and N.K. Gvosdev: The Receding Shadow of the Prophet, Praeger, London, 2004, p. 1; for quotes within the quote, see Takeyh and Gvosdev.
[8] J. Esposito: *The Islamic Threat;* Myth or Reality? (Oxford University Press; 1992); p. 175.
[9] P. J. Buchanan: Rising Islam may overwhelm the West; *New Hampshire Sunday News;* August 20; 1989.
[10] C. Krauthammer: The New Crescent of Crisis: Global Intifada; *Washington Post*; February 16; 1990.

Islam against Christianity, or against unbelievers. In Europe and the USA all these perceptions of threats exist, sometimes side by side and at other times separately. Sometimes they crop up suddenly and compete with each other, and at other times they are systematized and compounded, all depending on what is required or desired in a particular situation.[11]

Coming at the perfect time to confirm the post Cold War newly rediscovered truth there occurred 9/11. Some of the repercussions will be seen as the book progresses. In words, it put the Islamic agenda back to sometime before the First World War, except under new forms. Muslims, whether their works, movements, or private lives, including their copulating with their spouses, all came under careful Western and their allies' scrutiny. Of course, tens of thousands of Islamists/'terrorists' have since been slain, thousands disappeared, and the coffers of many organisations dried of funds. The act (9/11) not only legitimised and justified the previous and much else, it most of all re-confirmed the centuries old image: the evil side of Islam. Feverishly the whole and powerful Western apparatus of opinion making, regardless of its form, or political and ideological leanings, resumed the rhetoric now so well burnished since the medieval period. We shall see that in most chapters. In the meantime, everybody's else crimes were disappeared from the surface. Forgotten became the CIA's crimes, and so were the Serbs', Croats', colonial powers', mass murdering Christian Lebanese', Israelis' in Palestine, despotic mass murdering Muslim regimes', South and Central American death squad leaders', and whoever else slew and tortured en masse previously, or was still at it (in the Muslim world or of Muslims these days.) And each time people tended to deviate their focus, or slightly begin to forget, there the Islamist beast strikes again. Its outrages fuel the old diatribe and, of course, the by now necessary forceful retributions.

In the years 2000s War on (Islamic) Terror, led by Blair and Bush and their teams, setting aside what was happening in Afghanistan, at different interrogation sites (including in Muslim lands), and most of all in Iraq, to which we shall return, it seemed all Muslims had become guilty by association with the faith. In 2006, following a dawn raid by British police, and the arrests of two alleged Muslim 'terrorists' involved in a 'chemical' plot, to the remark by a journalist that the two arrested men were law-abiding citizens, a member of the British government stated that terrorists hide behind the law-abiding veneer.[12] Today, even kosher Muslims: drunkards, gamblers, drug takers, homosexuals (as in the recent Paris attacks (November 2015) and in Florida (12 June 2016,) are all at it: Islam the carrier of the terrorism gene as understood and explained by the leading experts (to whom we shall devote plenty of space in this work). In *De L'Islam en general et du monde moderne en particulier,* the Frenchman, Jean Claude Barreau, holds:

---

[11] J. Hippler and A. Lueg: Introduction; in *The Next Threat*; op cit; p. 1.
[12] Interview on Newsnight BBC2 2 June 06; seen by this author.

> What could be described as the "great humiliation", and what is indeed present in the basic disposition of the Muslims, can be explained by the origins of their religion: it is warlike, conquest-hungry and full of contempt for the unbeliever.[13]
>
> Islam as a whole is presented as the aggressor against the West. It embodies 'a theology of conquest and victory, but no theology of defeat'.[14]

According to the American news magazine *Time*,

> This is the dark side of Islam, which shows its face in violence and terrorism, intended to overthrow modernizing, more secular regimes and harm the Western nations that support them.[15]

All agree, even those with some empathy for Islam, such as the wonderfully humane Christian theologian, Hans Kung, who tells us how, unlike Christianity, Islam is corroded by violence in its very foundation:

> The question then, that I would ask Muslims in a religious dialogue is, can we say the same thing about Muhammad? Can he become in the same way a critical corrective, a court of appeals on these matters? Isn't it true that a Muslim who wishes to use violence in reaching his political/religious goals can invoke Muhammad in general and in particular, even as Marxist Leninist can invoke Marx and Lenin in staging violent and bloody revolutions? On this point, at least, Friederich Durrenmatt is surely right when he notes in his worthwhile essay on the relations between Judaism, Christianity and Islam: Muhammad, of course, has nothing in common with Jesus.... But Muhammad can well be compared to Paul and to Karl Marx.'[16] An important problem arises here, which needs to be discussed: Christians can never honestly invoke Jesus of Nazareth to bless violence, hatred, killing and war - even though this implies and creates a burden of pain for the peacemakers.[17]

In words, as Daniel notes:

> A wicked Muslim was thought to act out of the nature of his creed; a wicked Christian could always be found an excuse. All the sins of the Christians, generally the same sins as the Muslims', were either to be explained away, or at least condemned as contrary to Christian discipline.[18]

Indeed, an individual, or a group, can only act in an evil manner as directed by their religion if they were Muslims. Neither the IRA in Northern Ireland, nor the Maronites of Lebanon who slew tens of thousands of Muslims in Lebanon long before 'Muslim terrorists' discovered the thrills of killing unarmed men, women or women, small or old, have ever been accused of acting in the name of Christianity.[19] Likewise, the recent (22 July 2011) Norwegian mass murderer, Breivik, had nothing

---

[13] J.C. Barreau: *De l'Islam en General et du Monde Moderne en Particulier*, (Paris: Belfont le Pres aux Clercs; 1991).
[14] Ibid.
[15] 'The Dark Side of Islam'; *Time Magazine*; 4 October 1993; p. 62.
[16] *Collected Works*, Vol 29, pp. 54 f.
[17] H. Kung et al: *Christianity and the World Religions*; (Doubleday; London, 1986); p. 93.
[18] N. Daniel: *The Arabs and Medieval Europe*; Longman Librarie du Liban; 1975, p. 243.
[19] The list of their crimes would make shocking reading. Their massacres of Palestinians at Tell Azaatar, the Qarantaine, and throughout the 1970s, besides Sabra and Chatilla, are possibly some of the most horrific recorded in history.

whatsoever to do with Christian-White-Supremacists; he was just yet another bad apple; never mind if such bad apples fill few crates already, and we are not talking of the crates in the large depots of history. In a fairly recent programme on the BBC, a member of the panel noted that when children in the UK were asked "What is a Muslim?" the answer from all was: a terrorist.[20]

Many, if not most, if not all crimes and outrages committed in the name of Islam these days are simply acts that repel the senses of anyone, including Muslims'. The killing of the British soldier, Lee Rigby, in the late Spring of 2013, for instance, is simply a repellent act, and so is the killing of the two Scandinavian women in Morocco (17 December 2018). And we could say the same about the authors of acts such as in the Manchester Arena or stabbings in London (3 June 2017), and others. Beyond this, do these acts serve Islam? Only a subhuman could say yes to this. Under the Islamic beard and garb lurks the most vile. We experienced this in Algeria in the 1990s, and we know the vile genesis, nature, and ends of these acts. Anyone can be anyone, or anything, and then can claim to murder and slaughter in the name of Islam. Timur the Lame did it in the years 1388-1402. With the rarest of exceptions, the millions of his victims were Sunni Muslims.[21] Those who kill today in the name of Islam in Western streets as in the Muslim land do it on behalf, or under the patronage, of concealed dark agencies. These murders, just as the whole ISIS masquerade, are not easy to put in place. They demand considerable logistics only large state organisations (and many states working together) are capable of. The best of Muslims have been the chief targets of these murderers in recent decades. In the recent Syrian conflict were slain not just civilians, but also imams, scholars, and leading commanders and fighters amongst the Islamic resistance. At Istanbul Airport (Summer 2016) were gunned down tens of people, the veiled, the unveiled, the old and young. Anyone can kill if such killing(s) served strategic purposes of the Killing Agency, and dress the act in the by now convenient Islamist

---

[20] BBC 1 Question Time; early 2003, seen by this author.
[21] Ibn Khaldūn: *Kitāb al-ʿibar*, V: 506. See also Ibn Khaldūn, *Al-taʿrīf*, Lajnat al-taʾlīf wa-al-tarjamah wa-al-nashr, 1951; 382. In *Al-taʿrīf*, Ibn Khaldūn also refers to Timur and his troops as mughul numerous times (Ibn Khaldūn, Al-taʿrīf, 365). We also find them as altaṭar/al-tatar in numerous places (e.g. Ibn Khaldūn, Al-taʿrīf, 366, 380, 381, 382). Al Maqrizi: *Kitab as-Suluk*, MS Paris, No. 1728. For this and the following MSS, see de Slane, Catalogue des manuscrits arabes dans la Bibliotheque Nationale, Paris, 1883-1895.
Al-Manhal as-Safi, MS Paris, Nos. 2069-2071, and *an-Nujum az-Zahira*, ed. W. Popper, Berkeley, Vol. V, 1932-1936; Vol. VI, 1915-1923; History of Egypt (1382-1411) translated from the Arabic Annals of Ibn Taghri Birdi by W. Popper, University of California Publ. in Semitic Philology, Vols. 13 and 14, Berkeley, 1954.
J. Schiltberger: The Bondage and Travels of Johann Schiltberger, a native of Bavaria, in Europe, Asia, and Africa, 1396-1427; tr. from the Heildelberg Ms. Edited in 1859 by Friedrich Neumann; London, the Hakluyt Society; 1879; pp. 27-8. Sylvester de Sacy: Memoire sur une correspondence inedited entre Tamerlan et Charles VI; *Extrait du Moniteur*; No 226; 1812; pp. 7-8; A.S. Atiya: *The Crusade in the Later Middle Ages*; op cit; pp. 256-7.
J.H. Wylie: *History of England under Henry IV*; Longman; London; 1884. Timur to [John VII] the regent of Constantinople, 15 May 1402, in Alexandrescu-Dersca, M.M., *La campagne de Timur en Anatolie (1402)* (Bucarest, 1942, repr. London, 1977); pp. 123-4. Letter of Gerardo Sagredo, 12 Oct. 1402, ibid, p. 131. Clavijo, p. 93 (tr. Le Strange, p. 135). H. Moranville, Memoire sur Tamerlan et sa cour par un Dominicain, en 1403, *BBC* 55 (1894), pp. 441-64 (here p. 453). 65. Ibid., p. 454. *Chronographia regum Francorum*, III, p. 220.
Beltramo da Mignanelli, 'Vita Tamerlani' (1416), in Et. Baluze, ed., *Miscellanea novo ordine digesta et non paucis ineditis...*, new ed by J.D. Mansi, *N* (Lucca, 1764), p. 138; partial tr. Waiter J. Fischel, 'A new Latin source on Tamerlane's conquest of Damascus (1400/1401)', *Oriens* 9 (1956), pp. 201-32.

terror garb. These actions take place within the whole anti Islam framework, for purposes we shall look at this work. Their persistence is also fed by the fact that the Western media and Western academia (and its experts on Islam), politicians and other opinion makers, and their allies in the Muslim world give it credence (we shall see plenty of that in Chapter 3, and note how only a rumour or a claim is turned by these extremely influential voices into truth). It suits theirs and others' purposes, and is even their reason d'etre. The lives of Muslims or Westerners victims of 'Muslim terrorists' hardly, if at all, matter; more than often, in fact, the 'Islamist terrorist' does everyone a good service. Again, in Algeria we know one or two things about this: the French media and academia, politicians, and even the Catholic Church and so-called Human Right Agencies remain largely responsible in abetting and legitimising the 1990s macabre Islamist killing masquerade which cost 250,000 Algerian lives.[22]

We just said it: purposes, Aims. As during the past millennium, as to be shown in Chapters 2 to 5 and 8 to 12, Muslim misdeeds, real, imagined, invented, or exaggerated, are exploited by the West for a multitude of ends. Without such Muslim misdeeds again real, invented or exaggerated, and Western use of them, we would have to cut the history from the crusades (1095-1291) till Iraq 2003- and Syria 2011- by 90%. And it will be the same in the future if people are interested to know. It will be again in response to whatever came from the Muslim side that action would come from the Western side sometime in the mid late 2020s.

Without a doubt, there are awful Muslims out there, and one has come across quite many of them; their vileness at times surpassing that of the worst villains in films about villains. Surely, too, there are and there always be Muslim misdeeds and misdeeds committed in the name of Islam by vile, innate murderers, foolish, even mad Muslims, misdeeds which cannot be avoided even in a near perfect world. However, we all know that mass murderers and genocide perpetrators have always existed and even thrived in the Christian West.[23] It is not because they are now being disappeared from knowledge by the vast Western industry of distortions thriving in the media, academia, the Church, and cultural and political institutions that they never existed. Should anyone begin to put the focus on Western crimes, no encyclopaedia in 50 volumes would be large enough. Also examining the situation around, all what one can see is that the vastest majority of victims of organised terror and violence are Muslims themselves. Taking any moment at random in 2014, for instance, will show us true the odd Muslim outrage in Pakistan with the woman stoned to death by her family, or the woman condemned to death for apostasy in the Sudan, the hundred or so demonstrators chased away by Turkish police, and maybe one other forgotten event. The observer would also see the

---

[22] See Lounis Aggoun- Jean baptiste Rivoire: *Francalgerie: Crimes et Mensonges d'Etat*; La Decouverte; 2005.
[23] See, for instance:
-W. Howitt: *Colonisation and Christianity*: (Longman; London; 1838).
D. E. Stannard: *American Holocaust; The Conquest of the New World;* (Oxford University Press; 1992).

thousands being bombed and gassed in Syria, the thousands being slain in Egypt by the Western propped up latest dictatorship, and the tens of thousands more being daily tortured there, besides the thousands of Muslims being slain in Central Africa, and so on. The difference is, whilst the former outrages in Pakistan, the Sudan, and Turkey fill the Western news networks, the latter from Egypt, Central Africa, and elsewhere, hardly seem to benefit of any publicity, and, when they are briefly noted, they are generally explained away or dismissed through some other diversionary technique; this will form the focus of Chapter Two.

Muslims today are intellectually pathetic. Whether secularists or Islamists, the latter in particular, they have no solid intellect that can formulate a vision encompassing issues of economic, social, environmental or intellectual/artistic dimensions that challenge the Western (unfortunately we cannot tell you anything about this here, as it might lead us astray, but you can find more in our chapter 3 of the *West, Islam, Barbarism and Civilisation*, which explains to you how Muslim deciders operate). Lamentably, Muslim elites, or call them intellectuals if you want but they are not, cannot even formulate an adequate narrative of history or even a narrative of present reality, even their own. Let's give you an instance here. Relying on the lame condition of Turkish 'intellectuals'/elites (historians, cultural agencies, media...) (a couple of exceptions aside such as the now sadly defunct: Salahi Sonyel,) (lameness also shared by the whole Muslim world) the West has made of Turkey the chief criminal in history. 'The Turkish genocide of Armenians' during the First World War (1914-1918) is claimed to be the crime, the horror of the First World War, or any war for that matter.[24] In fact, Turkey is the only country in the world that has to carry this burden, and what is even worse is that it is made to carry it by 'its friends and allies.' And much worse even, it refuses to take appropriate measures to deal with the situation; but that is its choice. Never mind, this 'Turkish Crime' serves the central element of always having one common culprit of all world outrages: Islam. The crime is indeed attributed to the Ottomans when in reality Turkey, at the time of the alleged crime was ruled by a trio of incompetent thugs who could not even put in place a decent military operation throughout the whole First World War, and who, with their group (The CUP), about a decade earlier, in 1908, had ended Ottoman rule.[25] This 'Turkish crime' serves as cover up for the civilised (Turkey's friends and allies and authors of the Armenian genocide narrative) own crimes such as the mass eradication of natives in the Americas and elsewhere,[26] of their mass killings of Muslims, whether during the crusades, or their eradication in the West,

---

[24] The latest by AFP on yahoo news on 22 February 2014. Seen at 18.06. **World War I root of Mideast conflict, Armenian genocide;** by Philippe Alfroy.
[25] To have an idea on this, see this author's works on Turkey at MSBN Books, 2015-7. The readers should not look at what this author says but what the sources of the time themselves tell us, sources he details in great amount.
[26] Western Crimes in South East Asia, see: J. Crawfurd: *History of the Indian Archipelago*; Archibald Constable & Company; Edinburgh; 1820. W. Howitt: *Colonisation and Christianity*: Longman; London; 1838. W. Churchill: *A Little Matter of Genocide*; City Lights Books; San Francisco; 1997.

or the crimes of the colonial era, or the recent genocide of the Tutsis in Rwanda.[27] The Turks themselves were mass exterminated in the Balkans and Greece (millions of Turks were slain between 1806 and 1913 as detailed in chapter 9.)[28]

The West uses this generalised Muslim intellectual impotence to reshape every type of narrative. Even the recent massacres of Palestinians by Christians in Lebanon, the Bosnian genocide, the bloody invasions of Iraq, Lebanon and Afghanistan, and the tens of thousands of Muslims murdered by dictatorships sponsored by the West, all now are buried deep, and away from memory. Only this author annoys everyone by bringing some of it out (the rest of Muslim 'intellectuals' (exceptions aside) are too corrupt and too coward to say anything), although to be fair, this author does it unwillingly only to make an argument, and does his best to only bring out less than 0.1% of such filth. But such is the narrative of history today that, even France, the slaughterer in chief, responsible for the killing of millions of Algerians during its colonial period (1830-1962)[29] (as we shall see in chapter 10) has made itself into a nation of civilisers.[30] In regard to the latter, it must be said, a few exceptions aside, Algerian elites' lameness is responsible for this macabre hocus pocus.

Never mind, Daniel, again, makes a very interesting observation:

> Apparently, under the pressure of their sense of danger, whether real or imagined, a deformed image of their enemy's beliefs takes shape in men's minds. By misapprehension and misrepresentation, a notion of the ideas and beliefs of one society can pass into the accepted myths of another society, in a form so distorted that its relation to the original facts is sometimes barely discernible. Doctrines that are the expression of the spiritual outlook of an enemy are interpreted ungenerously and with prejudice, and even the facts are modified - and in good faith - to suit the interpretation. In this way is constituted a body of belief about what another group of people believes. A

---

[27] On French crimes in Algeria, see: H. Alleg; J. de Bonis, H.J. Douzon, J. Freire, P. Haudiquet: *La Guerre d'Algerie;* 3 vols, Temps Actuels; Paris, 1981.
On Crusaders mass killings, see: G.W. Cox: *The Crusades*; Longmans; London; 1874.
R. Finucane: *Soldiers of the Faith*; J.M. Dent and Sons Ltd; London, 1983.
On the eradication of Muslims in the West, such as in Spain, see: S. Lane-Poole: *The Moors in Spain;* Fisher Unwin; London; 1888.
-H.C. Lea: *The Moriscos of Spain*; Burt Franklin; New York; 1968 reprint.
-H. C. Lea: *A History of the Inquisition of Spain*, 4 vols; The Mac Millan Company, New York, 1907.
On the tragic fate of Muslims in the Balkans, see: J. McCarthy: *Death and Exile: The Ethnic Cleansing of Ottoman Muslims, 1821-1922*; The Darwin Press; New Jersey; 1995.
[28] W. Alison Phillips: *The War of Greek Independence 1821-1833*; Charles Scribner's Sons, New York; 1897; pp. 56-61; see also T. Gordon, *History of the Greek Revolution*, 2 vols; Edinburgh, William Blackwood, 1832.
See Foreign office reports; also R. Millman: *Britain and the Eastern Question*; Oxford; 1979; pp. 125-89.
 J. McCarthy: *Death and Exile: The Ethnic Cleansing of Ottoman Muslims, 1821-1922*; The Darwin Press; New Jersey; 1995.
-Gustav Cirilli: *Journal du siege d'Adrianople*; Paris, 1913.
-Ernst Jäckh; *Deutschland im Orient nach dem Balkan-Krieg;* Chapter 7: Deutsche und französische Augenzeugen von christlichen Massakers. (Die Balkangreuel des 30 jährigen Krieges); Martin Mörikes Verlag, Munich, 1913; pp. 83-98.
-P. Loti: *Turquie Agonisante*; Calman Levy; Paris; 1913.
[29] M. Lacheraf, in L. Blin: *l'Algerie du Sahara au Sahel*, l'Harmattan, Paris, 1990; note 3; p. 112.
See also D. Sari: *La Depossession des Fellahs 1830-1962;* SNED; Algiers; 1978.
[30] On 23 February, 2005, the French National Assembly passed an act which declared and imposed on high school teachers to teach the positive values of colonialism to their students (article 4, paragraph 2).

> 'real truth' is identified: this is something that contrasts with what the enemy say they believe; they must not be allowed to speak for themselves. This doctrine about doctrine is widely repeated, and confirmed by repetition in slightly varying forms. The experts, perhaps because being close to the facts is a constant stimulus to their zeal, contribute more to the process, and they are themselves of course wholly convinced by it.[31]

Repeating and confirming by repetition and claims that Islam/Muslims equate with the dark and barbaric now dwells deep in the Western psyche. It is quite revealing that in a recent book on Islam, when referring to the crusaders' capture of the city of Jerusalem in 1099 and the slaying of its entire Muslim and Jewish population by the Christians, the writer of the caption on this event, instead, writes:

> The capture of Jerusalem by the crusaders in 1099 was a bloody affair, in which the mostly Christian population was put to the sword.[32]

This error is not a reflection of an author's lapse of attention. It reflects the Western psyche towards Islam and Muslims today that evil can only come from the vile who is known to all since the medieval period.

We said it, already, intellectually or in any way, Muslims hardly help their cause, rather the opposite. Not only are they impotent intellectually or in any field for that matter, unless it is crass, they come out as threatening even in their vestments. The male imposes himself thanks to his darkish looks, thick beard, gandouras over trousers, or vice versa, or some clothing mish-mash none can decipher. The camera always makes sure to capture his facial expression at its worst deformity, or when he is applying the siwak on his teeth. For females, the focus is on burkas, and the darker and more off-putting the garment the better; and if the woman wears gloves on hot summer days, even greater focus is put on the detail. But why are we mentioning this stuff here? It is crucial as we show in chapter 2; especially in an age where the visual or image/picture conveys or reinforces the established preconceived views of the would be target(s) and justifies actions towards it/them (remember how the Nazis portrayed the Jews in the 1930s, it was more potent than any discourse by Goebbels).

When you have created this character threatening, unattractive (repulsive in fact) and the like, you can do to him or her, and to their whole tribe, not forgetting their progeny, anything you wish, you are only rendering a great service to humanity.

Of course, you can earn yourself more legitimacy if you manage to show these creatures' inferiority. Muslims being locked in the mess they are locked in today, it confirms their other barbaric nature (defined as antithesis to civilisation), also a fruit of their, by now agreed by all: vile faith. A whole Western academic apparatus is at work in confirming this and in spreading it wide, including via Muslim academics in their own lands and wherever they cogitate.[33] We shall, indeed, give

---

[31] N. Daniel: *Islam and the West;* (One World; Oxford; 1993); ed.; p. 12.
[32] P. Lunde: *Islam;* (Dorling Kindersley; London; 2002); p. 63.
[33] See works by S.E. Al-Djazairi who drowns you in instances of the sort so much so until you are convinced.

you a thorough idea about these academics and other clever people who write books, for, with the Church, they are responsible for 99% of Muslim woes throughout history, recent and even today in particular. Throughout this work, in fact, you will notice that those who carried swords or guns, or knives, to cull Muslims were inspired and guided by these clever clogs, whilst generally Church personnel danced in triumph at the sight of Muslim corpses, whether during in the Crusades (1095-1291) or in the Lebanese Civil War (1975-1980s) or in Bosnia (1992-1995).

Together with academia, the media, including in the Muslim world, bombards the minds with the same. Other than besmirching the faith, the wrong diagnosis of the causes of the Muslim malady (blaming the faith) makes the malady even worse. This, in turn, confirms the long (medieval) established Western views, thus legitimising both Western discourse and action on the ground, hence more Western meddling and bastonading of Muslims, and the same sorry saga goes on and on, and will go on and on for a long while to come.

This is what we try to narrate in this work

Structurally, this book is in 12 chapters (not counting this introductory one). It begins (chapter 1) by looking at the Western picture/view of Islam and Muslim societies, born in the Middle Ages and continuing down the centuries till our time, changing slightly in form but always retaining the same substance. Chapter 2 shows the manner such views and the exploitation of perceived Muslim threat/violence/barbarism in words, or even (when necessary) the pagan/heretical/and much else that Islam represents were reshaped or shaped so as to serve, justify, and legitimise Western retribution of the Muslim fiend. People, including Muslims, of course, blame what they call Islamophobia on the media. Of course, this is an idiotic claim, for Islamophobia or hatred of all things to do with Islam dates centuries before the media was born. The media is just a means in the hands of whoever owns it. *The Independent* in the UK and *Liberation* in France, for instance, used to be more left wing than this author, and now they are even more right wing than him (compared to his students days, he has shifted considerably to the right, in fact; but in his case it took tens of years, in theirs, as soon as the new man with the cash appeared, oops, everyone illico-presto moved to the other side.) The true culprits of anti Islamic rhetoric are the Church in the first place and Western academia and men and women of letters. We show throughout the role of the Church. We shall show the role of the others in chapter 3. Just like the Church, both academia and men and women of letters do, indeed, justify or legitimise, and even worse, give intellectual credibility to Western or anyone else (for that matter) reasons to punish Muslims; they, moreover, thanks to their eloquence and academic/intellectual veneer stir emotions to such levels as to make those who do the retribution of the Muslim fiend even harsher in their retribution. This justified/legitimised retribution is looked at in Chapters 4 and 5. As it proved to be an excellent method/technique, it was also applied in a few more places such as the

Americas (Chapter 6). As history breeds situations that carry much negative aspect or fall out, we are referring to the slave trade, issues of race, mistreatment of captives and women, the twin roles of Islam, as a dark agency, and Christianity/the West, as a force of good, take central stage. This is done in Chapters 7 and 8. Chapters 9-10-11 cross time and space bringing us to our millennium to show that everywhere, all the time, it is service as usual, nothing changed. Chapter 12 reinforces this previous and sad assessment: the failed coup in Turkey in 2016 was lamented, not the coup itself as some idiots might still be thinking despite all what we said already, but lamented for its failure; lamented mainly by the friends and allies of Turkey, and also friends/lovers of Muslims who deem coups of good services to Muslims. Which means, I am afraid to say….

One

TEN CENTURIES IN THE MAKING OF AN IMAGE

Daniel writes:
> The earliest Christian reactions to Islam were much the same as they have been until quite recently. The tradition has been continuous and it is still alive. Naturally there has been variety within the wider unity of the tradition and the European and the (American) West has long had its own characteristic view, which was formed in the two centuries or so after 1100, and which has been modified only slowly since. One chief reason for continuity has been not only the normal passage of ideas from one author to the next, but the constant nature of the problem. The points in which Christianity and Islam differ have not changed, so that Christians have always tended to make the same criticisms; and even when, in relatively modern times, some authors have self-consciously tried to emancipate themselves from Christian attitudes, they have not generally been as successful as they thought.[34]

Likewise, Rodinson remarks that, Western depictions of Islam 'for the most part, contemptuous and uncomprehending,' have continued basically unchanged since the Middle Ages.[35] For over fourteen centuries now, Scott observes, no religion has suffered more than Islam.[36] 'Nobody is afraid of Buddhism or Hinduism; vis a vis Islam, however, fear is the normal attitude,' points out Van Ess; and it does not date just from the oil crisis (of 1973) and the Islamic revolution (in Iran in 1979), but again, travels back to the Middle Ages, and remains constant at all epochs.[37] 'Imagination and fear,' Scott observes:
> Painted the Saracens as a race of incarnate fiends, whose aspect was far more frightful, whose atrocities were far more ruthless, than those of the Huns who had been routed by Aetius four hundred years before on the plains of Chalons. The lapse of twelve centuries has not sufficed to dispel this superstitious dread, and the Saracen, as a monster and a burglar, still figures in the nursery tales and rhymes of Central France.[38]

This long established onslaught based on lies, and meant to spawn the worst fears, has also been amply noted by Tolan,[39] Sardar and Davies,[40] Southern,[41] and others.[42]

---

[34] N. Daniel: *Islam and the West*; op cit; p. 11.
[35] M. Rodinson: *Europe and the Mystique of Islam*; tr. by R. Veinus; (I.B. Tauris and Co Ltd; London; 1988); p. 35.
[36] S.P. Scott: *History of the Moorish Empire in Europe*; 3 vols; (J.B. Lippincott Company, 1904); vol: 3; p. 58.
[37] J. Van Ess: Islamic perspectives, in H. Kung et al. *Christianity and the World Religions*; Orbis Books, 1993; p. 5.
[38] S. P. Scott: *History of the Moorish Empire*; op cit; Vol 3; p. 334.
[39] J. V. Tolan ed., *Medieval Christian Perceptions of Islam* (Routledge; London; 1996).
[40] Z. Sardar; M.W. Davies: *Distorted Imagination*; (Grey Seal Books; London, 1990).

The disgrace of the Christians [Daniel holds] was to attack Islam for so many reasons.... In this area we can only say that Europeans have on the whole maintained towards the Arabs a constant reserve which seems to run consistently through the whole medieval period up to the present day.[43]

So, Back to the Beginnings: The Middle Ages:

The firing shots came from the East. John of Damascus (c.675/676-749), wrote that there arose among the Arabs a man named Mamed, who became acquainted with the Old and New Testaments, and later, after discoursing with an Arian monk, 'established his own sect', which he imagined to be a new religion.[44]

The view of Islam as 'a satanic scheme' had its roots in the writings of eighth-century eastern Christian polemicists. Peter the Venerable (1092-1156) in turn considered Mohammed in relation to Anus and the Antichrist. In the Prologue to the *Summa* the abbot justified this connection by stating that:

In no way could anyone of the human race, unless the devil were there helping, devise such fables.... By means of them... this Satan had as his object particularly and in every way to bring it about that Christ the Lord would not be believed to be the Son of God and true God, the creator and redeemer of the human race.[45]

Just around that time, Gauthier de Compiègne (1010-1070) held that Mohammed was a poor child, but was raised by a baron who made his fortune in Persia, India and Ethiopia, and whose trust Mohammed wins, before a Christian hermit teaches him about the Old and New Testaments.[46] In *L'Entrée d'Espagne*, a later poem, the Prophet is described as a former Christian leader frustrated at being denied the Papacy,[47] hence driving him to start a new religion. Before then, it was a monk who became a cardinal named Nicolas, who to take revenge on his attackers, makes of the Prophet the instrument of his revenge. Then Nicolas becomes the Prophet himself, hence Mohammed was initially in Rome, celebrated and adulated, but because angry for not having been elected pope, founds a new rival religion.[48]

---

[41] In R.W. Southern: *Western Views of Islam in the Middle Ages*, (Harvard University Press, 1978).
[42] D.R. Blanks, and M. Frassetto *Western Views of Islam*; op cit. N. Daniel: *The Arabs and Medieval Europe*; (Longman Librarie du Liban; 1975).
[43] N. Daniel: *The Arabs*; op cit; p. 319.
[44] John of Damascus: *De Haeresibus*, Patrologia Graeca, vol. 94, 761.71; in G. Von Grunebaum: *Medieval Islam* (The Chicago University Press; 1969), p. 43.
[45] J. S. Geary: Arredondo's *Castillo Inexpugnable de la fee*: Anti Islamic propaganda in the Age of Charles V; in J. V. Tolan ed., *Medieval Christian Perceptions of Islam*, op cit; pp. 291-311; at p. 304.
[46] Gauthier de Compiègne: *Otia Machometi*; in E. Edelstand du Méril, *Poesies populaires latines du moyen âge* (Paris, 1977).
[47] *L'entrée d'Espagne, Chanson de Geste Franco-Italienne*; ed., A. Thomas; 2 vols (Paris; 1913), I, cii, II, 2444-64.
[48] E. Doutte: Mahomet Cardinal, in *Memoires de la societe d'agriculture... sciences et arts de la Marne*; Second serie; vol 1; 2nd part; (Chalons; 1899); pp. 233-43.

The Prophet becomes the agent of 'Perverse Jews,' and also heretic Christians: Nestorians, Jacobites, Arians, and so on, depending on who makes the attack on Islam.[49]

The dominant purpose of Christian polemics was to darken the character of the Prophet. Hence, in *The History of Charles the Great and Orlando,* the pseudo-Turpin (fl. 1130) says:

> The Saracens had a tradition that the idol Mahomet, which they worshipped, was made by himself in his lifetime; and that by the help of a legion [of] devils it was by magic art endued with such irresistible strength that it could not be broken.[50]

Hidlebert of Lemans (d.1133), Archbishop of Tours (France), describes the Prophet trying to prove his divine mission in the eyes of the people by the apparent miracle that

> A terrifying bull, secretly tamed and trained by the 'impostor,' kneels before him at his bidding.[51]

In the middle of the thirteenth century there appeared another biography of Mohammed by the French writer Vincent de Beauvais (1190-1264?). In his *Speculum Historiale* he explained the details of Mohammed's life in such a way as to make it easy to see the similarity of this biography of Mohammed to the account of the life of Anti-Christ.[52]

Vincent de Beauvais also tells us that Mohammed converted people to his faith 'with the sword, force and destruction'.[53] He maintains that the main method of conversion to Islam was by force: Mohammed seized the possessions of the weak by force and devastated the lands of neighbouring peoples to compel them to convert to Islam. At the same time the world of Islam is for Vincent de Beauvais also an upside-down world, a world of miracles where everything is

> The other way round: during fasting one is allowed to eat and drink, during pilgrimage one is allowed to worship idols, and in Paradise the righteous indulge in idleness and carnal pleasures.[54]

Vincent de Beauvais creates a dual image of the Islamic world-on the one hand it is the satanic world of the Anti-Christ, on the other, the world of miracles.[55] He portrays Mohammed as skilled in magic.[56]

Southern explains how a fictionalised negative image of Mohammed grew up in Europe in this period, and 'was elaborated and exaggerated according to

---

[49] M.T. D'Alverny: Pierre le venerable et la Legende de Mahomet: *A Cluny, Congres Scientifique*... 9-11 July, 1949; (CNRS; 1950); pp. 161-170; at p. 163; in M.T. D'Alverny: *La Connaissance de l'Islam dans l'Occident Medieval*; ed., by C. Burnett (Variorum; 1994).
[50] In D.C. Munro: The Western; op cit; at pp. 331-2.
[51] H. Prutz: *Kulturgeschichte der kreuzzuge* (Berlin, 1883), p. 81.
[52] S. Luchitskaja: The image of Muhammad in Latin chronography of the twelfth and thirteenth centuries; In *Journal of Medieval History*; vol 26; 2000; pp. 115-26; at p. 123.
[53] Vincentii Bellovacensis, *Speculum*, Lib. XXIII, cap. LXII.
[54] Ibid, cap. LX, LXIII.
[55] S. Luchitskaja: The Image of Muhammad; op cit; pp. 115-26; at p. 123.
[56] Vincent de Beauvauis: *Speculum historiale, Bibliotheca mundi* (Douai, 1624), vol 3, Lib. XXIII.

expectations as to how such an enemy of Christendom might behave.'[57] Hence, when Guilbert of Nogent (1055-1124) spoke about the Prophet in his *Gesta Dei per Francos*,[58] he may have garbled his name and pushed him a few centuries forward in time, and could neither separate fact from fiction, still he concluded: 'It is safe to speak of evil of one whose malignity exceeds whatever ill can be spoken.'[59]

Davenport also notes the repeated assertion that the Prophet was subject to epileptic fits 'to impute that morbid affection to the apostle of a novel creed as a stain upon his moral character.'[60]

The Message, the Qur'an, suffered the same fate as the Messenger. Many commentators, Frassetto notes, included slanderous accounts of the life of Mohammed and vehement denunciations of the Qur'an and Islam in their works.[61] According to Guibert of Nogent, it was a book of law which appeared by a false miracle on the horns of a cow (or bull or ox).[62] The Qur'an, according to one of the so-called Cordova martyrs, Eulogio (who was executed for insulting the Prophet in 859, in Cordova,) has for Mary the worst of thoughts. Eulogio says that 'He will say nothing about the horrible sacrilege about Mary (in the text),'[63] which, of course, can be easily disproved by any reading of the text. Surah 3-verse 42, for instance, says:

> 'The angels said to Mary: `Mary God has chosen you and made you pure. He has preferred you above all women.'

Muslims were deemed sexually perverse.[64] The associated vision of the Muslim was that of a figure of extremes, excessive in zeal, in cruelty, and in sensuality, a picture enduring for centuries.[65] Ademar of Chabannes, a French Monk of the late 10th-early 11th century (989-1034), describes the Muslims as

> Burning with concupiscence and without modesty, men lay with men, women with women... and people copulate with animals.[66]

His compatriot, Guilbert (of Nogent) (d. ca 1124), thus describes Muslims:

> The more they abandoned themselves in all ways, as if authorized by heaven itself, to all kinds of excess in these permitted vices, the more they covered up the wickedness of it, in praising the grace of God, who accorded, in his indulgence, these loose times. All the severity of Christianity was condemned

---

[57] R.W. Southern: *Western*; in John Sweetman: *The Oriental Obsession*; op cit; p. 6.
[58] *Gesta Dei per Francos*, bk.1, caput 3 in patrologia latina, ed., J.P. Migne (Paris, 1853), Vol 156; col. 689.
[59] In R.W. Southern: *Western Views of Islam in the Middle Ages* (Harvard University Press, 1978); p. 31.
[60] J Davenport: *An Apology for Mohammed and the Koran* (J. Davy and Sons; London; 1869), p. 14.
[61] M. Frassetto: The Image of the Saracen as Heretic in the Sermons of Ademar of Chabannes; in *Western Views of Islam* (Blanks-Frassetto ed); op cit; pp. 83-96; at p. 84.
[62] In N. Daniel: *The Arabs*, op cit, p. 233.
[63] Ibid; p. 41.
[64] In N. Daniel: *The Cultural Barrier* (Edinburgh University Press, 1975), p. 166.
[65] J. Sweetman: *The Oriental Obsession* (Cambridge University Press, 1987), p. 6.
[66] G. Duby: The Knight, the Lady and the Priest; tr. B. Bray; Chicago; 1983; pp. 57-120; in M. Frassetto: The Image of the Saracen as Heretic in the Sermons of Ademar of Chabannes; in *Western Views of Islam* (Blanks-Frassetto ed); pp. 83-96; at p. 89.

and given over to public insults; the teachings of honesty and virtue which had been laid down by the Evangels were accused of being hard, of being cruel; and on the contrary those that the cow had brought were called the teachings of generosity and were recognized as the only ones in accord with the liberty instituted by God himself. ... But since they did not place any restraint on the indulgence of the senses, one soon saw them giving themselves up to vices that even the ignorant animals ignore entirely and that are not even decent to mention...[67]

From *Le Couronnement de Louis,* we read that people were attracted to Islam by the pleasures of drinking and sexual gratification,[68] whilst Vincent de Beauvais holds that is the religion of indulging passions.[69]

Later in the medieval period, there was born the Humanist movement whose depictions and rhetoric addressed the other 'barbaric' form of Islam and Muslims. For Petrarch (1304-1374) Muslim was a metaphor for the dangerous and foreign Asia, so reviled by Ancient Greeks, and they represent barbarism itself. The Christian West, on the other hand, in his view, is the bastion of civilisation, manly courage and decency.[70] As Sweetman notes:

> The dominant picture [of Muslims], in the minds of the Latins, was of forces of aliens advancing from North Africa and raids which left ruins and burnt out churches and monasteries in Southern France. There is reason to believe that raids of vandals were hardly differentiated from raids of Saracens and it was practically certain that many of the raids of North Africa were of pagan Berbers, whose crimes were laid at the door of Islam because they came from a territory which was within the aegis of Islam, and pagans and Muslims alike were branded with the stigma of idolatry.[71]

Such medieval accounts, Sweetman points out, show how the ignorance of Islam persisted, and misconceptions about it have remained profound.[72]

Daniel, however, rightly notes that Western Christendom uses these identifications to explain Islam's great appeal, an appeal which is due to nothing else 'Than to its corruption of souls, offering people sensuous pleasures Christianity would never contemplate to even address.' Christianity since its early days,' [Daniel remarks,] 'had stressed the value of total sexual continence in a way that was foreign to Islam.'[73] Very often, Daniel, adds, Islam suffered untrue accounts which are deliberate, malicious misrepresentations, absurd, based on pure fantasy.[74] C.

---

[67] D.C. Munro: Western; op cit; p. 334.
[68] E. Langlois: *Le Couronnement de Louis*; 2nd rev; Paris; 1966; in Jo Ann Hoeppner Moran Cruz: Popular Attitudes Towards Islam; op cit; p. 58.
[69] Vincentii Bellovacensis, *Speculum*, cap. LX.
[70] F. Petrarca: *De vita solitaria*; ed. M. Noce; Milan; 1992; English translation: *The Life of Solitude*; ed., J. Zeidin; (Urbana; 1924). N. Bisaha: 'New Barbarian' or worthy adversary? Humanist Constructs of the Ottoman Turks in fifteenth century Italy; in Western Perceptions (Blanks-Frassetto ed); op cit; pp. 185-205; at p. 189.
[71] J.W. Sweetman: *Islam and Christian Theology;* op cit; p. 60.
[72] Ibid; p. 63.
[73] N. Daniel: *The Arabs and Medieval Europe*; op cit; p. 230.
[74] N. Daniel: *The Arabs*; op ct; p. 232.

Meredith Jones concluded that there was no better explanation for these misrepresentations than flagrant fanaticism.[75] Such depictions, however slanderous and based on lies, still went on, unaltered, in the following period.

In the 'Renaissance' (15th-17th Centuries):

Schwoebel notes how the Crusader views of Islam in the Middle Ages were carried over and perpetuated even 'after the main lines of the medieval world view had crumbled.'[76] Daniel, too, observes how the Europeans inherited from their mediaeval fathers a large and persistent body of ideas about Islam;[77] the same accounts of Islam recurring monotonously. Even travellers, who felt bound to describe Muslim doctrine with the authority of their experience, just repeated statements which had been, or might have been, lifted straight out of medieval accounts.[78] The representation of the Orient in tragedy in that period, for instance, reproduces the usual stereotypes:

> The imbecile cruelty of the rulers; the power of the Imams, and the rushed credulity of the Muslims.[79]

The contemporary Jean Germain (fl.1455), who contributed his fair share in exhorting crusades against the Muslims, wrote in refutation of Islam, one of his best known works being *'Le Debat du Chretien et du Sarrazin'* (Debate between the Christian and the Saracen). In this imaginary debate, held allegedly in the palace of 'the emperor of the Saracens,' Germain attacked 'the folly of Islam,' reviewed the evidence supporting the authenticity of Christ and other arguments in favour of Christianity, and in his view, exposed the motives commonly cited for abjuring Christianity in favour of Islam.[80] Schwoebel notes, how, arguing from 'the assumed authority of the Scripture and the superiority of Christianity,' Germain produced but another work of Christian polemic and contributed nothing new to the West's knowledge of Islam nor a more constructive approach to the Muslim world.[81]

Little had changed in comparison with the medieval period, indeed, except that the Islamic fiend was now the Ottoman Turk. As the Ottomans had become the leading force of Islam, it was all too normal that in the wars against them, they should be painted the way they were. Schwoebel notes how:

---

[75] C. Meredith Jones: The Conventional Saracen of the Song of the Geste, *Speculum*; 17; 1942; pp. 201-25.

[76] R. Schwoebel: *The Shadow of the Crescent: The Renaissance Image of the Turk* (Nieuwkoop; 1967), p. 147.

[77] N. Daniel: *Islam, Europe and Empire* (University Press, Edinburgh, 1966), Preface; xiii.

[78] Ibid; pp. 23-4.

[79] As in the play *Roxelane*; 1643; in P. Martino: *l'Orient dans la Literature Francaise au 17em et 18em siecles* (Librairie Hachette; Paris; 1906), p. 193.

[80] Paulin Paris: Les Manuscrits Francais de la Bibliotheque du Roi (Paris; 1836; Vol I; pp. 83-6. Abbe Bugniot: Jehan Germain, eveque de Challon sur Saone; 1436-1460; *Memoire de la Societe d'Histoire et d'Archeologie de Challon sur Saone;* IV; 1863; pp. 377-401; at pp. 394-401.

[81] R. Schwoebel: *The Shadow of the Crescent;* op cit; p. 108.

> The Turk was viewed as an infidel, a follower of the profane Mohammed, and a pernicious force dedicated to the destruction of Christendom.[82]

The Turk was, for most Frenchmen, according to Rouillard, the symbol of cruelty and lasciviousness.[83] When the ambassadors from Florence led by their venerable Archbishop Antoninus appeared at the papal court on May 24, 1453, Pope Calixtus spoke of his goal to take the offensive against the Ottomans.[84] After a long eulogy on Calixtus' virtues and fitness for his high office, Antoninus elaborated on the Ottoman problem. He denounced the Turks 'As cruel beasts, blasphemous, and enemies of Christ.' He described Mohammed II (the conqueror of Constantinople) as 'The son of Satan, the perverted enemy of the human race, and the personification of all evil.'[85]

In England, the attitude of publicists, the clergy, and statesmen towards the Turks differed very little from literary and popular attitudes.[86] When the news reached England in 1565 that the Ottoman siege of Malta had been lifted, a form of thanksgiving was ordered by the Archbishop of Canterbury to be read in all churches every Sunday, Wednesday and Friday.[87] This special order of services refers to:

> Our sworn and most deadly enemies the Turks, infidels, and Miscreants... who by all tyranny and cruelty labour to root out not only true religion, but also the very name and memory of Christ our only saviour and all Christianity.[88]

As in the medieval period, distortions and exaggerations took central stage. As Blanks points out

> Deliberate misrepresentations on the part of medieval writers who have access to accurate information has been an enduring issue in the historiography of pre-modern encounters between Europe and Islam.[89]

The technique of rejection could hardly be faulted, Daniel observes.[90] 'The dogmatic filter,' he adds, 'excluded every Islamic idea, except deformed to "prove" a Christian argument.'[91] Vitkus expands on this:

> The early modern image of Islam, as seen through Western eyes, is one that has been radically transformed by time, distance and cultural mediation so that it bears little resemblance to the religion and the culture that it purports to describe. In fact, the representation of Islam in medieval and Renaissance

---

[82] Ibid; p. 187.
[83] C.D. Rouillard: *The Turk in French history, Thought and Literature; 1520-1660* (Paris; 1941), pp. 641-5.
[84] R. Schwoebel: *The Shadow of the Crescent;* op cit; p. 37.
[85] Ibid.
[86] F.L. Baumer: England, the Turk and the Common Corps of Christendom; in J.S. Geary: Arredondo's *Castillo Inexpugnable de la fee;* op cit; p. 292.
[87] S.C. Chew: *The Crescent and the Rose* (Oxford University Press; 1937), p. 443.
[88] *A Short form of Thanksgiving to God...* ed., by W.K. Clay (Cambridge; 1847), pp. 532-33.
[89] D.R. Blanks: Western Views of Islam in the Pre-modern Period: A Brief History of Past Approaches; in *Western Perceptions* (Blanks-Frassetto ed); op cit; pp. 11-53; at p. 22.
[90] N. Daniel: *The Cultural Barrier*; op cit; pp.165-6.
[91] Ibid; p. 166.

> Europe is at times almost the opposite of its alleged original. Through a process of misinterpretation and demonisation, iconoclasm becomes idolatry, civilisation becomes barbarity, monotheism becomes pagan polytheism, and so on. And yet, these twisted stereotypes are, in a sense, real. They are real because, for the vast majority of medieval and early Europeans, they served as the only available means for understanding (or perhaps we should say misunderstanding) Islam. These representations are also 'real' in the sense that any such representation has a material and ideological impact as a historical phenomenon: it is a mode of perception that shapes the way people think and therefore the way they act.[92]

European visitors to the Muslim lands, under various guises, contributed to distort the picture further. Gunny focuses on Herbert, the attaché to the British Embassy in Persia (in 1626).[93] One of Herbert's claims was that:

> Some men keep a lock on top of the head by which Muhammad may distinguish them from Christians on Judgment Day and by which he will lift them to paradise....[94]

Herbert also states that it was from his parents that the Prophet: 'sucked knowledge of both religions.' Obviously Herbert failed to realise that the Prophet was an orphan. Herbert also holds that the Prophet, although circumcised, was baptized by Sergius, a 'Sabeeian heretic who denied the Trinity.' With such 'help' the Prophet 'concocted' the Qur'an and by money and force subjected the rest of his followers. Herbert adds that all Muslims invoke the Prophet four times a day, and expect his coming patiently.[95] Of course, this has no validity as any person can find by reading about Islam.

The Capucine friar, Gabriel de Chinon, visited Isfahan in the 1640s, learned Armenian, Turkish, Persian and other Oriental languages, and set up a mission of his order at Tauris and another in the mountains of Kurdistan. Like many of his peers, then, as in future centuries, he played on the Sunni-Shia differences, and gave them a more dramatic dimension than in reality. In his observations, the first three caliphs-Abu Bakr (632-634), Omar (634-644), and 'Uthman (644-656) appear like vile schemers who bribed people to join their party.[96] This story will form the central element of the main work on the First Caliphs by Wilfred Madelung centuries later (in 1997), a work for which, incidentally, he was widely acclaimed.)[97] Another Renaissance claim is by Wilf Chinon who tells us that Omar choked Abu Bakr to death because he wanted to make amends for Ali.[98] Nothing of the kind happened, of course, Abu Bakr proclaiming Omar as his successor after

---

[92] D.J. Vitkus: Early Modern Orientalism: Representations of Islam in 16th and 17th century Europe; in *Western Perceptions* (Banks-Frassetto ed); op cit; pp. 207-30; at p. 207.
[93] A. Gunny: *Images of Islam in Eighteenth Century Writing* (Grey Seal, London, 1996), p. 11.
[94] Ibid.
[95] Ibid.
[96] Ibid; p. 26.
[97] W. Madelung: *The Succession to the Prophet*, Cambridge University Press, 1997. For acclaims and awards, see Wikipedia: Type his name and book title.
[98] A. Gunny: *Images of Islam;* 26.

consultation with leading figures.[99] Chinon also makes the claim that the Persians invoke Ali to their help in preference to God himself.[100]

The Roman Catholic missionary to the Levant, father Michel Nau (1631-83), who was superior of the Jesuit mission in Aleppo, in his book *L'Etat Present de la Religion Mohametane*, praises Muslims for destroying idolatry, but accuses them of substituting their own idol. To him,

> Muslims simply merge all their idols into one which they elevate according to their whim and which is the image of a false god.
>
> Most Muslims imagine Him to be corporeal, and when Muslims sometimes call Him a pure spirit, they do so in complete ignorance and that at their best they take a spirit to mean nothing more than light.[101]

Nau considers Muslims as the most debauched of all people, and whilst there are Muslims of honour and moral integrity, they are only a minority, and this goodness is not the result of their religion but of their own natural goodness.[102]

Much that was imputed to Islam arose, indeed, in the imaginations of European writers.[103] Chew points out the absurd writing about the Qur'an seemingly including stories of beasts saluting Mohammed and of the moon descending from heaven to visit him.[104] The Qur'an, of course, contains no such stories, yet:

> The currency of these and other fables [Chew explains,] shows that hostile writers seldom troubled to acquaint themselves with the Latin text; and if they did so their prejudice blinded them to the beauty and grandeur which would else surely have glimmered, albeit obscurely, through the unworthy rendering of the original.[105]

Kabbani also explains how:

> The Elizabethan stage, preoccupied as it was with the melodramatic, the passionate and the violent, drew heavily on the available stock of eastern characters so vivid in the public imagination.[106] The Saracen, the Turk, the Moor, the Blackamoor and the Jew were key villains in the drama of the period, crudely depicted as such by the lesser playwrights, but drawn with more subtle gradations by a Marlowe or a Shakespeare. Although Shakespeare whitewashes Othello by making him a servant of the Venetian state, a soldier fighting for a Christian power, and most importantly, a killer of Turks, he still remains a savage - although a somewhat noble one. His excitable nature and his passionate instincts flaw him: his jealousy recalls a long tradition of Eastern jealousy, his revenge a confirmed consequence of that tradition.[107]

---

[99] For details and references, see this author's *First Caliphs*; MSBN 2016.
[100] A. Gunny: *Images*; op cit; p. 26.
[101] M. Nau: *L'Etat present de la Religion Mahometane;* (Paris; 1684); vol 1; p. 65; in A. Gunny: *Images of Islam;*; p. 27.
[102] Ibid; p. 28.
[103] N. Daniel: *Islam, Europe*; op cit; p. 23.
[104] Burton: The Anatomy of Melancholy; III; iv; i.3; in S.C. Chew: *The Crescent*; op cit; p. 438.
[105] S. C. Chew: *The Crescent*; p. 438.
[106] See: E. Jones: *Othello's Countrymen*: (London; 1965); S. Chew: *The Crescent and the Rose;* op cit.
[107] R. Kabbani: *Imperial Fictions*; op cit; pp.19-20.

In Milton's *Paradise Lost* (published in 1667), Evil comes from the East:
> Satan is an Oriental monarch (Lucifer the shining one - The Eastern Morning star) whose proud ambition was to defeat God and the angels is analogous to the aggressive imperialism of Eastern emperors such as the Ottoman sultan. According to this pattern of association, the West is angelic, the East is demonic.[108]

Distorting the reality of Islam and Muslims, then, as today, was acceptable as it brought otherwise divided Christians together. The French propagandist La Noue:
> I know we have some religious controversies in religion amongst us (Christians), which notwithstanding Protestant and Catholics are still brethren and grafted upon oneself... But with these profane Mahumatists, who worship an imaginary God, which is rather a devil and do pollute all honesty and sack the world, what conjunction and fellowship can we have? Against these enemies the ravishers of our goods, tormentors of our bodies, and poisoners of our souls are we to strive with our swords. But amongst those that bear one safe till all controversies ought to be ended in modesty and truth.[109]

Sexuality, again, as the notion of a veiled, hidden lust that masquerades as virtue and chastity is deemed a typical characteristic of the Islamic woman in Western European texts.[110] The virtuous Muslim woman often converts to Christianity 'saved' by the love of a good Christian man.[111] Sexual perversity is seen to be intrinsic in the teachings of Islam.[112] Hence, George Lengherand, mayor of Mons in Hainault, who visited Palestine and Egypt in 1486, stated that:
> Muslims believed blessedness consisted of food, drink, luxuries, and in all sensualities, and pleasures which excite the body, even sodomy. Mohammed decreed that those who did not live in such pleasures would perish... and His Alcoran was full of errors. I believe it is the greatest horror in the world.[113]

Christian writers not only criticised Islam for offering sensual pleasure as a reward to the virtuous in the next life, they also condemned the sexual freedom allowed in this life under Muslim law.[114] Islamic regulations governing concubinage, marriage, and divorce were at once misunderstood and reviled by Western Europeans.[115] Alexander du Pont in his *Roman de Mahomet* maintains that the Prophet permitted every Muslim to marry ten wives and every Muslim woman to marry ten times as well.[116]

---

[108] In D.J. Vitkus: Early Modern Orientalism: Representations of Islam in 16th and 17th century Europe; In *Western Perceptions* (Banks-Frassetto ed); op cit; pp. 207-30; at p. 219.
[109] F. La Noue: *The Politicke and Militarie discourse of the Lord de la Noue;* tr. E. A. London; p. 290.
[110] D.J. Vitkus: Early Modern Orientalism; op cit. p. 223.
[111] D. Metlitzki: *The Matter of Araby*; op cit; pp. 177 ff.
[112] Z. Sardar; M-W. Davies: *Distorted Imagination*; op cit; p. 41.
[113] *Voyage de George Lengherand*, ed., Charles Denys (Mons, 1861), pp. 181-2.
[114] D.J. Vitkus: Early Modern Orientalism: op cit; p. 223.
[115] N. Daniel: *Islam and the West*, op cit; pp. 135-40.
[116] Ibid; p. 145.

In the view of Western Christian polemists, the progress of Islam could only be due to sexual permissiveness combined with violence. Islam, as Vitkus notes, was defined and caricatured as:

> A religion of violence and lust-aggressive jihad in this world, and sensual pleasure promised in the next world. But if the doctrines of Islam were so obviously worthy of scorn, what could account for the widespread, rapid growth of Islam? Force of arms and successful military aggression, violent conversion by the sword - these are often cited by Christian writers in the early modern era as an explanation for the astonishing achievements of the Islamic conquests. The early Arab Muslims are described as powerful bandits and plunderers united by a voracious appetite for booty.[117]

In the view of Pope Pius II (Pope 1458-1464),

> Islam was a pernicious force, incompatible at all points with Christianity and dedicated by its very nature to the overthrow of the Christian religion.[118]

However, as Kabbani observes:

> The cruelty of the Oriental in narrative construction went hand in hand with lasciviousness. One favourite example that reappears with great frequency during this period is the story of the Turkish sultan who falls in love with a slave girl, so that he abandons all matters of state to her embraces.[119] Rebuked by his ministers and officers, who press him to attend to his army about to engage in battle, he is only enraged at their meddling. One evening, he bids his lover dress in her most revealing silks and attend to him at a banquet. He embraces her before his courtiers, then abruptly draws his sword and cuts off her head. Another version has him bid his ministers into his bedchambers, where he lifts the bedclothes to reveal to them the charms of his mistress. This done, he stabs her to death, and marches off to war.[120]

The 18th Century

In this supposed age of Enlightenment, we barely note any improved views of either faith or followers. Rather the contrary: Abbe (Abbot) Jean Luis Poiret (1757-1834) published his *Voyage en Barbary* (Travel to Barbary) in 1789.[121] He found that Muslims had

> A limited view of destiny, on the grounds that they made it apply to physical events and rarely to moral acts. Attached to the outward ritual of their religion, they indulged in ferocious deeds proper to their personality, without giving heed to the amorality of their actions.[122]

---
[117] D.J. Vitkus: Early Modern Orientalism; op cit; p. 217.
[118] R. Schwoebel: *The Shadow of the Crescent*; op cit; p. 72.
[119] N. Daniel: *Islam, Europe and Empire*; Edinburgh 1966; p. 18.
[120] R. Kabbani: *Imperial Fictions*; op cit; p. 19.
[121] J. L. Poiret: *Voyages en Barbary ou letters ecrites de l'ancienne Numidie pendant les annees 1785-6;* (Paris; 1789).
[122] Ibid; p. 105.

Poiret saw a number of contradictions in the actions of these 'ignorant and coarse people,' arising from the total lack of moral foundations for their acts, Muslims in his eyes, reminiscent of primitive people still in the state of nature as described by Rousseau in his *Discours sur l'Inegalite*.[123]

In his *Voyage au Levant* (Travel to the East), Paul Lucas says that he witnessed the execution of two Muslims convicted of theft, condemned to be burned alive in a public place.[124] This, as Gunny notes, might well be a figment of his imagination, for this is certainly not an Islamic punishment.[125]

In *An Account of South West Barbary,* translated by Ockley,[126] Muslims are described as

> Insufferably false and treacherous that neither their word, nor their oath, can be depended upon from the first to the last.[127]

The author shows great interest in the fate of women, stating that they are taught nothing by their parents other than to bake a little bread, clean their houses and serve their husbands who treat them like handmaidens rather than wives. Women themselves are conspicuous for their amorality for in spite of their strict upbringing, they have

> Will and invention enough to procure a great many opportunities favourable to their inclinations.[128]

According to the same author, the reason why Muslims do not lend money on interest is not the Qur'anic injunction against usury, but tax evasion. They appear poverty stricken, not only because of their laziness, but also because the appearance of affluence might lead to their being more severely taxed if not robbed of all their possessions.[129]

The generalised view was that Islam was nothing more than a heresy based on violence and sexual permissiveness. According to Prideaux, the Prophet gratified the Arabs:

> Passions and corrupt affections which he found them strongly addicted to, especially those of lust and war. In this way he found it easier to draw them into his party.[130]

In his *Memoires,*[131] Prevost (1697-1763) holds that the Turks, Moors and corsairs do not just have a shadowy existence, and an obsession for plunder, but also express sexual pleasures and cruelty, and all at once.[132] Antoine Galland (1646-1715), in his travels to the East, concentrated his attention on the expressions of

---

[123] A. Gunny: *Images of Islam;* op cit; pp. 32-3.
[124] P. Lucas: *Voyage au Levant,* (The Hague; 1705); 2 vols.
[125] A. Gunny: *Images of Islam;* op cit; p. 36.
[126] Ockely tr: *An Account of South West Barbary,* (London; 1713).
[127] Ibid; pp. 33-4.
[128] Ibid; p. 34.
[129] In A. Gunny: *Images of Islam;* op cit; p. 39.
[130] Prideaux; in D.A. Pailin: *Attitudes to Other Religions;* (Manchester University Press; 1984); p. 101.
[131] A. Prevost: *Memoires pour servir a l'Histoire de Malte* (Paris; 1741).
[132] A. Prevost: *Memoires;* in A. Gunny: *Images of Islam;* op cit; p. 170.

violence that were supposedly intrinsic to the East. This violence is often linked with sexuality.[133] This was a common theme of European travel writing: the all invasive seraglio with its crimes of passion was never far from the traveller's mind.[134]

Jean Andre Peysonnel (1694-1759) visited the Regencies of Tunis and Algiers in 1724-5, and wrote his impressions in the form of letters, which were published in 1838.[135] Peysonnel notes that women who had been found guilty of adultery with their Christian slaves are drowned in the sea. He also says that Christians are forced to abjure their faith and to become Muslims, otherwise they can be condemned to death - unless the matter can be bought with money.[136] This is a similar view to Voltaire's articles to the *Memoire* in 1745 based more on imagination than experience.[137]

J.G. De Saint-Sauveur (1757-1810) emphasises amongst the Muslims of North Africa the vice of lust:

> The Turks and Algerians, not anxious for large families, behave as true pirates on the marital bed. They ravage the field of sensual delight without making any effort to have them bear fruit. The women, resigned to their fate, suffer further insults since almost none of these petty sultans, taking Jupiter of Greek mythology as a model, hesitate to abandon Hebe for Ganymede.[138]

Abbe (Abbot) Vincent Mignot (1730-1790) wrote *Histoire de l'Empire Ottoman* etc, to the year 1740.[139] He insists that Muslims behave towards their womenfolk like 'the savage idol-worshippers' do towards their deities. They lavish presents on them, but they also ill-treat and worship them. Mignot also makes other scurrilous claims such as that Islam owes its expansion to its huge armies which subjugated many empires,[140] and that a religion that gave full indulgence 'to the ambition, the lusts and cruelty of mankind,' could not fail to gain proselytes.[141]

Muslim women are not free from censure, of course. Venture, for instance,[142] asserts categorically that there is no such a thing as delicate women (or men) amongst Muslims.[143]

Violence, sexual perversion and also despotism, all coalesce in the harems and households of the Muslim world. As Cirakman sums up in relation to Western views of the Turks:

> In the eighteenth-century images of Turkish women, one can perceive that the free-spirited and virtuous character of European women is not only

---

[133] R. Kabbani: *Imperial Fictions*; op cit; p. 25.
[134] Ibid.
[135] J.A. Peysonnel: *Voyages dans les regences de Tunis et d'Alger*; (1838).
[136] In A. Gunny: *Images of Islam*; op cit; p. 32.
[137] Ibid.
[138] J.G. De Saint-Sauveur's *Enyclopedie* in L. Valensi: *North Africa Before the French Conquest; 1790-1830*; tr., by K. J. Perkins (Africana Publishing Company; London; 1977), p. xx.
[139] V. Mignot: *L'Histoire de l'Empire Ottoman depuis son origine jusqu'a la paix de Belgrade en 1740;* (Paris; 1771).
[140] In A. Gunny: *Images of Islam;* op cit; p. 173.
[141] F. Atterbury: Sermons and Discourses; I; p. 130; in D.A. Pailin: *Attitudes;* op cit; p. 101.
[142] J. Michel Venture de Paradis: *Memoires sur la Barbarie en general* (Paris; 1983).
[143] Manuscript. BN, Fonds Francais 6430, commentary on f.76 at f.162; in A. Gunny: *Images of Islam;* op cit; p. 193.

contrasted with the stupid and sly Oriental women, but also with Turkish men who appear to be silly, weak, corrupt and despotic. Although the images of Oriental women somehow attempt to entertain the reader, they also tell about the scope of despotism and complete its depiction. From the diverse images of Turkish women one can perceive that despotic power encompasses every aspect of society to such an extent that even a plain Turkish man, who could be at the lowest level of the hierarchical order, could enjoy despotic power over somebody, such as his wife and children. These are assumed to be his slaves. Despotism as an Oriental mode of living is in fact assumed to be a complete system of oppression in which there is no position from which one can act with free will. In eighteenth-century thought about the Turks, every observation seems to affirm the logic of despotism and every analysis attempts to show that it could not be otherwise.[144]

The generalised view was that Mohammed led Muslims on the path of violence, Islam's use of the sword contrasting with Christianity, 'the religion of love', violence explaining the progress of Islam.

> The religion of Mohammed [according to Tillotson] is famously known to have been planted by force at first, and to have been maintained in the world by the same violent means.[145]

In *Les Ruines*, Volney (1757-1820) says that

> Mohammad succeeded in building a political and theological empire at the expense of those of Moses' and Jesus' vicars.

Or, in the scene where he has an imam speaking about the law of Mohammed,

> God has established Mohammad as his minister on earth; he has handed over the world to him to subdue with the sabre those who refuse to believe in his law.[146]

Volney denounces the

> Apostle of a merciful God, who preaches nothing but murder and carnage, the spirit of intolerance and exclusiveness that shocks every notion of justice; and that Christianity might be irrational, but it was gentle and compassionate.[147]

Rousseau wrote in 1762 a letter to Christophe de Beaumont, in which he expressed the most hostile views towards Islam.[148] He invented a story of a Parsee of Surat who secretly married a Muslim woman, was arrested and condemned to death for refusing to be converted to Islam. The dying Parsee starts by attacking the polygamy of Muslims, then he hopes to be reborn among them in order to teach them to become humane, forbearing and just. He accuses them of being blinded by

---

[144] A. Cirakman: *From the Terror of the World to the Sick man of Europe;* (Peter Lang Publishing; New York; 2002); p. 163.
[145] Tillotson: Works; I; p. 148; in D. A. Pailin: *Attitudes*; p. 103.
[146] Volney: Les Ruines; in Z. Sardar; M.W. Davies: *Distorted Imagination*; op cit; pp. 46-7.
[147] Ibid.
[148] J.J. Rousseau: *Oeuvres Completes* (B. Gagnebin and M. Raymond eds: Paris; 1964).

their fanaticism, of tormenting God's servants and of being cruel and bloodthirsty.[149]

Again, distortions play central stage. Alexander Ross, in his *Pansebeia*, dated from 1696, insists that the Muslims worship the sun and the moon,[150] which, of course, is not the case.

Herbelot in *Bibliotheque Orientale*,[151] dated 1779, claims that when Muslims refer to the Trinity, 'They easily accept that the first person - the father - is the essence of God, the second person - the Son - is wisdom and that the third -the Holy Ghost- is life.'[152]

This is wrong, for one of the main dividing lines between Islam and Christianity is this matter of Trinity, as in Islam the Oneness of God is absolute, and Mohammed and Jesus are Prophets only.

Herbelot also holds that

> Muslims believe that most mad people are saints and that some wisdom resides in madness.[153]

In reality, there is no sainthood, and mad people are not even allowed in mosques let alone listened to for their wisdom.

Boulanger writes[154] that everything took place on the tenth day of Muharram for the Persians: the floods, the same day the Qur'an was sent from heaven, and Hussein, Ali's son was killed at Kerbala by Omar's followers.[155] All of this, of course, has no true historical foundation, for neither was Hussein killed by Omar or his followers, but instead was killed during Umayyad rule (which began in 661, whilst Omar died in 644), and even more importantly, the Qur'an was not revealed in one day but in phases during the Prophet's life in Makkah and Madinah.

In his article, 'Sarrasins,' in the *Encyclopédie*, Diderot gives more credentials to the Western views, such as the fatalistic nature of Islam. He insists that the Prophet himself preached fatalism, a doctrine responsible for great courage and contempt for death and which teaches that prudence is useless.[156] This, of course, as Gunny notes, is completely wrong, for the Qur'an vigorously opposes fatalism, with its excuses for evading duties imposed by Divine law.[157]

Volney in *Voyage in Egypt and Syria*,[158] asserts categorically that Islam fails to fix the obligations or rights of individuals, groups and classes.[159] This, of course, is

---

[149] In A. Gunny: *Images of Islam;* op cit; p. 130.
[150] A. Ross: *Pansebeia, or A View of All Religions in the World;* London; 6th ed (1696); pp. 118 ff.; in D.A. Pailin: *Attitudes;* op cit; p. 82.
[151] B. Herbelot: *Bibliotheque Orientale* (Paris; 1697), (The Hague; 1777).
[152] In A. Gunny: *Images of Islam;* op cit; p. 52.
[153] Ibid.
[154] N.A. Boulanger: *L'Antiquite Devoilee par ses usages* (Amsterdam; 1766).
[155] Ibid; p. 99.
[156] Diderot and J. d'Alembert eds: *Encyclopedie;* (Paris, 1751-1780); 35 vols; vol 8; pp. 272-3.
[157] A. Gunny: *Images;* op cit; p. 164.
[158] C. Chasseboeuf (Volney): *Voyage en Egypte et en Syrie* (Paris, Mouton and Co; 1959 ed).
[159] Ibid; p. 372.

contradicted by the Qur'an. The index on legislation in the Qur'an includes matters such as bequests; arbitration, blood-money, bribery, charity, contracts, children...[160] Concluding on such distorted depictions of Islam by Christians, Pailin observes:

> With a few exceptions, Islam is examined in order to show that it is inferior to Christianity and offers no plausible threat to the various proofs of the truth of Christian revelation. Christian apologists are not interested in establishing and stating the truth about Muslim faith and practice. They use or abuse Islam in order to support their own convictions about the perfection of Christianity and to exhort their fellow believers to a better practice of their faith.[161]

19th-20th Centuries and First Decades of the 21st Century

Daniel notes how most of the scholars were personally convinced that Islam was inferior in point of morality and the reader of the great 19th century scholarly lives of the Prophet, by Weil, Muir, Sprenger, Noldeke, Dozy, Goldhizer, found no reason to alter the opinion with which he began.[162] William Muir, writing in the last years of the 19th century, thus, says:

> To put the matter shortly, each religion is an embodiment of its Founder. Mahomet sought power; he fought against those who denied his claims; he put a whole tribe to the sword. He cast aside, when they had served his purpose, the Jewish and Christian Scriptures, and he engrafted his faith on the local superstition of his birthplace. He did all these things under cover of an alleged divine authority, but he did no miracle.
>
> The life of Jesus is all in contrast. He spoke and taught as one having the inherent authority in Himself; but He could also say, 'The works that I do in My Father's name, they bear witness of Me'. He was holy, harmless, undefiled. He pleased not Himself. Though rich, he became poor, that we through His poverty might become, rich. He made Himself of no reputation, and took upon Him the form of a servant. He was despised and rejected. He humbled Himself, and became obedient to death, even the death of the cross.[163]

The same for J.D. Bate (1836-1923) who served as a missionary in India (1865-1897), and who also contributed many articles to the Missionary Herald and the Baptist Magazine:

> The credit for founding Islam is Muhammad's alone... its distinctive peculiarities are all his own. He alone is responsible for its faults and he alone is entitled to all the credit, whatever it may be, of being its sole founder.[164]

---
[160] M.M. Pickthall: *The Meaning of the Glorious Qur'an* (Ta ha Publishers; London; 1930), p. 463.
[161] D. A. Pailin: *Attitudes*; op cit; p. 104.
[162] N. Daniel: *Islam, Europe and Empire*; op cit; p. 29.
[163] Sir W. Muir: *Mahomet and Islam* (London; 1895), pp. 249-50.
[164] J.D. Bate: *The Claims of Ishmael* (London; W. Allen; 1884), p. 43.

The Catholic Cardinal, Newman, in 1853, considered that Islam consecrated nationalism, as Christianity did civilisation. Its partial truth, he said, wrought 'both a gloom and an improvement in the soul not very unlike the effect which some forms of Protestantism produce among ourselves.' He held that the ancient and momentous truths embodied in Islam made it 'undeniably beneficial so far as their proper influence extends, but as a religion, Islam 'was as debasing as it was false, to the population that received it.'[165]

Tens, if not hundreds, of similar claims were made by other authors and men of letters. We just rely on Stoddard (in regard to this theme) who gives us this overall view:

> What I desire to emphasise here is their (the religious nationalists) pernicious influence on the prospects of a genuine Mohammedan reformation as visualised by the true (liberals) whom I have described. Their malevolent desire to stir up the fanatic passions of the ignorant masses and their equally malevolent hatred of everything Western except military improvements are revealed by outbursts like the following from the pen of a prominent 'Young Turk' [who says]: 'Yes, the Mohammedan religion is in open hostility to all your world of progress. Learn, ye European observers, that a Christian, is in our eyes a being devoid of all human dignity. Our reasoning is simple and definitive. We say: the man whose judgment is so perverted as to deny the evidence of the One God and to fabricate gods of different kinds, cannot be other than the most ignoble expression of human stupidity. To speak to him would be a humiliation to our reason and an offence to the grandeur of the Master of the Universe. The worshipper of false gods is a monster of ingratitude; he is the execration of the universe; to combat him, convert him, or annihilate him is the holiest task of the faithful. These are the eternal commands of our One God. For us, there are in this world only believers and misbelievers, love, charity, fraternity to believers; disgust, hatred, and war to misbelievers. Amongst misbelievers, the most odious and criminal are those who, while recognising God, create Him of earthly parents, give Him a son, a mother; so monstrous an aberration surpasses, in our eyes, all bounds of iniquity; the presence of such miscreants amongst us is the bane of our existence; their doctrine is a direct insult to the purity of our faith; their contact a pollution for our bodies; any relation with them is a torture for our souls.
>
> While detesting you, we have been studying your political institutions and your military organisations. Besides the new arms which Providence procures for us by your own means, you yourselves have rekindled the inextinguishable faith of our heroic martyrs. Our Young Turks, our Babis, our new fraternities, all are sects in their varied forms, are inspired by the same

---

[165] In N. Daniel: *Islam, Europe and Empire*; op cit; p. 33.

thought, the same purpose. Toward what end? Christian civilisation? Never!'[166]

Such language, unfortunately, finds ready hearers among the Moslem masses. Although the liberal reformers are a growing power in Islam, it must not be forgotten that they are as yet only a minority, an elite, below whom lie the ignorant masses, still suffering from the blight of age-long obscurantism, wrapped in admiration of their own world, which they regard as the highest ideal of human existence, and fanatically hating everything outside as wicked, despicable and deceptive. Even when compelled to admit the superior power of the West, they hate it none the less. They rebel blindly against the spirit of change which is forcing them out of their old ruts, and their anger is still further heightened by that ubiquitous Western domination which is pressing upon them from all sides. Such persons are as clay in the hands of the Pan-Islamic and nationalist leaders who mould the multitude to their own sinister ends.

Islam is, in fact, today torn between the forces of liberal reform and chauvinist reaction. The liberals are not only the hope of an evolutionary reformation, they are also favoured by the trend of the times, since the Moslem world is being continually permeated by Western progress and must continue to be thus permeated unless Western civilisation itself collapses in ruin. Yet, though the ultimate triumph of the liberals appears probable, what delays, what setbacks, what fresh barriers of warfare and fanaticism may not the chauvinist reactionaries bring about! Neither the reform of Islam nor the relations between East and West are free from perils whose ominous possibilities we shall later discuss.[167]

Just as in the past, Islam remained in Western view a corrupt, sensual faith. Thus, E.A. Freeman, judges

> The West to be progressive, monogamous and Christian, the East as stationary, arbitrary, polygamous and Mahometan.[168]

For Chateaubriand, Muslims spend their time 'Either devastating the world, or sleeping on carpets amidst women and perfumes.'[169]

Which is also the claim made by J.D. Bate, who says that:

> Islam succeeded by corrupting its followers. Men had even converted to Islam to indulge their brutal appetites for sexual pleasure...[170]

Burton goes one step further, projecting every imaginable kind of sexual perversion onto the Orient, announcing to his contemporaries that whatever they could not find in their Victorian homes, they would find in the Orient, and that whatever was

---

[166] Sheikh abul Hak, in Sherif Pasha Organ, *Mecherouliette*, of August 1912. Quoted from A. Servier: *Le Nationalisme Musulman*; (Constantine; Algeria; 1913).
[167] L. Stoddard: *The New World of Islam*; (Chapman and Hall; Ltd; London; 1922).
[168] E.A. Freeman: *The History and Conquests of the Saracens*; London Mc Millan 1876), 3rd ed., pp. i.4.
[169] Chateaubriand: *Itineraire de Paris a Jerusalem;* op cit; pp. 908.
[170] J.D. Bate: *The Claims of Ishmael*; op cit; pp. 285; 253.

not permissible in England was permissible in Egypt where women are used to being treated as chattel.[171]

In Kabbani's words:

> The West argued that Muslims were not only lewd in every day life, but had conceived of a heaven that would permit endless sensual gratifications. The notion of the carnal delights of the Islamic heaven was sharply contrasted, in an effort to mock, with the angelic society of the Christian paradise. Christians were morally refined and longed for a bodiless heaven. Muslims were spiritually coarse and could not envisage bliss that was not corporal.[172]

Being sexually perverse apparently does not prevent Islamic society from enslaving women. In 19th century Westerners' eyes, women in Islam are only seen 'in terms of subjection, enslavement and concubinage.'[173] The Oriental men are, thus:

> Cruel captors who hold women in their avaricious grasp, who use them as chattels, as trading-goods, with little reverence for them as human beings.[174]

In the writings and paintings of the French Romantics movement, the woman becomes for the fanaticised, brutal Muslim a prize of war and piracy; the Muslim prowling upon her, and ravaging her.[175] Thus Helena, heroine of a poem by Alfred de Vigny, is violated by the Turks; an act de Vigny dwells upon in every single, morbid detail. In the *Orientales* of Victor Hugo, all women are prisoners at the Seraglio, and are offered to the beastly delectation of the Sultan. All these women are young and virgin.[176] These victims of Turkish beastly desires are generally convent girls kidnapped by pirates (Muslims), and taken to the Harem of the Sultan.[177] Countless tales in poems and fiction also speak of women enrobed in sacks and thrown alive into rivers' tumultuous waters,[178] and women instantly murdered by their husbands for raising their veils in the sight of another man.[179]

Muslim men's cruelties towards women hardly absolve Muslim women, who are deemed to be evil due to their faith. Thus, Lord Cromer's view on Muslim women is that due to Islam, they have on the whole a negative influence on others.

> They could not impart knowledge or moral training to their children. Nor could they instil in the East that refinement of manners which women had created in the West.[180]

By the early twentieth century, Islam had been subjugated in many or most lands. There descended on it thousands of missionaries from all over the Christian world

---

[171] In Z. Sardar; M.W. Davies: *Distorted Imagination;* op cit; pp. 51-2.
[172] R. Kabbani: *Imperial Fictions*; pp. 16-7.
[173] In N. Daniel: *Islam and the West*; op cit: p. 314.
[174] R. Kabbani: *Imperial Fictions,* op cit; p. 78.
[175] C. Grossir: *L'Islam;* op cit; p. 99 fwd.
[176] V. Hugo: *Les Orientales*; 1964; Les Tetes du Serail; IV; pp. 602-3.
[177] Ibid. *Chanson de Pirates*; p. 619.
[178] J. Merimee: la Double Meprise; in C. Grossir: *L'Islam;* op cit; p. 102.
[179] V. Hugo: *Les Orientales*; op cit; *Le Voile*; p. 625.
[180] Cromer: *Modern Egypt;* op cit; ii; pp. 155-60.

(they also descended on China and Russia) to convert the heathen to the true faith, and ended up confusing such heathen, as Christian missionaries represented so many contradictory schools, and so they made the heathen who listened to them even more heathen. Never mind these are some of their views as found in the main Missionary organ, *The Moslem World*. H.B. Young writes:

> After more than a century of Christian missionary effort in Moslem lands and in the light of the present uncertainties both at home and abroad, it would seem wise and logical to consider whether there is any justification for continuing missionary effort in Moslem lands and in the second place to consider, if there are to be missionaries to Moslems, what their function should be.
>
> The Christian witness to Moslems has been astonishingly discouraging down the years. 'We have toiled all night and caught nothing' (Luke 5.5) has often been used to describe the failures of the past decade. At Madras the statement was unequivocally made by the group of thirty five workers among Moslems who met in a special conference that the fact stands that Islam remains unresponsive, and that the signs of the times do not point in the direction of change.[181]
>
> The East today is increasingly coming to regard Christ as the norm to which all other religious standards and ideals must approximate. He captures the imagination of the Eastern mind because He is the suffering Servant and not the military leader, because He exemplifies love and sacrifice and service rather than power, worldly gain, and territorial expansion.[182]
>
> To be a missionary to the Moslems is perhaps the most difficult assignment given to any ambassador of Christ in the days that lie ahead. It requires all the passion and persuasion, all the prayer and perseverance that can be mustered.[183]

In another article, 'A Method of presenting Jesus Christ to the Moslems', the writer held:

> How can I best present my saviour to my Muslim brothers and sisters? This has been the question every missionary must have asked from the earliest days of missionary work. Many methods have been tried with the utmost devotion. Yet we still must all confess with heartfelt regret that the results so far have been meagre. In spite of all the missionary work of the Christian churches, yet proportionately how little, Islam still exerts its influence over three hundred million people created in God's image. Who willeth that all should be saved and come to the knowledge of the truth as it is in Jesus. Who is the express Image of God, the only Way to the Father.
>
> We can all put our finger on various reasons hindering and discouraging Moslems from confessing Christ as their Saviour and many of us are sure that

---

[181] World Mission of the Church; p. 140; *International Missionary Council*, (New York; 1939).
[182] W.W. Cash: *Christendom and Islam;* (Harper and Bros; New York; 1937); pp. 166-7.
[183] H. B. Young: The Future Missionary to Moslems; in *The Moslem World*; vol 31; pp. 235-40; at pp. 235-9.

many who have been buried in Moslem graves died with the love of Christ in their heart, as well as we know that there are many living today amongst us outwardly as Moslems who are only waiting to profess openly their faith to Jesus as their Saviour and Lord. Apart from the natural fear of persecution, ostracism, disinheritance and the like, there is another reason discouraging them. The Churches, Eastern and Western, are not showing any desire, in the main, that Moslems should be won and weaned from the power of Satan into fellowship with the one true God.[184]

Colonisation also brought many travellers to the Muslim world. Overwhelmingly, they gave the same image of both faith and adherents. Lane, for instance, writes that the Egyptians have much religious pride - the name of God is always on their lips - but their behaviour is most inconsistent with their profession.[185]

> They exhibit exemplary patience and fortitude, nearly approaching apathy. At the same time they are marked by their cheerfulness, and love amusement. They are most hospitable, but are lacking in gratitude... but their generosity is matched by their cupidity.[186]

For Lane, the Egyptians are sexually inflammable, and easily excited to quarrel.[187] They are incapable of telling the truth: 'Constant veracity is a virtue extremely rare in modern Egypt.'[188]

Eliot Warburton's *The Crescent and the Cross*, was a very popular work, and was edited eighteen times, the last as late as 1888. Warburton describes the Egyptian fundamentally as 'Sensualist and a slave.... He is only to be a subject in the basest of all kingdoms.'

The women have all the insipidity of children without their innocence or sparkling freshness. Their beauty, voluptuous and soulless, appeals only to the senses.' As for the male:

> The Muslim purchases his wife as he does his horse; he laughs at the idea of honour and of love.[189]

Kinglake in his work *Eothen* speaks of the intimidation that his dragoman, Dhemetri, a Middle East Christian of Greek origin, used as the only pragmatic means of gaining provisions and accommodations among the strange barbarians. Dhemetri resorted on occasions to the use of the horsewhip, and his tone in dealing with the Muslim Arabs, Kinglake relates, was not only firm and resolute, but at times

> Very violent and even insulting... This tone, which I always disliked, though, I was fain to profit by it, invariably succeeded.[190]

---

[184] A Method of presenting Jesus Christ to the Muslims: *The Moslem World*; vol 37; p. 255.
[185] E.W. Lane: *Manners and Customs of the Modern Egyptians* (London; 1836).
[186] Ibid; vol 1; pp. 377 ff.
[187] Ibid; p. 305.
[188] Ibid; p. 304.
[189] E. Warburton: *The Crescent and the Cross* (New York; Wiley and Putnam; 1845), I; p. 65 f.
[190] A. W. Kinglake: *Eothen;* (London; W, Blackwood; 1904); p. 235 ff.

But Kinglake salves his conscience a bit, and excuses Dhemetri, by pointing to the causes of his behaviour:

> He had lived for the most part in countries lying under Muslim governments and had witnessed (perhaps too suffered from) their revolting cruelties; the result was that he abhorred and despised the Mahometan faith and all who clung to it.[191]

Kinglake concludes of the Middle East:

> Behind me I left an old and decrepit world - religions dead and dying - calm tyrannies expiring in silence - women hushed and swathed and turned into waxen dolls - love flown and in its stead mere royal and 'Paradise' pleasures.[192]

Nearly a century later, in the 1980s, V. S. Naipaul captured the same picture. In *An Area of Darkness* (1964), *India: a Wounded Civilisation* (1977), and *Among the Believers* (1981), as he travels through India first, then through Egypt, Iran, Pakistan, Malaysia and Indonesia, he captures the villainy of Muslim society.[193] On the train to Cairo he observes a man across the aisle as:

> He hawked twice, with an expert tongue rolled the phlegm into a ball, plucked the ball out of his mouth with thumb and forefinger, considered it, and then rubbed it away between his palms.[194]

Still in Egypt he witnesses some ceremony, where people he describes seem to have come out from some dark leper house:

> As disquieting as the blood were the faces of some of the enthusiasts. One had no nose, just two punctures in a triangle of pink mottled flesh; one had grotesquely raw bulging eyes; there was one with no neck, the flesh distended straight from cheek to chest.[195]

Naipaul 'understood the sources of the evils of Muslim society': Islam. Muslims' failure in life 'led back again and again to the assertion of the faith.'[196] Islam, in his opinion, was merely a refuge from distress,[197] that achieved nothing, but was parasitic and uncreative.[198] Islam, to him, is

> A religion of fanaticism that leads to a sensation of utter futility; an archaic form of devotion in a rapidly progressing world. It is symptomatic of a renunciation of civilisation that can only marginalize those who are renouncing it by placing them in an intellectual vacuum from which there is no escape. The Islamic alternative to the Western pattern of social behaviour is an aberration, a contemptible failing in sophistication and skill.[199]

And in the Muslims' rejection of the West, Naipaul sees:

---

[191] Ibid; p. 328.
[192] Ibid; p. 355.
[193] Extracts of Naipaul's views are from R. Kabbani: *Imperial Fictions*; op cit.
[194] V.S. Naipaul: *An Area of Darkness;* (London; 1964 and 1981); p. 12.
[195] Ibid; p. 127.
[196] V.S. Naipaul: *Among the Believers: An Islamic Journey*; (London, 1981); p. 85.
[197] Ibid; p. 228.
[198] Ibid; pp. 158-9.
[199] In R. Kabbani: *Imperial Fictions*; op cit; pp. 134-5.

> Their rage - the rage of a pastoral people with limited skills, limited money, and a limited grasp of the world - is comprehensive. Now they have a weapon: Islam. It is their way of getting even with the world. It serves their grief, their feeling of inadequacy, their social rage and racial hate.[200]

The only person Naipaul appreciates in the whole Islamic land is an Indonesian poet, but not a Muslim, an animist instead, with Dutch education, married to a Dutch woman. Unlike the Muslims, all intellectually empty and lost, this Indonesian, Situmorang is:

> Placid and sane. He had achieved that calm by retrieving the heritage of his ancestors with the help of a European anthropologist.[201]

For his 'profound, erudite, and first class depiction of Islamic society,' Naipaul earned the Nobel Prize, and the greatest literary accolades from the West.

But, most auspicious of all qualities of Muslims is that same gene denounced by all and since the Middle Ages: the gene of violence, an intrinsic component of the Islamic faith. *The Moslem World*, again:

> Heathenism has no fanatics. Religion of the heathen is a tribal concern... The Mahommedan is quite different. Islam tolerates no other religions. God demands their suppression.. The heathen becomes a fanatic in such (Islamic) school. Once the Mohammedan knows how to perform his ablutions and the sacred rites with the appointed formulae, he becomes possessed by the feeling, 'I alone am clean among the unclean!'... Fanaticism is naturally what the Mohammedan convert acquires, first, because it needs no scholarship... Although, unfortunately, he may not be able to wield weapons against the all powerful Whites, he can mock and despise them in his heart. And all this is rendering service to God. Whatever religious zeal the heathen did possess bursts into a flame of glowing fanaticism.[202]

Likewise, Stoddard writes:

> There is among Muslim masses a great deal of genuine fanaticism caused not by European political domination but by religious bigotry and blind hatred of Western civilisation.[203]

Cantwell Smith says:

> It is the Muslim Arab's aggressive reaction to the attack of his world which he has already found to be almost overwhelming, then has leapt with frantic, sadistic joy to burn and kill. The burning of Cairo, the assassination of Prime Ministers, the intimidation of Christians, the vehemence and hatred in their literature - all of this is to be understood in terms of a people who have lost their way, whose heritage has proven unequal to modernity, whose leaders have been dishonest, whose ideals have failed. In this aspect, the new Islamic

---

[200] V.S. Naipaul: *Among*; op cit; p. 214.
[201] Ibid; p. 295.
[202] The Influence of Islam; in *The Moslem World*; vol 2; pp. 392-3.
[203] L. Stoddard: *The New World of Islam*; op cit; p. 65.

upsurge is a force not to solve problems but to intoxicate those who can no longer abide the failure to solve them.[204]

'In the Western depiction of Islam, its dangers and violence, it is difficult to know where reality ends and myths begin' (Esposito)[205]

> 'The Muslims are coming, the Muslims are coming![206] A caricature of Western fears? Exaggerated? Perhaps. However, when Dan Quayle, the vice president of the United States speaks of the danger of radical Islamic fundamentalism, grouping it with Nazism and communism, and magazines and newspaper editorials speak of Islam's war with the West and its incompatibility with democracy, and a respected national newspaper, the Boston Globe,[207] runs a four part series on Islam, whose general tenor is captured by the title of its introductory piece, 'The Sword of Islam,' it is difficult to know where reality ends and myth begins.'[208]

Recently, the American Time magazine told us:

> This is the dark side of Islam, which shows its face in violence and terrorism, intended to overthrow modern, more secular regimes and harm the Western nations that support them.[209]

Writing in 2003, supposedly to encourage understanding between the Islamic and Western worlds, Cox and Marks say:

> Understandably, terrorism is currently top of the agenda. But there is substantial evidence of a concerted and coordinated strategic attack over a long period on the fundamental principles of Western societies.
>
> Islam can provide Muslims with a religious justification for changing any existing society into an Islamic society. The aim is to make Islam supreme and to dominate every aspect of society. This is what is wanted not only by the leaders like those we have described - including Osama bin Laden - but by many Muslims all over the world according to their teaching, preaching and publications.[210]

Judiciously, or insidiously one must say, and just like the whole of their work, in fact, being a combination of selection and juxtaposition of facts and declarations, combining selected verses of the Qur'an with declarations by Bin Laden and others, the same Cox and Marks tell us:

> Muslims believe that when they die they go to the grave to await the day of judgement when Allah will decide, on the basis of works done on earth who goes to Paradise and who to hell.[211] The only way to guarantee going to Paradise - and avoid Allah's verdict on the day of judgment - is to die in jihad

---

[204] W. Cantwell Smith: *Islam in Modern History*; (Princeton University Press; 1957); pp. 158-9.
[205] J. Esposito: *The Islamic Threat*; op cit; p. 168.
[206] D. Pipes: The Muslims are coming! The Muslims are coming! in the *National Review*; November 19; 1990; pp. 28-31.
[207] Boston Globe: July 27; 1991.
[208] J. Esposito: *The Islamic Threat*; p. 168.
[209] *Time Magazine*: The Dark Side of Islam; 4 October 1993; p. 62; in A. Lueg: The Perception of Islam; op cit; pp. 7-31.
[210] C. Cox-J. Marks: *The West, Islam and Islamism*; op cit; p. 56
[211] Qur'an: 101: 6-9.

while fighting the enemies of Islam.[212] This provides a major religious motive for suicide bombers or others to volunteer for jihad.[213]

Bernard Lewis, in an article 'Roots of Muslim Rage,' speaks of the Muslim peril, as paraphrased in the American Atlantic Monthly:

> The struggle between Islam and the West has now lasted fourteen centuries. It has consisted of a long series of attacks and counterattacks, jihads and crusades, conquests and re-conquests. Today much of the Muslim world is again seized by an intense and violent resentment of the West. "Suddenly," a distinguished historian (Lewis) of Islam writes, 'America had become the archenemy, the incarnation of evil, the diabolic opponent of all that is good, and specifically, for Muslims, of Islam. Why?[214]

Islam and Muslims, Esposito notes, are, thus,

> Portrayed as the instigators and protagonists in fourteen centuries of warfare. Islam is the aggressor. Thus in the above statement, Islam and the acts of Muslims are described as aggressive - responsible for attacks, jihads, and conquests-while the West is described as defensive, responding with counterattacks, crusades, and re-conquests. Despite the portrayal of fourteen continuous centuries of confrontation, the reader is informed that "suddenly" America has become the archenemy, evil personified, and so forth. If the contemporary threat is "sudden," then the reader will logically conclude that Muslims have a historic propensity to violence against and hatred of the West, or else that Muslims are an emotional, irrational, and war-prone people.[215]

We shift to another issue that brings us closer to now (2020) that the very essence or source of Islam, today, is more questioned than even during the Middle Ages. Even the friends of Islam, such as Montgomery Watt, for instance, claim that 'whilst divine, the Qur'an includes errors':

> What other believers in God would hope for would be that Muslims would find a way of maintaining the general truth of the Qur'an, but without denying that in some secondary matters there were slight errors...[216]

Rippin, for his part, holds:

> The earliest non-Islamic source testifying to the existence of the Koran appears to stem from the eighth century. Indeed, early Islamic sources, at least those which do not seem to have as their prime purpose the defence of the integrity of the canon, would seem to witness that the text of the Koran may not have been totally fixed until the early part of the ninth century.

---

[212] Qur'an: 8:39; 4: 74; 9: 89.
[213] Extract from declaration of war by Bin Laden; leaders of the World Islamic Front for the jihad against the Jews and the Crusaders... quoted in R. Gunaratna: *Inside al-Qaeda: Global Network of Terror*; (London; Hurst and Company; 2002); pp. 1; 7; etc. All in C. Cox-J. Marks: *The West, Islam and Islamism*; op cit; p. 34.
[214] B. Lewis: Roots of Muslim rage; *Atlantic Monthly*; 226:3; September 1990; p. 2.
[215] J. Esposito: *The Islamic Threat*; op cit; pp. 177-8.
[216] W.M. Watt: *Muslim Christian Encounters* (Routledge; London; 1991), p. 137.

> Manuscript evidence does not allow for substantially earlier dating either... What Wansbrough has done has been to bring to the study of Islam and the Koran the same healthy scepticism developed within modern biblical studies (and modern studies in general).[217]

To the likes of Patricia Crone and Michael Cook and their adepts: Islam, the Qur'an, Makkah, the Prophet, the early history of Islam: all of them are inventions by Islamic zealots.[218] Their views are now widespread, and form particular focus of scholarship, such as found in the latest New Cambridge History of Islam.[219] Of course Western academia is today replete with scholars holding the same views. And so, today, in 2020, we are back precisely to when it all began in the medieval period, with the systemic denial of the Prophet existence, the Message, and the whole story of Islam. It is all explained to us by the powerful Christian lobby and also the powerful secular or anti Christian lobby, and even by many scholars of Muslim origins, the only difference between today and the medieval times being the means used today on top of the traditional means of communications, the internet and Youtube.[220]

---

[217] A. Rippin: *Muslims, their Religious Beliefs and Practices*; vol 1; (London; 1991); p. ix.
[218] P. Crone; M.A. Cook: *Hagarism; the Making of the Muslim World*; Cambridge University Press; 1977. P. Crone, *Slaves on horses: The evolution of the Islamic polity* (Cambridge, 1980); see also P. Crone, *Meccan trade and the rise of Islam* (Princeton, 1987; repr. Piscataway, NJ, 2004)
[219] Chase F. Robinson, Editor, vol 1; in Michael Cook (General Editor): *The New Cambridge History of Islam*; Cambridge University Press; in 6 vols, Cambridge 2011. Introduction; vol 1.
[220] *Gibson, Dan (2017). Early Islamic Qiblas: A survey of mosques built between 1AH/622 C.E. and 263 AH/876 C.E. Vancouver: Independent Scholar's Press..* Imprint of CanBooks.ca
——— *(2011). Qur'ānic Geography: A survey and evaluation of the geographical references in the Qur'ān with suggested solutions for various problems and issues'. Vancouver: Independent Scholar's Press.*
https://www.youtube.com/user/canbooks
See also:
https://www.google.com/search?q=dan+gibson%2C+makkah&oq=dan+gibson%2C+makkah+&aqs=chrome..69i57j0.6392j0j7&sourceid=chrome&ie=UTF-8

Two

TEN CENTURIES OF PRACTICE IN RESHAPING THE TRUTH

As Lueg points out:
> Instead of serious analyses, [they] are given to psychologising or to painting crude images of the Islamic world along racist lines. Certainly, not all elements of the stereotyped fear of the Islamic threat have been invented unaided. In Islamic societies examples of aggression, repression, fanaticism and so on are indeed to be found. But our perception of Islam as 'the enemy' still has little to do with reality, because only certain aspects of reality are used to cement our clichéd image.[221]

Esposito also writes:
> A selective presentation and analysis of Islam and events in the Muslim world by prominent scholars and political commentators too often inform articles and editorials on the Muslim world. This selective analysis fails to tell the whole story, to provide the full context for Muslim attitudes, events, and actions, or fails to account for the diversity of Muslim practice. While it sheds some light, it is a partial light that obscures or distorts the full picture. As a result, Islam and Islamic revivalism are easily reduced to stereotypes of Islam against the West, Islam's war with modernity, or Muslim rage, extremism, fanaticism, terrorism. The "f" and "t" words, "fundamentalism" and "terrorism," have become linked in the minds of many. Selective and therefore biased analysis adds to our ignorance rather than our knowledge, narrows our perspective rather than broadening our understanding, reinforces the problem rather than opening the way to new solutions.[222]

Smith notes how nearly all who had approached Islam did so only to vilify and misrepresent it, writing from preconceived positions.[223] A dark picture was painted of Islam to contrast with the light self-image of Christianity and every crime imaginable was popularly associated with the faith, Smith adds.[224]

Summing up the Western view of Islam, Daniel holds that nonsense was accepted, and sound sense was distorted.[225] Attacks on Islam, which Daniel notes, are 'most divorced from reality, and most remote from any contact with Islam.'[226] Bucaille, equally, has concluded that the erroneous statements made about Islam in the West are the result of systematic denigration.[227] Lueg insists that the threat of Islam often

---

[221] A. Lueg: The Perception of Islam; op cit; p. 8.
[222] J. Esposito: *The Islamic Threat*; op cit; p. 173.
[223] R.B. Smith: *Mohammed and Mohammedanism*; (London; 1874); p. ix.
[224] In C. Bennett: *Victorian Images of Islam*; (Grey Seal; London; 1992); p. 77.
[225] N. Daniel: *Islam and the West*; op cit p. 302.
[226] N. Daniel: *The Arabs;* op cit; p. 232.
[227] M Bucaille: *The Bible, The Quran and Science;* (Seghers; Paris; 1993); p. 1.

stems from a limited vision rather than reality, and that anything we hear from the Islamic world, we assume to be stated from an inferior position and in a religious context, i.e., that of Islam.[228] Van Ess, likewise, points to the anti Islamic clichés, which lie deep in the subconscious and meet with unanimous approval.[229]

We have shown many instances of distortions of the realities of Islam, already. We cannot, of course, deal with all misrepresentations, inventions or exaggerations of Muslim crimes and the techniques used, and each and every issue. This work as it proceeds will address many such issues that could have come under this heading. A dominant effort of ours is to try as much as possible to avoid repeating ourselves, and might only do so by accident in a few places. Also, in the following heading we shall focus on the work of academia and people of letters of how they contribute overwhelmingly to the creation of the Muslim monster which then draws action from others. Here we limit ourselves to dealing with some of the manners an unfavourable image of Islam and Muslims is created which generally contrasts with the image of the Westerner/Christian, and en passant touch on the work of mainstream media and how it reshape facts, and also the work of artists.

The first technique is central to our work. It consists in presenting a discourse of Islamic violence/threat based on isolated, or even untrue, incidents in order to justify Western/Christian intervention. For this, the West has a ten century old experience to draw from. Hence, when Pope Urban II called for the Crusades (in 1095) at Clermont in France, he described the Muslims as:

> An accursed race, a race utterly alienated from God, a generation forsooth which has not directed its heart and has not entrusted its spirit to God, has invaded the lands of those Christians and has depopulated them by the sword, pillage and fire; it has led away a part of the captives into its own country, and a part it has destroyed by cruel tortures; it has either entirely destroyed the churches of God... When they wish to torture people by a base death, they perforate their navels, and dragging forth the extremity of the intestines, bind it to a stake; then with flogging they lead the victim around until the viscera having gushed forth the victim falls prostrate upon the ground. Others they bind to a post and pierce with arrows... What shall I say of the abominable rape of the women? To speak of it is worse than to be silent.....[230]

Of course, the pope lied. He had other reasons to call for the crusades as we detail to great length in our book on the subject, but the most important of such reasons was that the Church realised the military strength of Islam was ebbing, and there were

---

[228] A. Lueg: The Perception of Islam; op cit; pp. 28; and 21.
[229] J. Van Ess: Islamic perspectives; in H. Kung et al: *Christianity*, op cit; p. 6.
[230] In D. C. Munro, "Urban and the Crusaders", Translations and Reprints from the *Original Sources of European History*, vol 1:2, (1895), pp. 5-8.

great sectarian divisions within the ranks of the Muslim foe.[231] 11th century Syria, Lamonte notes, was 'a crazy quilt of semi independent states,' resulting from previous divisions of it made by the Byzantines and the Fatimid Caliphate of Cairo.[232] So, the Church exploited such divisions in order to finish the business with Islam. The Pope, however, needed something concrete, so he relied on an incident thirty years old, when a group of Bedouins robbed some Christian pilgrims in 1064-5,[233] to turn it into an instance of generalised horrific Muslim crimes so as to justify both the launching of the crusades and their subsequent violence.

The same technique, as we shall see in the subsequent chapters, was used by the Catholic Church when it sought to eliminate the Muslims from Sicily and southern Italy (in the 13th-early 14th century) and Spain (through the late medieval period and finally in 1609-10), when their 'dangerous presence amidst Christians' was emphasised above anything else.[234] The same technique was resorted to in the wars against the Ottomans, when Turkish cruelties were blown beyond any relation to reality, also during the Franco-British colonial era of the Muslim lands of the 19th century, when 'Muslim piracy and barbarism' were invented and used to justify colonisation of Muslim lands, and recently in concocting Iraqi weapons of mass destruction to justify the invasion of Iraq, or in always labelling Muslims as murderous, fanatical terrorists so as to inflict any violent retribution on them that is deemed necessary.[235]

Daniel explains to us this:
> The Christian canon of Muslim behaviour, that is, the received Christian opinion as to what Muslims actually did, was partly formed by the tendency of misconceptions to snowball, and to confirm as well as to add to one another. Mere repetition is enough to bring unshakable conviction.[236]

Repeating the same claim, however unproven, has always worked wonders in Western/Christian dealings with their foes. Take, for instance, the scene of Indians

---

[231] See Ibn al-Athir: Kamil; op cit; vol viii; X; p. 186, 256; J. D. Breckenridge: The Two Sicilies; in *Islam and the Medieval West*; S. Ferber Ed; op cit; pp. 39-59 at pp. 46-7. Rodrigo de Zayas: *Les Morisques et le racisme d'etat*, ed., Les Voies du Sud; Paris, 1992; p. 173. Ibn al-Idhari: *Al-Bayan al-Mughrib*; ed., A. Huici Miranda; Tetuan; 1963; pp. 381-5.

[232] J.H. Lamonte: Crusade and Jihad: in *The Arab Heritage*, N.A. Faris editor; Princeton University Press, 1944; pp. 159-98; at p. 163.

[233] For the incident, the real causes of the crusades, Pope Urban's speech, see, for instance: D.C. Munro: The Western; op cit; N. Daniel: *The Arabs;* op cit; S. Runciman: *A History of the Crusades*, vol 1, op cit; W. Durant: *The Age of Faith*; op cit.

[234] For all this, see: J.P. Lomax: Frederick II, His Saracens, and the Papacy, in *Medieval Christian Perceptions of Islam*, edited by J.V. Tolan; Routledge; London; pp. 175-97. J. Taylor: *Muslims in Medieval Italy*; Lexington Books; New York; Oxford; 2003. D.W. Lomax: *The Reconquest of Spain*, Longman, London, 1978. J. McCarthy: *Death and Exile: The Ethnic Cleansing of Ottoman Muslims, 1821-1922*; The Darwin Press; New Jersey; 1995. S. Lane-Poole: *The Moors in Spain;* Fisher Unwin; London; 1888. H.C. Lea: *The Moriscos of Spain*; Burt Franklin; New York; 1968 reprint. H. C. Lea: *A History of the Inquisition of Spain*, 4 vols; The Mac Millan Company, New York, 1907.

[235] Ernst Jäckh; *Deutschland im Orient nach dem Balkan-Krieg;* Chapter 7: Deutsche und französische Augenzeugen von christlichen Massakers. (Die Balkangreuel des 30 jährigen Krieges); Martin Mörikes Verlag, Munich, 1913; pp. 83-98. E. Jäckh: *The Rising Crescent* (New York, 1944). P.T. Levin: *'From Saracen Scourge to Terrible Turks; Medieval, Renaissance and Enlightenment Images of the Other in the Narrative Construction of Europe;'* A Dissertation Presented to the Faculty of the Graduate School of University of Southern California, in Partial Fulfillment of the Requirements for the Degree Doctor of Philosophy (International Relations;) August, 2007. Z. Lockman: *Contending Visions of the Middle East*; Cambridge University Press; 2004. J. Salt: *The Unmaking of the Middle East*; University of California Press, 2008.

[236] N. Daniel: *Islam and the West*, op cit; p. 270.

yelling and brandishing axes, chasing after a stage-coach with White men and women on board as you see in all classic Westerns; it creates the very opposite image of reality. It conveys to you the notion that the Indians did the most and most heinous crimes, whilst in truth, as we shall see in chapter six, it is they who were mass eradicated, with barely any White people losses. The technique worked so well with the Turks as we shall see in chapter 8, whereby the mere repeat of claims 'of their barbaric acts' was enough to cause them to be removed en masse, whilst in truth, it was they who were slaughtered en masse.[237]

Related to this is yet another absolutely simple and yet uniquely effective, and Western, manner of making something into truth, a method we looked at in great detail in all our works, and we shall return to in heading three. It is this: Source A cites Source B who refers to C, who refers to D, who refers to A, and there you have a truth established. The whole Greek legend, i.e the role of Greece in the rise of modern civilisation, as we explained in our work: *Our civilisation* is the outcome of this trick. This is also the story of the Turkish genocide of Armenians, whereby people refer to Henry Morgenthau, Viscount Bryce, Toynbee, Christian Missionaries, and so on, whilst all these were, for the nearest amongst them, Morgenthau, in Istanbul, and he had heard of the crime allegedly from Turkish officials; whilst Bryce and Toynbee were in London, working for the British Ministry of Propaganda, and the American Missionaries had heard of the incident.[238] But, none, absolutely none of the persons on, or near, the alleged scene of the crime, most particularly the Russians and the Armenians fighting by their side had seen anything.[239]

The same with Arab/Muslim slave trading, as we shall see in chapter 7. It was reported by Christian missionaries who found human bones in some place, and was proven in fiction, films, sketches and drawings, but had anyone been witness to it? None.

The same with regard to Arab/Muslim market stalls where women captives are sold naked: you can see it in hundreds of drawings and paintings by Europeans; you can read about it in hundreds of books, and can see it in films. In reality, had anyone seen it? None. And if you think for a minute: do you really believe Islamic society allows half naked or even naked women to be exhibited in bazars, markets stalls, and the like?

Playing with definitions or expressions such as we noted with Bad Apples is a very good way of reshaping truth. Islamic opposition to their slayers is, thus, and always defined as fanatical terror, and described as organised hatred of the West. We shall

---

[237] *Foreign Office Reports*; such as F.O. 195-1185; No 73. F.O. 195-2438, no 6650; Lamb to Lowther, Salonica 3 December 1912, etc.
M. Gehri (Delegue du Comite International de la Croix Rouge): 'Mission d'Enquete en Anatolie, 12-22 Mai 1921,' *Extrait de la Revue Internationale de la Croix Rouge*, 3em Annee, No. 31, 15 juillet 1921, pp. 721-735. (Geneva, 1921.) P. Loti: *Turquie Agonisante*; Calman Levy; Paris; 1913. Halide Edib: *The Turkish Ordeal*; John Murray; London; 1928.
[238] Henry Morgenthau: *Ambassador Morgenthau's Story*; Double Day, Page & Company; 1919; A.J. Toynbee: *The Murderous Tyranny of the Turks*; Hodder and Stoughton, London, 1917. Viscount Bryce wrote in Toynbee's foreword.
[239] Rafael de Nogales y Mendez, *Memoirs of a Soldier of Fortune* (Garden City, NY: Garden City Publishing Co., Inc., 1932)
S.J. Shaw and E.K. Shaw: *History of the Ottoman Empire and Modern Turkey*; vol 2; Cambridge University Press; 1977.

get to that when we deal with the case of Iraq after the 2003 invasion in Chapter 10. During the colonial period, Meredith Townsend, an experienced Indian administrator, noted how:

> All Muslims in particular are assumed to have fanaticism, as if it were some separate mental peculiarity, belonging to the Mahommedan faith, which accounted for everything, and especially for any marked impulse. Thus Turks were called fanatics for sympathising with Arabi (the Egyptian officer who rose against the British in the early 1880s), and Arabi's soldiers were called fanatics when they were decently courageous; *The Times* said Arabi's success depended on fanaticism, and France was warned by the newspaper correspondents to beware of an outburst of it.[240]

Even as they slew or starved Muslims in their millions in the 19th century, colonial powers, as Rodinson notes, still held that it was 'fanatical Pan-Islamism'

> That was attempting domination, that bore an aggressive ideology, and was the fruit of international conspiracy.[241]

Likewise, the French saw the Algerians who fought for independence (1954-1962) as nothing but murderous terrorists aiming at reversing France's civilising mission in Algeria.

And today, much the same prevails. Charles Krauthammer writes:

> History is being driven by another force as well: the political reawakening of the Islamic world.[242] It is a challenge all the more ominous because it is Pan-Islamic. It is a "global intifada," embracing not only the Islamic heartland but also the peripheries of the Muslim world where Islam confronts the non-Muslim communities in Kashmir, Azerbaijan, Kosovo in Yugoslavia, Lebanon, and the West Bank.[243]

For his part, Raymond Aron warns of:

> The Islamic revolutionary wave, generated by the fanaticism of the Prophet and the violence of the people.[244]

As Esposito remarks, it suits such opinion-makers to alter reality whenever it suits them, on one hand highlighting Muslim divisions when it suits their political agenda, and at others stressing Muslim unity in the hatred of the West when it serves that same agenda.[245] Hence, Senator Albert Gore, speaking of Syrian-Iraqi relations noted

> Baathite Syrians are Alawites, a Shiite heresy, while the Iraqis are Sunnis. Reason enough in this part of the world for hatred and murder.[246]

Yet, Esposito notes, when equally convenient, Islam, the Arabs, and the Muslim world are represented as a unified block poised against the West.[247]

---

[240] Meredith Townsend: Asia and Europe; (Westminster; 1901); in N. Daniel: *Islam, Europe*; op cit; p. 468.
[241] M. Rodinson: *Europe;* op cit; p. 127.
[242] C. Krauthammer: The New Crescent; op cit.
[243] In J. Esposito: *The Islamic Threat;* op cit; p. 182.
[244] R. Aron: l'Incendie; *L'Express;* December 1; 1979.
[245] J. Esposito: *The Islamic Threat;* op cit; p. 183.
[246] Exit Lebanon; *The New Republic*; November 12; 1990.
[247] J. Esposito: *The Islamic Threat;* op cit; p. 183.

Let us step onto another level to show how Muslim barbarism is enhanced in perceptions when reality is otherwise. Here, reality is altered by what Fisher calls altering the real importance of events by degrees of emphasis, by making a short story long, or a long story longer than it ought to be.[248] Thus, important, crucial events are much trivialised, or quickly buried, and conversely, one single event with hardly any bearing can be stretched considerably. We can cite one instance here, in the Autumn of 2006, when there took place the near total suppression from the news of the number of Iraqi victims of the war (650,000),[249] and focus instead was placed on Muslim women wearing the *niqab* (the veil that covers a woman's face). In regard to amplifying Muslim crimes, there is no shortage of that, and few random instances suffice to highlight the issue. In September 2003, when a Kurdish man was tried for killing his daughter, his case was turned into the worst case of patricide in generations. Equally, in the same period, when a Kenyan Muslim infected his two mistresses with AIDS, he was the worst culprit of the sort in the history of the disease. Of course, Muslim terrorist acts are the most remembered of all misdeeds, kept alive all the times, and every year at the same date commemorated, even more dramatically than the killings of the World Wars. Understandably outrages committed in the West are the most focussed upon, but the global nature of the Muslim fiend is not ignored either. The truly barbaric hostage taking in a school in Beslan, Southern Russia, early in September 04, and its horrific end, was the worst crime ever perpetrated according to the Western media, even seeming to dwarf Nazi crimes of the Second World War. Its horrors and the criminal nature of Muslims filled the pages of Western dailies, the graphic and morbid details enhanced, and repeated, daily. Conversely, looking at the situation in 2014 (on 2 May 2014), when tens of Eastern, pro Russian-Ukrainians were set ablaze in a building in the city of Donetsk, hardly any uproar, or emotional wording of any sort took place, the incident so much toned down it just about briefly made the news. There was no sight of weeping relatives; no picture of coffins; no pictures of the victims; nothing on the extreme nature of the act or its perpetrators; no sustained analysis by experts on the causes of the tragedy, and the evil, barbaric, nature of its perpetrators, and their faith; hardly anything at all, one even ponders at times whether the misdeed truly happened.

Then there is the technique we can call of equalising incidents that are far from equal, and to explain this nothing better than the following examples. When in the Autumn of 2004 a British man, Ken Bigley, was murdered in Iraq, this murder was turned into the most barbaric deed of all, taking the front of all news and media broadcast, for weeks, whilst the American destruction of a city of 300,000 people, Felloujah, and the mass slaughter of thousands of its people, around the same time,

---
[248] D.H. Fischer: *Historians' Fallacies*, (London: Routledge & Kegan Paul, 1971); pp.149-50.
[249] Figures in the medical journal: The Lancet; released on 11 October, 06.

was hardly noted, and if and when done, was only deemed 'a disproportionate answer to Muslim terror'.

An earlier, and even more poignant instance is that of the Taliban's execution of a woman for the murder of her husband in 2001. Western television channels broadcast and re-played the same scene of execution countless times, broadcast by every channel, at all times of the day, most channels showing the scene twice every hour, thus, creating the image of the Taliban (who never murdered or raped one single woman) into the cruellest foes of women. The weekly, The Sunday Times went:

'Under the Taliban,... pictures showing medieval barbarity.... Anyone viewing this film will expect the international response to be markedly different.'[250]

The Guardian equated this incident with:

'Atrocities comparable to very worst scenes in Kosovo, or Chechnya.'[251]

The killing of one woman, for right or wrong reasons, is, thus, equated to crimes where thousands of Muslim women were murdered, and thousands more raped.

We must here cite the horror of the coup in Egypt (2013-,) whereby the killing of thousands of people, the incarceration of more than ten thousand men and women, death sentences passed in their thousands in sham trials, torture and other exactions committed on a huge scale, and yet, hardly, if any, murmur, from the West or 'Human Right' agencies. Rather, it seems all this is sound and is a proportional response to Muslim terror and threat. Indeed, in April 2014, an Egyptian court condemned to death over 1000 people for the murder of a policeman. How could a thousand persons reach the bugger and murder him seems only to make sense to the twisted minds of those who see nothing abnormal in this. In fact, the killing of thousands in this same coup was justified on the ground that Amnesty International produced a report which spoke of torture of people by pro Morsi supporters,[252] which hence justified the army to crush them, including crushing them into earth with bulldozers.

The role of academia will follow in the next heading, but let's have a look at the media, how it lies systematically, lying its reason d'etre. We pick some events from early in the new millennium just as a sample. In late 2001, when the USA was struck by a terror campaign with anthrax, supposedly the work of Islamic terrorists, this was to prepare for war on 'terror' in Afghanistan. On this matter, the BBC even found links of anthrax terrorists with Iraq. Yet, this very BBC, in March 2002, accepted that an American CIA expert was the author of the anthrax campaign.[253] Unrepentant, in another Panorama programme (9 February 03), the BBC insisted on the Iraqi links with terror to add to the justifications for the war on Iraq. Another

---

[250] The Sunday Times: 26 June 2001.
[251] The Guardian: 26 June, 2001.
[252] See *The Telegraph*; UK; 9 October 2013, referring to Brendan O'Neill: Did Amnesty International Unwittingly assist the Egyptian Military in its Bloody Crackdown; 20th August, 2013 (type all on internet).
[253] BBC; Newsnight; 14 March 2002; 10.30 pm; then all media May-June 2003.

BBC reporter, on a separate assignment in northern Iraq, even stumbled on a supposed chemical factory under the control of Islamic groups, hence proof of Islamic chemical terror in preparation. Once Iraq and the said building were bombed (March 03), it was proved that the building had no value of any sort. On 9 February 03, the British used 'an up-to-date dossier' to demonstrate Islamic terror with Iraqi links; and yet the report proved later to be a copy of a dissertation published nine years before, word by word, even, with the grammatical mistakes of one of the foreign authors being repeated. Then there was the 45-minute threat Iraq posed with its weapons of mass destruction, the biggest farce of recent times. Still it justified the war on Iraq in 2003. The BBC, most particularly, throughout the war in Iraq, in 2003, conveyed the view that death and mayhem, and the war itself, were a means to end Saddam's terror. In the early stages of the war it even turned into an agency of propaganda for the military and politicians, talking of the fall of Um Qasr on the first day of the war, when it did not happen; telling us of the surrender of the Iraqi southern army on the second day of the war, when it did not happen; telling us of the surrender of Basra on the third day of the war, when it never took place; talking of an uprising in Basra against the Iraqi rule on the eighth day, when there was none; reporting on the cold-blood execution of British soldiers by the Iraqis, when no evidence proved that it happened... and countless other distortions, which ended in the station going completely silent when the city of Felloujah was flattened in November 2004 by American forces. And yet, despite all this connivance, we are told and retold about the corporation's dedication to the truth. Incidentally, in regard to Felloujah, its destruction and the killing of countless thousands of its population was, in American words, 'to give back the city to its people,' 'to free it from terrorists,' 'to remove evil,' 'to prepare the city for democracy' and, finally, it had to be destroyed because, in the words of the devout Christian chaplain of the American army: 'Satan lives in Felloujah.'[254]

Patrick Cockburn's Story:

Here, we focus on this person' story to show you that how any story is used to do its work. We shall return to Cockburn and his involvement in the Shia-Sunni issue in Chapter 10.
In respect to the story, we don't know this person well, and have not read any of his many books to say what sort of person he is, indeed. He might be an angel of person, we don't know. He might be one of those happy to fan the Sunni-Shia sectarian violence, and he could also be a hater of all things Sunni, we cannot tell categorically. We definitely know that he cares very much for the Shia side and Iran, that he explains to us clearly as we show in Chapter 10.

---

[254] Christian military chaplain to the BBC on Newsnight 10.30, 24 November 04; and on BBC 24; on 24-5 November 04.

So let's begin with the story, first and raise the issues which we wish to raise that are relevant to our work.

First, if you consulted Wikipedia, you would find the best and most succinct summary of the affair that is of interest here. As, it is short we repeat what is relevant to us, and quote verbatim in order to avoid putting words in people's mouths:

> Cockburn was criticised for an apparent claim made in his 2015 book *The Rise of Islamic State* about the Adra massacre of Alawites and Christians during the Syrian Civil War.
>
> Idrees Ahmad pointed out that in the book Cockburn was apparently claiming to be a witness and noted that this claim disagrees with Cockburn's reportage at the time, in which he stated he learned of the killings via "a Syrian [Assad regime] soldier who gave his name as Abu Ali". Ahmad also questioned whether the massacre had taken place.[255]

We don't want to become involved in the controversy, but would advise everyone to check the following: Who is Lying about Syria's Christian Massacre by Muhammad Idrees Ahmad, updated Apr 14, 2017, available at:
https://www.thedailybeast.com/whos-lying-about-syrias-christian-massacre?ref=scroll

We are not of course, interested in Cockburn's defending himself because we leave that to him as he does in the page whose details we just gave you. The argument by Idrees Ahmed is also well expressed by himself on the same page, and we cannot match the form or substance of either Ahmed's or Cockburn's defence of their respective arguments.

Wikipedia does an excellent job in noting:

> Cockburn said that he had made no such claim; rather, he charged, an "obvious error" had been, at best, misconstrued by Ahmad. Cockburn confirmed that it was his contemporary report that was correct, that he did not witness the massacre and admonished Ahmad for doubting the fact of the massacre, mentioning "reports from the AP and Reuters news agencies" describing the massacre by Islamic militants and quoting local witnesses. Cockburn's publisher explained the error arose from the publisher summarising but misunderstanding writings by Cockburn, that Cockburn had never claimed to be a witness and that the error would be corrected in subsequent printings of the book. The publisher criticised Ahmad for using a "minor" mistake "made evident by text that surrounds and contradicts it" to "impugn the integrity" of Cockburn.[256]

---

[255] Wikipedia https://en.wikipedia.org/wiki/Patrick_Cockburn
[256] Ibid.

Here where we intervene. Indeed, this is the sort of story we have been dealing since we started and shall keep dealing with for the rest of this work, whether in respect to the Turkish horrors justifying the crusades, or the Missionaries who found bones by wells for them to argue this was as a sign of widespread and unequalled Muslim slave trading, or the paintings of naked Muslim women in bazaars to give ground to the story of Muslim trade in enslaved women, or Henry Morgenthau's witnessing the Turkish genocide of Armenians from Istanbul, whilst Bryce and Toynbee could see it from London, or Gladstone witnessing the massacres of Christians in Bulgaria from his Christian Seminary in London, in the 1870s, or Father Dan and other Christian Redemptionists who could see the plight of thousands of Christians in the dark dens of Algerian prisons in the 17th century, thousands which eventually grew to millions thanks to the genius of today's academia,[257] and we can go on. Indeed, it is always the same thing: everybody saw or was a witness to the Muslim crime, but in fact everybody relies on the reports of witnesses, who themselves might have heard of the incident thanks to the reports of those who refer to them. We set aside the crook, called the Pope, a liar, and also the crook Gladstone, another liar, and the crooks of today, whom we cannot name in order to avoid trouble, who also lied about Saddam Hussein's arms of mass destruction, and so on. This is indeed what concerns us, this ten century old story of always inventing or exaggerating the story of Islamic terror or threat, or violence, or barbarism.

What matters to us more importantly, is what Idrees Ahmad explained extremely well, but which Cockburn lamentably failed to deal with or even address busy as he were defending his integrity. Indeed, throughout the period related to the massacre Cockburn refers to, something we could witness at the time, perhaps by coincidence, articles and claims not just by Cockburn, were used by the Syrian regime to inflict terrible retribution on the opposition. The casualties amongst Muslims were considerable. This is precisely what happened in Algeria in the 1990s, whereby reports in the French media about Islamist barbarities, which they never saw in person, but wrote about in every detail, were followed by horrendous 'counter massacres' by supposedly anti Islamist groups. Historically, it all echoes perfectly, as we shall see further down, the response by the Christians when they read Gladstone's pamphlet, and hence slaughtered hundreds of thousands of Turks.[258] The killing of at least 600,000 Iraqis by the Americans and their allies also remains the result of a mistake: the false claim of Saddam's weapons of mass destruction.

---

[257] Such as R.C. Davis. *Christian Slaves, Muslim Masters: White Slavery in the Mediterranean, the Barbary Coast, and Italy, 1500–1800.* Basingstoke: Palgrave Macmillan, 2003.
[258] See J. McCarthy: *Death and Exile: The Ethnic Cleansing of Ottoman Muslims, 1821-1922*; The Darwin Press; New Jersey; 1995. S.J. Shaw and E.K. Shaw: *History of the Ottoman Empire and Modern Turkey*; vol 2; Cambridge University Press; 1977.

And we finish with Cockburn where we attack him directly: His book: *The Rise of Islamic State Isis and the New Sunni Revolution*. We ask: Are Isis truly a sign of Sunni Revolution? They are a symptom of Muslim failure and above all an outcome of Western meddling in Muslim affairs. They are just murderers who murdered Sunnis more than anybody else. This, Cockburn hardly refers to. What have ISIS got to do with Sunni Islam? We possibly hate them more than the Shias do. But first and foremost: Why this Western obsession with Sectarian aspects of Islam, of which we accuse Cockburn and his colleagues when we get to the chapter on Iraq, 10? It is he and his likes, and this we are left to tell in that chapter, who, with others involved in the Muslim world, academics, or diverse individuals and organisations who, knowingly, or maybe by instinct, have fanned and are still fanning the Sunni-Shia hatred. We shall show this. They can never stop for a minute and ask themselves about the power of words, and most of all, why do they have to always refer to someone as a Sunni or Shia, Arab, or Berber, Turk or Kurd? Cannot they just say: a murderer, a good person, or whatever, just as we do when we speak of Westerners, never referring to them as Protestants or Catholics? Can't they see that sectarianism is a dormant beast that only wakes up when it hears its name called? And that once it wakes up, the result is piles of mutilated bodies dumped in rubbish tips and human bits strewn all over the place, just blown up by a car bomb, maybe two.

The Use of Images

During the crusades, whilst the Christians were slaughtering their way into the Muslim world,[259] their draughtsmen were able to create a completely different image of both deed and foe. This is seen in the illustrations of the chronicles of William of Tyre (1130-90).[260] Muslims are distinguished from the Franks by their exaggerated physical features, to the limits of caricature. The reader would recognise the evil nature of the characters, as today villains in comics can be recognised easily.[261] Two late manuscripts, from 1285 and 1295[262] put in evidence the ugliness of the adversary. The Turkish defenders of Antioch wear turbans and black, dense beards, are dressed in simple tunics, with a grin on their face, the eyebrows dense and dark, the lips thick, eagle nosed, they appear in profile in an inferior position, which the draughtsman attributes to mediocre and inferior people.[263] These very features are found in another representation of the siege of Antioch, where grinning, tightly packed Turks behind their walls, can see advancing the heavy Christian cavalry, carrying spears topped by heads of Turks, easily recognisable: 'thick lips, strong noses, hair similar to that of Africans represented in

---

[259] See S. Runciman: *The Crusades*; (Cambridge University Press; 1962).
[260] M Balard; les Musulmans d'apres les illustrations de Guillaume de Tyr, in *De Toulouse a Tripoli*; Colloque held between 6 and 8 December, 1995, (University of Toulouse. 1997); pp. 143-51. Pictures pp. 152-166.
[261] Ibid; pp. 143-4.
[262] (Paris, Bibliotheque Nationale, ms. fr. 9082 and 9084).
[263] F. Garnier: *Le Language de l'image au Moyen Age*, (Paris, 1982), I, pp. 142-3; in M. Ballard: Les Musulmans, op cit; p. 146.

European Classical art.'[264] Thus, far from ignoring the Oriental world, the draughtsmen knew how to describe the adversary in caricaturing him with large features, their equipment incomplete, some physical features inferior, features which translate the diffuse perception that the West had in the 13th century of Islam: a world that was upside-down from Christian values, the archetype of evil, the ultimate enemy, 'that we can only fight to the death.'[265]

This technique of enhancing Muslim barbarism or cruelty via pictures became intensified in subsequent centuries as many instances in this work show. During the colonial era (19th-20th centuries), Muslim barbarism was caught in a number of paintings, which Kabbani describes with great skill. The artists recreated in their studios 'the cave of Ali Baba they had read about as children.' They also added the necessary tools of violence to depict what they imagined to be a particularly violent East. Gautier's description of Chasseriau's atelier illustrates this vogue: 'Daggers, swords, knives, pistols; fire arms...'[266] that represented an explosive and dangerous place where murder was an anodyne occurrence, where barbaric cruelty and opulence were displayed at once.[267]

Visiting another Orientalist painter's studio, Gautier's literary imagination provided him with the ready scenes of Eastern criminality to animate the space created by the presence of so many exotic objects: 'This room could serve as a background for some scenes of jealousy and murder; blood would not taint these deep purple carpets.'[268]

Gautier's perception of an Orient where gore and gems went hand in hand, where blood did not show a stain on the deep purple of exquisite carpets, was shared by most popular of Orientalist tableaux.[269]

Eugene Delacroix's 'La Mort de Sardanapale' was painted in 1827 before he actually made the journey East. It contains the images of Europe's Orient, derived from Byron's popular poem of that name.

> An Oriental despot sits enthroned on his luxurious bed (with its fantastic heads of elephants and its crimson drapery) detachedly watching all his earthly possessions being destroyed. His naked concubines are being stabbed to death by three dark villains, and his horse is being dragged away. All is chaotic, the brushstroke depicting the scene is an aptly 'romantic' and agitated one, while the canvas is crammed full of dramatic detail and incident, leaving no restful vacuum for the gaze.[270]

Henri Regnault's 'Execution sans jugement sous les rois maures' (Execution without Trial under Moorish Kings) of 1870 depicts a killing, the title giving it 'historical'

---

[264] M Balard: Les Musulmans d'apres les illustrations; op cit; p. 145.
[265] Ibid; p. 149.
[266] As quoted by Phillipe Julian: *Les Orientalistes*; (Paris; 1977); p. 72.
[267] R. Kabbani: *Imperial Fictions*; pp. 74-5.
[268] Phillipe Julian: *Les Orientalistes*; op cit; p. 73.
[269] R. Kabbani: *Imperial Fictions*; p. 75.
[270] Ibid.

validity: a guard has just executed a man who resembles him in colour, stature and facial features. He looks down unmoved at the severed head as he wipes the blood off the sword on his sleeve. The guard's massive figure is in sharp contrast to the soft lines of his tunic. The red of the blood on the floor is 'transfused into diffuse shades: the orange that bathes the whole scene; the pink robe that the guard wears which deepens into blood colour again between his feet, so that he seems to be wading in blood; and the red belt that is wrapped around the dead man's waist.' Nobody else is in the painting to witness the scene; it has been committed in secret, with little emotion, 'a killing without judgment as befits a capriciously cruel Orient.'[271]

The villain in Orientalist painting is almost always depicted as very dark or as black. In a painting entitled 'The Prisoner' painted by Filippo Baratti in 1883, two dark men appear to be relishing the humiliation of a frail old white man, who is bound and at their mercy. 'The roles,' Kabbani remarks, 'are polarised here, for the painters of this genre could not conceive of white and black as equals - one had always to be at the other's mercy, even when they both fell into the category of 'Orientals.'[272]

The use of images is even more effective today, especially due to the Muslim bearded subjects and other distinctive features, most particularly the Burqa, the object of hate of Westerners, the symbol of women oppression and medieval darkness par excellence. Hence, if one picks up a British daily, The Daily Mirror, in its edition of 25 January 03, straight behind the cover page, it shows the Prince of Wales talking to a Muslim woman completely shrouded in black, with the exception of her eyes. On the occasion, the Prince of Wales came across tens of Muslim women all wearing a diversity of less intimidating cloaks, and yet the paper, like the rest of the media, chose that image to define the Muslim woman. The same daily a week later, on 1 February, returned to the issue of a woman threatened with stoning in Nigeria for adultery, and again, used the very powerful image of she holding a small baby, turning the possible execution of a woman, something more current in the USA than anywhere else, into a crime against motherhood. This particular instance was the work of a columnist writing in the central pages, who preached for the life of a woman, and yet constantly supported the war in Iraq. Hence, by the power of an image, a person in favour of the military occupation of a nation turned into a carer for humanity. But let's stay with this Burqa issue which is used in the West today as a symbol of both Muslim relegating women to the days of medieval backwardness, a symbol of threat, an image that repulses. Look at this:

---
[271] Ibid; pp. 77-8.
[272] Ibid; p. 78.

The associated vision of the Muslim as a figure of extremes - excessive in zeal, in cruelty, in sensuality has been particularly enduring.[273] Hence the image of the beast, today; the largest picture one could find in the London *Sunday Times*.[274] His dark, large, bearded ghoulish face is surmounted with piercing black eyes; and the winter coat he wears adds to his monstrous feature as the 'Islamist murderer.' He murdered his sister who had been 'raped.' The six page long article in the weekly (Sunday Times) is given even more poignancy by the witness account of the Palestinian (Armenian born) Professor Shalhoub Kevorkian who states that raped Palestinian girls are killed by their families, and that she labours very hard against 'the barbarism' of society.[275] Looking at the photograph of the ghoul, who symbolises all Islamists, does not just highlight the plight of his victims, it amply justifies his eradication and that of his like. And their eradicator, whoever it is, becomes a modernist, and a saviour of humanity.

Esposito gives us a good instance of how modern media works to associate dramatic pictures with shocking headlines to enhance the fear and threat of Islam. He notes how:

> The stereotypical image of Islam and Muslims as menacing militant fundamentalists was reflected strikingly in B. Lewis' talk entitled "Islamic Fundamentalism," given as the prestigious Jefferson Lecture of 1990, the highest honour accorded by the U.S. government to a scholar for achievement in the Humanities. A revised version became a lead article, "The Roots of Muslim Rage," in the *Atlantic Monthly.*[276]
> The "packaging"- the new title, the magazine's cover, and the article's two pictures - of "Roots of Muslim Rage" reflects the pitfalls of a selective presentation. It reinforces stereotypes of Islamic revival and of Muslims and

---

[273] John Sweetman: *The Oriental Obsession*: (Cambridge University Press, 1987); p. 6.
[274] *The Sunday Times Magazine*; July 8, 2001.
[275] Ibid.
[276] B. Lewis: Roots of Muslim Rage; *Atlantic Monthly*; 226:3; September; 1990; 47; 51.

predisposes the reader to view the relationship of Islam to the West in terms 'of rage, violence, hatred, and irrationality.' Because of Bernard Lewis' international stature as a leading scholar and political commentator on the Middle East, his topic and its prominent public platform, "Roots of Muslim Rage" received widespread coverage nationally and internationally. It has had a significant impact both on Western perceptions of contemporary Islam and on many Muslim perceptions of how Islam and Muslims are viewed in the West.

The message and impact of "Roots of Muslim Rage" is reinforced by the picture on the front cover of the *Atlantic Monthly*, showing a scowling, bearded, turbaned Muslim with American flags in his glaring eyes. The threat motif and confrontational tone are supplemented by the two pictures used in the article, highlighting the typical Muslim perception of America as the enemy. The first is of a serpent marked with the stars and stripes seen crossing a desert (America's dominance of or threat to the Arab world); the second shows the serpent about to strike from behind an unsuspecting pious Muslim at prayer. Like other sensationalist stereotypes, pictures meant

'To be provocative, to attract the reader, feed into our ignorance and reinforce a myopic vision of the reality. Muslims are attired in "traditional" dress, bearded and turbaned, despite the fact that most Muslims (and most "fundamentalists") do not dress or look like this. The result reinforces the image of Islamic activists as medieval in life-style and mentality.'[277]

The title, "Roots of Muslim Rage," sets the tone and expectation.

Yet would we [concludes Esposito] tolerate similar generalizations in analyzing and explaining Western activities and motives? How often do we see articles that speak of Christian rage or Jewish rage?

Partial analysis which reinforces comfortable stereotypes and Western secular presuppositions must be transcended, if we are to avoid the ideological pitfalls and biases of a political analysis driven by an exaggerated threat.[278]

Cinema, television and the internet are the most powerful modern weapons to enhance the image of the evil Muslim. There is hardly, if ever, anything positive shown or said on Islam or Muslims throughout the Western television networks. Instead, there is a daily outpouring of news, views, images, reports, documentaries, and fictional stories, depicting Islamic 'evils.' And nothing can be more powerful than what grips people inside their own homes.

There is hardly any instance of films depicting Muslims favourably, either. Muslims are nearly always cast as villains, with the same gross physical features depicted above (thick lips, slimy expressions, and the like.)

---

[277] J. Esposito: *The Islamic Threat*; op cit; pp. 173-4.
[278] Ibid

And of course there is the image that tarnishes Islam more than any other: that of a 'Muslim' holding a knife about to behead someone. The internet is replete of the stuff, and 'Muslim terrorists' seem to think that it serves their cause and the cause of Islam. It just serves to the eradication of many thousands of Muslims today, and possibly hundreds of thousands one day when people will have enough and will descend into the streets to inflict their own retribution on any Muslim they will bump into.

Three

SCHOLARSHIP AND PEOPLE OF LETTERS' ROLE

The origin of Western learning about Muslims and Islam is the direct outcome of the failed crusades of the Middle Ages (1095-1291). In the late Middle Ages, some of the earliest thinkers of Western Christendom: John of Segovia, Bacon, Wycliffe, Humbert of Romans and others concluded that the Muslims could not be defeated by the direct military means used then, and as they put it:

> Their hearts were hardened, they despised the Scriptures, they rejected argument, they clung to the tissue of lies of the Qur'an.[279]

More effective, Bacon argued in his *Opus Maius*, would be the learning of languages and of philosophy in order to convert the infidels.[280] Ramon Lull (b.1232) also suggested writing books for the conversion of Jews and Muslims to Christianity and establishing monastery schools where future missionaries could learn Hebrew and Arabic.[281] Thus was proposed that an academic effort should be made, and that Arabic professorships should be established in Paris, Oxford, Bologna and Salamanca, and other places.[282]

Under the auspices of the Church and also at times some rulers, there began the search for the means and methods to defeat Islam. A group of very able visionaries came out with many works that provided a strategy to accomplish such an aim. Despite some variations, they all agreed on destroying the Islamic economic system, first, then, they invariably proposed a series of crusades once that was accomplished. Amongst such illuminaries, we could cite Thaddeo of Naples who wrote *Hystoria de Desolacione et Conculcacione*...., which was published in 1292 in the wake of the fall of Acre, the last crusader stronghold in the East.[283] Thaddeo exhorts the Pope as:

> Vicar of Christ among nations to eradicate paganism and redress the injury to the Saviour that his name may be honoured throughout the world.[284]

Thaddeo also calls on all kings and princes to put an end to their dissensions and act, not singly, but 'as one body in the bosom of the Church Militant.' He exhorts

---

[279] Ibid.
[280] Jo Ann Hoeppner Moran Cruz: Popular Attitudes Towards Islam; in *Western Perceptions* (Blanks-Frassetto ed) op cit; p. 69.
[281] Ibid.
[282] Z. Sardar; M.W. Davies: *Distorted Imagination;* op cit; p. 42.
[283] Thaddeo of Naples: *Hystoria de Desolacione et Conculcacione... Terre Sancte* in AD MCCXCI; edited by Comte Riant; Geneva; 1873.
[284] Ibid; 64-5.

all the faithful 'to avenge the bloodshed of Christians on Eastern soil and by force of arms to save the Holy Land which is 'our heritage.'[285]

All the others follow on more or less the same line. Fidenzio of Padua who wrote *Liber recuperationis terrae sanctae,* straight in the wake of the fall of Acre also repeats many similar themes.[286] The Armenian prince, Hayton of Corycus who wrote in 1307 a very influential treatise: *Flor des estoires*, which enjoyed a wide reputation, did the same.[287] The formerly mentioned, Catalan missionary and philosopher Ramon Lull's who in 1309 completed the *Liber de Acquisitione Terrae Sanctae,* incorporated the main thesis of his other work the *Liber de Fine* and re-presented it with a slight modification in arrangement.[288] Pierre Dubois (1250-1321) wrote in 1306 *De recuperatione terrae sanctae,*[289] which also outlines the conditions for the success of the crusades, which includes first and foremost peace amongst the Christians, and also, as preconized by Lull and others, the instruction of a number of young men and women in oriental languages and the natural sciences with a view to the government of Eastern peoples. William of Nogaret was also influential especially in his capacity as the leading counsellor of the French monarch, Philip the Fair between 1302 and 1313). Marino Sanudo (the Edlder) (1260-1338) completed the *Secreta* (or *Liber Secretorum*) *Fidelium Crucis,* otherwise called *Historia Hierosolymitana*, *Liber de expeditione Terrae Sanctae*, and *Opus Terrae Sanctae*. This work was offered to Pope Clement V as a manual for true Crusaders who desired the reconquest of the Holy Land.[290]

Perhaps the first man of letters who had the most impact was the father of Humanism, Petrarch (1304-1374). In the view of Petrarch, Muslim became a metaphor for the dangerous and foreign Asia, so reviled by Ancient Greeks, and Muslims represent barbarism itself. The Christian West, on the other hand, in his view, is the bastion of civilisation, manly courage and decency.[291]

> Turks, Arabs, Chaldeans… a naked, cowardly, and lazy people who never grasp the steel but endure all their blows to the wind.[292]

Petrarch, thus, as Bisaha observes, reduces formidable Muslim empires to an image of 'disorganised and uncivilised hunters and gatherers.'[293] For him, the

---

[285] Ibid; 65-6.
[286] Fidenzio of Padua: '*Liber Recuperationis Terrae Sanctae,*' Edition G. Golubovich: Bibliotheca Bio-Bibliografica Della Terra Santa; 5 vols; Florence; 1906-27; Vol II; 9 et seq.
[287] La Flor des Estoires de la Terre d'Orient, in *Receuil des Historiens des Croisades Armeniens*; vol ii; Paris; 1906; pp. 111-253.
[288] Munich MS. Lat. 10565 ff.. 89 ro-96 vo. See also Longpre, in *Criterion* (Barcelona, 1927), III, 266-78. R. Lull: *De Acquisitione Terrae Sanctae* (1309); in E. Kamar, 'Projet de Ramon Lull "De Acquisitione Terrae Sanctae", in *Studia Orientalia Christiana: Collectanea* No. 6 (Cairo, 1961), pp. 3-131 (text 103-31).
[289] Ed., V. Langlois; in Collection de texts pour servir a l'etude de l'enseignement de l'histoire; Paris; 1891.
[290] For all these works and details, see the works by N. Housely in particular: N. Housley: *The Later Crusades;* Oxford University Press; 1992.
-N. Housley: *Documents on the Later Crusades; 1274-1580*; Macmillan Press Ltd; London; 1996.
[291] F. Petrarca: *De vita solitaria*; ed. M. Noce; Milan; 1992; English translation: *The Life of Solitude*; ed., J. Zeidin; (Urbana; 1924). N. Bisaha: 'New Barbarian' or worthy adversary? Humanist Constructs of the Ottoman Turks in fifteenth century Italy; in Western Perceptions (Blanks-Frassetto ed); op cit; pp. 185-205; p. 189.
[292] *Petrarch's Lyric Poems;* ed and trans R. M. Durling; (Cambridge; 1976); pp. 76-7.
[293] N. Bisaha: 'New Barbarian;' op cit; p. 189.

Muslims are 'the same wild Saracens the Romans encountered a millennium earlier, not the advanced civilisation of vast trade networks, great armies, large cities, and extensive learning.'[294] Petrarch also stirs Christian feelings by bringing the case of Jerusalem.

> Christians of true valour and courage should not suffer the Holy Land, the Christian patrimony, to be overrun by Muslim thieves.[295]

Petrarch would remain the father of the Humanist movement which played a leading role in the anti Ottoman crusade. His role is central not only in giving foundations to the whole legend of Greece as the mother of civilisation, as we saw in *Our Civilisation* (vol one,) his other leading role is well caught by Bisaha:

> By looking back to the ancient period, Petrarch saw a much more expansive goal: domination of the entire Near East as the Romans had achieved. Rome conquered the East, and Christianity tamed it. This was the heritage or birthright that Petrarch longed to see reclaimed by the modern heirs of Rome-why stop with the Holy Land? Rather than diverting his attention from crusade, Petrarch's love of early Christian and pre-Christian Rome served to inspire great zeal for crusade and, in turn, conquest on a large scale. He offered not only religious and historical justifications for the conquest of Eastern areas but secular and cultural arguments of Western superiority.... He constructed an image of cultural decline in the East after the rise of Islam and the departure of Latin learning-an image that negates the brilliance of Arab learning.... Petrarch exhibits this tendency most noticeably in his headstrong conviction of the supremacy of Western civilization and his yearning for cultural and religious hegemony over the East. Petrarch and later humanists fashioned a sense of cultural hegemony over the East in the absence of political hegemony. In essence, Western thinkers imagined their culture as more powerful than that of the East long before they began to exert ruling power over these lands. In some respects, then, Petrarch's rhetoric may be seen as a bridge between classical ideas of East and West and the more damaging paternalistic discourse of colonialism.[296]

The first systematic study of Muslim society and Islam by Western Europeans dates from the late 16th century, when in 1587 regular teaching of Arabic was begun in Paris. It was the work of two medical doctors and a Maronite priest of Lebanon.[297] From Paris, the study of Arabic devolved to Leiden in Holland, in 1613. Twenty or so years later the subject was introduced in England, in Cambridge (1632), and

---

[294] Ibid.
[295] Ibid at p. 188.
[296] N. Bisaha: Petrarch's Vision of the Muslim and Byzantine East, *Speculum*, Vol. 76, No. 2 (Apr., 2001), pp. 284-314; at p. 286.
[297] P. Casanova: L'Enseignement de l'Arabe au College de France (Paris; 1910) in A. Hourani: *Islam in European Thought;* (Cambridge University Press; 1991); p. 12.

Oxford (1634).[298] Instrumental in establishing the Chair at Cambridge was William Bedwell, who summed up the main objectives of such endeavour, in providing:

> 'Good service of King and State in our commerce';
> 'In God's good time to enlarging the borders of the Church, and propagation of the Christian religion to them who now sit in darkness.'[299]

Cahen observes that:

> Cultivated by businessmen, administrators, missionaries, oriental history has very often been dealt with according to interests and ideologies that cared little for historical truthfulness.[300]

Indeed, the thousands of Westerners who have dealt with Muslims, Islam, faith and civilisation, with the rarest exceptions, have pursued every other aim except the search for, or the conveying of, truth, as here outlined by Edward Said:

> To the West, Asia had once represented silent distance and alienation; Islam was militant hostility to European Christianity. To overcome such redoubtable constants the Orient needed first to be known, then invaded and possessed, then re-created by scholars, soldiers, and judges who disinterred forgotten languages, histories, races, and cultures in order to posit them - beyond the modern Oriental's ken - as the true classical Orient that could be used to judge and rule the modern Orient. The obscurity faded, to be replaced by hothouse entities; the Orient was a scholar's word, signifying what modern Europe had recently made of the still peculiar East.[301]

Courtesy of these academics, Muslim society is thus made comprehensible and intelligible by a variety of structures and concepts, defining and controlling it, working together, since to know is to subordinate as Kabbani puts it 'The West had to reshape the Orient in order to comprehend it... to devise in order to rule.'[302]

Indeed, when Sir William Jones, a servant of the East India Company, inaugurated studies of the Orient, it was in order 'To increase Europe's acquaintance with the peoples it would exert control upon.'[303]

To Sardar and Davies, the expanding study of Muslim society and Islam involved academics interested in matters of the Orient but:

> To institutionalise ignorance via the use of reason and academic discourse.
> Unlike any other discipline - when, for example, one studies botany one shows certain respect for plants; when one studies entomology, one comes to appreciate insects; a zoologist has certain affinity for wild life; an ecologist cannot be expected to detest the environment - Orientalism came to be based on hate. The Orientalists loathed and feared, and to some extent still do, the subject of their study: Islam and Muslims. Apart from the obvious belief that

---

[298] A. Hourani: *Islam;* op cit; p.13.
[299] Quoted by J.D. Latham in Z. Sardar and M.W. Davies: *Distorted Imagination;* op cit; p. 42.
[300] C. Cahen: l'Histoire economique et sociale de l'Orient Musulman medieval; *Studia Islamica* Vol 3 (1955) pp. 93-115; at p. 94.
[301] E. Said: *Orientalism;* London; 1978, in J. Sweetman: *The Oriental Obsession*: (Cambridge University Press, 1987); p. 8.
[302] R. Kabbani: *Imperial Fictions;* op cit; p. 138.
[303] Z. Sardar and M.W. Davies: *Distorted Imaginations;* op cit; p. 43.

Western civilization was the norm for all cultures, they also believed that Biblical tradition was the norm for all monotheism. Thus, Orientalism sought not to understand Islam but to dominate it, not to seek empathy with it but to ridicule it, abuse it and demonstrate its inferiority and, once raped, to envelop it within Western civilization and to turn Muslims into nice, docile, subject people, an extension of the West.[304]

A major aim of Western academia dealing with Islam has been to use knowledge of the Islamic subject, divisions amongst its ethnic and religious groups, most particularly, to exploit them so as to subjugate the Islamic foe. Western attention to Islam is, as Arenal points out, to put focus on, and use every sign of local identity.[305] Throughout the centuries, for the sake of political and military purposes, conflicts have been stirred between Berbers and Arabs, Arabs and Turks, Turks and Kurds, Shias and Sunnis. During the colonial era, for instance, the French in Algeria and Morocco implemented diverse policies to divide and create tensions between Arabs and Berbers.[306] The English successfully conquered India by splitting Muslims between themselves, and by splitting them from their other subjects: Jats, Sikhs, and others.[307] Today, the same can be seen everywhere, all forms of divisions and differences amongst Muslims played upon to stir conflict between them and so ease domination and control over them. Thus, in Iraq, for instance, thanks to such academic knowledge, and a crafty combination of media reports,[308] political scheming, and selective bombings, assassinations and massacres, Sunnis and Shias, Kurds and Arabs have been brought to tear each other. When the war on Iraq was launched in 2003 we constantly heard and read that Saddam Hussein was a Sunni who mass murdered the Shias, whilst in truth, Saddam Hussein was the product of the West,[309] put and kept in power by the West, and never ruled as a Sunni, but as the leader of the secular, Christian dominated, Baath Party. We shall return to this matter in detail.

Garcia Arenal observes the same obsessions with decadent Islam.[310] In the words of Sardar and Davies:

> Armed with the tools of the new disciplines, Orientalist attacks on Islam became more intense, more confident, more pervasive, they ascribed ridiculously large and important roles to minorities: Christians, Jews,

---

[304] Ibid; p. 41.
[305] M. Garcia-Arenal: Historiens de l'Espagne, historiens du Maghreb au 19em siecle. Comparaison des stereotypes *ANNALES: Economies, Societes, Civilisations*: Vol 54 (1999); pp. 687-703, at p. 702.
[306] J.J. Cook: The Maghrib through French Eyes; 1880-1929; in *Through Foreign Eyes;* edited by A.A. Heggoy; (University Press of America; 1982); pp. 57-92; p. 91.
[307] E. Driault: *La Question d'Orient*; (Librairie Felix Alcan; Paris; 1921); p. 63.
[308] Hence the UK Daily, *The Guardian,* in its edition of 10 January 04, asserted that the bombing of a Shia Mosque the previous day was the work of Sunni extremists. How could the paper convincingly assert this when aware of the Iraqi mayhem, where it is literally impossible to know who is doing what, and when no Western journalists can operate safely outside the secure Green Zone of Baghdad (as reported in *The Guardian* itself 12 March 07; media section page 3).
[309] See various media reports following his execution on 30 December 06, such as the Independent 30 December 06; cover page and page two.
[310] M. Garcia-Arenal: Historiens de l'Espagne, op cit; p. 702.

> Ismailis, assassins, Hellenists, certain features of Sufi thought (Hallajism is a 'religion of the cross'), anyone or anything which to their mind represented the antithesis of Islam and could undermine its basis.[311]

The many works by such 'specialists' of Islam such as Bosworth, Brett, Lewis, Rippin, Crone, Cook, Madelung, J. Jones, and many others (including those of Muslim background), are proof of this relentless undermining of the faith and its adherents and stirring as much as can muddle or confuse.[312]

Western academic expertise in conveying that which aims to corrupt has a long life. We have seen many instances in previous chapters. Here we look at some techniques as studied by Holt through the writing of Prideaux. Prideaux, Dean of Norwich (d.1724), compiled his work on the Prophet: *The True Nature of Imposture etc*, completed in 1697.[313] Prideaux presents an apparently well documented work, so that he

> May not be thought to draw this Life of Mahomet with design to set forth his imposture in the foulest of colours the better to make it serve (his) present purpose.[314]

In his account Prideaux lists 36 Arab authors or works, and makes great display of their names in his footnotes. This, of course, seeks to give his work legitimacy. However, as Holt observes, upon examination, it becomes clear that his knowledge of them was second hand, either from translations or quotations in the works of Orientalists. Together with these 'Arabic' sources, Prideaux uses the writings of anti Muslim controversialists. Thus, as Holt notes, the resulting biography is a combination of Muslim tradition and Christian legend, 'inspired by a sour animosity towards its subject.'[315] And commenting on Prideaux's work, Daniel holds that it 'outdoes almost any medieval writer in its virulence.'[316] The same techniques, albeit more sophisticated, are used today. Disappearance of facts, over-use of anti Islamic authors, using the wrong Muslim sources, or the right ones but in the wrong context, disappearing some works from bibliographies, misuse of footnotes, overuse of shallow Arabic expressions, and quite a few other techniques form the guide book to today's experts on Islam.

We cite the role of Muslim civilisation in the rise of modern sciences and civilisation, and see how such role is systematically suppressed from knowledge.[317] As a rule, make centuries disappear from history, centuries (7th–14th), which correspond to

---

[311] Z. Sardar-M.W. Davies: *Distorted Imagination*; op cit; p. 43.
[312] See the horrendous: W. Madelung: *The Succession to Muhammad; a Study in the Early Caliphate*, Cambridge University Press, 1997.
-P. Crone; M.A. Cook: *Hagarism; the Making of the Muslim World*; Cambridge University Press; 1977.
-M. Cook general editor: *The New Cambridge History of Islam*; in 6 vols; Cambridge University Press; 2010.
[313] P.M. Holt: The Treatment of Arab History by Prideaux; Ockley and Sale; in *Historians of the Middle East*; ed., B. Lewis and P.M. Holt (Oxford University Press; London; 1962), pp. 290-302; at pp. 291-4.
[314] Ibid; p. 293.
[315] Ibid; p. 294.
[316] N. Daniel: *Islam and the West*; p. 309.
[317] See Al-Djazairi: *The Hidden Debt*; op cit.

the very period of Islamic ascendancy, and the Islamic foundation of Western science and civilisation.[318] When these centuries are removed from the record, as Glubb notes, it makes 'the subsequent story of the rise of Europe largely incomprehensible.'[319] If centuries are easy to erase, it is even easier to erase unwanted facts. Each author goes further than his/her predecessor in the suppression of the facts that either speak favourably of Islam, or unfavourably of Western Christendom.[320] Any subject of history, eventually, ends up cleansed of all unwanted facts and their sources. To legitimise such a cleansed history, modern historians refer to each other, quote each other (and praise each other) and promote each other, and praise and promote those amongst Muslims who serve the same agenda.

Western academia is today generously granting the noble to the Christian West, and eagerly granting the vile to Islam. Whether piracy,[321] which apparently justified French colonial intervention in North Africa,[322] the oppression of minorities,[323] genocides, the African slave trade,[324] which also served to justify the colonisation of Africa 'in order to end the trade,' the persecution of women,[325] and many other dark instances of history, all are removed from the Western heritage and tossed into the Islamic court instead.

Many Western academics who deviate from this line are severely censored. Amongst these, we can cite Fisher, for instance, who condemned the Barbary corsair legend,[326] and who drew upon himself extreme hostility;[327] Singer who spoke favourably of the Islamic role in the rise of modern technology; Castro who insisted on the Muslim influence on Spain;[328] Menocal for the same;[329] or Justin McCarthy who showed that rather than the Turks committing genocides, they were

---

[318] As noted by P. Benoit and F. Micheau: The Arab intermediary: in *A History of Scientific Thought*; ed M. Serres; (Blackwell, 1995); pp. 191-221; p. 191.

[319] John Glubb: *A Short History of the Arab Peoples*; (Hodder and Stoughton, 1969); p. 135.

[320] G.T. Emeagwali in Science and Public Policy; *Journal of the International Science Policy Foundation*, Surrey; UK; Vol 16; No 3; 1989.

[321] C. Brockelmann: *History of the Islamic Peoples*; (Routledge and Kegan Paul; London; 1950) reprint; p. 292; p. 397.

[322] The myth of Barbary Piracy and its use by France as justification for colonization has been well dealt with by authors such as L.Valensi: *Le Maghreb avant la Prise d'Alger*; (Paris; 1969). G. Fisher: *Barbary Legend*; Oxford; 1957. P. Earle: *Corsairs of Malta and Barbary*; (London; 1970). A. Thomson: *Barbary and Enlightenment*: (Brill; Leiden; 1987); final Chapter: Towards Conquest.

[323] P. Conrad: *Histoire de la Reconquista*; Que Sais je? (Presses Universitaire de France; Paris; 1998); pp. 22-3.

[324] M. Gordon: *Slavery in the Arab World*; originally published in French: *L'Esclavage dans le Monde Arabe*; (New Amsterdam; New York; 1989). H.A.L. Fisher: *A History of Europe (from the Beginning of the 18th century to 1937)*; (Eyre and Spottiswoode; London; 1952); p. 1033.

[325] Any Western publication or form of opinion makes this claim. But see as an instance, Betty Mahmoody: *Not Without my Daughter*; (New York; St Martin's Press; 1993). Elizabeth Altschull: *Le Voile Contre l'Ecole (The Veil Against School)* (Le Seuil; Paris; 1995).

[326] G. Fisher: *The Barbary Legend*; (Oxford; 1957).

[327] A. Thomson: Barbary; op cit; p. 125.

[328] A. Castro: *Espana en su historia. Cristianos, moros y judios*; (Buenos Aires: Losada, 1948), 709 pp; see *The Structure of Spanish History*, English translation with revisions and modifications by E. A. King; (Princeton: Princeton University Press, 1954), 689 pp.

[329] Maria Rosa Menocal: *The Arabic Role in Medieval Literary History*, (University of Pennsylvania Press, Philadelphia, 1987).

the principal victims of genocides whether in the second half of the 19th century or the first decades of the 20th.[330]

Cleansing away 'bad' academics also means cleansing their names away from bibliographies, references, and eventually from all knowledge. Philip Conrad's History of Spain, for instance, in his bibliography (pp. 125-6), gives prominence to all historians hostile to anything Islamic: Perez, Lapeyre (on whom more further on), Menendez Pidal, and of course, Albornoz.[331] From his bibliography are suppressed sources such as Castro, Levi Provencal, Lea, Lane Poole, Dozy, and others who not only recognised the Islamic impact on Spanish history, but also highlighted the crimes of the Catholic Church.
Regarding the few scholars of Muslim origins who can be found in most social sciences and history departments, few exceptions aside such as M. Uyar, A. Djebbar, R. Rashed, F. Sezgin, the rest are mainly busy fanning divisive matters of religious, political and ethnic nature of their countries of origins.

What academia does, most particularly, is to come to the succour of the media and other mind shaping agencies to intellectualise and legitimise their anti Islamic stances. Even more gravely, this same academia spreads the crooked knowledge of Islam to its students, who eventually are blighted by it in their positions as political leaders, journalists, military officers, or any other functions. Once upon a time, there was a counter Western opinion that was pro-Islamic, but such a counter force is now being reduced to fewer and fewer voices. Its output is also being reduced not just because the anti Islamic force is powerful, but also because of a threatening new development: knowledge on the internet. Today, a certain type of knowledge is selected, and it occupies nearly the whole space on the internet, and any different narrative is disappeared entirely. It is in this respect the crooked form of knowledge of Islam which in not too long will be sole dweller of screens and minds. The days of the physical library and printed books are no more, and only knowledge in electronic form is the majesty; hence we are entering the age of smut as knowledge of Islam.

Academia is here to also cleanse the Christian/Western Past:

Cutting the numbers of victims of genocides (Indians, Black Africans, Muslims, Jews, and others) is a common technique. We take the case of women, and their burning in the millions as witches. Levack, the culprit 'historian' chosen here, thus writes:
> Some estimates, ranging as high as nine million executions,[332] have been grossly exaggerated. The totals have been inflated both by the claims of

---
[330] J. McCarthy: *Death and Exile: The Ethnic Cleansing of Ottoman Muslims, 1821-1922*; Darwin Press; New Jersey; 1995.
[331] P. Conrad: *Histoire de la Reconquista*; Que Sais je? (Presses Universitaire de France; Paris; 1998).
[332] A. Dworkin: *Woman Hating*; (New York; 1974); p. 130.

witch-hunters themselves, who often boasted about how many witches they had burned, and by subsequent writers, who for different reasons wished to emphasize the gravity of the process they were discussing.[333] Detailed scholarly studies have generally led to a downward estimate of the total numbers of victims. It has long been believed, for example, that an early seventeenth-century witch-hunt in the Basque-speaking Pays de Labourd in France resulted in 600 executions, but it now appears that the actual figure was closer to 80.[334] In Bamberg, where another 600 witches were allegedly burned between 1624 and 1631, the totals are probably closer to 300.[335] And in Scotland, where Henry C. Lea claimed that 7,500 persons were executed for witchcraft, the actual tally is probably less than 1,500.[336]

In estimating the size of the hunt it is also imperative that we distinguish between the number of trials and the number of executions. There were some witch-hunts in Germany in which virtually all suspects were tried and executed, but these were exceptions to the rule.[337] Table I establishes the execution-rate of witches in a number of European regions. The numbers of trials upon which these rates are calculated are very small, since they include only those cases whose outcomes are known. In most regions the execution-rate was less than 70 per cent and in some areas, such as Essex Count Ostrobothnia and Geneva, it was less than 25 per cent. Only in the Pays de Vaud did the execution rate reach the severe level of 90 per-cent. Even if we make allowances for trial records that have been lost or destroyed, the total number of persons who were actually tried for witchcraft throughout Europe probably did not greatly exceed 100,000.[338]

Then three pages down, the same author, Levack, writes:

The figures regarding total prosecutions and executions also fail to provide any indication of the effect that witch-hunts had on individual towns and villages. Only when we break down the composite figures year by year and village by village can we appreciate the full intensity of the witch-hunt. When we learn, for example, that 274 persons were executed for witchcraft in the Prince Bishopric of Eichstatt in just one year, and that 133 witches were executed in the lands of the Covent of Quedlinburg in just one day in 1589, we gain a much better sense of the toll that witch-hunting could take than when we calculate figures for an entire country during a 300-year period.[339]

For men living in the sixteenth and seventeenth centuries the main statistical

---

[333] Ludovico de Paramo boasted that inquisition alone had executed 30,000 persons for witchcraft by the middle of the 16th century; in H. C. Lea: *Materials Toward a History of Witchcraft*; (New York; 1957); iii; p. 549.
[334] G. Henningsen: The Papers of Alfonso de Salazar Frias; *Temenos*; 5; 1980; pp. 23-5; and 480-1.
[335] C. Larner: Crimen exceptum; the crime of witchcraft in Europe? In V. Gattrell et al. (ed): *Crime and the Law*; (London; 1980); p. 52.
[336] H.C. Lea: *A History of the Inquisition of the Middle Ages*; op cit; pp. 246-7; C. Larner: *Enemies of God; The Witch hunt in Scotland*; (Baltimore; London; 1981); p. 63.
[337] H. C. Midelfort: *Witch Hunting in South-Western Germany; 1562-1684*; (Stanford; 1972); p. 147.
[338] B. P. Levack: *The Witch Hunt*; (Longman; London; 1987); p. 19.
[339] H. C. Midelfort: Heartland of the Witch-Craze: Central and Northern Europe; *History Today*; 31; 1981; p. 28.

> question as far as witchcraft was concerned was not how many witches had been executed but how many were still loose. Some of these estimates were astonishingly high. In 1571 a French witch by the name of Troi-Eschelles told King Charles IX that there were 300,000 witches in his realm, and in 1602 the demonologist Henri Boguet used this figure to project a total of 1,800,000 for all of Europe. According to Boguet, there were witches by the thousands everywhere, 'multiplying upon the earth even as worms in a garden'.[340] The number of participants at the witches' assemblies was estimated to be at least 500 by one demonologist and as high as 100,000 by another.[341] These estimates help to explain why the educated classes in Europe were so frightened of witchcraft. They also help to explain why they prosecuted witches with such ferocity. A threat of this size could not be ignored; it had to be met head-on with all the judicial power that European states could muster.[342]

From these two extracts by Levack, we not only note the technique he uses to cut the numbers of the victims of witch-hunting (first quote), we also note a major contradiction. By first (p. 19) (first quote) trying to reduce the number of victims of the witch hunt, he cuts their numbers. Then by wanting to show how serious a problem it was (p. 22) (second quote), he gives high figures of witches, failing to notice in the process that his second set of figures (p. 22) completely contradicts his first set (p.19), and that he contradicts himself, too, in his central claims.

Muslim Spain (8th-13th centuries) was a model of cohabitation of diverse faiths, yet, modern historians, such as Menendez Pidal,[343] Lapeyre,[344] Al-Bornoz,[345] and others, now claim the contrary. Conrad, speaks of physical discrimination and daily humiliations inflicted by Muslims upon Christians and Jews; their over-taxation, and the cleansing of Jews and Christians from parts of cities, and herding them into segregated areas cut off from the Muslims.[346] The image built by Conrad relies on some limited evidence, which he generalises to the whole history of Muslim Spain. He fails to take into account the crucial fact that Christianity did not suffer under Islam. He fails to note that Christian populations were allowed freedom and privileges, and that the Jews were protected under Islam.[347] He sets aside the evidence about the leading part played by both Christians and Jews in Islamic government.[348] Conrad also sets aside the fact that the Jews controlled the vast

---

[340] J. Bodin: *De la Demonie des sorciers*; (Anvers; 1586); p. 365;
H. Boguet: *An Examen of Witches;* tr. E.A. Ashwin, ed. M. Summers; (London; 1929); pp. xxxii and xxiv.
[341] N. Remy: *Demonolatry*; tr. E.A. Ashwin; ed. M. Summers; (London; 1930); p. 56.
H. C. Lea: Materials; op cit; 1957; III; p. 1297.
[342] B. P. Levack: *The Witch Hunt;* op cit; p. 22.
[343] Ramon Menéndez Pidal, *Espana y su historia* (Madrid: Minotaure, 1957).
[344] H. Lapeyre: *Geographie de l'Espagne Morisque;* (SEVPEN, 1959).
[345] S Albornoz: *L'Espagne Musulmane*, French translation of earlier Spanish version, (Paris, 1985).
[346] P. Conrad: *Histoire de la Reconquista*; Que Sais je? (Presses Universitaire de France; Paris; 1998); pp. 22-3.
[347] See S. P. Scott: *History of the Moorish Empire*; op cit; vol 1.
[348] See S. Lane Poole: The Moors; op cit; E. Levi Provencal: *Histoire de l'Espagne Musulmane*; 3 vols; (Paris, Maisonneuve, 1953); S. P. Scott: *History*; op cit;

majority of Islamic trade and finance.[349] And contrary to what he says, instead of Muslim cleansing of others, it was in fact Muslims who were eliminated by Western Christendom. As Araya Goubet points out, religious tolerance - Islamic in inspiration - permitted the harmonious coexistence of Christians, Muslims and Jews. Christian dominance on the other hand, led to the exclusion, subjugation, and expulsion of the other two, starting in 1492.[350]

However, the mass removal of Muslims in Spain and other places is made acceptable 'for good reasons.' Lapeyre, tells us:
> During the re-conquista (in Spain), the acquisition of land led to fierce fighting, and the Muslim population, in general, was expelled by force. This was a brutal solution, but it made things much more simple.[351]

Jean Richard, along with the majority of modern Western historians, blames the massacre of the whole Muslim population of Jerusalem (1099) by the crusaders on the fact that the crusaders:
> Had been infuriated by the insults hurled (by the Muslims) at the procession they had made beneath the ramparts.[352]

During the Algerian war of colonisation (began 1830), General Pelissier smoked to death tens of thousands of Algerians in caves, but writing to the Minister of war Soult, Bugeaud (Pelissier's superior) held:
> That rigorous methods had to be applied to submit the country, without which there would be no colonisation, administration, or civilisation.[353]

The same noble effort justified the killing of an extra million Algerians during the War of Independence (1954-62).[354]

In the early 1990s, Serbo-Croat intellectuals legitimised the cleansing of Europe from the scourge of Islam. Dabic insisted on 'the Muslim threat' posed to Great Britain, Italy and France,[355] whilst Todorov explained how the Muslims in Bosnia were motivated by their 'Islamic way of life,' alien to European civilisation, warranting its removal.[356]

Recently, the mass slaying of Iraqis was presented as a war of liberation, or a war to bring democracy to Iraq, or, plainly 'to rebuild Iraq.'

Keneth Cragg justifies further rough treatment of Muslims:
> The current (1960s) suspension of democratic forms (in Arab countries, and ensuing repression of Islamists) arises not only from the fact, evident

---

[349] S.D. Goiten: *A Mediterranean Society*, 5 vols, (Berkeley; 1967-90).
[350] Guillermo Araya Goubet: The Evolution of Castro's theory; in *Americo Castro, and the meaning of Spanish Civilisation*. Edited By J. Rubia Barcia: (University of California Press, Berkeley, 1976); pp. 41-66; p. 51.
[351] H. Lapeyre: *Geographie de l'Espagne Morisque*; (SEVPEN, 1959); p. 119.
[352] J. Richard: *The Latin Kingdom of Jerusalem;* tr J. Shirley; (North Holland Publishing; Amsterdam; 1979); vol A; p. 15.
[353] H Alleg et al: *La Guerre d'Algerie*: op cit; vol 1; p. 69.
[354] Alain-G. Slama: *La Guerre d'Algerie*, (La Decouverte, Paris, 1996). Benjamin Stora: *Histoire de la Guerre d'Algerie*, (La Decouverte, Paris, 1993). P. Evno- J. Planchais: *La Guerre d'Algerie*, (La Decouverte, Le Monde, 1989). H Alleg et al: *La Guerre d'Algerie*: op cit.
[355] Interview with Vojin Dabic: Polumesec muci zapad (The Crescent worries the West), *Evropske Novosti (New Europe)*, 14 April 1993, p. 18.
[356] N. Cigar: Serbia's Orientalists; op cit; p. 151.

everywhere in the world, that government in these days of high dams, flooding populations and industrialisation must be direct and efficient. It springs also from the fact that democratic processes to be secure, require standards of general education and traditions of citizenship which often do not obtain and for lack of which the democratic process play into the hands of exploiters and vested interests. Moreover, viable and valid democracy demands a vigorous party system and the concept of the dignity of the opposition - elements still wanting, for a variety of reasons in the structure of most Islamic communities.[357]

We find at work the trusted method of cutting down the numbers of Muslim victims of Christians. In Spain, the millions of Muslim victims have now been reduced to a mere few thousands.[358] In a passage, Lapeyre (the culprit in chief) refers to Regla 'who had the great merit of destroying the legend of the 50,000 Moors of Catalonia, whom the historians piously transmitted without any critical effort. Even he (Regla) has overestimated these figures. By admitting 10,000 he still remains above the true figure.'[359] In the Kingdom of Valencia, for instance, the number of Muslims at the beginning of the 16th century is put at just about 70,000.[360] If Lapeyre is correct, where have the millions of Muslims who lived in Spain gone? If one takes the population of medieval Muslim Cordova as an illustration, archaeologists excavating parts of the city suggest that the population was as much as a million on account of the very great area covered by the Muslim city, which Levi Provencal says was about 8 times the size of the modern city.[361] A figure of a million inhabitants of the city would accord well with the figures given by the various authors, most of them very conservative and very reliable, cited by al-Maqqari: 200,000 houses for the common people and 60,300 for the more important elements; or even 300,000 houses.[362] This completely contradicts the ridiculous figures given by Lapeyre, and leaves open the question: where did the millions of Muslims in Spain go?

Lapeyre, again, admits that the Spanish Muslim population was en masse ethnically cleansed, but as he puts it, it was 'a brutal solution, perhaps, but it simplified things.'[363] 'The power of resistance of strong minorities is not to be demonstrated, especially when this is a faith as tenacious as Islam', he adds.[364]
For Perez, another historian:

---

[357] K. Cragg: *The Dome of the Rock*: Jerusalem Studies in Islam, (S.P.C.K; London; 1964); p. 189.
[358] H. Lapeyre: *Geographie de l'Espagne Morisque*; op cit.
[359] Regla; la expulsion, p. 263; in H. Lapeyre: *Geographie*; p. 98.
[360] H. Lapeyre: *Geographie de l'Espagne*; op cit; pp. 29-30; in L. Cardaillac; J.P. Dedieu: Introduction a l'Histoire des Morisques; in *Les Morisques et l'Inquisition*: ed L. Cardaillac; (Publisud; Paris; 1990); pp. 11-28; at p. 15.
[361] E. Levi Provencal: *Histoire de l'Espagne Musulmane;* op cit; pp. 362-3.
[362] Al-Maqqari: *Nafh Al-Tib.* Translated by P. De Gayangos: *The History of the Mohammedan Dynasties in Spain*; 2 vols; (The Oriental Translation Fund; London, 1840-3); pp. 214-5.
[363] H. Lapeyre: *Geographie;* op cit; p. 119.
[364] Ibid; p. 120.

> The minorities living under the status of protected minorities first under Muslims, then under Christian, had a pejorative meaning; ... Once the reconquista completed, no reason was there to maintain such a situation. Spain had now become a nation like others in Christian Europe...The Moors, descendants of the Mudedjares, had refused to assimilate; they had to be expelled in the early 17th century.[365]

According to Cardaillac and Dedieu:
> The Moors were building alliances with the enemies of Spain in North Africa and with the Turks, and other European enemies to invade the country. Denunciations of such Moors multiplied, and they were not without foundations.[366]

And:
> Why expulsion? Why now? Political considerations won, and the decision was justified by the rising threat and all the fears just described.[367]

Conrad sides with Menendez Pidal, who in his *Historia de Espana*, concludes that:
> After many centuries of forced neighbourhood with the Christians, this exotic race never integrated into Spain, neither to its faith nor to its collective ideals, nor to its character, the Moors never assimilated and lived like a cancerous growth in the Spanish flesh.[368]

These justifications for the elimination of the Muslims fail to make the parallel with the Christians living under the Muslims in crusader times, or under the Ottomans, in later centuries. During the crusades, the local Christians, Maronites and Armenians, in particular, sided with the crusaders and the Mongols, and massacred Muslims in considerable numbers.[369] Yet once the Muslims (led by the Mamluks) took the upper hand, they could have wiped out every Maronite and Armenian on account of their alliance with the crusaders and the Mongols, and on account of their direct participation in the mass slaughter of Muslims. None of this happened though. Both Maronites and Armenians have survived to our day amidst Muslim communities.

The Myths of Islamic barbarism

We are still trying to explain why the myths of Islamic barbarism have been with us for the last ten or so centuries. We also spend countless energies showing via facts that the myths cultivated abut Islam over the past ten or so centuries are based on distortions. We have already shown plenty of that and we cannot

---

[365] J. Perez: Chretiens; Juifs et Musulmans en Espagne; Le Mythe de la tolerance religieuse (VIII-XV e siecle); in *Histoire*, No 137; October 1990.
[366] L. Cardaillac; J.P. Dedieu: Introduction; op cit; p. 24
[367] Ibid; p. 25.
[368] R. M. Pidal: *Historia de Esapana dirigida por Ramon Menendez Pidal*; vol 2; (Madrid; 2nd ed; 1966); p. 41.
[369] See, for instance, J.J. Saunders: *Aspects of the Crusades*, op cit. S. Runciman: *A History of the Crusades*, op cit. K.S. Salibi: The Maronites of Lebanon under Frankish and Mamluk rule; 1099-1516; *Arabica* IV; 1957.

reproduce all what we said in our works here. We will just take brief note here and give you plenty of references that can guide you to the truth much better than this author.

Contrary to what is generally claimed, it was in the Christian West where countless numbers of people were burnt at the stake for their 'heresy,' not in the Islamic world.[370] The Inquisition which quartered, hanged, disembowelled and burnt, was a medieval Christian institution, not an Islamic one.[371] Equally, if historical reality is brought into focus, without one single exception, it shows Western Christian genocides - not Islamic, at all epochs in history. During the crusades (1095-1291), millions of Muslims were murdered;[372] wholesale rape, torture, mutilations, and even cannibalism took place on the part of the Christians.[373] There was not a single town or city that was taken from Muslims without its population in its entirety being butchered.[374] In Sicily and other parts of Europe, the Muslims were wiped out.[375] In Spain, it is three million Muslims, at least, who were removed.[376] Over ten million Algerians died as a result of French colonisation.[377] During the Balkan Wars in 1912-1913, terrible deeds were inflicted on the Turkish/Muslim population,[378] possibly, some of the worst instances of atrocities ever seen in history.[379] It is very likely that up to 10 million Turkish lives were wiped out between 1806 and

---

[370] See J.W. Draper: *A History of the Intellectual Development of Europe*; op cit. J.W. Draper: *History of the Conflict Between Religion and Science;* Henry S. King & Co; London; 1875.
[371] H. C. Lea: *A History of the Inquisition of Spain*; op cit.
[372] Josiah Cox Russel: Late Ancient and Medieval Population, *Transactions of the American Philosophical Society*, vol. 48/III, 1958; A.N Poliak: The Demographic Evolution of the Middle East: population trends since 1348, *Palestine and the Middle East*, vol X; no 5, 1938.
[373] G. Le Bon: *La Civilisation des Arabes*; op cit; p. 247. S. Runciman: *A History of the Crusades*, op cit. J.J. Saunders: *Aspects of the Crusades*; op cit. J.W. Draper: *A History of the Intellectual Development of Europe*; op cit; vol I.
[374] J.W. Draper: *A History;* op cit; vol 2; pp. 21 fwd.
[375] See N. Daniel: *The Arabs*; op cit.
[376] H. Lea: *A History of the Inquisition of Spain*, op cit. S.P. Scott: *History of the Moorish*; op cit; vol 3, in particular.
[377] C. Ageron: *Modern Algeria*, tr., by M. Brett, Hurst and Company, (London, 9th ed, 1990). H Alleg; J. de Bonis, H.J. Douzon, J. Freire, P. Haudiquet: *La Guerre d'Algerie*: op cit.
[378] Contemporary literature under various forms is available to the non lazy, and includes material in previous note, and also: W. Alison Phillips: *The War of Greek Independence 1821-1833*, Charles Scribner's Sons; New York; 1897.
M. Jacquot to *Journal des Debats* in Paris. 2 July 1877. *The extermination of Turkish people by Russia, and the true policy for England* (London, 1878), pp. 1-4. *Russian atrocities in Asia and Europe during the months of June, Jully*, and August 1877 (Constantinople, 1877), p. 12. Governorate of Tulca to the ministry of interior, 23 June 1877.
Foreign Office (FO) Layard to Earl of Derby, 26 July 1877.
See Alfred Austin, Tory Horrors or the Question of the Hour, A Letter to the Right Hon. W. E. Gladstone (London: Chatto and Windus, 1876). H.F. Baldwin: *War Photographer in Thrace; An Account of Personal Experiences During the Turco-Balkan War 1912;* Fisher and Unwin, London, 1913. Foreign office reports; also R. Millman: *Britain and the Eastern Question*; Oxford; 1979; pp. 125-89. F.O. 195-1185; No 73.
Or media reports such as: Telegram from Mr. Gay to "Daily Telegraph," London. Pera, July 14th, 1877.
Telegram from Mr. Englander to Reuter's Agency, London. Constantinople, July 22nd 1877.
Débats, Post, Times, Telegraph, Manchester Guardian, Examiner, New York Herald, and Gazette de Cologne.
[379] Ernst Jäckh; *Deutschland im Orient nach dem Balkan-Krieg;* Chapter 7: Deutsche und französische Augenzeugen von christlichen Massakers. (Die Balkangreuel des 30 jährigen Krieges); Martin Mörikes Verlag, Munich, 1913; pp. 83-98.
-P. Loti: *Turquie Agonisante*; Calman Levy; Paris; 1913.

1913.[380] Also millions of natives suffered extinction in the diverse continents, and not at Muslim hands.[381]

The notion that Islam, as a faith, is source of violence is contradicted by the faith itself. From page one to its final page the whole thing the Qur'an admonishes the faithful to do is to be kind, just, humane, generous, not to kill or harm the innocent, not to mutilate, and demands all one wishes for human beings to be. The Qur'an Chapter 2-Verse 190 insists that believers are only to fight in self defence and not go beyond the limits of what is necessary, since God does not like the transgressors. All forms of torture are condemned.[382] Forgiveness is emphasised as better than retaliation in Qur'an 5:45:
'We ordained therein for them: "Life for life, eye for eye, nose or nose, ear for ear, tooth for tooth, and wounds equal for equal." But if any one remits the retaliation by way of charity, it is an act of atonement for himself. And if any fail to judge by (the light of) what God hath revealed, they are wrong-doers.'
Qur'an 3:133-134 says:
'Be quick in the race for forgiveness from your Lord, and for a Garden whose width is that (of the whole) of the heavens and of the earth, prepared for the righteous, Those who spend (freely), whether in prosperity, or in adversity; who restrain anger, and are forgiving toward mankind;- for God loves those who do good.'
If some Muslim individuals fail to abide by the maxims of the faith (because they are criminals in essence) or are misled by anyone, this is not the fault of the faith. Moreover, as we said many times, behind the bloody, bearded, cagouled, knife brandishing, murderer, could be a captain of any secret service. Should people read *The Secret Agent* by Joseph Conrad (or see the film),[383] and changed Russian anarchists into 'Muslim extremists,' they would find logical answers to many dark

---

[380] *Foreign Office Reports*; such as F.O. 195-1185; No 73. F.O. 195-2438, no 6650; Lamb to Lowther, Salonica 3 December 1912. Foreign office reports; such as F.O. 195-1185; No 73; Layard to earl of Derby, 26 July 1877. FO. 371-1762, no 55161; Greig to Crackanthrope, Monastir, 19 November 1913.
-M. Gehri (Delegue du Comite International de la Croix Rouge): 'Mission d'Enquete en Anatolie, 12-22 Mai 1921,' = *Extrait de la Revue Internationale de la Croix Rouge*, 3em Annee, No. 31, 15 juillet 1921, pp. 721-735. (Geneva, 1921.)
-Gustav Cirilli: Journal du siege d'Adrianople; Paris, 1913.
-H. Edib: *Memoirs* (London, 1926). -H. Edib: *The Turkish Ordeal*; John Murray; London; 1928.
-T. Gordon, *History of the Greek Revolution*, 2 vols; Edinburgh, William Blackwood, 1832.
-Ernst Jäckh; *Deutschland im Orient nach dem Balkan-Krieg;* Chapter 7: Deutsche und französische Augenzeugen von christlichen Massakers. (Die Balkangreuel des 30 jährigen Krieges); Martin Mörikes Verlag, Munich, 1913; pp. 83-98.
-P. Loti: *Turquie Agonisante*; Calman Levy; Paris; 1913.
-M. Pickthall: *With the Turk in Wartime*; J.M. Dent &Sons; London; 1914.
-M. Philips Price: *War and Revolution in Asiatic Russia*, George Allen & Unwin Ltd, London, 1917.
-A.J. Toynbee: *The Western Question in Greece and Turkey;* Constable; London, 1922.
-Salahi R. Sonyel: Disinformation, the Negative factor in Turco-Greek Relations, *Perceptions*, March-May 1998, pp. 39-48.
-Syed Tanvir Wasti: The 1912-13 Balkan wars and the Siege of Edirne; in *Middle Eastern Journal*; 40 (2004); pp. 59-78.
-J. McCarthy: *Death and Exile: The Ethnic Cleansing of Ottoman Muslims, 1821-1922*; The Darwin Press; New Jersey; 1995. J. McCarthy: *The Ottoman Peoples and the end of Empire*; Bloomsbury; 2001.
-S.J. Shaw and E.K. Shaw: *History of the Ottoman Empire and Modern Turkey*; vol 2; Cambridge University Press; 1977.
[381] See D. Stannard: Genocide; op cit; R. Garaudy: *Comment l'Homme;* op cit; etc.
[382] As in Tabari, 1954, ii: 190; in A. Gunny: *Images of Islam;* op cit; p. 36.
[383] Acting cast includes David Suchet, Patrick Malahide, Peter Capaldi, and Janet Suzman.

deeds of the recent past. But who would dare looking for he who hides behind the cagouled monster. Not this author, definitely.

A word or two on the Turks to say that their persistent labelling as barbaric, cruel fiends and enemies of science and progress, has no basis in reality, but has other motivations. With regard to the Seljuks, hostility to them, as to the Mamluks for that matter, derives from the simple fact that during the Western Christian onslaught on the Islamic lands in the crusades era (1095-1291), they were the main foes of the crusaders. Any person reading the history of the crusades, from Muslim or Christian sources, old or new, should realise this, and if it had not been for the Seljuk Turks, Muslims might have ran the risk of being entirely exterminated.[384] As for the Ottomans, the same argument holds for, from the 14th until the early 20th century, they were the main Christian military foe, facing Christendom on countless fronts.[385] It was the Ottomans, who, as history shows us, protected the entire Muslim world from Western annihilation.[386] Thus, there is little surprise in coming across such vilification of the Ottomans, vilification which is amply noted by Fisher,[387] or Davenport, who concluded that the Turks' being the principal Islamic foe of the Christian West for centuries was the major reason for violent anti-Turkish rhetoric.[388] Galland (1646-1715) also earlier observed how the Turks were wrongly vilified: it suffices to name them to signify to Europeans 'a coarse, barbarous, thoroughly ignorant nation.'[389]

Regarding the other aspect of Islamic barbarism, i.e enmity to civilisation, we can categorically claim as we showed at great lengths in our works devoted to civilisation that it was the 'theocratic' Islamic state that spurred science, learning and civilisation to a level no other state did before, in fact dragging Arab society from an age of utter ignorance and barbarism into a state, power, and civilisation that then ruled the world.[390]

The Muslim force which conquered southern Europe had a profound impact on Andalusia, which 'has never been as productive of able men and valuable ideas as it was during the centuries of Islamic rule.'[391] By the end of the rule of Islam, this same

---

[384] Ibn al-Adim: *Bughyat al-talab*; partial ed Ali Sevim (Ankara; 1976). T.A. Archer: *The Crusades* (T. Fisher Unwin; London; 1894). Ibn al-Athir: *Tarikh al-dawla al-Atabakiya Muluk al-Mawsil*; in *Recueil des Historiens des Croisades* (Orientaux); 11/ii (Paris; 1871), pp. 1-394. Ibn al-Athir: *Kitab al-kamil*; ed K.J. Tornberg; 12 vols (Leiden; 1851-72). Baha Eddin: Ibn Shadad: *Nawadir asultania*; in *Receuil des Historiens Orientaux*; III (Paris; 1884). C.R. Conder: *The Latin Kingdom of Jerusalem* (The Committee of the Palestine Exploration Fund; London; 1897). G.W. Cox: *The Crusades* (Longman; London; 1874). Z. Oldenbourg: *The Crusades*; tr., from Fr by A. Carter (Weinfeld and Nicolson; London; 1965).
[385] Samuel Chew: *The Crescent and the Rose* (New York; 1974). P. Coles: *The Ottoman Impact on Europe* (Thames and Hudson; 1974).
[386] Refer to the Turkish assistance to the Maghreb in face of Christian onslaught in the 16th century, or the Turks fighting the Portuguese in the Indian Ocean. See, for Instance, F.F Armesto: *Before Columbus*: MaCMillan Education; London, 1987. C.R. Boxer: *The Portuguese Seaborne Empire; 1415-1825*; Hutchinson; London; 1969. G. Casale: *The Ottoman Age of Exploration*; Oxford University Press; 2010.
[387] G. Fisher: *The Barbary Legend*; op cit.
[388] J. Davenport: *An Apology for Mohammed and the Koran*; op cit.
[389] A. Gunny: *Images*; op cit; p. 45.
[390] S.E. Al-Djazairi: *The Golden Age*; op cit.
[391] E. Hyams: *A History of Gardens and Gardening*; op cit; p. 82.

southern Europe civilised the rest of Western Christendom,[392] or as Lombard puts it, it was Islam, which 'dragged Western Christendom out of its 'barbarian night.'[393] It was Islam which promoted trade and culture, and the Islamic advance, which dragged the West into 'an astonishing progress and the re-launching of its civilisation'.[394]

> The dark ages of Europe [says Smith] would have been doubly, nay trebly dark but for the Arabs who alone by their arts and sciences, by their agriculture, their philosophy, and their virtues, shone out amidst the universal gloom of ignorance and crime, who gave to Spain and to Europe an Averroes and an Avicenna, the Alhambra and the Al-Kazar..... It was the Arabs who developed the sciences of agriculture and astronomy, and created those of algebra and chemistry; who adorned their cities with colleges and libraries, as well as with mosques and palaces; who supplied Europe with a school of philosophers from Cordova, and a school of physicians from Salerno.[395]

Without a single exception, the first parts of Europe 'to emerge from barbarism' were those most directly under the influence of Muslim culture: the Spanish Marches of Catalonia, Provence, and Sicily.[396] To these places can be added Lorraine, as noted by Haskins, Thompson, and Welborn.[397] Another region that also witnessed a leap into science and subsequently diffused its learning was Salerno, the town south of Rome, which received medical learning from Tunisia, and then stood at 'The head of medical knowledge in the Christian West,' according to Durant.[398]

And what better quote on this than this one by Arthur. C. Clark:

> Almost all the Alternative History computer emulations suggest that the Battle of Tours (CE 732) was one of the crucial disasters of mankind. Had Charles Martel been defeated, Islam might have resolved the internal differences that were tearing it apart and gone on to conquer Europe. Thus centuries of Christian barbarism would have been avoided, the Industrial Revolution would have started almost a thousand years earlier, and by now we would have reached the nearer stars instead of merely the further planets....
>
> But fate ruled otherwise, and the armies of Islam turned back to Africa. Islam lingered on, a fascinating fossil, until the end of the twentieth century. Then abruptly, it dissolved in oil.

---

[392] See For instance: C.H. Haskins: *The Twelfth Century Renaissance*; op cit; R. Briffault: *The Making of Humanity;* op cit; J. Vernet: *Ce que la Science;* op cit.
[393] M. Lombard: 'Nous vivions dans des clairières. L'Islam, lui, brillait de tous ses feux...'. The article appeared in *Le Temps Stratégique* No 20, Spring 1987.
[394] Ibid.
[395] R.B. Smith: *Mohammed*; op cit; pp. 125-6; and 217.
[396] R. Briffault: *The Making of Humanity*, op cit; p. 207.
[397] C.H. Haskins: *Studies*; op cit; M.C. Welborn: Lotharingia; op cit; J.W. Thompson: The Introduction of Arabic Science; op cit.
[398] W. Durant: *The Age of Faith;* op cit; p. 457.

(Chairman's address: Toynbee Bi-Centennial Symposium, London, 2089).[399]

In respect to the claim that Islam is the source of chaos and mess, and even filth, of Muslim society of the recent past and that can easily be seen today and everywhere, this again is a profoundly gross error. Islam is innocent of this grand sickness affecting today's Muslim society. Setting aside what has been said in regard to the role of the faith in the origins of the Grand Islamic state and civilisation, everything in the faith points to, and insists on absolute order, harmony, perfection, and symmetry, on top of beauty and cleanliness. Muslim society used to be green, clean, orderly and book and garden loving.

In respect to the essential concept that shapes and is at the source of civilization, and that you can never find in today's Muslim society, that is the concept of search for perfection, this is a central element in Islam. The Qur'an is perfection in every respect, and it constantly stresses the search for excellence and perfection in respect to each and everything. Performing prayers demands from the faithful the perfect approach, in mind, in hygiene, in its performance, and when in a group in alignment, movement, behaviour, and so on. Timing and direction of prayers have also to be perfect. And so it goes for every single aspect of the faith, whether fasting, alms giving, reciting the Qur'an, going on pilgrimage, dividing inheritance...[400] This constant demand for perfection shapes and affects everything, especially as in Islam, faith and deeds, whatever their nature, are one and continuous, and daily. This explains what early Islamic civilisation, inspired by the faith, accomplished: from setting up the foundations of the modern sciences, which require precision and accurateness to the designs of exquisite arts and edifices of perfect symmetry and dimensions;[401] from the manufacturing of glass, paper, textiles, and steel to the setting up of the first industrial workshops known to us, which all require organisation, order, and perfect discipline;[402] from the establishment of the first public libraries to the management of the first prototypes of the modern hospitals

---

[399] A.C. Clarke: *The Fountains of Paradise;* Pan; 1979; p. 87.

[400] See appropriate chapters and explanations in both: M.A.S. Abdel Haleem: *The Qur'an;* Oxford University Press; 2004-5. M.M. Pickthall: *The Meaning of the Glorious Quran;* Ta ha Publishers; London; first printing 1930.

[401] R. Briffault: *The Making of Humanity* (London: George Allen and Unwin Ltd, 1928), p. 188. A. Mieli: *La Science Arabe et son role dans l'evolution scientifique mondiale* (Leiden: E.J. Brill. 1938), p. 99. B. Dodge: *Muslim Education in Medieval Times* (The Middle East Institute, Washington D.C, 1962), p. 27. G.M. Wickens: 'What the West borrowed from the Middle East,' in *Introduction to Islamic Civilisation,* edited by R.M. Savory, Cambridge University Press, Cambridge, 1976, pp. 120-5. E. Wiedemann: *Beitrage zur Geschichte der Natur-wissenschaften. X. Zur Technik bei den Arabern.* Erlangen, 1906. E. Wiedemann: 'Zur mechanik und technik bei der Arabern' in *Sitzungsherichte der Physikalisch-Medizinischen Sorietat in Erlangen* (38), 1906. J. Vernet: *Ce que la Culture doit aux Arabes d'Espagne,* translation by Gabriel Martinez Gros, Paris, 1985. D. Talbot Rice: *Islamic Art;* Thames and Hudson; London; 1979. H. Terrasse: *L'Art Hispano Mauresque des Origins au 13em Siecle;* Paris; 1933. H.R. Turner: *Science in Medieval Islam,* Austin Texas, 1997.

[402] T. Glick: Technological Diffusion; in T. Glick, S.J. Livesey, F. Wallis Ed: *Medieval Science, Technology and Medicine;* An Encyclopaedia; (Routledge; London; 2005); pp. 470-2; at p. 471. E. Gerspach: *L'Art de la Verrerie* (A Quantin Imprimeur, Editeur; Paris; 1885), p. 97. C.S. Smith: *A History of Metallography*; (Chicago; 1965); p. 33 ff. R.E. Mack: *Bazaar to Piazza; Islamic Trade and Italian Arts, 1300-1600*; (University of California Press; Berkeley; 2002); p. 4. L. Viardot: *Historia de los Arabes y de los Moros de Espana;* (Barcelona; 1844); p. 239. M. Lombard: *The Golden Age of Islam*; tr., J. Spencer (North Holland Publishers; 1975), p. 192.

which demand again order, discipline, and organisation of the utmost;[403] from the erection of splendidly designed gardens where everything was a delight to the eyes in forms and symmetry to the most minutely devised irrigation works where hardly a drop of water was wasted;[404] from the establishment of the first observatories where calculations captured every single move of the planets observed to the erection of scientific academies which served as the source of modern sciences and civilisation;[405] and from the construction of whole dazzling towns and cities out of sand to the building of dams and other engineering structures designed and constructed with such skills as to still function to this day in places after ten or so centuries of existence.[406]

---

[403] M. Quatremere: Memoires sur le gout des livres chez les Orientaux; in *Journal Asiatique*; VI; (1830); pp. 35-78. H. Purgastall: Additions au memoire de M. Quatremere sur le gout des livres chez les Orientaux; *Journal Asiatique*; XI (1848), pp. 178-98. F. Reichmann: *The Sources of Western Literacy* (Greenwood Press; London; 1980), p. 205. M al-Rammah: The Ancient Library of Kairaouan and its methods of conservation, in *The Conservation and Preservation of Islamic Manuscripts*, Proceedings of the Third Conference of Al-Furqan Islamic Heritage Foundation (1995), pp. 29-47; p. 29. M.M. Sibai; *Mosque Libraries: An Historical Study* (Mansell Publishing Limited: London and New York: 1987), p. 58. Issa Bey: *Histoire des Hopitaux en Islam*; Beirut; Dar ar ra'id al'arabi; 1981. A. Whipple: *The Role of the Nestorians and Muslims in the History of Medicine*. Microfilm-xerography by University Microfilms International Ann Arbor, Michigan, U.S.A. 1977.

[404] J. Harvey: *Medieval Gardens* (B.T. Batsford Ltd; London; 1981), p. 37. J. Sourdel Thomine: *La Civilisation de l'Islam* (Paris; 1968), J. Dickie: Nosta Sobre la jardineria arabe en la espana Musulmane; *Miscelanea de estudios arabes y hebraicos* XIV-XV (1965-6); pp. 75-86. G. Marcais: Les Jardins de l'Islam; in *Melanges d'Histoire et d'Archeologie de l'Occident Musulman*; 2 Vols (Alger; 1957), pp. 233-44. F.F Armesto: *Millennium*; A Touchstone Publication, (Simon and Shuster New York; 1995), p. 35. D.R. Hill: *A History of Engineering in Classical and Medieval Times* (Croom Helm; 1984), p. 26. F.R. Cowell: *The Garden as a Fine Art* (Weidenfeld and Nicolson; London; 1978), p. 72. A.M. Watson: A Medieval Green Revolution; New Crops and Farming Techniques in The Early Islamic World, in *The Islamic Middle East 700-1900*; edited by A. Udovitch (Princeton; 1981), pp. 29-58.

[405] M. Hoskin and O. Gingerich: Islamic Astronomy; in *The Cambridge Concise History of Astronomy*; ed., by M. Hoskin (Cambridge University Press; 1999), pp. 50-62. H. Suter: *Die Mathematiker und Astronomen der Araber und ihre Werke* (1900; reprint APA, Oriental Press, Amsterdam, 1982). A Sayili: *The Observatory in Islam*, Turkish Historical Society (Ankara, 1960). B. Hetherington: *A Chronicle of Pre-Telescopic Astronomy* (John Wiley and Sons; Chichester; 1996). F. Sezgin: *Geschichte des arabischen Schrifttums* (vol vi for astronomy); 1978. B. Rosenfeld and E. Ihsanoglu: *Mathematicians, Astronomers and Other Scholars of Islamic Civilisation*; Research Centre for Islamic History, Art and Culture; (Istanbul; 2003). P. Kunitzsch: *The Arabs and the Stars: Texts and Traditions on the Fixed Stars, and Their Influence in Medieval Europe* (Variorum; Aldershot; 1989) in S.L. Montgomery: *Science in Translation*; p. 133. C. Burnett: The Introduction of Arabic Learning into British Schools in *The Introduction of Arabic Philosophy into Europe*; C.F. Butterworth and B.A Kessel ed (Brill; Leiden; 1994), pp. 40-57; pp. 44. K. Krisciunas: *Astronomical Centers of the World* (Cambridge University Press; 1988), pp. 36-8. T. Glick: Communication; T. Glick, S.J. Livesey, F. Wallis Editors: *Medieval Science, Technology and Medicine; An Encyclopaedia*; (Routledge; London; 2005); pp. 135-8; at p. 138.

[406] Z. Oldenbourg: *The Crusades*; tr., from the French by A. Carter (Weinfeld and Nicolson; London; 1965), pp. 476; 498. A. Castro: *The Spaniards; An Introduction to their History*; (University of California Press; 1971); p. 226. W. Blunt: *Splendours of Islam*; Angus and Robertson; (London; 1976); p. 37. Joseph McCabe: The Splendour of Moorish Spain; in W. Blunt: *Splendours of Islam*; p. 37. G. Marcais: l'Urbanisme Musulman, in *Melanges d'Histoire et d'Archeologie de l'Occident Musulman*; Vol 1; (Gouvernement General de l'Algerie; Alger; 1957); pp. 219-31; at p. 219. A.L. Udovitch: Urbanism in *The Dictionary of the Middle Ages*; op cit; Vol 12; pp. 306-10. E.E. Herzfeld: *Geschichte der Stadt Samarra* (Hamburg; 1948), p. 137. Al-Maqqari: *Nafh Al-Tib*. Partial translation by P. De Gayangos: *The History of the Mohammedan Dynasties in Spain* (extracted from *Nifh Al-Tib* by al-Maqqari); 2 vols (The Oriental Translation Fund; London, 1840-3), Vol 1; p. 87. M. Acien Almansa and A. Vallejo Triano: Cordoue, In *Grandes Villes Mediterraneenes du Monde Musulman Medieval*; J.C. Garcin editor (Ecole Francaise de Rome; 2000), pp. 117-34; at p. 117. D.R. Hill: *A History of Engineering in Classical and Medieval Times* (Croom Helm; 1984).

Four

THE MEDIEVAL MODELS: THE CRUSADES AND MUSLIMS OF SICILY

In launching the crusades (in 1095), Pope Urban II (Pope 1088-1099) spoke of:
> An accursed race, a race utterly alienated from God... has invaded the lands of those Christians and has depopulated them by the sword, pillage and fire... They (the Turks) perforate navels... (and inflict terrible cruelties on the Christians, depicted in great detail by the Pope) .... What shall I say of the abominable rape of the women? .... Accordingly undertake this journey for the remission of your sins, with the assurance of the imperishable glory of the kingdom of heaven.[407]

By this speech, Urban legitimised Christian aggression, making it for the whole Western community a case 'of kill or be killed.'[408]

To spread this message, Finucane notes, priests and prelates in different styles and tones, exercised 'all the tricks of the orator's trade, cajoling, threatening, promising; using allegory, hyperbole, anaphora; rousing with revenge motifs.'[409] Thus, Balderic (Baldricus), archbishop of Dol, goes:
> We have heard, most beloved brethren, and you have heard what we cannot recount without deep sorrow how, with great hurt and dire sufferings our Christian brothers, members in Christ, are scourged, oppressed, and injured in Jerusalem, in Antioch, and the other cities of the East..... Base and bastard Turks hold sway over our brothers.[410]

The Turks according to Fulcher of Chartres,
> Have killed and captured many, have destroyed the churches and devastated the Kingdom of God.[411]

For Guibert of Nogent, unspeakable cruelty has been inflicted on the pilgrims.[412]

All atrocities [Munro points out] highly spiced to suit the spirit of the time, and influence the Christians to take up arms, inciting many to take the Cross and flock to the Holy Land for revenge.[413]

Of course all these claims had no foundations, for the Pope lied. He, in truth, sought to bring the Orthodox Church under the Catholic in a show of unity against the Turks, releasing fighting spirits from Europe and unleashing them on the Muslim

---

[407] In D. C. Munro, "Urban and the Crusaders", Translations and Reprints from the *Original Sources of European History*, vol 1:2, 1895, pp. 5-8
[408] N. Daniel: *The Cultural*; op cit; p.158.
[409] R. Finucane: *Soldiers of the Faith*; (J.M. Dent and Sons Ltd; London, 1983); p. 30.
[410] In A. C. Krey, *The First Crusade: The Accounts of Eyewitnesses and Participants*, (Princeton University Press; 1921); pp. 33-36.
[411] D.C. Munro: The Western attitude; op cit; at p.329.
[412] In N. Daniel: *The Arabs*, op cit; p. 253.
[413] D.C. Munro: The Western; op cit; p. 329.

foe, exploiting the divisions between Muslims (who were slaughtering each other) in order to crush Islam once and for all. Most likely, he was seeking to gain a good seat somewhere in the hereafter as the one who crushed the devil. Definitely, he was doing a deal with the Italian cities to share out spoils of the East, and he did it for whatever else went through his head.[414]

Nonetheless, also stirred by various reasons, including the redemption of their countless sins, the search for glory, the dream of finding a field or a bazar, or just for the sake of slaying a few pagans, hordes departed from Europe. 'Clergy, nobles, all the people, the chaste, the incestuous, the adulterers, robbers, all who professed the Christian faith,' grasped the opportunity for penance, and went on the crusade.[415] They 'emerged in bands on all sides, equipped themselves with food and arms that they needed to get to Jerusalem,' says Albert of Aix, and were 'burning with fire and divine love.'[416]

Once reaching the Muslim East, they committed terrible atrocities such as when they took Ma'arrat an-Nu'man in 1098. The terrified population hid in their homes, but to no avail. For three days the slaughter never stopped; the crusaders killed more than 100,000 people.[417] The chronicler of nearby Aleppo, Ibn al-Adim (d. 1262), speaks of the carnage:

> They (the Franks) killed a great number under torture... They destroyed the walls of the town, burned its mosques and houses and broke the minbars.[418]

Robert the Monk says:

> Our men walked through the roads, places, on the roofs, and feasted on the slaughter.... They cut into pieces, and put to death children, the young, and the old crumbling under the weight of the years. They did that in groups....[419]

Radulph of Caen said how:

> In Maarra our troops boiled pagan adults in cooking pots; they impaled children on spits and devoured them grilled.[420]

In fact, as the chronicler, William of Tyre notes, it was a common practice for the crusaders to roast and eat the flesh of the Muslims they slew.[421] The daughter of the Byzantine Emperor, Anna Comnena, accused Peter the Hermit's followers of chopping up babies and impaling others on spits to roast over fires, while the elderly were subjected to a variety of tortures.[422] At Ma'arrat, to avoid such a fate,

---

[414] For the pope's true reasons to unleash the crusades, see D. Hay: *The Medieval Centuries*; (Methuen and Co; London; 1964); p. 81; pp. 90-1. W. Durant: *The Age of Faith*; op cit; p. 586.
[415] N. Daniel: *The Arabs;* op cit; p. 122.
[416] Ibid; p. 123.
[417] Ibn al-Athir: *Kitab al-Kamil*; ed., K.J. Tornberg; 12 vols; (Leiden; 1851-72). X; p. 190.
[418] In Y. Tabba: Monuments with a message, in *The Meeting of Two Worlds*; ed., V.P. Goss; (Kalamazoo; Michigan; 1986); pp. 223-40; at p. 233. See Kemal Eddin: *Muntakhabat min Tarikh Halab*; in *Recueil des Historiens Orientaux*; (Paris; 1872); ff. vol iii; pp. 586-7.
[419] Robert the Monk, in G. Le Bon: *La Civilisation,* op cit; p. 248.
[420] In J. Abu Lughod: *Before European Hegemony*; (Oxford University Press; 1989); p. 107.
[421] C.R. Conder: *The Latin Kingdom*; op cit. p. 45.
[422] *The Alexiad of Anna Comnena*, tr. E.R. A. Sewter; (Harmondsworth; 1969); pp. 311; 437.

many Muslims were said by a Christian writer to have jumped down wells to their deaths.[423]

These massacres were generalised to all towns and cities taken by the crusaders, from Antioch, to Jerusalem to Caesarea..., and lasted for more than a century. Then, in the 1250s, in alliance with the Mongols, the Christians threatened to exterminate the whole Muslim entity.[424] Had it not been for the Seljuk and Mamluk fight-back, principally, the Muslims would have been extinguished.[425] It is likely that over ten million Muslims were slaughtered by both crusaders and their Mongol allies.[426]

The mass killings of Muslims had a deeper justification other than their 'agression.' As Sweetman points out, Islam was represented to the popular mind as the religion of the 'pagan Saracens,' and they were all too often regarded solely as the traditional enemy, 'against whom it was an act of piety and penance to take up the banner of the cross.'[427] According to the contemporary Christian polemicist, Petrus Tudebodus, the Muslims are: 'Our enemy and God's... saying diabolical sounds in I know not what language.'[428]

The geographical and ethnic distinctions between these enemies are confused at one point Tudebodus describes a castle 'Full of innumerable pagans: Turks, Saracens, Arabs, Publicans, and other pagans.'[429] Many of the place names are familiar from the Bible; Tudebodus and other chroniclers associate the pagans with the places where antichrist is born and raised: Babylon and Corosan.[430]

Whilst the crusaders are seen as the new apostles, the Muslims take on the familiar role of the Pagan Roman persecutors; their paganism and barbarism a necessary counterpart to the steadfast devotion of the crusaders/apostles.[431] Tolan explains how the association of Islam with paganism justified the crusades as a vengeance against 'such pagans.'[432] Thus, during the first crusade (1095), according to Tudebodus, the crucifix, confronted with an idol of 'Machomet,' began to bleed miraculously.[433] Here the idol 'Machomet' fights Christ on the crucifix, and the crucifix wins.[434] The Amiravissus (apparently the Muslim ruler of Jerusalem)

---

[423] R. Finucane: *Soldiers of the Faith;* op cit; p. 106.
[424] Baron G. D'Ohsson: *Histoire des Mongols,* in four volumes; (Les Freres Van Cleef; la Haye and Amsterdam; 1834). J.J. Saunders: *Aspects of the Crusades*, op cit.
[425] Ibn al-Qalanisi: *Dayl tarikh Dimashk;* ed. H.F. Amedroz; (Leiden; 1908). Herbert. M. J. Loewe: The Seljuqs: in *The Cambridge Medieval History*, op cit; pp. 299-317. Ibn al-Furat: *Tarikh al-Duwal wal Muluk;* ed. M. F. El-Shayyal; unpublished Ph.d.; University of Edinburgh; 1986.
[426] A.N Poliak: The Demographic Evolution of the Middle East: *Population Trends since 1348, Palestine and the Middle East*, vol X. no 5, 1938. E.G. Browne: *Literary History of Persia;* (Cambridge University Press; 1929). Baron G. D'Ohsson: *Histoire des Mongols,* op cit.
[427] J. W. Sweetman: *Islam and Christian Theology;* (Lutterworth Press; London; 1955); part two; p. 57
[428] Petrus Tudebolus: *Historia de Hierosolimitanorum;* (edited by J and L. Hill; Paris; 1977); p. 51.
[429] Ibid; p. 128.
[430] Ibid; p. 73; 77; 148; etc.
[431] J.V. Tolan: Muslims as pagan idolaters in Chronicles of the First Crusades; in D.R. Blanks, and M. Frassetto ed: *Western Views of Islam in Medieval and Early Modern Europe;* St. Martin's Press; New York; 1999; pp. 97-117; at p. 101.
[432] Ibid; p. 105.
[433] Petrus Tudebodus: Historia; in J.V. Tolan: *Muslims*; p. 105.
[434] Ibid.

subsequently laments the imminent fall of the city (1099) and twice invokes 'Machomet and other gods.'[435] The confrontation between God's army and the pagan army, as between the crucifix and the idol of 'Machomet,' can have only one outcome: Christian victory. 'Themes essential to Christian history: pilgrimage, martyrdom, and the fight against idolatry, combining to form a powerful apology for the crusade,' Tolan remarks.[436]

In the wake of the Christian capture of Jerusalem (July 1099), the Muslim population was butchered en masse to the delight of everyone present or who subsequently heard of it. A contemporary, Abbot Raymond of Agiles of the French town of Du Puy, present during the dramatic moments, wrote with glee:

> When our men took the main defences, we saw then some astonishing things amongst the Saracens. Some were beheaded, and that's the least that could happen to them. Others were pierced through and so threw themselves from the heights of the walls; others after having suffered in length were thrown into the flames. We could see in the roads and in the places of Jerusalem bits and pieces of heads, hands, and feet. Everywhere we could only walk through cadavers. But all that was only little... [The abbot's description moves onto the Mosque of Omar, where]: there was so much blood in the old temple of Solomon that dead corpses swam in it. We could see hands floating and arms that went to glue themselves to bodies that were not theirs; we could not distinguish which arm belonged to which body. The men who were doing the killing could hardly bear the smoke from the corpses.[437]

For Raymond this massacre of 70,000 Muslims, at least, was sweet revenge. He says:

> This was truly a judgment of God, that that place should receive their blood, since it endured for such a long time their blasphemies against God.... I say that this day saw the weakening of paganism, the confirmation of Christianity, and the renovation of our faith.[438]

St Bernard was the main preacher of the second crusade (1148), which was eventually to end in great failure outside Damascus. His inflammatory rhetoric to mobilise the Christians went as follows:

> This we altogether forbid, that for any reason they should enter into an alliance with (the Muslims), neither for money nor for tribute, until with the help of God either their religion or their nation has been destroyed.

St Bernard denounces

> Muslim fanaticism and that an exposure of Islam would only increase the disgust which Christians felt for a religion characterized by sensualism and

---

[435] Ibid.
[436] J.V. Tolan: Muslims as pagan idolaters; op cit; p. 105.
[437] Abbot Raymond of Aguilers; in G. Le Bon: *La Civilisation des Arabes*; Syracuse, 1884; p. 249.
[438] Raymond D' Aguilers: *Liber*, ed., J.H and L. I. Hill; (Paris; 1969); pp. 150-1.

violence.[439] The Christian rejoices in the death of a pagan because Christ is glorified.[440]

The soldier of Christ, he asserts:

> Carries a sword not without reason; for he is the minister of Christ for the punishment of evil-doers, as well as for the praise of good men. Clearly when he kills a malefactor he is not a homicide but as I should say a malicide, and he is simply considered the avenger of Christ on those who do evil and the protector of Christians. But when he himself is killed he is known not to perish but to survive.
>
> Therefore the death which he proposes is for the profit of Christ; and that which he receives, for his own. The Christian glories in the death of the non-Christian, because Christ is glorified; in the death of the Christian the liberality of the King appears, as the soldier is led to his sword..... Not indeed that even non-Christians ought to be killed if there were some other way to prevent them from molesting or oppressing the faithful; but now it is better that they should be killed than that the rod of sinners should certainly be left over the fate of the just: lest perchance the just reach out their hands to iniquity.[441]

Not only, therefore, is Christ glorified in the death of the infidel, but killing is justified 'if only because the Christians may begin to pick up the ways of the Arabs.'[442]

Another contemporary, Humbert of Romans, was a back-room expert who summarised the theory as it stood in the thirteenth century. He made a collection of his crusading sermons, and his reputation in this field stood so high that he wrote his Threefold Work to brief the Fathers at the Council of Lyons in 1274.[443] His view is thus summed up by Daniel:

> A just war must cause the innocent to suffer, as so often happened in Europe to poor farmers, and hospitals and leper-colonies; but, he argued, the Muslim nation was culpable in the highest degree. There must be a sufficient cause to justify war, nothing like injured pride, or avarice, or vainglory; but the army of God fought for something better than even a material right, it fought for the faith. A just war must be fought on adequate authority; but the Crusade was fought on the authority of God, and so it was a just war in the highest degree. The Church wields two swords, against heretics and against rebels; but Muslims destroyed the body like the latter and the soul like the former... When it was objected that it might happen that innocent Christians suffered more than guilty Muslims, [Humbert pointed out] that this was not so, and

---

[439] J.W. Sweetman: *Islam and Christian Theology;* op cit; p. 76.
[440] St Bernard: *Opera* (ed Mabillon); vol I; col. 549.
[441] St Bernard in N. Daniel: *The Arabs and Medieval Europe*; Longman, Librairie du Liban; 1975; pp. 252-3.
[442] Ibid.
[443] N. Daniel: *The Arabs and Medieval Europe*; p. 253.

instanced the splendid occasion when the blood of the Arabs came up to the horses' knees, at the capture of Jerusalem in 1099.[444]

The doctrine of the just war received impetus from the Crusade. Apparently some objectors contrasted the behaviour of Christ and the Apostles with this shedding of blood, but Humbert pointed out that conditions had changed: Christians then had had no power and so been compelled to proceed by humility; now it was quite different; then they had miracles, now they had arms.[445]

Muslims deserved to die, for 'they were guilty' of polytheism, the worship of statues and representations of the Prophet.[446] In William's epics,[447] the Muslims, other than being 'hideous, treacherous, cowardly, arrogant, and willing to sacrifice their first-born sons, adore the gods: Mahomet, Cahu, Appolyon, and Tervagant, which are all earthly idols.'[448] Fulk of Chartres who took part in the first crusade (launched 1095) and lived in Jerusalem for over a quarter of a century says that in the Dome of the Rock the Muslims 'used to pray to an idol made in the name of Mahumet.'[449] Epics associated with Aymeri of Narbonne and his son, William of Orange, (written ca 1200, but legendary from the previous century), portray the Muslims as idol worshippers, and wicked creatures.[450] Pagans and Muslims were one and the same in the *Ars Fidei Catholicae* of Alanus de Insulis (b.ca 1128), where he has a section '*contra paganos seu Mohometanos*',[451] whilst Jacques de Vitry wrote:

> As often as the followers of Mohammed possess the Temple of Solomon, they set up his statue in the Temple and permit no Christian to enter.[452]

The Prophet is also said to have made himself adored as an idol, and even as a god, the *Gesta Francorum* speaking of gods, and of oaths taken by Muhammad as a god.[453] For Sigebert of Gembloux (d.1112), 'This is the Muhammad to whom the Gentiles, hitherto offer the worship of a deity.'[454] For the Englishman, Mathew Paris:

> A sort of infernal lightning, which, however, descended from the skies, had suddenly set fire to and destroyed the temple of Mahomet, together with his statue; and that again a second explosion similar to the first, had reduced the said temple to small bits; and that a third had, as we believed, thrust the ruins into an abyss in the earth. After this, he said, this fire, which burned with a most devouring heat, though it did not give a bright light, crept along under the earth, like the fire of hell, consuming even rocks in its way, and could not

---

[444] Ibid.
[445] Ibid.
[446] C. Pellat, 'L'idée de Dieu chez les «Sarrasins» des chansons de geste', *Studia Islamica*, 22, (1965), pp. 524.
[447] *Guillaume d'Orange; Four Twelfth Century Epics;* tr. John Ferrante (New York; 1974), pp. 63-139.
[448] In Jo Ann Hoeppner Moran Cruz: Popular Attitudes; in *Western Perceptions* (Blanks-Frassetto ed) op cit; p. 58.
[449] Fulcheri Carnotensis…in B. Z. Kedar: *Crusade and Mission;* (Princeton University Press; 1984), at p. 89.
[450] *Aymeri de Narbonne, Chanson de Geste*; (Louis Demaison; Paris; 1887), 2 vols.
[451] J.W. Sweetman: *Islam and Christian Theology* (Lutterworth Press; London; 1955), Vol I; Part II, p. 66.
[452] D.C. Munro: The Western attitude toward Islam during the period of the Crusades; *Speculum* Vol 6 No 4, pp. 329-43; pp. 331-2.
[453] Ibid.
[454] Sigebert of Gembloux, quoted in B.Z. Kedar: *Crusade*; op cit; p. 86.

even yet be extinguished. And thus the whole city of Mecca, and the country in its vicinity, were consumed with inextinguishable fire.[455]

Tancred (a crusade leader) was heard in 1099 to have found a silver idol of the Prophet in the Temple of 'the Lord,' a fable which was the result of a misunderstanding and mistranslation of the chronicler Fulcher of Chartres, but as Munro points out, taken up by today's scholars.[456] When the Byzantine Emperor, Manuel I Comnenus (1143-80), sought to show that it is inaccurate to equate Islam with idolatry he found himself censored by the ecclesiastical hierarchy.[457] Even prominent figures, such as the Bolognese professor of civil law Azo (1150-1230) wrote a commentary on the Code of Justinian that says that

> The pagans, that is the Saracens, worship innumerable gods, goddesses, and indeed demons.[458]

All these depictions conflict with the truth knowing that Islam's first deed was to destroy idols, but such distorted views helped justify the killings of Muslims. Thus, the 'Saracens' in the Song of Roland (who worship Antichrist, Lucifer, Termageunt and Diana among other idols), justified European heroics. Such 'Saracens' are to be killed by Christian knights.[459]

Muslims, finally here, are the authors of every kind of evil,
> Hating God and actively seeking Satan; they eat their prisoners, betray their oaths, and sell their own womenfolk.[460]

According to the Dominican Missionary, Riccoldo da Montecroce, who was in Baghdad in 1291, Muslims were 'Confused, mendacious, irrational, violent, and obscure.'[461]

Marco Polo in his Travels (1298)[462] is very full of admiration for the Mongols and their commander Hulagu who had slain millions of Muslims and destroyed the Caliphate, and is also full of praise for the idolaters, primarily Buddhists and Hindus.[463] As for the Muslims, he details with pleasure the overthrow of the Caliphate in 1258, and he describes Muslims as

> Treacherous, prone to great sinfulness, and as dogs not fit to lord it over Christians.[464]

As to their faith, it is the:

> Accursed doctrine of the Saracens [is that] every sin is accounted a lawful act even to the killing of every man who is not of their creed.[465]

---

[455] Mathew Paris' English History, vol III, p.231 in J. Dahmus: *Seven Medieval Historians* (Nelson-Hall, Chicago, 1982), p. 172.
[456] D.C. Munro: The Western; op cit; pp. 331-2.
[457] G.L. Hanson: Manuel I Comnenus and the 'God of Muhammad' A Study in Byzantine Ecclesiastical politics; in J. V. Tolan ed., *Medieval Christian Perceptions of Islam* (Routledge; London; 1996), pp. 55-84.
[458] Azo: Summa Aurea, to Cod.1.11; Lyons; 1557; col 7a; in B. Z. Kedar: *Crusade and Mission*; op cit; p. 88.
[459] R. Kabbani: *Imperial Fictions*; op cit; p. 15.
[460] In Jo Ann Hoeppner Moran Cruz: Popular Attitudes; op cit; pp. 56-7.
[461] In Z. Sardar; M.W. Davies: *Distorted Imagination;* op cit; p. 38.
[462] *The Travels of Marco Polo;* Trans R. Latham (New York; 1958).
[463] In Jo Ann Hoeppner Moran Cruz: Popular Attitudes towards Islam; op cit; p. 67.
[464] Ibid.
[465] Ibid; p. 68.

In Sicily

Muslim troops, from Aghlabid Tunisia, captured Sicily from the Byzantines beginning in 827. Muslim rule lasted there until the mid 11th century. Around this time, conflict between diverse Muslim factions led to the Norman capture of the Island. This took place over the period 1061-1091. At first Muslim-Norman cohabitation went fine as Muslims were needed to run the entire country, whether its economic, military, administrative institutions, or, more importantly, its financial system or Exchequer.[466] However, the accommodation of Muslims was quite precarious indeed, especially under William 1, the Bad (ruled 1154-1166). Muslim merchants were massacred en masse in Palermo in 1160. In 1161, the Lombards invaded the royal domain and slaughtered the Muslims wherever they found them.[467] Muslims fled en masse, westward to safer areas, where the population was still predominantly Muslim.[468] The Lombards destroyed Muslim communities with no distinction for sex or age, both those who lived mixed up with Christians in different towns, and those, who, living apart, possessed their own villages.[469] A few Muslims escaped disguised in Christian dress to the temporary safety of Muslim towns in the south.[470]

Despite that and considerable loss of power and status, somehow a Muslim community survived under the Norman and their Hohenstaufen successors. This was not pleasing to the Church as well as many rulers from outside of Italy. By the time of the rule of Frederick II (King of Sicily 1198-d. 1250), the situation reached levels such as that the Popes had enough of such Muslim presence. This, eventually, led to their removal.

What we are interested here is to show how once more the removal of such Muslims had to be justified on account of the dangers or threat they represented to Christianity.

Daniel tells us that:
> When William of Apulia is describing the capture of Palermo in his *De Rebus Gestis Normannorum in Sicilia*, he describes Roger's offer of safety and favour to the Muslim inhabitants. At the same time he destroys all the mosques, and turns the principal mosque into a church of the Virgin, so that where demons had sat should now be the seat of God and a fitting

---

[466] For Norman Sicily see, E. Pontieri (Malaterra): *De Rebus Gestis Rogerii... Malaterra*, Fonti per la Storia d'Italia; Bologna; 1927- V. de Bartolomeis (Amatus): *Storia dei Normanni di Amati di Montecassino;* Rome; 1935; D. Mathew: *The Norman Kingdom of Sicily*: Cambridge University Press; 1992. A. Metcalfe: *Muslims and Christians in Norman Sicily*; Routledge; London; 2003; H. Huben: *Roger II of Sicily*; Cambridge University Press; 2002. S. Cusa: *I Diplomici greci ed arabi di Sicilia...*; Palermo, 1868-82; reprinted Koln, Wien, 1982.
[467] N. Daniel: The Arabs; op cit; p. 151.
[468] D. Abulafia: *Commerce and Conquest; op cit*; p. 108.
[469] N. Daniel: The Arabs; op cit; p.151.
[470] N. Daniel: The Arabs; op cit; p.151.

doorway to heaven.'[471] 'This is not a bad summary of the mercy that Europe would always offer the Arabs: conditional on the destruction of their religion, and, ultimately of their separate identity,' says Daniel[472]

According to estimates, at its peak, the Muslim population of Sicily reached as much as half a million.[473] Early in the fourteenth century, the whole Muslim presence was wiped out of the island. The elimination of the Muslims from Sicily owes to slow, but relentless pressure put upon Frederick and his successors (Manfred and Conradin), to remove the Muslims from amidst the Christians. In fact this was not just the case in Sicily but was a common policy throughout Christendom. The Fourth Lateran Council, during the pontificate of Innocent III (1198-1261), for instance, imposed distinctive dress on the Muslims (canon 68), and barred them from holding public office over Christians (c.69).[474] In 1266, Pope Clement IV (d.1268) urged the expulsion of the Muslims, telling Jayme of Aragon, that his reputation would suffer greatly

> ...If in view of temporal profit he should longer permit such opprobrium of God, such infection of Christendom as is caused by the horrible cohabitation of Moors and Christians.[475]

Back to Sicily, Pope Clement V (Pope 1305-1314) justified the final removal of Muslims on account that their presence amidst Christians was 'an insult to the Creator.'[476] His predecessors, from Gregory IX (Pope 1227-1241) to Boniface VIII (1294-1303) hounded the successive lords of Lucera (the last colony of Muslims) about their Muslim subjects.[477] Frequently the popes listed the mere existence of the colony among the casus belli for the series of crusades that Pope Innocent IV and his successors launched against the Hohenstaufen rulers of Sicily and subsequent enemies of the papacy in southern Italy.[478] Scott comments on this:

> The centre of the Papal power and of the various states subject to its immediate jurisdiction—a jurisdiction already important, but not as yet exercised with undisputed authority—could not fail to be profoundly impressed by the proximity of this anomalous empire; where Christian symbols and Koranic legends were blended in the embellishment of cathedrals; where the crucifixion and the mottoes of 'Mohammedan' rulers were impressed together upon the coinage of the realm; where eminent prelates owed investiture, rendered homage, and paid tribute to the secular power; where Moslem dignitaries not infrequently took precedence of Papal envoys; and the hereditary enemies of Christendom

---

[471] In N. Daniel: *The Arabs and medieval Europe*; Longman Librarie du Liban; 1975; p. 148.
[472] N. Daniel: The Arabs; op cit; p. 148.
[473] A.L. Udovitch: Islamic Sicily; in Dictionary of the Middle Ages; Vol 11; pp. 261-3; p.262.
[474] Lucy K Pick: Rodrigo Jimenez de Rada and the Jews, Pragmatism and patronage in 13th century Toledo: *Viator* 28; pp. 203-22; at p. 204.
[475] H.C. Lea: *The Moriscos of Spain*; (Burt Franklin; New York; 1968); pp. 4-5.
[476] V. Green: *A New History of Christianity*; Sutton Publishing; Stroud; 1996; pp. 90-1.
[477] N. Housley: The Italian crusades; 40; 62; 64-5 In J.P. Lomax: Frederick II, His Saracens, and the Papacy, in *Medieval Christian Perceptions of Islam*, Edited by J.V. Tolan; Routledge; London; pp. 175-97; p. 189.
[478] Housley: The Italian crusades; 40; 62; 64-5 In J.P. Lomax: Frederick II, p. 189.

fought valiantly under the standard of the Cross. Nor was the effect of this ominous example confined to localities where daily familiarity had caused it to lose its novelty.[479]

Scott just noted how Muslims served faithfully the Sicilian crown, even when the Sicilians participated either in the Crusades in the East under Frederick II in particular (in 1229 and after) or in the bloody invasions and sacking of North African towns. North African sages were bewildered by the presence of Muslims in the armies and navies of the Norman kings, including during the attack on Alexandria in 1174.[480] Lowe remarks how Muslims were some of the most faithful and loyal servants any Christian Sicilian lord or ruler could hope for.[481] What was unforgivable, though, was peaceful intercourse with Muslims (as Frederick experienced in the wake of his 'peaceful' crusade in the East, or to show mercy to Muslims as Philip of Mehdia experienced in the wake of the Sicilian invasion of Bona in Algeria in 1146.[482] On that occasion, Roger II's eunuch, Philip, a very close to the King himself,[483] was denounced as a hidden Muslim:

> Under the cloak of the Christian name, he preserved a hidden soldier of the devil; while as far as outward appearance was concerned he showed himself to be a Christian, he was wholly Muslim in mind and deed; he hated Christians and greatly loved pagans (Muslims); he went into the churches of God reluctantly, and visited the synagogues of the malignants (mosques) more often. He supplied them with oil for arranging the lights and other things necessary. Not respecting Christian tradition at all, he did not stop eating meat on Fridays or in Lent; he sent messengers with offerings to the tomb of Muhammad, and commended himself greatly to the prayers of the priests of that place.'[484]

As a punishment, Philip was dragged violently at the heels of a horse to the square before the palace and thrown into the fire to die.[485] His 'accomplices' were also executed. The King did not interfere to show that he was 'a most Christian prince and a Catholic.'[486]

Gradually Muslims lost wealth and status, and the remnant of the Muslim population was forced into western Sicily by aggressive Latin settlement at the eastern end of the island.[487] Muslims were recurrently removed from their lands

---

[479] S. P. Scott: History of the Moorish Empire; op cit; p. 29.
[480] D. Abulafia: *Commerce and Conquest in the Mediterranean, 1100-1500*, Variorum, 1993; p. 112.
[481] A. Lowe: *The Barrier and the Bridge*, G. Bles; London; 1972. p. 92.
[482] The case of the Admiral Philip has been discussed with varied conclusions by most writers on the reign of Roger II, notably by Amari, *Romualdi Salemitani Chronicon*, ed. C. A. Garufi, R.I.SS, Muratori, new edition, Citta di Castello, t. vii, pte. I, pp. 234-6; and also by V. Epifanio, 'Ruggero II e Filippo di Al Mahdiah', in *Arch. star, sic.*, n.s., t. xxx, pp. 471 seq.
[483] In N. Daniel: The Arabs; p. 149.
[484] In N. Daniel: *The Arabs and medieval Europe*; Longman Librarie du Liban; 1975. p. 149.
[485] In N. Daniel: The Arabs; p. 149.
[486] In N. Daniel: The Arabs; p. 149.
[487] J.P. Lomax: Frederick II, His Saracens, and the Papacy, in *Medieval Christian Perceptions of Islam*, Edited by J.V. Tolan; Routledge; London; pp. 175-97; p. 177.

by Christians, violence was widespread.[488] Most rural Sicilian Muslims eventually found themselves reduced to the servile status of villains under Christian overlords.[489] Under papal pressure, Frederick deported them to the Italian hinterland, to Lucera, where they were supposed to offer no danger. Papal pressure, however, mounted for their complete removal. According to Lomax, `The bitter and inflammatory rhetoric with which the popes consistently assailed the Muslims of Lucera, and often their royal masters, reveals the depth and character of papal animosity.'[490] Pope Gregory IX urged Frederick to

> Shatter the presumptions of these Muslims so that they would dare not disturb the hearts of God's faithful even a little, especially since particular injury will seem to be done to our Redeemer if the sons of Belial, who are bound by the shackle of perpetual servitude, assail the sons of light within our borders or damnably imagine themselves to be equal to them in privileges.[491]

The Pope announced he was directing Dominican friars to evangelise them. Gregory urged Frederick to support the Dominicans:

> With the material sword, without which their mission might fail; indeed, to drag this people, who are openly deceived by the error of perdition, to the font of regeneration and renewal by means of terror, because then their servitude will be more fruitful, since the one God shall have come to you and to them.[492]

Frederick insisted that Muslims of Lucera represented no kind of threat to the Church or to their Christian neighbours.[493] Unhappy with this response, in February 1236, Gregory Charged Frederick with numerous crimina manifesta (manifest crimes) in a letter entitled Dum preteritorum consideratione, which includes:

> Buildings in which the divine name is honoured are forced to become places where the damnable Muhammad is adored....

Then he added about the Muslims who are:

> Placed almost in the middle of the kingdom, can more easily corrupt the Catholic faith by the venom of their infidelity. Thence greater dangers take hold, for Christians are mixed in with them. Through companionship with pagans the flocks of the faithful depart from the Lord's fold.[494]

Gregory used the threat of excommunication to force Frederick to back down, but Frederick defended the reverse view, that he had moved the 'Saracens' at great

---

[488] J. Taylor: *Muslims in Medieval Italy*; Lexington Books; New York; Oxford; 2003; p. 3.
[489] See Annliese Nef, "Conquetes et reconquetes medievales: La Sicile normande est-elle une terre de reduction en servitude generalisee?" *Melanges de l'Ecole Francaise de Rome (Moyen Age)* 112-2 (2000): 579-607.
[490] J.P. Lomax: Frederick II,; p. 179.
[491] MGH (Monumenta Germaniae Historica) Epist. Saec. XIII 1:398-9; No 494 in J.P. Lomax: Frederick II, p. 180.
[492] M.GH (Monumenta Germaniae Historica) Epist. Saec. XIII 1:447-8; No 553 in J.P. Lomax: Frederick II,; p. 182-3.
[493] Frederick would later maintain that the proximity of Muslims to Christians had produced more Muslim converts to Christianity; in J.P. Lomax: Frederick II, p. 183.
[494] MGH Epist. Saec. XIII 1:574-5; No 676 in J.P. Lomax: Frederick II, p. 185-6.

expense, and placed them in the midst of Christians who daily served as an example to them.[495]

In October 1238, Gregory sent the third and final excommunication warning; followed by other threats. Papal ire over the existence of the Muslim enclave at Lucera, and the legal arguments with which Gregory IX supported his attacks on it and its imperial patron, persisted long after Gregory's death in 1241 and that of Frederick in 1250.[496]

Preparations for a crusade against Manfred (successor of Frederick) and the Lucerine Muslims were launched in the spring of 1255.[497] In May of that year, Pope Alexander issued the crusade bull *Pia Matris* in which he denounced the Muslims for having assisted Manfred 'an enemy of the Church.'[498] The contemporary chronicler, Matthew Paris, reported that in 1255 the pope sent Cardinal Ottaviano degli Ubaldini with an army of 60,000 to destroy Lucera, which was still Manfred's base.[499] Despite the demands of organising such an operation, that May, Pope Alexander also saw to the promotion of a crusade against Muslims in North Africa.[500] The papal army sent to Apulia against Manfred was sizeable, but Manfred's forces managed nevertheless to repulse it. Despite Manfred's victory, the conflict dealt a severe blow to the social and economic stability of both Foggia and Lucera. People were forced to flee their homes and hunger struck the region.[501]

In June 1263, Urban IV, the new pope, made a number of concessions to Charles of Anjou (France) in order to secure his support for an expedition in Sicily against Manfred.[502] The Pope granted a tenth of all Church income from the kingdom of France and the county of Provence to Charles for a period of three years.[503] To win popular support for the campaign, the cross was preached, not only against Manfred but also against the Muslims of Lucera, in France as well as in Lombardy, Tuscany, the March of Ancona, and the lands bordering on the Kingdom of Sicily.[504] Those taking the cross against Manfred and the Muslims were granted the same indulgences, privileges, and immunities as participants in crusades to the Holy Land.[505] Urban wrote that Manfred had entered into 'alliances of malice with the Saracens of Lucera.' With their help, he had set about the takeover of the kingdom. The pope evoked images of war and conquest designed to provoke fear.[506] In order

---

[495] In J.P. Lomax: Frederick II, p. 186.
[496] J.P. Lomax: Frederick II, p. 188.
[497] J. Taylor: *Muslims in Medieval Italy*; Lexington Books; New York; Oxford; 2003; p. 131.
[498] *Annales de Burton, A.D. 1004-1263, Rerum britannicarum medii aevi scriptores*, Rolls Series 36, *Annales monastici*, ed. Henry Richards Luard, vol. 1. (1864; Vaduz: Kraus Reprint Ltd., 1963) pp. 352-3.
[499] Matthew Paris, *Cronica maiora* p. 351.
[500] *Les Registres D'Alexandre IV*, vol. 1, 142, no. 483; Cf. *Les Registres D'Alexandre IV*, vol. 1, 260-1, no. 873.
[501] Muscio and Altobella described a period of "crisis" for Apulian agriculture after the conflicts of the mid- 13th century: Muscio and Altobella, "Natura vergine" p. 68.
[502] Pope Urban IV, *Les Registres d'Urbain IV (1261-1264)*, eds. MM. Leon Dorez and Jean Guiraud, 2nd ser., vol. 2 (Paris: Ancienne Librairie Thorin & Fils, 1901). Pope Urban IV, *Les Registres*, vol. 2, 125-6, no. 272.
[503] J. Taylor: *Muslims in Medieval Italy*; op cit; p. 133.
[504] Pope Urban IV, *Les registres*, vol. 2, 125-6, no. 272.
[505] J. Taylor: *Muslims in Medieval Italy*; op cit; p. 133.
[506] Pope Urban IV, *Les registres*, vol. 2, 390-3, no. 804.

to present Manfred as a danger to society and to win support, Urban frequently described Manfred's army as being made up of "Saracens and infidels."[507] The alliance of the Muslims of Lucera with Manfred was given centre stage in a grave, nearly apocalyptic, portrayal of the threat posed to the Church.[508] On 20 July 1264, Urban launched an attack on several of Manfred's supporters, alleging that they had introduced an army of Muslims and other 'infidels' into the lands of the Church. He accused them of directing forces 'against the Catholic faithful.'[509]

On 20 March 1265, just over a month after being consecrated pope, Clement called for the preaching of a crusade against Manfred and his Muslim supporters.[510] Clement used many of the same policies which had been employed by his predecessors in order to gather support against Manfred. He told the count of Poitou that because of Manfred many inhabitants of the Sicilian kingdom had been massacred, churches had been occupied, and prelates had been captured and sent into exile.[511]

The French Angevins were brought by the Papacy as an ally to deal with the Sicilian issue, and eventually they resolved it amidst great bloodshed.[512] Once the Muslim population came under French rule, the issue arose of how to proceed with their final removal. In order to justify such removal, Muslims were once more depicted as a threat residing in the midst of Christendom. In his crusades sermons, Eudes of Chateauroux charged the Lucerine Muslims with abducting married Christian women, robbing them of their virginity, and forcing them into concubinage.[513] Such charges were designed to play on Christian fears of a violent destruction and profanation of Christian society by Muslims.[514] In order to incite people against the colony, Eudes also wrote about the alarming possibility of an alliance between the Lucerines and foreign Muslim powers.[515] Then, at last, in 1300, the Muslims were totally wiped out on the island,[516] many sold into slavery, the rest simply disappearing into the obscurity of history. Pope Boniface VIII was delighted on hearing the news of the destruction of the last Muslim colony in Sicily.[517]

---

[507] Pope Urban IV, *Les registres*, vol. 2, 413-414, no. 859; Pope Urban IV, *Les registres*, vol. 4, 75, no. 2992; Pope Urban IV, *Les registres*, vol. 4, 74, no. 2990.
[508] Ibid. J. Taylor: *Muslims in Medieval Italy*; op cit; p. 134.
[509] J. Taylor: *Muslims in Medieval Italy*; op cit; p. 134.
[510] Pope Clement IV, *Les Registres de Clement IV (1265-1268)*, ed. M. Edouard Jordan (Paris: Thorin & Fils, Editeurs, 1893-1945) 451, no. 1444; *Thesaurus novus anecdotorum*, eds. Edmond Martene and Ursino Durand (Lutetiae Parisiorum, 1717) vol. 2, cols. 70-73.
[511] J. Taylor: *Muslims in Medieval Italy*; op cit p. 135.
[512] Iohanees de Tayster: Annales, MGHS, vol 28; ed Felix Liebermann; (Stuttgart: Anton Hiersemann;) 1963; p. 591.
[513] Crusade and Rhetoric against the Muslim Colony of Lucera: Eudes of Chateauroux's sermons de Rebellione Sarracenorum; ed. Christoph Maier; *Journal of Medieval History*; 21; 1995; sermon 2, 380.
[514] J. Taylor: *Muslims in Medieval Italy*; op cit; p. 143.
[515] Crusade and rhetoric; sermon 1; 379.
[516] D. Abulafia: *Commerce and Conquest in the Mediterranean, 1100-1500*, Variorum, 1993; p. 4.
[517] N. Housley: The Italian crusades; p. 65. In J.P. Lomax: Frederick II; p. 189.

Five

THE RENAISSANCE, THE OTTOMAN 'THREAT' AND THE MOORS' QUESTION

The later Middle Ages Western crusading ideology came in the wake of the failed crusades of 1095-1291, and has been admirably studied by the likes of Atiya,[518] and most of all by Housley.[519] Following the fall of the last crusader stronghold: Acre, to the Muslims in 1291, late medieval Western ideologues, strategists, Popes, and various learned figures, put in place a new strategy to defeat the Muslim foe as we noted above (Chapter 3). They agreed a vast programme consisting in the destruction of the Muslim foe wherever it dwelt, either in North Africa or Arabia. They also, with interest to us here, agreed on Western Christians advancing through Asia Minor, removing the Turks, abolishing the 'Heretic' Greek Orthodox Church, and then recovering the Holy Land. These policies and strategies can be found expounded in a number of treatises.

One of the earliest such treatises, *Liber recuperationis terrae sanctae,* was written by Fidenzio of Padua straight in the wake of the fall of Acre in 1291.[520] He suggested a crusader advance across Europe to Constantinople, and then through Anatolia and Armenia. The 'peregrini Christiani' who proceed by this way would march through friendly Christian countries, with the exception of Muslim Turkey.[521] Once removing the Turkish obstacle the way was free to conquer the Holy Land.

The Armenian prince, Hayton of Corycus wrote in 1307 *Flor des estoires*, which enjoyed a wide reputation.[522] He, too, suggested the trans-continental route to the Hellespont, beyond which the roads of Asia Minor could be secured by the Tartars for the Christians until their safe arrival in Armenia.[523] His route anticipated the actual progress of the Crusade of Nicopolis (1396).[524]

The Catalan missionary and philosopher Ramon Lull's completed in 1309 the *Liber de Acquisitione Terrae Sanctae,* in which he incorporated the main thesis of his other work the *Liber de Fine* and re-presented it with a slight modification in arrangement.[525] According to him, a detachment of crusaders, after seizing

---

[518] A.S. Atiya: *The Crusade of Nicopolis;* Methuen & co. Ltd; London; 1934. A.S. Atiya: *The Crusade in the Later Middle Ages*; Methuen & Co. Ltd; London; 1938.
[519] N. Housley: *The Later Crusades*; Oxford University Press; 1992. N. Housley: *Documents on the Later Crusades; 1274-1580*; Macmillan Press Ltd; London; 1996.
[520] Fidenzio of Padua: '*Liber Recuperationis Terrae Sanctae,*' Edition G. Golubovich: Bibliotheca Bio-Bibliografica Della Terra Santa; 5 vols; Florence; 1906-27; Vol II; 9 et seq.
[521] Ibid; 51.
[522] La Flor des Estoires de la Terre d'Orient, in *Receuil des Historiens des Croisades Armeniens*; vol ii; Paris; 1906; pp. 111-253.
[523] In A.S. Atiya: *The Crusade of Nicopolis*; op cit; p. 23.
[524] Ibid.
[525] Munich MS. Lat. 10565 ff.. 89 ro-96 vo. See also Longpre, in *Criterion* (Barcelona, 1927), III, 266-78.

Constantinople, may proceed through Asia Minor and recover the Holy Land from the Mamluks.[526] This latter idea stipulated the destruction of the Orthodox Church, first.[527] Countless other authors argued the same strategy, including amongst them Burcard (fl.1332), Pierre Dubois (1250-1321), William of Nogaret (the leading counsellor of the French monarch, Philip the Fair between 1302 and 1313), and Marino Sanudo (1260-1338).

As will be seen in the following, it was precisely that which happened on the ground; Christian armies setting out one after the other to invade Asia Minor with the aims of removing the Turkish presence, destroying the Orthodox Church en passant, and reaching and 'Recovering the Holy Land.' It was a plan that was adopted for centuries in fact until its ultimate success, ie., the capture of the Holy Land (in 1917), but with two notable failures. First, there was the failure to destroy the Orthodox Church, in large measure thanks to the initial protection the Ottomans afforded to it, before Russia rose as a world power and took over the protection of that same Church. Secondly, the Ottomans were not defeated as planned. We focus on the second point to show that, unlike claims that blame the Ottoman threat as a cause of the Christian crusades, it was the other way round. We shall return in chapter 8 to deal with the issue of how Turkish barbarism was used to remove the Turks en mass now that the Ottomans had grown weak.

In 1303 there arrived to fight alongside the Byzantine Empire a Western Christian army led by Roger de Flor, reinforced with a fleet.[528] One of Roger's first encounters in Anatolia was with Othman. Roger defeated the Turks in 1304, before his undisciplined army led raids against both Turks and Greeks impartially.[529] The murder of Roger de Flor ended this venture. This was the first of many subsequent Western assaults against Turkey, of which only a few we cite here. In 1332, there was formed an anti-Turkish force that included all Catholic powers.[530] The object of this league was supposedly to 'clear the Aegean of Turkish Pirates,' but its real purpose was to make the seas safer for the passage of the projected crusade to the East.[531] This resulted in the first military engagement of note between the Christian and Turkish fleets, and eventually the destruction of the Turkish fleet in a series of engagements, the last of them in the Gulf of Adramyttium in September 1344.[532]

In 1343, Pope Clement VI (Pope 1342-1352) called for a crusade against the Turks throughout Western Europe.[533] The crusade was promoted into a holy league to attack the Turks.[534] A large fleet was put in place, its object being Smyrna. The fleet

---

[526] Munich MS.f.90. ro. F. 91 ro. See A.S. Atiya: *The Crusade in the Later Middle Ages*; op cit; p. 85.
[527] R. Lull: *De Acquisitione Terrae Sanctae* (1309); in E. Kamar, 'Projet de Ramon Lull "De Acquisitione Terrae Sanctae", in *Studia Orientalia Christiana: Collectanea* No. 6 (Cairo, 1961), pp. 3-131 (text 103-31), at 108-13, 130; in N. Housley: *Documents on the Later Crusades*; op cit; p. 47.
[528] E. Pears: The Ottoman; op cit; p. 657.
[529] S. J. Joseph Gill: *Byzantium and the Papacy 1198-1400*; Rutgers University Press; New Jersey; 1979; p. 189.
[530] P. Lemerle: *L'Emirat d'Aydin, Byzance et l'Occident*; 1957; p. 54.
[531] S.J. Joseph Gill: *Byzantium and the Papacy*; op cit; p. 196.
[532] Ibid.
[533] N. Jorga: Latins et Greeks d'Orient; *Byzantinische Zeitschrift*; XV; 1906; pp. 179-222; p. 189.
[534] A.S. Atiya: *The Crusade of the Later Middle Ages*; op cit; p. 291.

reached the port, and after setting most of the Turkish ships stationed there on fire, the Christian host landed safely.[535] The Crusaders captured the town itself on the hillside, before proceeding to massacre the Muslims among its inhabitants on 28 October 1344.[536]

In 1366, yet another anti-Turkish crusade took place, the Crusade of Amadeo of Savoy.[537] The Pope published a number of bulls by which he granted Amadeo the financial privileges due to a crusading prince.[538] Amadeo's expedition was regarded by the Church, not merely as an attempt to relieve the Byzantine Empire, but mainly as a *'passagium generale'* aimed at the ultimate recovery of the Holy Land.[539] The crusade resulted in the capture of Gallipoli and the massacre of its Muslim population.[540]

The Ottomans, of course, did not remain idle. Under Othman's son, Orkhan (1281-1362), the Ottomans captured the whole south coast of the Sea of Marmara and the Adriatic shore.[541] In 1371, the Ottomans crushed an alliance of Serbs, Hungarians, Wallachians and Napolese at the battle of Cernomen.[542] In 1375, crossing the Balkans, the Ottomans took Nissa, one of the strongest fortresses of the Byzantine Empire.[543] In 1380 the Ottomans captured Sofia and Nish, the northern Serb capital. Then, in 1389, the first Great Battle of Kosovo took place, where the Serbs were crushed.[544]

Sigismund, King of Hungary and brother of the Emperor of the West, together with Pope Boniface IX (Pope 1389-1404) preached a Crusade in 1394.[545] The resulting Crusade of Nicopolis in 1396 ended in a total disaster for Christian Europe; the elites of many nations were killed, a defeat that spread great dismay amongst their countrymen and the monarchs of Europe.[546]

Even Timur the Lame's attack against the Ottomans was in alliance with Christian nations, and his devastation of the realm was greatly celebrated in Christendom.[547]

---

[535] Ibid; p. 294.
[536] P. Daru: *Histoire de la Republique de Venise;* 9 vols; 4th ed.; Paris; 1853; I; p. 598.
[537] A.S. Atiya: *The Crusade of the Later Middle Ages*; op cit; p. 381.
[538] Bollati di Saint-Pierre: *Illustrazione Della Spedizione in Oriente di Amedeo VI*, documents nos. VI-XII, 344-67; *Viaggio di Levante*, Mazzo JO, no. 8; Bollati di Saint-Pierre, XIII, p. 368.
[539] A.S. Atiya: *The Crusade of the Later Middle Ages*; p. 388.
[540] Ibid.
[541] D. Vaughan: *Europe and the Turk*; (Liverpool University Press; 1954); p. 10.
[542] D. Vaughan: *Europe;* op cit; p. 21.
[543] S. Lane Poole: *Turkey;* (Khayats; Beirut; 1966 ed., originally published in 1908); p. 40.
[544] P. Wittek: The Ottoman Turks, from an Emirite of Marsh warriors to an Empire; in *Royal Asiatic Society of Great Britain and Ireland*; 1965; pp. 33-51; reprinted in *The Islamic World and the West;* edited by A.R. Lewis; op cit; pp. 106-18; at pp. 114-5.
[545] A.S. Atiya: *Crusade, Commerce and Culture;* (Oxford University Press; London; 1962); p. 148.
[546] E. Pears: The Ottoman Turks; op cit; p. 676.
[547] J.H. Wylie: *History of England under Henry IV*; Longman; London; 1884; p. 313 ff in particular. Michel Balard, *La Romanie genoise,* 2 vols with continuous pagination (Genova, 1978). N. Iorga, N., 'Notes et extraits pour servir a l'histoire des croisades au XV" siècle *ROL (Revue de l'Orient Latin)* 4 (1896), pp. 25-118, 226-320, 503-622., Byzantine relations with Timur are discussed in John W. Barker, *Manuel II Palaeologus 1391-1425. A Study in Late Byzantine Statesmanship* (New Brunswick, NJ, 1969), pp. 504-8 (appendix XVIII). Timur to [John VII] the regent of Constantinople, 15 May 1402, in Alexandrescu-Dersca, M.M., *La campagne de Timur en Anatolie (1402)* (Bucarest, 1942, repr. London, 1977); pp. 123-4.

However, instead of being finished by the blow it had received from Timur, the realm rose stronger and more vigorous.[548] The recovery was timely, for soon after, the Christians launched yet another crusade, the Crusade of Varna in 1444. Prior to the crusade, the Christians signed a peace treaty with the Ottomans, the Treaty of Sezged, which induced Sultan Murad II to withdraw from Rumelia into Asia. The Christians profited from this to block his return as their armies advanced to clear the Turks off Europe before crossing into Asia Minor in the belief that the Ottoman realm was now weak.[549] Murad was able to cross back the Straits into Europe, join his son, Mohammed II, and at Varna, on 10 November 1444, he crushed the Christian armies.[550]

In 1439, the Byzantine Emperor agreed to put the Orthodox Church under Catholic sway (through the Act of Union). This was loathed by the Greek population and intensely dreaded by the Ottomans as it would bring the armed forces of Western Christendom onto the Turkish borders.[551] Further developments between Byzantium and the Ottomans made the capture of Constantinople unavoidable.[552] The capture of Constantinople took place in 1453 after it submitted to three successive assaults in two days (May 28-9).

This Ottoman success caused an outpouring of Christian anti Turkish rhetoric. Pope Nicholas V on September 30, 1453 addressed a crusade bull to all Christendom. In it he denounced Mohammed II (the conqueror of Constantinople) as:

> The cruellest persecutor of the Church of Christ, the son of satan, the son of perdition, the son of death who thirsted for the blood of Christians. He pronounced the sultan to be the great red dragon with seven heads crowned by seven diadems and with ten horns described by St John.[553]

Pius II (Pope 1458-1464) represented the Turks as the natural enemies of the Christian faith. 'As a nation,' he wrote, 'the Turks are the foes of the Trinity.'[554] In his first oration before the congress of Mantua he proclaimed his intention of protecting the faith, which the Turks were doing everything in their power to destroy.[555]

Letter of Gerardo Sagredo, 12 Oct. 1402, ibid., p. 131. Clavijo, p. 93 (tr. Le Strange, p. 135). Hippolyte Noiret, ed., *Documents inedits pour servir a l'histoire de la domination Venitienne en Crete de 1380 a 1485* (Paris, 1892), pp. 129-30. Letter of Giovanni Cornaro, 4 Sept. 1402, in Alexandrescu-Dersca, M.M., *La campagne*; pp. 125-6.

[548] Lane Poole: *Turkey*; p. 75.
[549] E. Pears: The Ottoman Turks; op cit; p. 691.
[550] See M. Chasin: The Crusade of Varna; in K. M. Setton ed., *A History of the Crusade*; vol 6; op cit; pp. 276-310.
[551] For further details on these issues, see: S. Runciman: *The Fall of Constantinople; 1453*; Cambridge University Press; 1965. Doukas: *Decline and Fall of Byzantium to the Ottoman Turks;* Wayne State University Press; 1975.
[552] See E. Pears: *The Destruction of the Greek Empire*; Longmans; London; 1903. F. Babinger: *Mehmed the Conqueror*; tr. from German by R. Manheim; ed by W.C. Hickman, Bollingen Series, Princeton University Press, 1978.
[553] L. Pastor: History of the Popes; ed., and tr. F. Antrobus; p. 276; in R. Schwoebel: *The Shadow*; op cit; p. 31.
[554] *The Commentaries of Pius II*; tr., and ed. L.C. Gabel and F.A. Gragg; Smith College Studies in History. (Northampton Mass., 1936-1957). Commentaries; II; 116.
[555] Pius II: Commentaries; III, 141.

Chroniclers repeated the tales of Turkish atrocities with meticulous pains, and did not tire in describing them, and in attributing every conceivable crime to the enemies of the faith.[556] An English chronicler exclaims:

> If I should write, the detestable murder of men, the abominable and cruel slaughter of children, the shameful ravishment of women and virgins, which were perpetrated and done by the unmerciful pagan and cruel Turks, I assure you that your ears would abhor the hearing, and your eyes would not abide the reading, and therefore, I pass them over.[557]

The details of the story, Schwoebel notes, differ from one chronicler to another but in general they cover the same ground emphasising the brutality of the Turks.[558]

Jacques de Clerk described the scene when the Turks found many women inside the Church of Holy Wisdom:

> They (the Turks) enjoyed their carnal proximity; using force in contempt of God our Creator.[559]

European 'Humanists,' in particular, dwelt on Turkish atrocities, the slaughter of all people aged over six, mass rape, and Westerners, at any rate, accepted these rumours and humanists did not miss the opportunity to sell lurid tales of rapes on the high altar of Hagia Sophia in their accounts and letters.[560]

One such humanist, Aeneas Silvius Piccolomini (later to become Pope Pius II) thus held:

> What utter slaughter in the imperial city would I relate, virgins having been prostituted, boys made to submit as women, nuns raped, and all sort of monks and women treated wickedly? ... Those who were present say that the foul leader of the Turks, or to speak more aptly, that most repulsive beast, raped on the high altar of Hagia Sophia, before everyone's eyes, the most noble, royal maiden, and her young brother, and then ordered them killed.[561]

Of course Piccolomini Pius II) was speaking about facts he imagined from the distance, a method adopted before him by many other popes, and to be adopted by other Christian zealots, Gladstone, the future British Prime Minister, amongst others; but what mattered was, as Bisaha remarks, most Westerners, believed even the most sensational reports of violence and savagery that came their way.[562] Schwoebel also notes how imagination encouraged writers to invent specific details... 'The Turkish peril,' he holds, being viewed as the last phase in the centuries-old assault of Islam upon Christendom.[563] And for their evaluation and understanding of the problem, he explains, Europeans of the time drew heavily

---

[556] R. Schwoebel: *The Shadow;* op cit; pp. 12-3.
[557] Ibid; p. 13.
[558] Ibid.
[559] Jacques de Clerq: *Memoires*; ed., J.A. Buchon in Chroniques d'Enguerrand de Monstrelet; vol xiii. (Paris, 1826); p. 147.
[560] See, for instance, Aeneas Silvius Piccolomini's *Letter to Leonardo benvoglienti;* ed. Pertusi; La Caduta; vol 2; pp. 62-4.
[561] In N. Bisaha: *Creating East and West: Renaissance Humanists and the Ottoman Turks*; Philadelphia, Pennsylvania: University of Pennsylvania Press, 2004, p. 63.
[562] N. Bisaha: 'New Barbarian' or worthy adversary? Humanist Constructs of the Ottoman Turks in fifteenth century Italy; in *Western Perceptions* (Blanks-Frassetto ed); op cit; pp. 185-205; at p. 192.
[563] R. Schwoebel: *The Shadow;* op cit; p. 13 preface: ix-x.

upon the medieval corpus dealing with Islam and the Levant. They just clung tenaciously to established categories and adapted a large body of new information to the forms of thought and expression developed in the anti Muslim crusading literature of the Middle Ages.[564] All of the images, Levin notes, depicting

> The Muslim Other as God's Scourge, Antichrist, Pagan, Heretic, Chivalrous, and/or Lustful – were extended to the new foe, some more frequently than others.[565]

Just as they applied the old on the new, Western Christians now identified the old with the new. Setton, notes how from

> The later fourteenth century to the beginning of the twentieth, Europeans tended to identify Islam with the Ottoman Empire, and biblical texts were recast into anti-Turkish prognostications.[566]

Sixteenth century military and naval confrontations with the Ottomans were 'the logical continuation of a struggle long ago undertaken and never since abandoned.'[567]

Histories of the Turks, like that of Michel Baudier (1625), were written 'On the anti-Islamic bias of the monkish literature of the middle-ages.'[568]

Tolan also note how there was little new, rather, the solutions of the thirteenth century were now being recycled: Popes and publicists urging princes to crusade against the "Turk" in much the same language as their thirteenth-century counterparts (albeit at times in humanistic Latin style)...[569]

This is clearly seen in Arredondo's *Castillo inexpugnable defensorio de la fee etc*, written for Charles V (Emperor 1500-1558), whose English title goes as follows:

> Inexpugnable castle, defender of the faith and admirable discourse to conquer all enemies, both spiritual and corporal. And true account of marvellous things, both ancient and modern. And exhortation to pursue the Turk, and to conquer him, and to annihilate the sect of Muhammad, and every heresy, and to win back the Holy Land with Great and Joyous Triumph.[570]

Geary explains that Arredondo (the author) (fl.1528) 'espoused' many of the standard medieval stereotypes of Islam, just as many Renaissance authors, 'taking their cue from a long list of medievals, resorting to caricature and distortion in their

---

[564] Ibid; preface; ix-x.
[565] Paul T. Levin: *'From Saracen Scourge to Terrible Turk: Medieval, Renaissance, and Enlightenment Images of the Other in the Narrative Construction of Europe.'* A Dissertation presented to the Faculty of the Graduate School University of Southern California in partial requirements for the degree of Doctor of Philosophy (International Relations) 2007; p. 200.
[566] K.M. Setton: *Western Hostility to Islam and Prophecies of Turkish Doom*; Philadelphia: American Philosophical Society, 1992, p. 17.
[567] P. Coles: *The Ottoman Impact on Europe*; (Thames and Hudson, London; 1968); p. 126.
[568] Paris, 1626; see k. Setton Western hostility; p. 52.
[569] J.V. Tolan: *Saracens: Islam in the Medieval European Imagination;* NY: Columbia University Press, 2002, pp. xvii-xix; See the excellent work by Paul T. Levin just referred to above, a couple of footnotes back, for the great outlines of old and modern literature dealing with this subject. Levin's work is so good that its publishing in book form ought be carried out if that has not been the case yet.
[570] J.S. Geary: Arredondo's Castillo inexpugnable de la fee: Anti Islamic propaganda in the Age of Charles V. Published on June 23; 1528 by Juan de Junta; in J.V Tolan ed., *Medieval*; op cit; pp. 291-311; pp. 293-4.

accounts of Islamic religious ideas.'[571] The *Castillo* pursued a particular medieval tradition in which perceptions and misrepresentations about the Prophet and Qur'anic revelations are rooted in the theological conception of Christian unity.[572] Arredondo most certainly borrowed from Antoninus when in chapter 53 he offered an explanation why God permitted the infidels to possess the city of Jerusalem:

> God does not want Christians to sin in the Holy City in which the son of God suffered for the sins of mankind. At the same time God takes no offence at the presence of the Muslims in that city because they are dogs, and they were allowed to guard the gates of the city by an angry God who was no longer willing to tolerate the sins that proliferated among His flock.[573]

As Geary notes:

> Whereas Arredondo's efforts to malign Islam and the Turks were based to a significant degree on theological arguments, legendary underpinnings, and the use of opprobrious language, it was primarily by means of portraying the Ottomans as violent and avaricious people that the author's propagandistic goals were achieved. This type of portrayal was commonplace during the period in question, for as Schwoebel has shown, "the inhumanity of the Turks was emphasized above all else, and the stereotyped Turk - savage and bloodthirsty, swooping down upon innocent Christians, and massacring them indiscriminately - was firmly established in the traditions of the West.[574]

To this end several chapters of the *Castillo* recounted the events leading to the Christian defeat at the citadel of Rhodes. Sultan Suleyman appears as a deceitful and false leader, having betrayed an oath sworn to the Grand Master of Rhodes. In reality Suleyman treated the defenders in the best possible way, allowing them to go free, and it was they who subsequently betrayed their oath, when they moved to Malta and re-started their attacks against Turks and other Muslims.[575] Still, according to the chronicler:

> Like a perverse and cruel tyrant, an enemy of truth, on Christmas Day, in order to cause Christians grief, he [Suleyman] tore down the gate to the city, and with his banners and armed men, and with a great uproar, he entered the city and profaned and defiled the Church of St. John, and he destroyed the holy statues and the altarpiece, and he worshiped Muhammad in this same temple, and he had the same done in all the temples and churches, and he didn't uphold a thing that he had promised, like infernal Lucifer.[576]

The text thus sought to establish a trifold relationship, based on deception, between the Prophet Mohammed, his successor, Suleyman, and 'their mutual agent, the Devil.' This notion of the diabolical sect, strategically reinforced

---
[571] J.S. Geary: Arredondo's; p. 292.
[572] Ibid.
[573] Ibid; p. 303.
[574] R. Schwoebel: *The Shadow;* op cit; p. 13.
[575] J.B. Kinross: *The Ottoman Centuries*, op cit; p. 176 ff. See this author's *Barbary Pirates*; MSBN Books; 2015.
[576] Fol 46; in J.S. Geary: Arredondo's Castillo; op cit; p. 304.

throughout the *Castillo,* could hardly have resulted in an ambivalent response. The message was clear enough: 'the Devil and his allies must be annihilated.'[577]

Arredondo used both his knowledge of history and contemporary European affairs with his rhetorical skill in order to present a picture of Islam and the Turks intended to make a marked impression on his readers, many of whom, he must have assumed, would consist of Christian princes and noblemen whom he might persuade to wage the holy war on the foe. Toward the end of the *Castillo* he issued one last plea on behalf of the Church, reminding members of the nobility of their responsibility to support the Emperor:

> Go, go and defend the holy law of your Lord and God Who gave you the estates, dominions, and incomes that you possess. Now we will see who among you is truly a Catholic knight, how much sincerity you have in serving your God, your King and Emperor, how much you love your country, how much charity you have for your faithful brother Christians and how much hate toward the evil unbelievers. Arm yourselves, oh noble knights, with both material and spiritual weapons so that you may destroy the enemy, these dogs, the Turks.[578]

Even as Ottoman power began to wane, in the 17th century, and as there was realistically no Turkish threat of any sort, there continued the same rhetoric. Thus, d'Avity writes:

> There is no nation in the world so arrogant. And this insolence growes in them from the many victories that these barbarians have obtained in all parts, and by reason of the wonderful largenesse and extent of their prince's dominions.' 'They are exceedingly given to whoredom and all kind of uncleanness, yea euen to sodomy itself, which they use publicly... They are treacherous and disloyal as may be, and make no scruple of breaking their promises so as this infidel has been the ruin of many Christians, which trusting to their words, have often yielded themselves into their hands, who afterwards were miserably massacred or led into captivity.[579]

For Abercomby and other contemporaries, the Turks have an ambition to destroy Christianity and they are now 'the powerfullest nation in Europe.'[580]

Knolles, equally, states that the history of the Turks 'Is a record of the ruin of the greater part of the Christian commonwealth.'[581]

For Marsh, it is lawful to make war on the Turks because they are:

> So ignorant and barbarous that they are incapable of government, their constitutions are so unnatural as that of slaves governing freeman: that of

---

[577] J.S. Geary: Arredondo's Castillo; op cit; p. 304.
[578] Fol 61; in J.S. Geary: Arredondo's Castillo; op cit; p. 305.
[579] P. D'Avity: *The Estates, Empires and Principalities of the World;* tr., by E. Grimestone; (London; 1615); p. 948.
[580] D. Abercomby: *The Present State of the German and Turkish Empires;* (London; 1660); p. 15.
[581] R. Knolles: *The General Historie of the Turks....;* (London; 1687-1700,) in A. Cirakman: *From the Terror;* op cit; p. 85.

murder in case of expending: that of commonese of women: that of prohibiting learning etc, that mankind by a league of nature, and the tacit consideration of humanity, should rise against them as the reproaches of humane monsters of mankind, as the very shame of nature.[582]

The Frenchman La Noue insists that an offensive should be undertaken by a united force of all Christendom,

> A war that must be undertaken to rescue the souls infected by Islam, and to set the bodies free from the most horrible bondage that ever was.[583]

Throughout the period, disseminating the image of 'the bloodthirsty Turkish beast' was the work of scholar-publishers-pioneers of the first half–century of printing.

> Combining a sharp eye for business, a passion for scholarship, and some spirited concern for the moral issues of the day [Schwoebel notes] they quickly wielded their presses in defence of the faith. Publishing news and reports of the Ottoman advance, the tales of travellers, histories, and a wide variety of publistic pieces, the printers kept the Turkish peril before the eyes of an ever expanding reading public.[584]

Their printed texts, often accompanied by pictorial illustrations, further stimulated the sense of crisis. The large volume of works made available for the new reading public of the Renaissance presented the Eastern peril in terms and proportions inconceivable in the Middle Ages.

The stereotyped Turk, savage and bloodthirsty, swooping upon innocent Christians, and massacring them indiscriminately, thus, became firmly established in the tradition of the West.[585] In England, for instance, as Baumer notes, the attitude of publicists, the clergy, and statesmen toward the Turk in the 16th and 17th centuries differed very little from literary and popular attitudes.[586] To the French Turquerie meant the rude, the cruel, the bad; to the Spaniards everyone bad was a "turco", whilst for the Germans a rich vocabulary applied to the Turks, words such as "Türkenhund" (Turkish dog), "Türkenknecht" (Turkish farm-hand), "Kümmeltürke" (caraway Turk), and in the Austrian countryside, even today, children are called in from play, "Es ist schon dunkel. Türken kommen. Türken kommen" (It's already dark. The Turks are coming! The Turks are coming!)[587] To some Christian theologians, the word Turk came from "torquere", torture, whilst a popular theory identified the Turks with the Scythians, who were considered a particularly cruel race.[588] Even more frightening was the legend of the dog-Turk, a man-eating

---

[582] H. Marsh: *A New Survey of the Turkish Empire*; (London; 1664); pp. 65-6.
[583] F. La Noue: *The Politicke and Militarie discourse of the Lord de la Noue*; tr. E. A. London; p. 247.
[584] R. Schwoebel: *The Shadow;* op cit; p. 166.
[585] Note 47: Cf. M. Gilmore: *The World of Humanism; 1453-1517*; (New York, 1952); pp. 20-1; who believes that such a view of the Turk was the product of the literature of the 16th century.
[586] F.L. Baumer: England, the Turk and the Common Corps of Christendom; in J.S. Geary: Arredondo's Castillo inexpugnable de la fee: Anti Islamic propaganda in the Age of Charles V. Published on June 23; 1528 by Juan de Junta; in J.V Tolan ed., *Medieval*; op cit; pp. 291-311; at p. 292.
[587] I. Karlsson: The Turk as a Threat and Europe's Other; in *International Issues and Slovak Foreign Policy*; issue 1, 2006; pp. 62-72; at p. 63.
[588] Ibid.

creature, half animal and half human, with a dog's head and tail.[589] This identification of the Turk with the beast of the apocalypse lasted for centuries.[590] Whilst the Turk was strong, it only resulted in wars which Turk could deal with, but when the power of the Ottomans went on the wane, then it resulted in the mass removal of millions of Turks and would have ended in the removal of Turkey itself had it not been for the great Turkish fight of 1919-1922. We shall return to this in Chapter 8.

The Fate of the 'Moors' of Spain

According to Scott:
> The sumptuous (Muslim) edifices which abounded in every city have disappeared or have been mutilated almost beyond recognition. Barbaric violence has annihilated the palaces which lined the Guadalquevir, and whose richness and beauty were the admiration of the world. Ecclesiastical malignity has demolished to their very foundations or sedulously effaced the characteristics of the innumerable temples raised for the propagation of a hostile religion, and the extent of this systematic enmity may be inferred from the suggestive fact that of the seven hundred mosques required for the worship of the Moslem capital, but one has survived. Diligent antiquarian research has failed to establish even the sites of all but three or four of the remainder, of whose existence and splendour both history and tradition afford abundant and indisputable evidence. The ignorance and prejudice of successive generations have, in addition to the above named destructive agencies, contributed their share, and no unimportant one, to the obliteration of these memorials of Arab taste and ingenuity.[591]

Philip II (1527-1598) went as far as ordering that every stone in Toledo which bore Arabic inscription to be destroyed.[592]

Academia, both Muslim and non Muslim, due ineptness and corruption, continues the work of vandalism. Muslim influence on the culture of Spain is inadequately presented in major universities today.[593] It has been set aside in ways other contributions have not been.[594] This exclusion, of course, as we noted above, hampers the understanding of Spanish history.[595] However, and again, we contrast

---
[589] Ibid. 64.
[590] By far, the best outline of Western depictions of the Turks is by A. Cirakman: *From the Terror of the World to the 'Sick Man of Europe;'* (Peter Lang Publishing; New York; 2002).
[591] S.P. Scott: *History of the Moorish Empire*; in 3 vols; The John Lippincott Company; Philadelphia; 1904; vol 2; pp. 557-8.
[592] Ibid; p. 576.
[593] J.T. Monroe: The Hispanic-Arabic World: in *Americo Castro and the Meaning of Spanish Civilisation;* J. Rubia Barcia ed; University of California Press, Berkeley, 1976, op cit; pp. 69-90; p. 87.
[594] Maria Rosa Menocal: *The Arabic Role*; op cit; p. 92.
[595] Ibid.

old and new scholarship. An old source, Lea's *History of the Inquisition*, reveals many of the horrors that had been inflicted on Muslims.[596] Scott, likewise, recaptures the tragic fate of Muslims.[597] Contemporary Spanish sources, including soldiers' accounts, also speak of the woes of Muslims. Perez de Hita, for instance, who fought the civil wars of Grenada (1568-71),[598] recounts how Muslim women, terrified at the advance of the Spanish forces:

> Unable to withstand the attack, they went out on a cliff overlooking the sea, and embracing each other, and shouting their pain and sorrow, plummeted to their deaths. Others sought to put the idea of Christian mercy to the test and constructed crude crosses knot out of pieces of wood. Kneeling before the soldiers they would cry: 'I Christian sir, I Christian'. But no one in that squadron offered any Christian charity, and the Moorish women were forced to jump from the cliffs.[599]

Perez de Hita conceals neither the cruelties of the soldiers, nor his admiration for Muslim strong adherence to their faith and heritage.[600]

Modern and today's works, with rare exceptions, such as the excellent British historian of Spain, L.P. Harvey,[601] offer a completely different picture. Conrad, for instance, refers to the taking of Barbastro by the Christians in 1064, but omits to speak of the massacre that ensued, and the mass rape of Muslim women.[602] He does not fail, however, to mention, that when the Muslims retook the town the following year they slew the Christian garrison.[603] Other recent sources, Cardaillac, Dedieu, Fletcher, and most modern authors,[604] also follow on the same lines in creating an altogether different picture from that of old.[605] We have already seen a few instances of this in chapter 3, how today's historians clean Church history, and attribute the crimes to the Islamic side, instead. Let's now show how the descendants of Muslims, the so-called Moors, were gradually removed on account of their heresies, threat, and so on.

'Heresy' was punished by burning. It is more than certain that tens of thousands of Muslims were burnt alive at the stake.[606] Zurita says, that by 1520, the Inquisition of Seville had sentenced more than 4000 persons to be burnt, and 30,000 to other punishments. Another author estimates the total condemned by this single tribunal,

---

[596] H.C. Lea: *A History of the Inquisition of Spain*, 4 vols; The Mac Millan Company, New York, 1907.
[597] S.P. Scott: *History;* op cit.
[598] Perez de Hita: Guerras civiles; Blanchard-Demouge ed; 2 vols; in Rhona Zaid: The Guerras civiles de Granada: the idealisation of assimilation; (vol ii, 79) in J.V. Tolan ed. *Medieval Christian Perceptions of Islam*; Routledge; London; 1996; pp. 313-30.
[599] Ibid; pp. 326-7.
[600] Ibid.
[601] L.P. Harvey: *Islamic Spain, 1250-1500*, University of Chicago Press, 1990.
L.P. Harvey: *Muslims in Spain, 1500-1614*, University of Chicago Press, 2005.
[602] P. Conrad: *Histoire de la Reconquista*; Que Sais je? Presses Universitaire de France; Paris; 1998; p. 49.
[603] Ibid.
[604] In June 2004 the Church came out with a new, cleansed history of Spain.
[605] *Les Morisques et l'Inquisition*: edited by L. Cardaillac; Publisud; Paris; 1990. R. Fletcher: *Moorish Spain*.
[606] H.C. Lea: *A History of the Inquisition;* op cit; See volume three.

within the same period, to 100,000.[607] In 1531, the Valencia tribunal had fifty eight trials for heresy, with some 45 burnings in person, most of whom were Muslims.[608] In this city alone, an average of at least one Muslim was burnt alive every week, and this happened for twelve years, 1528-1540.[609] Over the period 1549-1622, the Inquisition of Saragossa had burnt 1,817 men; and 758 women.[610] The burnings went on for centuries; Hernando de Palma, a Muslim, accused of teaching and conducting Islamic ceremonies, denied and overcame severe torture, then confessed. He was burnt in Toledo in 1606.[611] The Dominican Inquisitor, Bleda, writing in 1604, also commented that:

> When they are about to be burnt alive, the Muslims always read their Islamic lines (shahada), and threw a curse on the 'Holy Church,' [and he concluded that] they should have their mouths gagged so as to stop them from insulting our true faith.[612]

In today's works, both these acts and their sources are suppressed from knowledge, the claim being that the crimes of the Inquisition were exaggerated, and that Muslims suffered hardly any persecution.[613]

As in previous epochs, and as elsewhere, the Church, again, played a central role in the mass removal of Muslims. It justified this on many grounds. The Archbishop of Grenada, Guerrero, returning from Trente, in 1563, passed through Rome (The Vatican) and paid a visit to Pope Pie (Pius) IV (1559-1565). The Pope listened with 'commiseration,' and praised the zeal of this 'salvager of souls' who informed him that the flock (the Moors) were only new Christians by name. The Pope gave him a letter for Philippe II, the Spanish king (1556-1598), remonstrating the latter that

> The scandal had lasted long... It was necessary to rid the country of this evil sect.[614]

The Inquisitors themselves described

> The Moriscos as Moors who would always be Moors and, if the Inquisition did not convert them, it at least compelled them to sin with less publicity and thus diminished their evil example.[615]

In the work of the Portuguese Dominican, Damian Fonseca, the presence of the Moors

> Was intolerable because they were a cancer, and so as not to infect the whole body, that rotten limb had to be amputated.[616]

---

[607] Anales, tom. iv. fol. 324; note 54; in W.H. Prescott: *The Reign of Ferdinand and Isabella*; 2 vols; A.L Burt; New York; 1837; vol 1; p. 205.
[608] Arch. Hist. Nacional, Inquisition de Valencia, Legajos 98, 300; H.C. Lea: *A History of the Inquisition in Spain*; op cit; p. 358
[609] A. Thomson; M.A. Rahim: *Islam in Andalus*; Taha; London; 1996; p. 187.
[610] Les Morisques et leur temps; *Table Ronde Internationale*: 4-7 July 1981; Montpellier; CNRS; Paris; 1983; p. 527
[611] H.C. Lea: *A History of the Inquisition in Spain*; op cit; pp. 199-200.
[612] In R. De Zayas: *Les Morisques et le Racisme d'Etat*; ed Les Voies du Sud; Paris; 1992; pp. 471-2.
[613] Recent Studies by the Catholic Church have completely absolved the Inquisition of its crimes towards Muslims.
[614] Rodrigo de Zayas: *Les Morisques;* op cit; p. 229.
[615] Archivo hist.nacional, Inq.de Valencia, Leg.5, fol.185. 186 etc.
[616] Damian Fonseca: *Lusta expulsion de los moriscos de Espana*; Madrid 1612.

The 'Moors' were also accused of treason, murder, kidnapping, blasphemy, sacrilege, and for Don Juan Ribera (1532-1611), Archbishop of Valencia, even the destruction of the Armada (in 1588) was 'a divine judgment for the indulgence exhibited towards the enemies of the faith, and that the recent occurrences of earthquakes, tempests and comets was also attributed to the same cause.'[617] The Dominican Inquisitor Bleda (1550-1622), likewise, held:

> The sins of these people are such that there are eyes to see them and hands to touch them, that even the plague which has devastated the kingdom in these latter years also come from their presence, and also resulting from their presence are all the woes and miseries which we suffer from, as well as the maritime disasters affecting us. Oh Lord, give us a land that is purified and freed from heretics, and heavens will be given to you in exchange. If you expelled these heretics from our land, you will obtain the help of God to exterminate your enemies.[618]

Throughout much of the period preceding the final elimination in 1609-1610, a number of policies were put in place to gradually remove Islam and eventually end the Muslim presence. Emphasis was put on the demolition of baths and wash rooms, on account, as Scott puts it:

> Of the scandal the sight of apartments devoted to ablution and luxury caused every good Christian, as well as for the reason that their use was always considered entirely superfluous in a monastic institution.[619]

Further measures such as the pragmatic published on 2 January 1567, included:
-The scrapping of the Arabic language.
-The removal of Islamic way of dress
-The doors of Muslim homes to remain open on Fridays and other feast days (to see whether they were doing any prayers);
-And the baths and washing facilities, public and private, (symbols of Islam (and of sin) were to be razed to the ground.[620]

The Dominican Inquisitor Bleda, in 1604, outlines how the 'Moors' are false Christians, and suggests ways to Christianise them:

> On Muslim fasting: They work all day, and those amongst them who buy fruit in markets would not taste a single one during the day.
> Often, the Muslims are made to eat meats, which they are told are not of pork, or meats they are told have not been cooked in animal fat. Days later, they are told, they have been cheated, and what they had eaten days before contained pig substance. Then you see them making themselves vomit, even four days after they had eaten the thing, whilst the children burst into tears once told this.

---
[617] S.P. Scott: *History*; op cit; vol 3; p. 311.
[618] In R. De Zayas: *Les Morisques*; op cit; pp. 468-9.
[619] S.P. Scott: *History*; op cit; vol 2; p. 261.
[620] Rodrigo de Zayas: *Les Morisques*; op cit; p. 230

> When figs have been smeared with pork substance, or even fig trees, Muslims would not touch the fruit again, and even pick axes and cut the fruit trees.
> None of their men will become a monk, and none of their women will ever turn nun.
> They grow wine trees but only to eat grapes, or sultanas, and never drink wine.
> They never accuse a member of their community in a Christian court of any deed.
> Thus:
> Muslims ought to be forced to rear pigs, and to eat their meat, and also to eat food that is made of pork fat.
> It is highly crucial that they should be banned from using Arabic.[621]

The Venetian envoy, in 1595, described the Moriscos 'as constantly increasing in numbers and wealth; they never go to war but devote themselves exclusively to trade and gain.'[622] In the Castilian cortes of 1592, which represented to Philip that previous ones had asked him to remedy the evils of the Granadan Moriscos scattered through the land. These evils, they say,

> Are daily increasing, for the longer the cure is delayed the greater are their numbers; they have obtained possession of trade, especially in provisions, which is the crucible in which money is melted, for they gather and hide it at the harvest time so that the crops must pass through their hands. For this purpose, they become shopkeepers, caterers, bakers, butchers, innkeepers, water-carriers etc., whereby they get and hoard all the money. They never buy land and thus become rich and powerful so that they control the secular and ecclesiastical courts which so favour them that they live openly in disregard of religion. They daily emigrate to Barbary; they marry among themselves and never ask for dispensations but celebrate their weddings with zambras and they bear arms publicly. The most atrocious crimes committed within these ten years are their work. It is evident that they can cause the State some disquiet — for all of which a remedy is sought at the king's hands. The remedy was an edict ordering all the magistrates of the kingdom to enforce with rigor the severe restrictive legislation directed against them.[623]

There was, thus, no escaping the fateful decision: the final removal of the Muslims in the years 1609-1610, an episode needless to dwell upon too long here except for one or two instances.[624] On December 9, 1609, the edict was sent to San German

---

[621] Summed up from R. De Zayas: *Les Morisques*; op cit; 465-501.
[622] *Relazioni Venete*, Serie I. Tom. V. p. 451.
[623] Janer, p. 270. — Bleda: *Cronica*, p. 905. — Nueva Recop. Lib. viii. Tit. ii. ley 24; Lea: *Moriscos*; p. 210-211.
[624] For details, see, for instance:
-Jan Read: *The Moors in Spain and Portugal*, Faber and Faber, London, 1974.
-H.C Lea: *A History of the Inquisition in Spain*, The MacMillan Company, New York, 1907.

from Seville; the galleys and troops were brought from Valencia as soon as they could be spared, and on January 12, 1610, the edict was published. It required the 'Moriscos' to depart, under the pain of death and confiscation, without trial or sentence; it gave them thirty days in which to make preparations... to take with them no money, bullion, jewels or bills of exchange.... just what they could carry...'[625] At Val del Aguar, the Muslim survivors of a massacre, starved, frozen and dying were conducted to the port of embarkation to North Africa; many perished; women and children were stolen by soldiers and sold as slaves; and amongst those embarked, few reached Africa.[626] According to Le Bon, the expulsion was carried in such a way that most 'Moors' should be massacred during emigration. Religious figures delighted that three quarters were killed on route.[627] In one expedition alone, which was taking 140,000 to North Africa, 100,000 were massacred.[628] On the boats, or on their way through France, the same stories of wretchedness; masters of the private vessels which they chartered had no scruples in robbing or murdering them. Many who sailed were never accounted for as arriving, and those who passed via France were pillaged.[629]

All in all Spain was emptied of its Muslim population. The figures of the 'expelled' vary according to Western historians; from a low of 120,000 (Vincente and Fuentes) to a maximum of 3 millions (Navarrete).[630] Modern Catholic historians such as Lapeyre reduce the figure to just a handful of thousands,[631] who generally were massacred by their Arab brethren in Oran,[632] although the city was under Spanish rule at the time.[633] Older historians such as Sedillot, quoted by Le Bon, speak of three million Muslims altogether eliminated, but beginning from an earlier time (1492).[634]

This act, according to Le Bon, was worse than any act of barbarism committed by the worst barbaric invaders.[635] Following the 'expulsion,' however, a letter from the king to Arch-Bishop Ribera, confided 'in the divine favour, that he had resolved on the expulsion of this evil race.'[636]

An inscription was laid on all highest marble and copper plates to commemorate the expulsion of the Moors. It read:

> The supreme Pope Paul V ruled the Church when Philippe the Third, King of Spain, true Catholic, expelled from Spain all Muslims, who had pretended to

---

-H.C. Lea: *The Moriscos of Spain*; op cit;.
[625] H.C. Lea: *The Moriscos*; op cit; p. 345.
[626] H. C. Lea: *A History*; op cit; Vol III; p. 398.
[627] G. Le Bon: *La Civilisation*; op cit; p. 206.
[628] Ibid.
[629] H.C. Lea: *The Moriscos of Spain*; op cit; pp. 360-1.
[630] In H.C. Lea: *The Moriscos of Spain*; op cit; p. 359.
[631] H. Lapeyre: *Geographie de l'Espagne Morisque*; SEVPEN, 1959.
[632] Ibid; p.155.
[633] Rodrigo de Zayas: *Les Morisques*; op cit; p. 273.
[634] G. Le Bon: *La Civilisation*; op cit; p. 206.
[635] Le Bon, it must be reminded, is no great lover of Islam, the Turks, Berbers (and Jews for that matter,) although his admiration for Islamic civilization is immense.
[636] H.C. Lea: *The Moriscos*; op cit; p. 316.

have received the faith for many years, and had committed the crime of apostasy. They were guilty of the highest crime of treason against the republic. They were transferred to the provinces of Africa, France and Italy, because they were given the possibility to choose which they preferred, with the great support of the Christian people. The Duke of Lerma, Marquese of Denia, don Francisco de Sondoval y Rojas, persuaded the king and carried out that said expulsion. Thanks to his advice, and by the authority of the king who invested it in him, in few months, and with great courage and great diligence we were able to undertake this grandiose action. It was accomplished, and we reached the aim we planned, and were consequently admired by all.

Many kings of Spain had gloriously freed provinces from Muslim oppression by conquering them little by little during so many years. But the invincible Philippe the Third protected all Spain, and freed it all from this obvious danger, which threatened it. It is necessary to consider with reason, and applaud the father of the nation, victor of the enemy, and salvation of his kingdoms of which he rid its enemies once for all, and put them in disarray. Even if the victories of his predecessors were heroic, he supersedes them all thanks to the Lord of the armies who grants victories.

This memorable expulsion took place between the months of October 1609 and September 1610.[637]

Historical narrative comes to cleanse this inglorious page from the history books of the Catholic Church. The numbers of the descendants of Muslims removed from Spain in the years 1609-1610 is now standing at less than ten thousand; each Western scholar cut the numbers of their predecessors, until from a around 3 millions such numbers have fallen to this low. French Catholic historians have done the work. Cardaillac, Dedieu, Martinez, and others, following Lapeyre, have taken the lead in cutting down Muslim populations even in their large concentrations such as Valencia.[638] Justifying such low estimates, Lapeyre blames Muslim demographic crises and emigration.[639] So-called leading historians of the subject, such as Francois Martinez,[640] and the emeritus professor Trevor J. Dadson,[641] challenge old sources that speak of high figures, and instead argue much lower figures. Most historians today, in fact, find attenuating circumstances for the elimination of Muslims/their descendants from Iberia. Lapeyre, the chief Catholic historian, justifies the mass cleansing of Muslims on account of the

---

[637] R. de Zayas: *Les Morisques;* op cit; p. 261.
[638] H. Lapeyre: *Geographie de l'Espagne Morisque*; SEVPEN, 1959; pp. 29-30 in L. Cardaillac; J.P. Dedieu: Introduction a l'Histoire des Morisques; in *Les Morisques et l'Inquisition*: op cit; pp. 11-28; at p. 15.
[639] Ibid; p. 13.
[640] F. Martinez: *La Permanence morisque en Espagne après 1609 (discours et realites)*, Lille, Atelier de reproduction des theses, 1997.
[641] See his remarkable carrier, accomplishments, etc… https://www.qmul.ac.uk/sllf/modern-languages-and-cultures/people/emeritus-academic-staff/profiles/dadson.html

tenacity of their faith, Islam.[642] Perez, for his part, blames Muslims for their refusal to assimilate, hence necessitating their removal.[643] Cardaillac and Dedieu, just like all historians, today, with perhaps one or two exceptions, blame it all on the threat Muslims represented to Christianity, hence making their removal necessary.[644] Conrad, just as Menendez Pidal, see it as thus:

> This exotic race never integrated into Spain, neither to its faith nor to its collective ideals, nor to its character, the Moors never assimilated and lived like a cancerous growth in the Spanish flesh.[645]

---

[642] Lapeyre; p. 119-120.
[643] J. Perez: Chretiens; Juifs et Musulmans en Espagne; Le mythe de la tolerance religieuse (VIII-XV e siecle); in *Histoire*, No 137; October 1990.
[644] L. Cardaillac; J.P. Dedieu: Introduction; op cit; p. 24
[645] R.M. Pidal: *Historia de Esapana dirigida por Ramon Menendez Pidal*; Vol 2; Madrid; 2nd edition; 1966; p. 41.

Six

THE CONQUEST OF 'BARBARIANS' AND THEIR MASS CLEARING

This issue is quite important for us to look into, for it shows how the technique of painting someone inferior or a threat can be used to unleash terrible retribution on that someone. The story of the Jews shows how their depictions have eventually led to their mass killings. The story of the Natives we deal with here has the other distinction of showing us that had the Muslims been subdued such as such Natives they could have suffered the same fate. It was simply thanks to Islam, which united Muslims in their fight back, that Muslims survived. The American Natives lacked such unifying bond and were destroyed in turn, and generally, armed by Europeans, they were made to tear each other. Islam also helped Muslims avoid that which killed Natives en masse, notably alcohol. Just on the latter point before we address the Natives story, Wagner, a German scholar who was marching with the French army in Algeria, in the 1830s, wrote:

> The sober and frugal habits of that people, also an unchanged feature of their ancestors, is a great hindrance in the way of civilization; it makes their improvement as difficult as their expulsion or destruction. The North American red men were defeated and driven from the country of their fathers by the "fire-water;" wherever those savages tasted spirits, they were-enslaved by them, and lost both energy and freedom. But such means are of no avail with the Arabs.... Spirits never become necessities with them, and all the remembrance of the merriment caused by wine is not able to wrest out a boojoo from their pocket. I never saw a drunken Arab during all my stay in Africa. Only milk and water are tasted in the encampments, and yet this people is not inferior to any other, either in bodily strength or mental energy.[646]

There is in the West a long tradition of associating with barbarism (cruel, violent, murderous, inferior, enemies of reason and sciences, primitive, animal-like) the people intended for subjugation. Aristotle (384-322 BC), for instance, assumed that humanity was naturally divided into masters and servants, civilised people and barbarians.[647] Centuries on, Petrarch (1304-1374) deemed the natives of Africa a Little better than beasts, and they seemed to him closer to the wild man tradition than to the classical celebration of primitivism: solitary, sub-rational, instinctive yet still human creatures.[648] The pirates reported by Hemmerlin likened them to dogs and monkeys and accused them of barking and howling

---
[646] M. Wagner: *The Tricolor on the Atlas*, London; T. Nelson and Sons, 1854; pp. 144-5.
[647] Aristotle: *The Politics*; (Harmondsworth; 1981); book I; in U. Bitterli: *Cultures*; op cit; p. 120.
[648] Petrarch: *De Vita Solitaria*; vi; 3rd ed; A, Altamura; (Naples; 1943); pp. 125-6.

speech, disgusting table manners, and eating uncooked food. And those broad, flat faces observed by the pirates, suggest cromagnoid origins, lust and degeneracy.[649] A work written for the edification of the future Queen Isabella of Spain 'The Catholic,' in 1468, held:

> It is said that the barbarous people are those who live without law; the Latin, those who have law: for it is the law of nations that men who live and are ruled by law shall be lords of those who have no law, because they are by nature the slaves of the wise who are ruled by law.[650]

When early in the 15th century, Europeans came into greater contact with Black Africans, Catholic intellectuals, such as Zurara, saw them

> Like beasts, with no law of reasonable creatures ... nor knowledge of good, only of surviving in animal sloth. In the previous generation [according to him] they seemed drawn from bestiality.[651]

He found the first slaves directly shipped from Africa

> So deformed in their faces and bodies as almost to resemble shadows from the nether world.[652]

Which in his view justified their servitude and, by implication, their incapacity for legitimate self government.[653] The Blacks, Armesto sums up, were readily classified by contemporaries in a category not far removed from that of the apes, as men

> Made degenerate by sin, cursed with blackness, as well as being condemned to slavery.[654]

The theologian Juan Gines de Sepulveda (1489-1573) deemed it lawful to subdue the natives of America by armed force due to their barbaric vices.[655]

This condemned the Natives encountered by Christians. In the centuries under consideration here, the Indian population of North and Central America was cut by 80-90% of its total numbers.[656] How this happened is summed up here.

First, Western Christian expansion overseas was given legitimacy by the papacy. Pope Alexander VI (1492-1503):

> Conceded and granted those (American) islands with all their dominions, cities, castles, places, villages, rights, jurisdictions and all that pertained to them, to you and your heirs and successors, the monarchs of Castile and Leon, in perpetuity.[657]

---

[649] F. Fernandez Armesto: *Before Columbus;* op cit; Chap 9; pp. 240-1.
[650] M. De Cordoba: *Jardin de nobles doncellas*; ed. H. Goldberg (Chapel Hill; 1974); pp. 138-9.
[651] G. E. de Zurara: *Cronica de Guine;* op cit; chs 79-82; I; pp. 295-310.
[652] Ibid; pp. 107-12.
[653] Ibid; vol I; pp. 141-7.
[654] Ibid; p. 227.
[655] Textual quotations from Juan Gines de Sepulveda and Fray Bartoleme de Las Casas: *Apologia*; ed., by A. Losada, Madrid, Editoria Nacional; (1975); pp. 61; 142.
[656] U. Bitterli: *Cultures in Conflict*; Polity Press; tr., from German; Cambridge; 1989; p. 33.
[657] Palacios Rubios, *De las islas del mar oceano*, ed. Silvio Zavala, Mexico City, 1954; p. 128.

> The Pope [says Robertson] as the vicar and representative of Jesus Christ, was supposed to have a right of dominion over all the kingdoms of the earth...... He granted in full right to Ferdinand and Isabella of Spain (and to the Portuguese) all the countries inhabited by Infidels which they had discovered, or should discover; and in virtue of that power which he derived from Jesus Christ... and as it was necessary to prevent this grant from interfering with that formerly made to the crown of Portugal, he appointed that line, supposed to be drawn from pole to pole, a hundred leagues to the westward of the Azores should serve as a limit between them.[658]

First to arrive on the American scene was Columbus (1492) whose initial impression of the Island of Hispaniola are told in his diary:
> I, in order that they might feel great amity towards us, because I knew that they were a people to be delivered and converted to our holy faith rather by love than by force, gave to some among them some red caps and some glass beads, which they hung round their necks, and many other things of little value. At this they were greatly pleased and became so entirely our friends that it was a wonder to see. Afterwards they came swimming to the ships' boats, where we were, and brought us parrots and cotton thread in balls and spears and many other things.[659]

More importantly, even, he said:
> It only needs people to come and settle here, and to give orders to the inhabitants who will do whatever is asked of them. I myself, with the few men at my disposal, can travel all through these islands without risk. I have already seen three of my men land alone, and by their mere presence cause the flight of a whole crowd of Indians, although they had no intention of harming them. The Indians have no weapons and are quite naked. They know nothing about the art of war and are so cowardly that a thousand men would not stay to face three of our men. One can see that they are well able to do whatever is asked, and they only need to be given orders to be made to work, to sow or to do anything useful.[660]

Then there arises the issue of: how could Western Christendom put to death tens of millions of friendly, semi naked, innocuous, people? Justification arose as in the *Requerimiento* (Requirement), which proclaimed that:
> The pope had bestowed overseas territories upon the Kings of Spain, commended the Indians to submit to Spain and accept Christianity, and

---

[658] In W. Howitt: *Colonisation and Christianity*; Longman; London; 1838. p. 20.
[659] *The Journal of Christopher Columbus;* tr., C. Jane; revised by A.A. Vigneras; London; 1960; p. 23.
[660] C. Columbus: Journal, in Cioranescu. Oeuvres [91]; p. 113 in P. Chaunu: *European Expansion*; op cit; p. 164.

warned that if they refused they would be subjugated by warlike means and set to forced labour.[661]

This still did not explain their treatment. The following, does, however, as expressed by many Christian figures of the time. The theologian Juan Gines de Sepulveda maintained that it was lawful to subdue the natives of America by armed force because they were:

> All barbarous in their customs and most of them by nature have no letters of good sense, and they are infected with many barbarous vices.[662]

The worst vice imputed to the native Indians was cannibalism. In his journal, Columbus wrote that the Indian Caribs eat human flesh,[663] yet Columbus provides no evidence to support his statement.[664] Still, the argument of Indian cannibalism was applied everywhere the Europeans decided to install themselves, using the same rhetoric about the native cannibalism and vices to justify their deeds.[665] Indian 'cannibalistic practices,' amply justified their genocide.[666] The myth of the cannibal Indians, Traboulay remarks, thrived in the Christian West throughout the extermination period, that is until the eighteenth century when there never was any evidence of such cannibalism.[667]

Once the excuse was found, it was the eradication policy which could have posed some problems. However, native Indians showed both incapacity and reluctance to fight back. As Howitt remarks, unlike the Muslims who offered determined opposition to Western domination, and which certainly has accounted for their survival,[668] newly discovered peoples in the Americas, just as elsewhere, because of their ineffectual weaponry or their good natured compliance, were used as an almost inexhaustible supply of forced labour or sexual gratification.[669] Columbus, it was, who introduced Indian slavery, suggesting that it would be lucrative enough to compensate for the small supply of gold found.[670] Under Columbus' governorship, the Lucayan Indians of the Bahamas were lured to Espanola by the Spaniards who promised them that they would meet their departed loved ones on that island.[671] On Espanola the Indians found 'neither father, mother nor loved ones but iron tools and instruments and gold mines instead, where they perished

---

[661] U. Bitterli: *Cultures in Conflict*; Polity Press; tr., from German; Cambridge; 1989; p. 120.
[662] Textual quotations from Juan Gines de Sepulveda and Fray Bartoleme de Las Casas: *Apologia*; ed., by A. Losada, Madrid, Editoria Nacional; 1975; pp. 61; and 142.
[663] See the letter of Dr. Chanca of 1493; in *Select Documents illustrating the four voyages of Columbus*; ed., and trans by Cecil Jane; 2 vols; London; 1930-2; pp. 18-103; see also Jalil Sued Badilla: Los Caribes: realidad of Fabula; Rio Piedras; P. R. 1978.
[664] D. M. Traboulay: *Columbus and Las Casas*; University Press of America, New York, 1994. p. 32.
[665] See: P. Boucher: *Cannibal Encounters. Europeans and Island Caribs; 1492-1763*; Baltimore; The John Hopkins University; 1992.
[666] R. Garaudy: *Comment l'Homme devient Humain*; Editions J.A, 1978; p. 256.
[667] D.M. Traboulay: *Columbus and Las Casas*; op cit; p. 32.
[668] W. Howitt: *Colonisation;* op cit; pp. 174-5, notes how the capacity for Muslim led India as elsewhere to resist Western onslaught saved them from being extinct as the Indians in America were.
[669] R. Robertson: Introduction, in U. Bitterli: *Cultures in Conflict*; op cit; p. 5.
[670] D.M. Traboulay: *Columbus and Las Casas*; p. 26.
[671] Ibid; p. 34.

in no time.' Subsequently, to find 'a single Lucayo alive was almost a miracle.'[672] Their population fell from 1 million in 1492 to only a few thousands in 1510.[673] Much greater fall according to other sources, the Indian population in Espanola in 1496 estimated around 3.77 millions; by 1508 it was just a mere 92,000; and by 1570, there were only 125 survivors.[674]

The same happened on the rest of the continent, where the Indians were worked to death. The stench of the dead corpses in the mines, according to one contemporary, was so great that it brought pestilence, especially in the mines of Huaxican, in whose vicinity 'there was difficulty in walking except on corpses and bones.'[675] Indians were chained together at the neck and marched in columns to toil in gold and silver mines, any who did not walk quickly enough were decapitated.[676] Las Casas' *Short Account of the Destruction of the Indians* appeared in 1552, after its author had finally returned to Spain.[677] Indian inability to fight, compounded by the ravages inflicted by Western sexual diseases and epidemics introduced amongst them, led to the death of up to 90% of their populations.[678] Central Mexico, once with a population of 25 million people, seventy-five years later had just over 1 million.[679] A catastrophic fall also noted by Traboulay for the same country, from the estimated initial population of 25 million to only one million in 1600.[680] 95 out of every 100 people had perished, just as in the whole of Central America, as in western and central Honduras, where 95% of the native people were exterminated in half a century, and in western Nicaragua, where the rate of extermination was 99% in just sixty years.[681] Wachtel speaks of about 8 million people in Peru at the conquest in 1530;[682] this fell to 1.3 million in 1590.[683] Traboulay, on the other hand, puts the initial population of Peru at 32 million in 1520, falling to 5 million by 1548.[684] Mickle, for his part, reminds how the once great and flourishing empires of Mexico and Peru were in the end steeped in the blood of forty millions of their people.[685] It is likely that 70 million people from the Indies to the Amazon perished as a result of the European invasion even before the end of the 16th century.[686]

---

[672] Ibid.
[673] R. Garaudy: *Comment l'Homme;* op cit; p. 257.
[674] D.M. Traboulay: *Columbus and Las Casas*; op cit; p. 56.
[675] Father Motolinia: letters to Charles Quint; in R. Garaudy: *Comment;* op cit; p. 258.
[676] D E. Stannard: "Genocide in The Americas" in *The Nation*, (October 19, 1992; pp. 430-434)
[677] J.H. Parry: *The Spanish Seaborne Empire*; London; 1966; p. 143.
[678] U. Bitterli: *Cultures in Conflict*; op cit; p. 33.
[679] D.E. Stannard: "Genocide in The Americas; op cit.
[680] D.M. Traboulay: *Columbus and Las Casas*; op cit; p. 56.
[681] D.E. Stannard: "Genocide in The Americas; op cit.
[682] N. Wachtel: *The Vision of the vanquished;* Hassocks; 1977.
[683] R. Robertson: Introduction, in U. Bitterli: *Cultures in Conflict*; p. 15.
[684] D.M. Traboulay: *Columbus and Las Casas*; op cit; p. 56.
[685] Mickle in W. Howitt: *Colonisation*; op cit; p. 15.
[686] P. Chaunu: *European Expansion; op* cit; p. 310; D E. Stannard: "Genocide; op cit.

The same story was repeated North of the continent. Beginning with Indian friendly reception of the Westerners, such as when the vessel Giovanni da Verrazzano arrived at the mouth of the St Lawrence River in 1525, a sailor fell overboard and was washed ashore by the current. The crew watched in horror as their comrade was surrounded by Indians who began lighting a fire.[687] Their relief was great when the Indians did nothing more than dry the Frenchman's clothes and give him something to eat: 'With the greatest kindness, they accompanied him to the sea, holding him close and embracing him; and then to reassure him, they withdrew to a high hill and stood watching him until he was in the boat.'[688]

In 1534 there began the Frenchman's Jaques Cartier's voyages to Canada; in Hochelaga, a fortified centre of the Indian Huron tribes, the seafarers received an enthusiastic welcome from over a thousand Indians, and presents were exchanged.[689] Cartier's expedition, tradition has it, was only saved from dying of scurvy by a mysterious plant which the Indians had recommended as a remedy.[690] The same kindly reception was shown by Indians to arriving English and pilgrims from Holland.

Indian friendly reception could hardly conceal the fact, as Stannard puts it 'that they stood in front of Western designs for their land and riches, which demanded their removal.'[691] Just as south of the continent, natives were depicted as animal-barbaric fiends. In the White American perception, the Native Indian was inferior, and so had no right to impede 'the obvious designs of Providence,' Fontana says.[692] He would survive while 'There remained corners of land on which he could find refuge from the advance of civilisation, but his destiny in the long run was extinction,'[693] Fontana adds.

Indian land and stock were seized; game was killed off; Indian hunters were attacked for hunting within state lines; Indians were bribed to sell their land, and land titles were obtained through fraud.[694] American government agents were planted among the Indians to advocate removal, while Indian chiefs were bribed with gifts and grants to speak favourably of the policy.[695]

More often, Le Bon points out, whole Indian populations were eliminated, just hunted like beasts for fun.[696] In 1703, Boston's Reverend, Solomon Stoddard, urged the Massachusetts governor to train a large pack of dogs to hunt down those who remained: 'Such dogs would be an extreme terror to the Indians [he

---

[687] U. Bitterli: *Cultures in Conflict*; op cit; pp. 27-8.
[688] L.C. Wroth: *The Voyages of Giovanni da Verrazzano*; 1524-1528; New Haven; 1970; p. 135.
[689] U. Bitterli: *Cultures*; op cit; p. 88.
[690] *Les Francais en Amerique pendant la premiere moitie du XVIem siecle*; ed., C. A. Julien; Paris; 1946; pp. 168-9.
[691] D E. Stannard: "Genocide; op cit.
[692] J. Fontana: *The Distorted Past*; op cit; p. 118.
[693] Ibid.
[694] E.R. Wolf: *Europe and the People Without History*; (University of California Press; Berkeley; 1982); p. 285.
[695] Ibid.
[696] In G. Le Bon: *La Civilisation*; op cit; p. 468.

said] and would "catch many an Indian that would be too light of foot for us.[697] Recognising that the more humane might think his plan to hunt Indians as they do bears to be a little extreme, Stoddard acknowledged, 'that he might agree if the Indians were as other people but in fact the Indians were wolves and are to be dealt with as wolves.'[698]

One of the early famed leaders of the new nation, Andrew Jackson, called native peoples "savage dogs" and boasted: I have on all occasions preserved the scalps of my killed," Jackson at one time supervising the mutilation of 800 or so Creek Indian corpses, cutting off their noses to count and preserve a record of the dead, and slicing long strips from their bodies to tan and turn into bridle reins.[699]

It was President Jackson who was responsible for the infamous Trail of Tears, when U.S. Army troops drove the remnants of the Cherokee nation out of their homes and across the country in a march, in which most perished; something 'alongside which the Bataan Death March, the most notorious Japanese atrocity in all of World War II, pales by comparison.'[700]

In America, as Howitt, notes:
> Once the country was born, the American Republicans, followed faithfully, not their own declarations, but the maxims and the practices of their progenitors. The Indians have been declared savage and irreclaimable. They have been described as inveterately attached to hunting and a roving life, as a stumbling block in the path of civilisation, as perfectly incapable of settling down to the pursuits of agriculture, social arts, and domestic habits.[701]

Ward Churchill points out, how:
> From aristocrats like Jeffrey Amherst to the lowliest private in his army, from the highest elected officials to the humblest of farmers, (all) described America's indigenous peoples as vermin, launched literally hundreds of campaigns to effect their extermination, and then revelled in the carnage which resulted. Martial glory was attained by more than a few officers who proudly boasted in later years of having instructed their troops, when attacking essentially defenceless native communities, to 'Kill and scalp all, little and big [because] nits make lice.' The body parts taken by soldiers in such slaughters remain prized possessions, discreetly handed down as trophies through the generations of all too many American families.[702]

Venereal diseases introduced by Westerners helped wipe out larger numbers of Native Indians. Epidemics introduced by Cartier on the Saint Lawrence in 1535, just as the nameless plague spread by de Soto's exploration of the deep south in

---
[697] D.E. Stannard: "Genocide in The Americas" op cit.
[698] Ibid.
[699] David E. Stannard: "Genocide; op cit.
[700] Ibid.
[701] W. Howitt: *Colonisation and Christianity;* op cit; pp. 390-1.
[702] Ward Churchill: *A Little Matter of Genocide*; op cit; p. 2.

1538 began a history in which almost every attempted European settlement infected the natives.[703] In Canada, fur traders confused the Indians by their unbridled sexuality and introduced alcohol.[704] When drunk, the Indians went berserk in the slaughter of each other.[705] Throughout the 17th century most particularly, both English and French armed the Indians, intoxicated them with alcohol, and then set them against each other, then, using the most atrocious acts committed by them, branded them 'as most fearful and bloody savages,' and for that reason drove them out of their rightful possessions, or butchered them.[706] The burning of entire Indian towns and surrounding cornfields, and the poisoning of whole communities were systemic.[707] Indians were also burnt en masse in huge auto da fe. William Bradford, the governor of Plymouth Colony, described the reaction of the settlers to one such mass immolation:

> It was a fearful sight to see [the Indians] thus frying in fire and the streams of blood quenching the same, and horrible was the stink and scent thereof; but the victory seemed a sweet sacrifice, and [the settlers] gave the praise thereof to God, who had wrought so wonderfully for them.[708]

By the close of the 17th century there was, at most, one native person of New England alive for every twenty who had greeted the English colonists less than a hundred years earlier; a 95-percent die-off.[709] In the Carolinas, for instance, the fate of the Indians may be summed up in a single passage by an early contemporary:

> Two wars were carried on against the natives of the most extravagant description. All the wandering or fixed nations between the ocean and Appalachian mountains were attacked and massacred without any interest or motive. Those who escaped being put to the sword, either submitted or were dispersed.[710]

The number of people living north of Mexico prior to the European invasion remains (of course) a subject of much academic debate, from a low of about 7 million to a high of 18 million; but by the close of the 19th century the indigenous population of the United States and Canada totalled just around 250,000; thus from the first arrival of Europeans in the 16th century to the infamous massacre at Wounded Knee in the winter of 1890, between 97 and 99% of North America's native people were killed.[711]

However, in Western perception, Armesto notes:

> Humanists, missionaries and jurists were the writers most interested in newly discovered peoples and their respective accounts can be treated as a

---

[703] F. Fernandez-Armesto: *Millennium;* A Touchstone Book; Simon and Shuster; New York; 1995; p. 276.
[704] U. Bitterli: *Cultures in Conflict;* op cit; p. 98.
[705] Ibid; p. 119.
[706] W. Howitt: *Colonisation;* op cit; p. 317.
[707] D E. Stannard: "Genocide; op cit.
[708] Ibid.
[709] Ibid.
[710] Abbe Reynal in W. Howitt: *Colonisation;* op cit; p. 340.
[711] David E. Stannard: Genocide; op cit.

basis for classifying the material. Secular chroniclers and conquerors or would be conquerors who sometimes wrote accounts or characterisations of their intended victims, usually in supplications addressed to popes, shared, on the whole, the jurists' perspective: their interest lay in establishing that their victims were fair game for enslavement or war, bereft of true sovereignty and consigned to inferior juridical categories.[712]

Narrative of history in our universities, colleges, in books and documentaries, the internet and films, comes today to cleanse everyone's misdeed. Ward Churchill notes how:

> Today, we discover, while perusing the texts of orthodox scholarship, that much of this never happened, or to the extent that some things must be at least partially admitted, was 'tragic,' 'unavoidable,' and unintended.' The decimated natives were peculiarly responsible for their own demise, having never bothered to develop immunities to the host of pathogens unleashed among them by the ever increasing numbers of Old World Settlers swarming to their shores. In North America, where the practice of denial is most accomplished, successive waves of historians and anthropologists harnessed themselves to the common task of advancing the pretence that the aboriginal population of the continent was but a small fraction of its real number. Thus, the death of people who never existed need not be explained, nor can there be serious questions as to the original ownership of territory which was uninhabited until the settlers came. The formal term is land vacant and therefore open to whomsoever might wish to claim it.[713]
> In the relatively rare instances where even this complex of denial and evasion is insufficient - the 1864 Sand Creek Massacre and its 1890 counterpart at Wounded Knee, for example, are too well known to be simply 'disappeared'- orthodoxy frames its discourse in terms of madmen and anomaly.[714]

Contemporary accounts such as those of Las Casas', which described genocides of natives in America, are today deemed to be the result of their author's insanity.[715] The mass extinction of Indians in America, just as that of the aborigines in Australia, we are told, was only the result of individual, uncontrollable settlers, Western policy being always to protect such natives.[716] The Western man in America is today described as a victim, as Fontana notes.[717] 'The redskin we see in our films is the villain who cruelly slays settlers and scalps them (though the scalping business was

---

[712] F. Fernandez Armesto: *Before Columbus*; op cit; pp. 228-9.
[713] See: J. Axtell: Beyond 1492: *Encounters in Colonial North America;* (Oxford University Press; 1992); pp. 261-3; F. Jennings: *The Invasion of America; Indians; Colonization and the Cant of Conquest;* (Chapel Hill; University of North Carolina Press; 1975); pp. 15-31.
[714] Ward Churchill: *A Little Matter*; op cit; pp. 2-3.
[715] U. Bitterli: *Cultures in Conflict*; Polity Press; tr from German; (Cambridge; 1989); p. 83.
[716] Channel Four Programme: Empire; seen on Welsh version S4C, 11 February 2003.
[717] J. Fontana: *The Distorted Past;* op cit; p. 119.

a white man's invention to facilitate payment by heads to the Indian hunters,)' Fontana adds.[718]

Stannard comments further how this crime is justified today by the likes of Krauthammer:
> Nonetheless, says Charles Krauthammer in an essay in *Time*, while duly insisting that he would never "justify the cruelty of the conquest, the fact is that "mankind is the better for it (the genocide of Indians).[719]

Ward Churchill notes how Charles Krauthammer, one of *Time Magazine*'s regular political columnists, used an entire column on May 27, 1991, 'to lambast as 'politically correct' opportunists anyone who dared express regrets over the killing of millions of innocent people and the destruction of entire ancient cultures in the Americas. What happened in the wake of the European invasion was only what has always characterised human history, Krauthammer claimed... The real question is, he noted, 'what essentially grew out on this bloodied soil?' For, regardless of the level of destruction and mass murder that was visited upon the indigenous peoples of the Western hemisphere, it was, in retrospect, entirely justified because in the process it wiped out such alleged barbarism as the communally based Inca society (which really was only a 'beehive,' Krauthammer said) and gave the world 'a culture of liberty that endowed the individual human being with dignity and sovereignty.'[720]

Krauthammer is not alone. Arthur Schlesinger Jr., writing in *The Atlantic* for September (1992), held that while
> In general, the European record in dealing with the indigenous peoples of the Americas was miserable - and indefensible.... there are benefits, too, and these require to be factored into the historical equation.[721]

Schlesinger contends that these societies of dazzling accomplishment would most likely have preserved their collectivist cultures and their conviction that the individual had no legitimacy outside the theocratic state, and the result would have been a repressive fundamentalism comparable perhaps to that of the Ayatollah Khomeini in Iran. And had the Westerners not conquered and destroyed the Aztecs and the Incas, these societies might have continued indefinitely with their unpleasant practices of "ritual torture and human sacrifice.[722]

Schlesinger was not content to build his case on the purported shortcomings of the ancient societies of the Americas. No, he gazed into his crystal ball and asserted.... that without the European conquests and slaughter at least some

---
[718] Ibid.
[719] In David E. Stannard: "Genocide in The Americas"; op cit.
[720] In D. Stannard: The Politics of Holocaust Scholarship: Uniqueness as Denial; in A.S. Rosenbaum; ed: *Is the Holocaust Unique? Perspectives on Comparative genocide*; Boulder; CO: (Westview Press; 1995); p. 165.
[721] In David E. Stannard: "Genocide in The Americas"; op cit.
[722] Ibid.

New World societies today would be sufficiently unpleasant places to live so as to make acceptable the centuries of genocide that were carried out against the native people of the entire Western hemisphere.[723]

Left radicals, likewise, scarcely deviate from such views. The postulations of the Revolutionary Communist party, USA, published nearly a decade before the quincentenary, held that the pre-Columbian population of North America was about half that admitted at the time by even the thoroughly reactionary Smithsonian Institution, that the people were so primitive that they were forced to regularly consume their own fecal matter in order to survive, and that only European conquest and colonisation had lifted them from their state of perpetual degradation to the level of rudimentary humanity.[724]

---

[723] D. E. Stannard: The Politics; op cit; pp. 165-6. Schlesinger's Atlantic piece ran in the September 1992 issue.
[724] The RCP: 'Searching for a Second Harvest; In Ward Churchill ed: *Marxism and Native Americans*; (Boston; South End Press; 1983).

Seven

WOMEN

Whilst the first half of this book dealt with the history of the myths about Islamic barbarism, showing the medieval origins of both myth and techniques in its fabrication, and explained the reasons for it genesis, this second half brings us to the period elapsing from the 18th century till our day in 2020. It will only be returned to pre 18th century history if and when necessary regarding some issues, and even this will be kept succinct as this period of history (pre-18th) has received its share in the first half, and henceforth focus is on matters of our times principally.

Muslim 'Oppression of Women'

We have seen in chapter 1, principally how early Christian saw Islam and Muslims in respect to matters of sexuality and the treatment of women. So, we pick the matter in the 18th century.
In the *Lettres Persannes* Montesquieu (1689-1755) emphasises the essential differences between the East and the West by contrasting stereotypical images of Oriental women with that of Western women. In his letter 67, he states that the:
> Mohammedan faith deprives women of their freedom, … and Mohammedanism locked women behind bars… and had that religion conquered the earth, women would have been imprisoned everywhere.[725]

In letter 24, he asserts that this religion (Islam) is so much
> …Discriminating against women, that they are not just forbidden to read the scriptures, but also that they were not to enter paradise because of their sex.[726]

Obviously, Montesquieu shows little knowledge of the Qur'an. Among several verses referring to women having their reward in paradise is one in Surah 4 (known as Surah an-Nisa – the Women) verse 124:
> 'If any do deeds of righteousness - be they male or female - and have faith, they will enter Heaven, and not the least injustice will be done to them.'

As he argues in *The Spirit of the Law,* it seems that despotism is related to the servitude of women while the spirit of monarchy promotes the liberty of women:
> In despotic governments women do not introduce, but are themselves an object of luxury. They must be in a state of the most rigorous servitude. Everyone follows the spirit of government, and adopts in his own family the customs he sees everywhere established. As the laws are very severe and

---
[725] Montesquieu; Pensees; p. 508; 1622; in Pauline Kra: *Religion in Montesquieu's Lettres Persanes*; Institut et Musee Voltaire (Geneve; 1970), p. 113.
[726] Montesquieu: Letter 24; in P. Kra: *Religion*, op cit; p. 114.

executed on the spot, they are afraid lest the liberty of women should expose them to danger... as princes in these countries make a sport of human nature, they allow themselves a multitude of women; and a thousand considerations oblige them to keep those women in close confinement.[727]

For Montesquieu, polygamy is a case for the

> Abuse of slavery, because slavery should be calculated for utility, not for pleasure. However, in Mohammedan states women are born only to be subservient to the pleasure of others... this servitude is alleviated by the laziness in which such slaves spend their days; which is an additional disadvantage to the state.[728]

The French work *Difficultés sur la Religion* etc, also dating from the same century, makes countless false assertions about Islam such as in the eighteenth *verité* (truth) where it implies that Muslims carry out circumcision as a holy act, which the rest of the world finds absurd as it finds absurd the burning of widows in India.[729] In the author's mind, the Muslims, by believing that circumcision pleases God and that ablution cleanses sin, attribute a weakness to God. The author also asserts that Islam is responsible for the destruction of morality and true virtues, and amongst others also claims that the Qur'an excludes women from paradise.[730]

Answering Lady Montague (1689-1762), the wife of the British Ambassador at Constantinople, who had praise for the condition of women in Turkey, Eton insists that Turkish women are deceitful but never free. Although women look for opportunities to become unfaithful to their husbands, and the proposition generally comes from them, it also involves great danger.[731] Thus, they live a "stupid solitary life' surrounded by slaves or by women as ignorant and spiritless as themselves.[732]

In a similar vein, Hunter observes, as against Montague's description, that Turkish women are quite unhappy and live a slave's life:

> In a country where plurality of wives is authorized by law, and... the sex must infallibly be tyrannized over and degraded. It is deprived of its natural rights. It is denied its natural protection... It is robbed of its dignity and its honour.. It is compelled to pay obedience to a wretch whom it despises, and whilst it despises to submit to the gratification of his lust.[733]

On the one hand, polygamy is denounced as a shameless and insulting tyranny, achieved by the powerful and strong over the weak and helpless. On the other hand, polygamy is conceived as suitable for a Turkish man; in fact, it is considered as a very good and necessary maxim for the Turks:

---

[727] Montesquieu: *The Spirit of the Laws;* 1749; tr., by T. Nugent; (New York and London; Hafner Publishing Company; 1966); p. 102.
[728] Montesquieu: *The Spirit of the Laws;* op cit; p. 242.
[729] R. Mortier ed., *Difficultes sur la religion proposees au Pere Malebranche;* (Brussels; 1970); p. 113.
[730] In A. Gunny: *Images of Islam;* op cit; p. 103.
[731] W. Eton: *A Survey of the Turkish Empire;* op cit; p. 243. See A. Cirakman: *From the Terror;* op cit.
[732] Ibid; p. 243.
[733] W. Hunter: *Travels in the Year 1792;* (London; 1796); pp. 375-6.

> Wives, slaves, and concubines, promiscuously granted them without control and every tenet of their faith, and practice of their lives, combining jointly to indulge their wishes in the gross enjoyment of a sensual appetite.[734]

Slavery of women in Turkey is also contrasted with the liberty of European women. This is best illustrated in a play about the character named Maria Cecilia who is portrayed as daughter of Grand Signor, Ahmet III (Sultan 1703-1736). She went to Europe and became a Christian. According to Turkish standards she has an outrageous life style: she is educated in Italy, residing in France, in love with a knight of Malta (the fiercest enemy of the Turk). Sultan Ahmet who is depicted as a particularly effeminate and soft ruler is astonished to see his daughter in Western clothes. He is also appalled by the fact that Maria has a quite improper attitude towards him. Then, he asks:

'What god do you serve? ... My daughter must be a Christian!'
Just for Maria to declare:

'I avow it openly, the respect I owe my God is above my fear of a father.'[735]

Antoine Galland (d.1715), the translator of the One Thousand and one Night in French, recounts the story of a mistreated slave girl made desperate by her keeper:

> A slave from Constantinople having been mistreated by many blows with a stick on her feet by her master, entered into a deep despair, that she set fire to the house and hanged herself after that, thus seeking to punish the cruelty of her master, and free herself at the same time.[736]

The theme of enslaved Muslim women fills the 19th century narrative in all its forms. In literature, woman for the fanaticised, brutal Muslim is a prize of war and piracy; the Muslim prowling upon her and ravaging her.[737] Helena, heroine of a poem by the Frenchman Alfred de Vigny is violated brutally by the Turks; an act de Vigny dwells upon in every single, morbid detail. As for her women folk, in the *Orientales* of Victor Hugo, another Frenchman, they are all prisoners at the Seraglio, and are offered to the beastly delectation of the Sultan. Of course, all these women are young virgins.[738] The victims of Turkish beastly desires are generally convent girls kidnapped by (Muslim) pirates, and taken to the Harem of the Sultan.[739]

Similar picture is expressed in contemporary Western paintings, which, even more than the written, enhance the plight of the female slaves in Muslim clutches. Generally, they depict scenes from supposed Muslim slave markets, where naked women are exhibited and sold. Kabbani looks at a number of such paintings.[740] John Faed's 'Bedouin exchanging a slave for armour', dating from 1857 shows the Bedouin with an almost entirely naked slave-girl exhibited in the stall of a sword

---

[734] A. Hill: *A Full and Just Account;* op cit; p. 91.
[735] J. Lavalee: *Maria Cecilia or Life and Adventure of the Daughter of Ahmet III, Emperor of the Turks*; (London; 1788); pp. 209-10.
[736] A. Galland: *Journal; 1672-3;* edited by C. Shefer; (Paris; 1868); 2 vols; vol ii; p. 19.
[737] C. Grossir: *L'Islam des Romantiques;* op cit; p. 99 fwd.
[738] V. Hugo: *Les Orientales;* (1964); Les Tetes du Serail; IV; pp. 602-3.
[739] Ibid. Chanson de Pirates; p. 619.
[740] R. Kabbani: *Imperial Fictions;* op cit; pp. 78-9.

merchant. The girl's body is inspected in such a meticulous, very searching manner, her worth assessed in armour. Her expression, Kabbani notes, 'is a piteous one, ... completely helpless; naked, bound, female, and a slave.' The oriental man is predatory, lecherous, gross, and loathsome.

Another famous slave-market scene is Gérôme's 'Le Marché d' Esclaves,' where the slave girl is in the midst of would-be purchaser men. The girl, again, is naked, offered to the gaze of her captors and would-be buyers. The Muslim owner, holding her head veil is 'a ghoulish-looking man,' just as Muslims are depicted: frightening with their gross, dark complexions, their hairy faces, big, bulging eyes, thickened lips... Four other victims await their turns for inspection, still huddled in their veils.[741] In every scene, the delicate features of the woman contrast with the beastly appearances of her Muslim male captors and traders.

Kabbani points out how:

> Oriental males are almost always portrayed as predatory figures in Orientalist paintings. They are mostly as ugly or loathsome, in contrast to the women who are beautiful and voluptuous. This leaves the woman free for the abduction of the viewer's gaze since she is not attached within the painting, being mismatched with a male who is her obvious inferior. Thus, she must desire to be saved from her fate in some way. By such projection, the European fantasised about the Eastern woman's emotional dependency on him. This appealed to his sense of himself as romantic hero.[742]
>
> Their (oriental men's) villainy is compounded by the fact that they are portrayed as traders in female bodies. They are the cruel captors who hold women in their avaricious grasp, who use them as chattels, as trading-goods, with little reverence for them as human beings. This idea was highly important in distinguishing between the barbarity of the Eastern male and the civilised behaviour of the Western male. One tied women up and sold them at slave auctions; the other revered them and placed them on pedestals. The European cherished the notion of his gentlemanliness among savages. It was one added way of convincing himself that he was born to rule over them.[743]

For Christian writers and Missionaries the fault lies with Islam. E.A. Freeman (1823-1893), judged

> The West to be progressive, monogamous and Christian, and the East stationary, arbitrary, polygamous and Mahometan.[744]

A view that was shared by his contemporary, J.D. Bate, who served as a missionary in India (between 1865 and 1897), saying that:

---

[741] Ibid.
[742] Ibid; pp. 79-80.
[743] Ibid; pp. 76-7.
[744] E.A. Freeman: *The History and Conquests*; op cit; pp. i.4.

> Islam succeeded by corrupting its followers. Men had even converted to Islam in order to indulge their brutal appetites for sexual pleasure... the great Arabian reformer made permanent provisions for the flesh.[745]

These and similar claims have no foundations, Smith pointing out how Islam won the hearts and the minds not because it was a sensuous religion; the fast, daily prayer, almsgiving, Smith notes,

> Appeal little to lazy, sensual or selfish people. Nothing could be more destitute of truth than to argue that a religion owed 'its permanent success to bad morality.[746]

However, to maintain this false image of Islam, as Daniel notes:

> The Christian canon of Muslim behaviour, that is, the received Christian opinion as to what Muslims actually did, was partly formed by the tendency of misconceptions to snowball, and to confirm as well as to add to one another. Mere repetition is enough to bring unshakable conviction; and once it had been asserted that Islamic teaching was sexually lax, every example of laxity would be noticed from that moment, and, once notified, attributed to the doctrine.[747]

Missionary Literature brought out the same issue early in the 20th century, emphasising most particularly the role of Western colonisation in freeing Muslim women. Writing from Fort National, in Greater Kabylia (Algeria), J.T.C. Blackmore, in an article: 'France: A Disintegrator of Islam', says:

> Recently a French friend of some years standing, now risen to an important official position, said to me: 'I want to tell you now that I am coming to see more and more that the French cannot advance very far in North Africa unless we overthrow the Moslem religion.
>
> This growing antagonism to Islam in official quarters does not come from a spirit of religious fanaticism, but because of the hindrance Islam is found to be in the social and economic development of the country.
>
> To my friend's declaration I replied:
>
> 'And I want to tell you that actually France is one of the forces that is contributing the most to the undermining of Islam.'
>
> His pleased smile confirmed to me his desire to see the country rid of Mohammedanism, but he said:
>
> 'I don't see that. On the contrary we are stupidly and constantly Islamising the Berbers.' He then enumerated a few things in support of his statement, e.g. the native students entering the normal college for school teachers in Algiers when registering, after the question, "What religion?" are obliged to put down, 'Islam'. Only with great difficulty recently have Christian converts been able to avoid this.

---

[745] J.D. Bate: *The Claims of Ishmael*; (London; W.H. Allen; 1884); pp. 285; 253.
[746] R.B. Smith: *Mohammed*; op cit p. 196.
[747] N. Daniel: *Islam and the West*; op cit; p. 270

> 'Yes I said, 'officially and intentionally a brave attempt is still being made to fulfil the old promise not to disturb the religion and customs of the country, but unconsciously France is working powerfully and surely to the disintegration of Islam....'

Then, the author (Blackmore) goes on to describe the trial of a Kabyle/Berber who beat his wife, and how he appealed against the tribunal that decided in favour of his wife. His appeal was rejected, and the following is an extract of the decision:

> Whereas it appears from the previous decisions of judges and from diverse documents that numerous protestations have already been made against the barbarous custom which forbids the Kabyle woman, brutalised by her husband, to ask for the rupture of the conjugal tie, that a new and more humane conception of woman's rights has at last seen the day in Kabylia, and the evolution of this idea has reached a sufficiently advanced stage to constitute a new custom, which has taken the place of the old one, and that the moment has arrived for the courts to recognise and adopt it - the appeal, whilst allowable as to its form as to its purport, is rejected.
>
> Mankind throughout Kabylia are beginning to tingle with indignation. Womankind are beginning to laugh discreetly. But the law goes on in its might.
>
> Thus, France gently but surely is overthrowing Islam.[748]

Stoddard sums up for us the great work of colonisation:

> The importance of Western education in the East is nowhere better illustrated than in the effects it is producing in ameliorating the status of women.... As an English writer well puts it: 'Ladies first,' we say in the West; in the East it is 'ladies last.' That sums up succinctly the difference in the domestic ideas of the two civilizations.
>
> Under these circumstances it might seem as though no breath of the West could yet have reached these jealously secluded creatures. Yet, as a matter of fact, Western influences have already profoundly affected the women of the upper classes, and female education, while far behind that of the males has attained considerable proportions. In the more advanced parts of the Orient like Constantinople, Cairo and the cities of India, distinctly modern types of women have appeared, the self supporting, self-respecting and respected woman school-teacher being especially in evidence.
>
> The social consequences of this rising status of women, not only to women themselves but also to the community at large, are very important. In the East the harem is, as Vambéry well says, the "bulwark of obscurantism."[749] Ignorant and fanatical herself, the harem woman implants her ignorance and fanaticism in her sons as well as in her daughters. What could be a worse handicap for the Eastern intellectual than his boyhood years spent 'behind

---

[748] J.T.C. Blackmore: France: A Disintegrator of Islam; in *The Moslem World*; vol 14; 1924; pp. 136-9.
[749] Vambery: La Turquie d'aujourdhui et d'avant Quarante ans; p. 32.

the veil?' No wonder that enlightened Oriental fathers have been in the habit of sending their boys to school at the earliest possible age in order to get them as soon as possible out of the stultifying atmosphere of harem life. Yet even this has proved, merely a palliative. Childhood impressions are ever the most lasting, and so long as one-half of the Orient remained untouched by progressive influences, Oriental progress had to be begun again *do novo* with every succeeding generation. The increasing number of enlightened Oriental women is remedying this fatal defect. As a Western writer says:

> 'Give the mothers education and the whole situation is transformed. Girls who are learning other things than the unintelligible phrases of the Koran are certain to impart such knowledge, as daughters, sisters, and mothers, to their respective households. Women who learn housewifery, methods of modern cooking, sewing, and sanitation in the domestic economy schools, are bound to cast about the home upon their return the atmosphere of a civilised community. The old time picture of the Oriental woman spending her hours upon divans, eating sweetmeats, and indulging in petty and degrading gossip with the servants or with the women as ignorant as herself, will be changed. The new woman will be the companion rather than a slave or a toy of her husband. Marriage will be advanced from a stage of a paltry trade of bodies to something like a real union, involving respect towards the woman by both sons and fathers, while in a new pride of relationship the woman herself will be discovered.'[750]

The issue of women enslavement in Islam as against Western liberation of them still dominates 20th century perception. Some Western writers go further into the issue to explain why Muslims encourage the trade of women slaves. A leading voice in the subject, Murray Gordon, writes:

> Even in the slave states of the antebellum American South, where relations between the races were governed by strict codes of behaviour, often stiffened by anti-miscegenation or anti-cohabitation laws, it was not uncommon for slave owners to keep one or more slave girls as mistresses, although rarely as wives. However, this aspect of slavery was incidental to the real purpose of slavery, which was to provide, at an economic price, black slaves to work the cotton fields which were the economic backbone of the South. In this order of things, male slaves, who became the main toilers in the fields, generally commanded a higher price than women slaves of comparable age and health. In contrast, what distinguished the domestic trade in Africa and the export to the Muslim world of young female slaves was the degree to which acquiring concubines was a compelling and conscious motive.[751]

---

[750] L. Stoddard: *The New World of Islam*; op cit; pp. 258-9.
[751] A.G.B. Fisher and H.J. Fisher: *Slavery and Muslim Society in Africa*; (London; C. Hurst and Company; 1970); p. 99.

Acquiring one or more concubines was an irresistible attraction to men that pervaded all social ranks of Muslim society. After being brought into her master's household, the concubine performed routine domestic chores; it was not uncommon for talented slave women to receive instruction in art, poetry, or singing and then to spend much of their time performing for the benefit of their owners. Notwithstanding the various roles they assumed, the primary purpose of most men in acquiring a concubine was sexual. The concubine offered men a religiously approved way of gratifying their sexual desires and fantasies in ways that were often not possible in normal marital life.

In Islamic society, a man could have no contact at all with his intended wife until the consummation of their marriage. Koranic law, for reasons having to do with female modesty and chastity, forbids women to be in the company of any men, except their husbands or persons so closely related to them as to come within prohibited degrees for marriage. Included in this category were close relatives, slaves, particularly eunuchs, and children too young to be aware of differences of sex. A woman unlike her husband, who could avoid the constrictive embrace of a sexually frustrating marriage by taking as many as four wives at any one time and buying as many concubines as he wished, had no such options. She had to live a monogamic life under conditions that placed severe limits on her physical movements in a society which restricted her meeting other men.

Such restrictive courting practices, which few women dared flout, were bound to create, in time, serious strains in marital ties. Personal problems arising from differences in temperament or sexual incompatibility were scarcely avoidable for men and women who were almost strangers to one another upon marriage. The unhappy or sexually frustrated women, rarely a matter of concern to the male-dominant society whose mores she had to follow, had to resign herself to remaining faithful to an uncaring or insensitive husband or to seeking a lover. Adultery, however, when committed by a woman, remained an unpardonable act in Muslim society; under Islamic law it is punishable by death. Such a rule was applied, *a fortiori*, to a woman who owned male slaves as well. While a woman could own slaves in her own right, she was not permitted to have sexual relations with any of them - a restriction that did not apply to her husband. A man who discovered that his wife shared her bed with a slave could have her pay for such a transgression with her life....[752]

Gordon then adds:

The availability of concubines, moreover, offered a man a measure of relief from the unhappiness of marriage that was sexually un-gratifying. Before purchasing a slave whom he intended to use as a concubine, a man was

---

[752] M. Gordon: *Slavery in the Arab World*; originally published in French: *L'Esclavage dans le Monde Arabe*; (New Amsterdam; New York; 1989); pp. 84-5.

> careful to make sure that she was responsive to his amorous advances. This could be managed in the privacy of special stalls that were set aside in slave markets for the close examination of female slaves by prospective buyers, here men would take liberties with these hapless girls in a manner they would not dream of when courting a woman they wished to marry. In Cairo, despite laws regulating the proper and moral conduct of public affairs, including slave market practices, these regulations were often flouted by interested customers of female slaves. This opportunity to choose a concubine after first approaching her in an intimate manner offered for a man a far more promising way of developing a sexually gratifying relationship than with a wife.[753]

And Gordon concludes:

> The merger of this form of slavery into the structure of family life helped make slavery into a formidable institution in the Islamic world and says much about why it became so difficult to do away with it.[754]

A Lueg, together with J. Hippler, has completed one of the most remarkable works on the Western perceptions of Islam,[755] a work which raises many fundamental issues, especially in respect to the issue we are discussing here. Lueg sums up the overall Western view of women:

> There is little variation in the image of the Islamic woman offered by the media: she serves man and is oppressed by him, be it (based on past ideas about harems or polygamy) as one among many other wives, or as the cleaning lady in the West who must always walk three steps behind her husband, or even as the woman who lives the spoilt 'life of luxury' in the Arab ruling houses so beloved by the tabloids - she remains passive and dependent. From the gossip column to the feminist magazine, Islamic women are mainly this: victims. As such, they are merely objects of reporting, never allowed to speak for themselves. Women from Islamic countries are sometimes even perceived as a threat because they are victims. They are seen as emigrating to the West from their homelands *en masse*. One Western official, who requested anonymity, put it this way:

'Consider that there are one billion Muslims in the world, so we're talking hypothetically about 500 million women who might want out.'[756]

Under the title 'A Stick in the Back, a Child in the Belly' *Der Spiegel* describes the 'quiet and hidden martyrdom' of Turkish women in Germany, 'whose billowing robes and old-maid scarves' have made them a laughing-stock.[757] 'They are terrorised and beaten, and live in constant fear of their violent

---

[753] Ibid; p. 86.
[754] Ibid; p. 91.
[755] J. Hippler, A. Lueg: *The Next Threat: Western Perceptions of Islam*, Pluto Press, 1995.
[756] A.L. Bardach: Tearing off the veil, *Vanity Fair*; (August 1993).
[757] *Der Spiegel*: No 44; 1990; p. 99.

husbands, brothers or male relatives who have total power over everyone in the family who wears a dress.'[758]

'Women's refuges in Germany', writes *Der Spiegel*, 'are full of Turkish women.' Instead of Turkish women themselves, it is a sociologist from Frankfurt, 'Mrs Konig, expert on the Turks', who tells us all about the conditions in Turkish families. The title of a special issue of the feminist magazine *EMMA-WOR* (The Effects of Male Madness and how Women Offer Resistance) is adorned by the picture of a Muslim woman veiled in black from head to toe, with a blood red crown of thorns placed on her head by a photo montage, the symbol of Jesus, who, according to Christian tradition, sacrificed himself on the cross.[759]

Betty Mahmood's best-seller *Not Without My Daughter* drew in its wake a wave of publications on the life of women in Islamic countries or married to Muslims.[760] The more dramatic and brutal the story the better. The women allowed to give their accounts in these publications had to be 'Prisoners in their own country', 'Sold into slavery by their own fathers' or 'Sentenced to death by their own families'.[761]

The veil is deemed the symbol par excellence of Islamic oppression of women. As Lueg notes, the harem, the veil and the Turkish cleaning lady with a headscarf are the clichéd images that the West associates with women and Islam. Oriental women appear mostly shrouded in threatening black yards of material: the chador.[762] 'The Headscarf Affair' soon becomes 'a chador war' in the French media.[763] Since the end of the nineteenth century, the veiling of women has been seen in the West as a symbol of the backwardness of the Islamic countries. Veiling - to Western eyes, the most visible marker of the differentness and inferiority of Islamic societies – has become a symbol now of both the oppression of women ... and 'the backwardness of Islam, and the open target of colonial attack and the spearhead of the assault on Muslim societies.'[764]

Another author who captures well the issue, perhaps much better than most, is Kabbani. We give her space in her own words. She writes:

> One of the reasons I wrote this book was to disprove the commonly held and oppressive assumption that Western culture is superior to other cultures; that it is somehow more humane, civilised or tolerant, less violent and less misogynistic. Such assumptions formed the bedrock of nineteenth-century

---

[758] Ibid.
[759] A. Lueg: The Perception of Islam in Western Debate; p. 18.
[760] A.K. Reulecke: Die Befreiung aus dem Serail,' *Feministische Studien*; 9 Jargang 2, November 1991; pp. 8-20. Betty Mahmoody: *Not Without my Daughter*; (New York; St Martin's Press; 1993).
[761] A. Lueg: The Perception of Islam; op cit; p. 18.
[762] Ibid; p. 17.
[763] '*Mit Kopftuch in die Schule,'* Frankfurter Rundschau, 7 December 1992.
[764] L. Ahmed: *Women and Gender in Islam*; (New Haven; Yale University Press; 1993); p. 152.

imperialist thought, and provided the intellectual justification for colonizing other peoples' societies.

But imperial ideas did not perish with empire. They serve as much of a manipulative political function today as they did a hundred years ago. In the decade that has elapsed since the book was written, I have observed nineteenth-century ideas about the superiority of the West's treatment of its women superimposed on the heated debate about the nature of Islam and its treatment of women. Islam, at the end of the twentieth century, has been made into the religion the West loves to hate; a seething cauldron of sexism, and a dumping ground for all blame.

In the nineteenth-century, the colonial view was that Islam should be thrown off by Muslims so that they would become easier to rule. Muslim women in particular were the focus of this call. Lord Cromer, British Viceroy of Egypt, a lifelong hater of female suffrage in Britain, nevertheless championed emancipation for Egyptian women. In seeking to 'liberate' Muslim women from their religious culture, he was hoping to break the back of the anti-colonial resistance, which had strong religious overtones.

Today, the imperial torch has been passed to a new group of Orientalists, a great many of them American feminists. It has become intellectually fashionable for American women-writers - with little or no experience of the Muslim world, with no knowledge of Muslim history - to spew forth, in books and articles, on the 'pathetic' state of women under Islam. What is worrying about this growing literature, which is always popular with a Western readership that can never get enough about the 'horrors' of Islam, is that it re-establishes the old racial stereotypes at a time when it is quite disastrous to do so, given an already taut situation between the Muslim world and the West.

This literature also builds on some very dubious foundations:

That Western women have it all, and Muslim women have nothing; that, for Muslim women to earn status and respect from Western feminism, they must denature themselves by throwing off their religious culture in its entirety. These assumptions are real traps for feminism, as they pander to patriarchy, and assure Western men that they are superior in the way they have managed things. They also reek of a paternalism that is as infuriating as it is blinkered.

(Then Kabbani relates a very interesting personal experience, where the Western 'expert' on Muslim women only contributed by her writing to distort the picture further):

When the article appeared it was one more unrelieved catalogue of horrors about Islam. It was illustrated with a huge blow-up photograph of ghostlike women, veiled from head to foot. It ignored any of the important debates within Islam about the rights of women....

> But the whole Western debate about Muslim women is a dishonest one.... The study of the Muslim world by the West has never been a neutral and scholarly exercise.[765]

Both Lueg and Kabbani give us very interesting explanations for this Western obsession with the fate of Muslim women. Lueg, first:

> As I see it, it is often the Western point of view and not so much Islam that ascribes the role of victim to women in Islamic countries', says Martina Sabra.[766] Indeed while travelling through Islamic countries one does come across many women who simply do not play the role of victim, and who do not see themselves in this light at all. Clearly, the cliché of the oppressed Islamic woman serves the purpose of distracting us from things that are wrong in our own society. These defects appear more acceptable if someone else's experience is even worse. As far as Islam as the 'enemy' is concerned, the problem of women's oppression can be pushed far aside, on to other equally 'Islamic countries', which differ from our 'secular states'. Such a point of view allows us to look down on the Islamic countries and reassure ourselves about our own superiority. 'In the mass media, the stylisation of the "oppressed woman behind the veil" (functions) as a symbol of the "medieval backwardness" of Islamic states, and provides fodder for the outlined discourse on the superiority of the West', writes Anne Kathrin Reulecke.[767]
>
> Moreover [Lueg insists] Islamic women should speak for themselves, and we should accept them as individuals. We will not be doing the situation justice as long as we continue to take cover behind the cliché of the Islamic woman as victim. We must analyse discrimination against women by taking into account the real social conditions, as we do for women in the West, instead of assuming we 'know' in advance that this is due to mainly religious reasons. A more equal dialogue could be achieved in this way.[768]

Kabbani points out, how the 'noble' sentiments for Muslim women are generally the outcome of emotional/physical perversions.[769] One of Burton's group of associates, Milnes, had a very active interest in flagellation, and had written a poem on the subject, for which Burton suggested the title 'The Birchiad.'[770] Burton, of course, is famed for his translation of the *One Thousand and One Nights*, and also his *Personal Narrative of Pilgrimage to al-Maddinah and Meccah.*[771] Both he and Milnes were fascinated by sexual deviancy, which cemented their friendship considerably. In Milnes' library was the work of Hankey (another member of the group), whose

---

[765] R. Kabbani: *Imperial Fiction*; op cit; pp. ix-x.
[766] M. Sabra: Frauenrecht-Menscherencht, *Blatter des iz3w,* No 172; March-April 1991; pp. 26-9.
[767] A.K. Reulecke: Die Befreiung; op cit.
[768] A. Lueg: The Perception of Islam; op cit; p. 20.
[769] R. Kabbani: *Imperial Fictions;* op cit; pp. 55-61.
[770] In a letter of 26 April 1862.
[771] London, 1855-6.

books were extremely outrageous; and who also had a passion for collecting instruments of torture as well as pornographic books and objects. Hankey watched the execution of a woman murderer whilst being sexually attended to by prostitutes; all peculiarities highly appreciated by Burton.[772] Kabbani notes that this very Burton, who expressed deep contempt for Egyptians, Persians, Turks and Arabs, was telling of sexual mutilation abroad, whilst his own compatriots were mutilating women via clitoridictimies and ovary removal.[773] Burton is also the translator of *The Perfumed Garden* of Shaykh Nefzawi, a work he regretted had left out explicit scenes of sodomy and homosexuality.[774]
And this hardly differs from what we have today.

Throughout the whole historical experience and to this minute at no moment did Muslims note Christian magnanimity to women folk. During the crusades, for instance, the sight of Christians eating rotten Muslim corpses was seen by the Muslims as particular evidence of Christian depravity,[775] but it was mass rape of Muslim women by the crusaders, which literally shattered that most sacred pillar of Islamic society, the sanctity of womenfolk.[776]
Mass rape of Muslim women by Christian armies was generalised, whether east or west. In Barbastro (Spain), in 1064, after the capture of the town, Christian accounts describe rapes as taking place in the mosques, or in front of fathers, brothers, and husbands.[777]
We leap over the centuries, and look at the more recent times to note Muslim women butchered and raped en masse, in Kosovo;[778] in Bosnia,[779] and elsewhere. Has anyone raised any concern for the brutal treatment of women in prisons by the present military dictatorship in Egypt? Or denounced the same regime for blowing off the heads of countless women with high velocity bullets in the Summer of 2013? Does anyone denounce the same military for violent treatment of female demonstrators? None of course, for these are the wrong women, and, most of all, this is the right regime, the sort loved in the West.
Not that Christians ever showed kindness to their own women. During the so-called Western Renaissance (15th-17th centuries), millions of women were burnt alive for their 'heresies or witchcraft.'[780] One can cite briefly, at random, how in the 16th century, Jean Bodin, prosecutor for the King of France, and Nicolas Remy, judge and general prosecutor of Lorraine, both wrote on demons, the latter sending to the stake, as a judge, about three thousand sorcerers and sorceresses.[781] Between 1590

---

[772] R. Kabbani: *Imperial Fictions*; op cit; p. 61.
[773] See Dr E.W. Cushing quoted in B. Ehrenreich and D. English: *Complaints and Disorders*; (London; 1974); p. 35.
[774] Nafzawi Chaikh: tr., and ed., R.F. Burton: *The Perfumed Gardens*; (London; 1886).
[775] R. Finucane: *Soldiers of the Faith*; (J.M. Dent and Sons Ltd; London, 1983); p. 64
[776] C. Hillenbrand: *The Crusades, Islamic Perspectives*, op cit; p. 298.
[777] N. Daniel: *The Arabs*; op cit; p. 83.
[778] Slaughter and rape of Muslim women, see media and the Hague Trial Reports 1999-2002.
[779] Read accounts by Maggie O'Kane: *The Guardian*: August 1992-January 1995.
[780] A. Dworkin: *Woman Hating*; (New York; 1974); p. 130.
[781] R. Pernoud: *Pour en finir avec le Moyen Age*: (Editions du Seuil, Paris, 1977); p. 103.

and 1597, 1,500 women were executed for witchcraft in Scotland alone.[782] By the 17th century, the number of trials for witchcraft increased to mad proportions.[783] There was hardly any region in France, where famous trials cannot be evoked, whether Loundun, Louviers, Nancy, in Normandy etc.[784] It was the same in most parts of the Western Christian world. From 1603 to the end of the century, 3192 individuals were condemned and executed in Great Britain alone under the accusation of witchcraft, sorcery or conjuration.[785]

We leap over the centuries and draw attention to a piece of news on the BBC in 2002, which reported that a club to train American women to use fire arms was opened in Oregon. The aim was to teach women to shoot their male partners when the latter attacked them. The reason: 3,000 American women are killed every year by their husbands or partners.[786] We can also remind those with short memories what happened in the 1970s and 1980s in South and Central America, when thousands of female left-wingers were inflicted upon horrific cruelties, things that not even the worst amongst Muslims has ever inflicted on women folk.

Here we draw the final veil. Western women are entitled to seek their freedom the way they wish. No Muslim, definitely not this author, would ever interfere in their story in any way whatsoever. The same entitlement for Muslim women: they are also free to decide on their matters, and nobody, Western, or male, has the right to interfere in their story. The reason, however, why Muslim women will never follow the Western model, whatever Western males in particular bark, is simple, it is in history, and it is in these pictures; they are absent from Muslim history. Millions of them cram Western-Christian history:

---

[782] Channel Four; 9-10 pm; 30 January 03.
[783] R Pernoud: *Pour en finir*; op cit; p. 103.
[784] For a summary on this see: Jean Palou: *La Sorcellerie*, Edition Que sais je?, no 756, 5ed, 1975, notably.
[785] J. Davenport: *An Apology*; op cit; p. 112.
[786] BBC 1 News: 10 p.m. 15 May 02.

Never has this been done to women in the land of Islam.

Eight

CAPTIVES, SLAVES, AND RACISTS

For centuries, once more, according to the established Western view, the Muslims have been cruel captors of Christians, pitiless slave traders, and vindictive racists, the whole concept of Islam, in fact, said to be based on the persecution of others, and relying on slavery. The few voices amongst Western Christians such as Sir Geoffrey Fisher, a British Ambassador in Algiers, who denounced the myths of Muslim piracy and cruel treatment of Christian captives, or Davenport and Smith who denounced the myths of Muslim slave trading, were ferociously rebuked. The image that has endured of Muslims is their cruelty to Christians and Black people alike. Some quite recent works, in fact have made the picture much worse, for instance, making 'Muslim piracy,' the most brutal of all deeds, resulting in the mass enslavement of millions of White Christians.[787] Colonisation itself, it is claimed, aimed 'at ending Muslim piracy and cruel treatment of Christians, and putting an end to Muslim slave trading of Africans, besides, of course, civilising Muslim society.' In another work, this author has looked at the specific subject of piracy, including the treatment of captives.[788] Here this matter will be just summed up, and greater focus given to other issues such as slave trading and racism, comparing Western rhetoric with reality on the ground.

Muslim 'Cruel Captors of Christians'

The era of the Muslim Barbary (Algeria, Tunisia and Libya) corsairs (16th-18th centuries), with its large number of Western Christian captives, coincides with the intensification of such depictions. According to Postel (ca. 1550) Christians in North Africa suffered

> 'An infinity of martyrdoms' and the seamen thought Algiers 'that Citie fatall to all Christians and the butchery of all mankind.'[789]

Printed accounts of Turkish or Barbary galleys attacking Christian merchants confirm the Western stereotypes associating Islam with acts of violence, treachery, cruelty, and wrath.[790] From the Saracen knights of medieval romance to the Barbary pirates and Turkish pashas of early modern 'report,' tales of hostage taking and

---

[787] R.C. Davis: *Christian Slaves, Muslim Masters: White Slavery in the Mediterranean, the Barbary Coast and Italy, 1500-1800*; Palgrave McMillan; 2003.
[788] *Barbary Pirates*; MSBN BOOKS; 2017.
[789] In N. Daniel: *Islam, Europe;* op cit; p. 14.
[790] N. Matar: The Renegade in English 17th century Imagination, cited in D.J. Vitkus: Early Modern Orientalism: Representations of Islam in 16th and 17th century Europe; in *Western Perceptions* (Banks-Frassetto ed); pp. 207-30; p. 221.

captivity have been emphasised in Western narratives about the Islamic world.[791] These

> Islamic villains usually come to a violent end, howling obscene curses and shrieking as their souls go straight to hell.[792]

This myth easily found its way into 17th century popular culture.[793] A newsletter of 1640 speaks of 3000 English in

> Miserable captivity, undergoing insufferable labour, such as rowing in galleys, drawing carts, grinding in mills, with diverse such un-Christian like work most lamentable to express, and most burdensome to undergo, withal suffering much hunger and many blows on their bare bodies, by which cruelty many, not being able to undergo it, have been forced to turn Mahomedan.[794]

In literature and legend, Islamic 'Saracens, Turks and Moors' frequently appear as ranting, irrational, fanatical killers who practice treachery, oath-breaking, double-dealing, enslavement, piracy, and terrorism.[795]

The biggest fear was that captured Christians would lose their faith to Islam, and be damned for eternity, a conversion equated with every form of crime. Samuel Hartib confirmed in his 'Remonstrance of 1644 that poverty made 'Many who would live honestly to cheat, lie, steal, kill, turn Turk, or anything.'[796]

Matar notes how:

> When a money collector entered a village public house and church, he told tales of horror about the captors, thereby projecting a frightening image of the Turks and Moors. The certificates often included a formula warning people that unless they offered money, the captives would remain un-ransomed and would subsequently 'turn Turk' and so be lost to their families and country. To villagers whose knowledge of the 'Mahumetans' may have exclusively derived from wandering players or parish preachers, the collector provided what might have seemed as the most authentic description of Muslims: cruel infidels who compelled Christians, with torture and savagery, to renounce their much-loved God and monarch.[797]

These depictions and fears associated with them lasted until the colonial period. French colonisation of North Africa used piracy and cruel treatment of Christians as justifications.

Today, we are treated to the images of Western hostages about to be beheaded by 'Muslim' extremists (oddly enough always masked, although telling us on their web-

---

[791] N. Matar: The Renegade; op cit; p. 221.
[792] D.J. Vitkus: Early Modern Orientalism: Representations of Islam; op cit; p. 221.
[793] M. Morsy: *North Africa 1800-1900*; (Longman; London; 1984); pp. 72-3.
[794] Calendar of State Papers Domestic 1640, p. 231; in C. Lloyd: *English Corsairs on the Barbary Coast;* (Collins; London; 1981); p. 124.
[795] See N. Matar: The Renegade; op cit; p. 221.
[796] S. Hartib: *The Hartib Papers*; CD Rom; (1995).
[797] N. Matar: Introduction; in *Piracy, Slavery, and Redemption*; edited by D.J. Vitkus; (Columbia University Press; New York); 2001; p. 25.

sites who they are. Such images reinforce the bestial side of Muslims, which, of course, makes the task of their slayers a noble one.

True, many Muslims are truly vile individuals, and in every respect. However, when comparing the conditions of captives, both Muslims and Christians, especially during the period when large numbers of Christians fell into Muslim captivity, we realise the more enviable Christian fate in Muslim captivity, and the far harsher lot of Muslims.

a. Muslims under Christian Captivity

In the medieval period considerable numbers of Muslims fell under Christian captivity. As a rule, all Muslims were put to death except those few deemed worth enslaving. In 1191, for instance, Acre was retaken by the Christians who had not just the defenders beheaded but the whole population (something hardly any historian mentions today).[798] At the very decisive battle of Navas de Tolosa, in 1212, Al-Nasir's much superior Muslim army was crushed. In the wake of battle, 70,000 Muslim prisoners were slaughtered at the order of the Bishops of Toledo and Narbonne who were at the scene.[799] In contrast, not long before, on 18th July, 1195, Abu Yusuf Yaqub al-Mansur inflicted a crushing defeat on Alfonso VIII of Castile at Alarcos.[800] After the victory, Abu Yusuf freed twenty thousand Christian prisoners without even demanding a ransom.[801]

If and when Muslims were not slain, their fate was not enviable either. The late 12th century Muslim traveller, Ibn Jubayr, who went to crusader-held territory, devoted some of his most emotional lines to a description of the captive Muslim men stumbling in shackles and doing hard labour like slaves, and the captive Muslim women plodding along with iron rings on their legs.[802] Muslims had been enslaved during the crusader conquest and many were captured and enslaved again during subsequent warfare.[803] Muslims seeking to escape risked losing their legs when caught.[804]

Subsequently, in the so-called Barbary Corsair era (16th-18th centuries), the treatment of Muslim captives remained equally bad.[805] In their galleys, the French tried West African Blacks and Iroqois Indians, both unsuccessfully; and the elites of

---

[798] P.W. Edbury: *The Conquest of Jerusalem and the Third Crusade*, (Scolar Press, 1996); p. 97. F. Guizot: *History of France*; London; 1872; 8 vols; p. 439 fwd; E. Gibbon: *The Decline and Fall*; op cit; VI; p. 119. M. Hodgson: *The Venture*, op cit; p. 267.
[799] T.B. Irving: Dates, Names and Places: The end of Islamic Spain; in *Revue d'Histoire Maghrebine*; No 61-62; 1991; pp. 77-93; at p. 81.
[800] J. Glubb: *A Short History*; op cit; p. 190.
[801] Ibid.
[802] Ibn Jubayr: Travels; p. 322; in B. Z. Kedar: The Subjected Muslims of the Frankish Levant, in *Muslims Under Latin Rule, 1100-1300*, ed J.M. Powell (Princeton University Press, 1990), pp. 135-74; at p. 153.
[803] In B. Z. Kedar: The Subjected Muslims; op cit; p. 153.
[804] Ibid; p. 170.
[805] P. Earle: *Corsairs of Malta and Barbary*; (Sidgwick and Jackson; London; 1970).

such galleys remained the Muslims of North Africa.[806] Turkish or North African slaves were always preferred for galleys, particularly those of France, because they were a tougher breed than convicts.[807] Experts considered the Turks, and especially the North Africans, to have no equal as rowers, and it was felt essential to have at least one Muslim slave per bench.[808] Spanish, Neapolitan, and Papal galleys were also a destination for Muslim slaves sold in Malta.[809] The life of a galley slave has been described by a Frenchman who had experienced it:

> Picture to yourself six men chained to a bench, naked as they were born, one foot on the stretcher, the other lifted and placed against the bench in front of him, supporting in their hands a heavy oar and stretching their bodies backward while their arms were extended to push the loom of the oar clear of the backs of those in front of them... sometimes the galley slaves row ten, twelve and even twenty hours at a stretch, without the slightest rest or break. On these occasions the officer will go round and put pieces of bread soaked in wine into the mouths of the wretched rowers to prevent them from fainting. Then the captain will call upon the officers to redouble their blows, and if a slave falls exhausted over his oar (which is quite a common occurrence) he is flogged until he appears to be dead and is thrown overboard without ceremony.[810]

Christians who had converted to Islam, when caught, were handed over to the Inquisition.[811]

As Lloyd points out, compared with the hard life of a seaman on board a merchant vessel, not to say the navy which was worse, a common seaman cannot have found life in bagnio (Muslim prison) much harder, certainly as many have left on record, it was preferable to life in a European gaol.[812] Edward Coxere, who was freed after Blake bombarded the port of Tunis, became a Quaker and, as soon as he returned home, was imprisoned under the Conventicle Act. This is how he compared his captivity in Yarmouth prison with that of Tunis:

> They allowed us water enough to drink, but nothing to eat, nor bread to be brought us, nor nobody to come near us... Such unkind usage I never had when I was a slave under the hands of the Turks, such as Christians call Infidels, that though I was chained a nights with great iron chain, and was made to work a days, and sometimes beat, yet they gave me bellyful of bread to eat with my water; but here, among my countrymen and such as called

---

[806] See for instance: P. Bamford: Slaves for the galleys of France; 1665-1700; in John Parker (ed) *Merchants and Scholars*; (Minneapolis; 1965); and Ibid: The Procurement of Oarsmen for the French galleys; 1660-1748; *American Historical Review*; Lxv (1959).
[807] C. Lloyd: *English Corsairs*; op cit; p. 146.
[808] P. Earle: *Corsairs of Malta and Barbary*; op cit; p. 170.
[809] Ibid.
[810] Quot Bradford 33.
[811] C. Lloyd: *English Corsairs*; op cit; p. 146.
[812] Ibid; pp. 25-6.

> Christians, they gave me not the privilege as they gave their dogs, for they would deny anyone to give them a crust of bread.[813]

We shall see that Christians in Muslim captivity could obtain their freedom and did so nearly always. It was quite the reverse for Muslims in Christian captivity. Earle speaks about a Muslim slave from Damietta who petitioned for his freedom in 1682. He said that he had been a slave for fifty four years, fifty of which he had spent as an oarsman in the galleys.[814] On two occasions he had been promised his liberty for special services. The first was at the battle of the Dardanelles in 1656. Twenty years later he was again promised his liberty for his services in burying infected slaves during the plague of 1676. Neither of these promises had been honoured, however, and

> Now the poor supplicant is over eighty years old and desires to finish his life in his own country, for which reason he begged that 'he could be placed in the number of old slaves who are being sent to liberty as a result of alms sent from Barbary.[815]

There is an interesting account of the end of the Muslim captives in Malta:

> In 1749, an alleged slave plot led to a trial when nearly all the slaves were condemned to death. They were tortured and executed in batches. Most of the 'Infidels' were marched through the streets of Valetta and led to high scaffolds erected in the public squares on which they were birched, branded and finally hanged, beheaded or quartered. Those who consented to be baptised were put to death without further torture. These cruel scenes went on for a whole month, the (Christian) knights showing themselves pitiless avengers.[816]

The Inquisition was a medieval Catholic invention. Its purpose was to remove 'heretics' from the midst of Christians. Its main victims were the Muslims and Jews. Generally, they ended up tortured in dungeons, confessing whatever their accusers sought to make them confess, burnt at the stake, or disappeared for ever, their properties confiscated, their families thrown into perpetual want.[817] The following extracts say:

> The Inquisitors felt it their duty to investigate their (the Muslims' and Jews') minds, and to eliminate anyone whose words or deeds confirmed their suspicion. Their methods were even more callous and efficient than the ones which had been employed by the medieval Inquisition in France. According to Mariana:

---

[813] E. Coxere: *Adventures by Sea*; ed., E.H.W. Meyerstein; (1945); p. 100.
[814] P. Earle: *Corsairs of Malta and Barbary*; op cit; pp. 171-2.
[815] *Archives of the Order of Malta*; 646; p. 215.
[816] T. Zammit: *History of Malta*; (Valetta; 1929); p. 248.
[817] H.C. Lea: *The Moriscos of Spain*; (Burt Franklin; New York; 1968 reprint). H. C. Lea: *A History of the Inquisition of Spain*, 4 vols; (The Mac Millan Company, New York, 1907).

> What caused the most surprise was that children paid for the crimes of their parents, and that accusers were not named or made known, nor confronted by the accused, nor was there publication of witnesses: all of which was contrary to the practice used of old in other tribunals…. And what was most serious was that because of these secret investigations, they were deprived of the liberty to hear and talk freely, since in all cities, towns and villages there were persons placed to give information of what went on. This was considered by some the most wretched slavery and equal to death.[818]

Countless numbers of Muslims, tens of thousands, at least, were burnt alive at the stake. Even in their death, the Muslims had crowds standing armed with stones ready to throw at them as soon as they began reciting their final prayers.[819]

The treatment of Muslim prisoners during the colonial period as in French Algeria (1954-1962) is well documented as in works by Alleg *et al*:

> Claude Lecerf resides in a camp, where between 150 and 200 Algerians are crammed, waiting for their deaths, sleeping on straw-covered floors. Every day and every night, more operations bring in more prisoners. Above the camp is situated the interrogation centre, where torture is systematic, many leaving in a coma, many more dying under torture. The soldiers load the corpses into trucks and take them for mass burial somewhere in the countryside.
> At night the paratroopers force their way inside homes, which they ransack and loot,… (and bring in more prisoners).
> Often, 'attempts to escape by prisoners' are simulated; then the prisoners are shot in the back…
> Lecerf has seen many killings of prisoners in cold blood. One evening, Captain P gathers prisoners, gives them lessons on morality, and then shoots two in the head. Other officers fire in the air in direction of the rest, who run, and get cut by barbed wire… That was a recreation for the French….
> All over the city (of Algiers), more prisoners are brought in to more camps. Those who have been tortured are taken out to identify more suspects. They have their heads covered in black cagoules, with two openings for their eyes. Traitors, perhaps, but surely people who because of torture have lost all control and mind. Their task is to point at others in the crowd of Algerians, who are then picked, thrown into trucks, just like dogs, and conducted to more centres for torture…
> On top of torture, prisoners are disappeared in their thousands, the general secretary of Algiers prefecture citing the figure of 3,000 disappeared before the end of March 1957, and the countless thousands more who were not even counted… Interrogation centres abound, in villas, private apartments, farms, sites under construction, caves…

---

[818] A. Thomson-M.A. Rahim: *Islam in Andalus;* op cit; p. 121.
[819] H.C. Lea: *The Moriscos of Spain*; op cit. H. C. Lea: *A History of the Inquisition of Spain*, op cit.

Anyone who faints during torture is executed. The rule is that someone who had been tortured could not be liberated. The same is applied to intellectuals. At night more sorties are carried out in covered trucks, collecting in all centres of interrogation the countless many. Everyone is thrown on board, the half dead from torture included, all taken to large mass graves, and there the men of unit O liquidate everyone with pistols and knives... Others are taken by helicopters above the sea, and there, a large piece of concrete is tied to their feet, and they are thrown down never to resurface again. There are also many buildings being erected, and in the concrete, in the foundations of these buildings, many corpses are buried.'[820]

During the recent war on terror between 2001 and 2010, Muslim captives in their hundreds at least, if not thousands, completely vanished as if earth had swallowed them.[821] Abu Ghreib, Guantanamo Bay, and Baghram Airport are the best-known instances of mass mistreatment of Muslims. In Iraq, as in many other countries, the dirtiest work: torture and extra-judicial killings of thousands of suspects and 'insurgents' was done by proxies' death squads[822] (which Western and other media attributed to sectarian or terrorist killings). Countless numbers of Muslims who sought refuge in the West were delivered to 'Muslim' regimes who then proudly showed Westerners how to do it: drilling, cutting, burning, raping, and one or two other unsavoury acts.[823]

b. Christians in Muslim Captivity:

The picture of innocent Christian victims impaled outside Muslim city gates is still revived occasionally, symbol of Muslim mistreatment of Christians during the Pirates era.[824] Earle and Bono,[825] Matar, Belhamissi,[826] and above all Fisher, the rare historians who compared Muslim and Christian misdeeds at sea, condemned this Barbary corsair legend and its cruelties.[827] Other than the usual Christian propaganda, stories of Muslim cruelties were by professionals concerned with raising money for ransom, and from escaped prisoners selling their adventures in a popular market that expected sensation.[828] This is noted by Cervantes who in his

---

[820] H. Alleg, J. de Bonis; H.J. Douzon; J. Freire; P. Haudiquet: *La Guerre d'Algerie*, (Temps Actuels; Paris; 1981); vol 2; pp. 463 ff.
[821] See various reports by Human Rights Agencies in 2005-6 on such disappeared Muslims.
[822] See various sources already cited above (as in chapter one), and The Times online - January 10 2005 (http://www.timesonline.co.uk/tol/news/world/iraq/article410491.ece).
[823] The issue of rendering prisoners to these countries, and plane flights carrying prisoners between the West and other parts, has been widely publicised in 2006; See G. Monbiot in *The Guardian* 8 May 07; p. 25.
[824] BBC 2: Timewatch; 10 January 2003.
[825] P. Earle: *Corsairs of Malta and Barbary*; op cit; S. Bono: *I Corsari Barbareschi*; (Torino; 1964).
[826] Moulay Belhamissi: Captifs Chretiens en Algerie a l'Epoque Ottomane: Histoire ou hysterie? in *Le Maghreb a l'Epoque Ottomane*; ed. A El-Moudden; (Casablanca; 1995); pp. 75-84.
[827] G. Fisher: *The Barbary legend*; op cit.
[828] N. Daniel: *Islam, Europe*; op cit; p. 14.

Persiles shows false captives busy cheating 'curious crowds.'[829] Much, thus, was made by propagandists in Europe to stress the hardships of life in 'this Gulag Archipelago of the Mediterranean,' Lloyd says.[830] Rehbinder was particularly scathing about the Catholic priests and their bigoted anti-Islamic writings.[831] This was particularly true of the Redemptionist fathers who told lies about the condition of the slaves 'in order to excite the charity of the faithful.'[832] De Tassy explains that:

> It is normal that those whose duty is to buy off slaves had great interest to arouse great emotions within a public from whom they expect donations... They vaunt the services they render to the public by going to Barbary to redeem bogus slaves, who roam the world as beggars and tell tales of their slavery in North Africa.[833]

The 'Peres Redempteurs' were concerned to present the North Africans in the worst possible light in order to arouse their readers' sympathies and to raise the money to buy back the captives who, in their eyes, risked not only their lives, but most of all their salvation at the hands of the 'Infidels.'[834] The aim was also, above all, to excite Christian zeal against the Muslim 'Infidel.'[835] A French Marine Commissary who lived in Algiers in the first half of the eighteenth century and dedicated his book on Algiers to the French Consul in that city, while recognizing the relatively 'uncivilized' or unpolished character of life in Algiers, flatly denied that Christian captives were in general badly treated. Having himself been a prisoner of war of the Spanish in 1706, he says that he 'would prefer ten years of slavery in Algiers to one in Spain.'[836]

In his account of captivity, Richard Haleston recalled the torture he had endured under his Catholic captors (on the rack and in solitary confinement) and the kindness shown to him by an old Algerian who protected and fed him. Meanwhile, his wife was going around London describing his 'most vile slavery and miserable bondage,' not under the Catholics, but under the Algerians.[837] A contemporary, De La Croix, insists:

> We should agree, it is better to fall in the hands of the worst Bey (Turk) galley, than in the hands of the Viceroy of Naples.[838]

The general behaviour of the Muslim corsairs when capturing a ship was very much better than that of their Maltese rivals, and incomparably better than that of a contemporary English privateer.[839] Fisher notes the contrast drawn by Sir Henry

---

[829] In D. Brahimi: *Opinions et regards;* op cit; p. 122.
[830] C. Lloyd: *English Corsairs on the Barbary Coast;* op cit; p. 116.
[831] Rehbinder: *Nachrichten und Bemerkungen uber den algierischen Staat,* 3 vols. (Altona, 1798-1800); vol 1; pp. 9 fwd.
[832] Chevalier d'Arvieux: *Memoires;* (Paris; 1735); iii; p. 458.
[833] Laugier de Tassy *Histoire du Royaume d'Alger;* (Amsterdam; 1725), in Denise Brahimi: *Opinions et regards des Europeens;* op cit; p. 122.
[834] A. Thomson: *Barbary and Enlightenment;* op cit. p. 19.
[835] Ibid; p. 26.
[836] Laugier de Tassy: *Histoire du Royaume d'Alger;* (Amsterdam; 1735); p. 329; in N. Barbour: *A Survey of North Africa;* (Oxford University Press; 1959); p. 37.
[837] Guildhall Library; London; Ms 9234/2; in N. Matar: Introduction; op cit; note 101; p. 46.
[838] De la Croix; in N. Daniel: *Islam and the West;* op cit; p. 309.
[839] See, K.R. Andrews: *Elizabethan Privateering;* (Cambridge; 1964); pp. 40-3.

Blount between the barbarism of English seamen and the 'extraordinary civility of the Turks,'[840] which appears to be endorsed by Admiral Badiley, who had a long experience of the Levant trade. At a critical juncture he warned a colleague of the case of a converted Turk who reverted to his old religion after witnessing the excesses on shore of some English sailors.[841]

English writers and observers agree that enslavement on Muslim ships was better than on French, Italian, or Spanish galleys.[842] Some sailors, such as Webbe, Hasleton, and Coxere, experienced captivity at the hands of both Muslim and Christian slave masters and were able to compare treatment: they described far more horrible treatment at the hands of Italian and Spanish captors than that received from North African privateers.[843] In 1635 Henry Kebell wrote that he and his companions would have preferred to

> Have fallen into the Turks' hands than into Frenchmen's, for they [the French] would have hoysed them overboard.[844]

Instead, many of the Christian captives were taken straight on as sailors, divided into batches under the eyes of the soldiers.[845] Although when off duty they were normally confined, they seem to have been chained up only when the ship was actually going into action.[846] Women were almost always well treated. Anyone who touched a woman in a sensual manner ran a very great risk of being bastinadoed.[847] Pananti goes so far as to advise future captives to give any gold or other valuables that they might have to the female passengers 'as the Turks hold their persons sacred.'[848]

On land, Christian captives lived in huge bagnios or courtyards under the direction of a guardian or a warden Pasha and a guard of janissaries. By the 17th century, the bigger bagnos were able to provide considerable comforts that must have made the life of a slave much easier to bear.[849] Captives were put to work in household service, in farming, gardening, building, animal husbandry, or in business.[850]

> We were suffered to work upon any manner of trade or occupation wherein we were any way expert... and what we did or made, we sold to the Turks, and they gave us money for the same [wrote Edward Webbe in 1591.][851]

The 18th century Spanish captive, Joseph de Leon, stated that there were captives who worked in shops, as he did, and in steel and ammunition factories, while others

---

[840] G. Fisher: *Barbary Legend*; op cit; p. 129.
[841] T.A. Spalding: *Life of Admiral Badiley*; (Westminster; 1899); p. 135.
[842] See, for instance, E. Neau: *An Account of the Sufferings of the French Protestants*; (London; 1699).
[843] N. Matar: Introduction; op cit; p. 21.
[844] *CSPD; Charles 1, 1634-5*, 7:325, in N. Matar: Introduction; op cit; p. 21.
[845] See experience of the American sailor John Foss: *A Journal of the captivity and suffering of John Foss; several years prisoner at Algiers*; (Newburyport; 1798); p. 9.
[846] P. Dan: *Histoire de la Barbarie et de ses corsairs*; (Paris; 1637); p. 262.
[847] P. Grandchamp: Une Mission delicate en Barbarie au XVII em siecle: J.B. Salvago, drogman Venitien, a Alger et a Tunis; *Revue Tunisienne*; xxx (1937); p. 473.
[848] F. Pananti: *Narrative of a residence in Algiers*; (1818); p. 355.
[849] S. Bono: *I Corsari barbareschi*; op cit; pp. 225-49 discusses the life of slaves.
[850] N. Matar: introduction; op cit; p. 18.
[851] E. Webbe: *The Rare and most wonderful things....* Edited by E. Arber; (London; Alex Murray and Son; 1868); p. 27.

opened taverns in which both captives and Moors congregated.[852] In the bagnos there was usually a chapel and a hospital, where father Dan noted that seven priests celebrated Mass at an improvised altar before dawn to 600 captives.[853] Chapels, Catholic, Protestant, and Orthodox, served mainly by captured priests or visiting Redemptionist fathers were found in most bagnos, shops and medical facilities were provided, and later slave hospitals were built, and there was even the possibility of relaxation.[854] One should add that women and priest captives in the 'Barbary Coast' were exempted from work.[855]

Many captives commented on the latitude shown to them by their Muslim captors, the like of which was never regularly shown to Muslim captives in England, Spain or France.[856] Thomas Smith recalled his captivity in Algiers as 'the happy time of my slavery,' Francis Knight had 'an honest moral man' for a captor, and William Okeley was tempted not to escape to England, where there was civil unrest and poverty, but to stay instead with his captors who had gainfully employed him.[857] Joshua Gee recalled the generosity of one captor who shared his food with him; Joseph Pitts was adopted by his last master, who treated him as his son.[858] Nash and Parker, two merchants, were captives in Sallee (Morocco) for four years, during which time they learned the language and trade of the country, and then

> Set up a House in Tetuan in the Year that the English quitted Tangier [1684], which House has continued ever since; and it is said those Gentlemen before they left Barbary got better fortunes in it, than they lost by being taken.[859]

Chevalier d'Arvieux wrote of his experiences in the Regency of Tunis as an envoy of Louis XIV in that country between 1665-1675, where he helped secure the freedom of Christian slaves through negotiations with the Turks. When he negotiated a treaty at Tunis in 1666 he was surprised at the tolerance shown to captives and the comforts enjoyed by domestic slaves

> They live very commodiously for their state of life and provided they are willing to work, pretty much at their ease.[860]

His *Memoires* were only published long after his death in 1702, he wrote:

> What I saw in Tunis has convinced me these people are full of humanity, as I witnessed that our slaves on the boats waiting to sail were fed every day (fruit, meat, bread...)... and some of these slaves demanded that they stayed with their masters until the day they left for home; and I agreed.[861]

---

[852] C de la Veronne: *Vie de Moulay Ismail...* (Paris; Paul Geuthner; 1974); pp. 157-8.
[853] C. Lloyd: *English Corsairs on the Barbary Coast*; op cit; p. 115.
[854] S. Bono: *I Corsari barbareschi;* op cit; pp. 225-49.
[855] M. Morsy: *North Africa 1800-1900*; op cit; p. 66.
[856] N. Matar: Introduction; op cit; p. 19.
[857] Ibid.
[858] Ibid; p. 20.
[859] Captain Braithwaite: *The History of the Revolutions in the Empire of Morocco;* (London; 1729); p. 67.
[860] D'Arvieux: *A Levantine Adventurer* by W.H. Lewis; (1962); p. 124.
[861] Chevalier D'Arvieux (1995): Tunis: Le sort des esclaves chretiens; pp. 457-61; vol iii: in Denise Brahimi: *Opinions et regards des Europeens sur le Maghreb aux 17em et 18em siecles*; (SNED; Algiers; 1978); pp. 75-6.

D'Arvieux said of the slaves of Mehmed Beg, the son of the Pasha of Tunis, that they were so well treated that they had forgotten their own country, 'where they knew they would never be so much at their ease, as they were with him.'[862] As Earle insists, often, indeed, it might be hard to tell who was a slave and who was master, so important did the slave become in the domestic economy of Islam. It is therefore wise, he advises, 'to treat with caution the horrific descriptions of the life of slaves in Barbary.'[863] Many Christian captives did so well under Muslim captivity that they had no desire to leave. A captive who had made a success of business in 'Barbary' might well pay off his ransom, and continue as a free Christian merchant.[864] One can mention the examples of the American John Cathcart who, as a captive in Algiers, became relatively wealthy by running taverns (which Christians, though prisoners, were allowed to do) and who, when freed, asked to be posted to North Africa; he thus became the USA's first consul in Tripoli in 1799.[865] The American consul named that same year in Algiers, Richard O'Brien, had also been a slave there for ten years, whilst Simon Lucas, British consul in Tripoli (1793-1801), had been a captive in Morocco.[866]

Many of the Christian captives not only did not return home, but also converted to Islam, and settled permanently in the Muslim world.[867] In the 'Barbary States' the 'renegados' (i.e. converts to Islam) rose to high positions, whilst in Turkey itself, Polish, Hungarian, and other Eastern Europeans entered the stream of Islamic life.[868] After learning of the large number of Christian converts who had risen in power and prominence in Algeria and Tunisia, Robert Burton concluded that the Christians who 'will turn Turk... shall be entertained as brother.'[869] When the Scottish traveller, William Lithgow, visited the Englishman Captain Ward in 1616 in North Africa, Ward was living in great style, retired from the sea and enjoying the fruits of his labours. He had 'turned Turk' and built there an exquisite palace, beautified with rich marble and alabaster stones.[870] Chevalier D'Arvieux also describes the pomp and status the slave Don Manuel attained in Tunisia in the 1660s.[871] A few Christian renegades acquired even greater power, even becoming Bey or Dey, (i.e. the country's leaders or regional governors.)[872] All these stories, as Matar points out, explain why the Algerian scholar Moulay Belhamissi has insisted that the study of captivity accounts should discriminate between what is "histoire"

---

[862] L. D'Arvieux: *Memoires du Chevalier d'Arvieux*; op cit; p. 499.
[863] P. Earle: *Corsairs of Malta and Barbary*; op cit; p. 82.
[864] Ibid; p. 91.
[865] M. Morsy: *North Africa 1800-1900*; op cit; p. 66.
[866] Ibid.
[867] N. Matar: Introduction; op cit; p. 2.
[868] In N. Daniel: *Islam, Europe and Empire*; op cit; p. 10.
[869] R. Burton: *The Anatomy of Melancholy*; ed Holdbrook Jackson; (London; Dent; 1977); p. 349.
[870] W. Lithgow: *The Total Discourse of the Rare Adventures*; (1632; repr. 1906); p. 315.
[871] L. D'Arvieux: *Memoires du Chevalier d'Arvieux*; op cit; pp. 438-9.
[872] P. Earle: *Corsairs of Malta and Barbary*; op cit; p. 31.

and what is "hysteric," between what actually happened and what captives, their relatives, and modern historians have projected.[873]

Moving forward in time to the period French onslaught on Algeria (1830 onward) little mercy was shown towards the indigenous population. A French officer, on one of the countless expeditions, recounts:

> Order was given to deliver a war of devastation... So our soldiers acted with ferocity... women, children were slaughtered, homes burnt down, trees razed to the ground, nothing was spared... Kabyle women wore silver bracelets to the arms and around their ankles. Soldiers cut off all their limbs, and they did not always do it to the dead only.[874]

And yet, when Emir Abdelkader (who led the resistance against the French), freeing his French prisoners said to them: 'I have nothing to feed you; I cannot kill you, thus I send you back home....' the prisoners full of admiration for the Emir, according to the French general St Arnaud: 'had their minds diseased,' and had been 'brainwashed.'[875]

Muslim 'Pitiless Slave Traders'

Denouncing 'Muslim slave trading' and praising the role of both Church and Empire in its abolition, H.A.L. Fisher writes:

> The Destruction of the Portuguese slave trade within the western hemisphere was made possible only by the vigour of the British navy.
> There remained the difficult and almost intractable problem of liberating Africa from the Arab slave gangs and the domestic slave trade which was carried on in the heart of the continent. A system of marine patrols, however excellent - and in the forties a sixth of the British navy was employed on the African patrol work - was clearly inadequate to cope with so vast an evil. The career of David Livingstone, the Scottish missionary, who, mostly on foot and with few native companions, crossed Africa between 1853 and 1856, opened out a new epoch and pointed to a new way. Livingstone's African journeys brought home to the imagination of the British public the horrors of the Arab slave trade, which had its centre in Zanzibar, and led to the revival of the Abolitionist activity, the first fruit of which was the treaty between Britain and Zanzibar in 1873, which closed the great slave mart in that city.[876]

---

[873] Moulay Belhamissi: *Captifs Chretiens en Algerie a l'Epoque Ottomane: Histoire ou hysterie?* in *Le Maghreb a l'Epoque Ottomane*; ed. A El-Moudden; (Casablanca; 1995); pp. 75-84; in N. Matar: Introduction op cit; p. 20.
[874] P. Gaffarel: *l'Algerie: Histoire, conquete et colonisation*, ed. F. Didot, (1883); in H.H. Alleg; et al: *La Guerre d'Algerie*, op cit; p. 77.
[875] General St Arnaud in a letter of 16 May 1842.
[876] H.A.L. Fisher: *A History of Europe (from the Beginning of the 18th century to 1937)*; (Eyre and Spottiswoode; London; 1952); p. 1033.

Cardinal Lavigerie, who played the leading role in seeking to spread Christianity in Algeria during French colonisation of the country (1830-1962), explains that:

> The expansion of this evil (slave trade) is due initially to the traditions of the Muslims of North Africa, those of Egypt and Turks. The Mahometans cannot, for reasons of debauchery and laziness, do without slaves, who infuse them with new strength and new blood.... Reducing a Negro to slavery, I was going to say, is one of their fundamental religious rules. They teach in their Qur'an that the Negro does not belong to the human race; that he is between man and the animal, even lower than the latter.... He (the Muslim) finds glory in reducing the blacks.[877]

(Where the cardinal found the passages he refers to in the Qur'an is impossible to trace.)

Opposition to Lavigerie enraged him:

> The free thinkers and the Turks of Europe have truly a sad courage when they assert that Mahometanism fights slavery. To the contrary, Islam legitimises slavery, absolutely, here in the Sudan, in Syria, everywhere...[878]

Literary fiction, just like the cinema, abounds with the same depictions. Hassan is the Slaver in Rider Haggard's *Allan and the Holy Flower*, published in 1915. Hassan is cruel and deceitful. Here he is trying to dissuade with lies the Christian hero from advancing inland from the coast:

> The people in the interior are savages of the worst sort, whom hunger has driven to cannibalism.

Here he is attempting a more subtle deceit:

> I see, honoured lord, that you are man of mettle not easily to be turned from your purpose. In the name of God the Compassionate, land and go wheresoever you like.

We easily realise that 'we are in a nest of slave traders, and this Hassan is their leader.' And Hassan uses the language of religion, not only for the benefit of those he hopes to deceive, but naturally, for example, when his slaving is proved: 'God is great!' muttered the discomfited Hassan...

As for the cruelty of the Arabs, it is communal - not confined to Hassan at all - and ingrained...

> These Arabs, being black-hearted, kill those who can walk no more, or tie them up to die. If they let them go, they might recover and escape, and it makes the Arabs sad that those who have been their slaves should live to be free and happy.[879]

---

[877] Cardinal Lavigerie: *lettre sur l'Esclavage Africain, et l'esclavage Africain*, Conferences, Paris, (St Sulpice) and Brussels (Ste Gudule).
[878] In N. Daniel: *Islam; Europe*; op cit; p. 307.
[879] Ibid; p. 302.

Christian Missionaries are the main witnesses of Muslim crimes and cruelties. A Catholic missionary in 1888 describes how an African slave market was crowded with slaves, joined by cords or chains in long lines, and with others, revealing signs of starvation, in the streets. Nearby was a cemetery where the dying as well as the dead were left for the hyenas.[880]

The missionary A.J. Swann, on his way to Lake Tanganyika 'saw' caravans of slaves who had journeyed 1,000 miles and had an additional 250 miles to go, and who were chained by the neck in long files, some of them in six foot forks, and with many of the women bearing babies on their backs. They were in filthy condition and many of them were scarred by the cuts of the hide whip.[881]

Narrative today brings back to life these terrible experiences. Gordon writes:

> Europeans who travelled the Fezzan-Kawar route often recorded with horror the human skeletons with which it was strewn. Blanched bones, usually those of women and children were often piled up around wells, the telltale monuments of desperate effort to reach water.
>
> While on the road, slaves often fell victim to disease or were killed or captured by marauding bands of brigands. The privations of the journey and short rations, often the result of indifference or penny-pinching attitudes of cost-minded merchants, made many of the slaves susceptible to illness and disease. Moving from one disease environment to another in a debilitated physical condition made slaves ready victims of contagious diseases such as cholera and smallpox. An epidemic among slaves in transit, whether by land or sea, was much to be feared. A caravan afflicted by smallpox might be condemned to wander in the desert, like a plague ship, shunned by all.[882]

Gordon, in fact, is the guru who inspires and feeds others with the truth, acting a bit a la Toby E. Huff, or Renan, or whoever leads in any field and to whom everyone refers in such a field. So, let's listen to this guru. In *Slavery in the Arab World*.[883] Gordon opens his book in capital letters, as follows:

'SLAVERY IN THE ARAB WORLD ANTEDATED BY MORE THAN a millennium the establishment of this appalling institution by Europeans in the New World. It continued to flourish, moreover, for more than a century after the tocsin had sounded for it in the West. As many as eleven million Africans, approximately the same number estimated to have been taken from Africa's West Coast in the European-controlled triangular slave trade, were forcibly removed from their families and communities to do service in Arab households, harems and armies.

Despite the long history of slavery in the Arab world and in other Muslim lands, little has been written about this human tragedy. Except for the few abolitionists, mainly in England, who railed against Arab slavery and put pressure upon Western governments to end the traffic in slaves, the issue has all but been ignored in the

---
[880] R.W. Beachey: *The Slave Trade of Eastern Africa;* (London; Rex Collings; 1976); p. 187.
[881] A. J. Swann: *Fighting the Slave hunters in Central Africa*; (London; 1910); p. 48.
[882] M. Gordon: *Slavery in the Arab World*; (New Amsterdam; New York; 1989); p. 160.
[883] M. Gordon: *Slavery in the Arab World*; op cit.

West. In contrast to the endless flow of books and articles that have enriched our understanding of slavery and the traffic in slaves from West Africa to the New World, the slavery that for centuries was an integral feature of Arab society has escaped the attention of Western scholars. Ignorance of Arab history or perhaps a bad conscience about the West's shameful record in this sordid business may help account for these vast gaps in Western historiography.

Something better might have been expected of Arab historians. Yet, here too, a conspiracy of silence has prevailed and has blocked out all light on this sensitive subject.'[884]

In Gordon's view, Islam, of course, is to blame for slave trading:

'Arab writers and jurists, to the limited extent that they touched upon slavery, have done so with approval. No moral opprobrium has clung to slavery since it was sanctioned by the Koran and enjoyed an undisputed place in Arab society.'[885]

'The decision by Arab states to abolish slavery during this century was taken for reasons that had little to do with the moral aspects of the issue. Pressure from Western powers, the introduction of a money economy, and the realization that maintaining slavery would forever bar Arab nations from entering the councils of international society provide a much better explanation for their announced policy. That slavery and the slave trade were inherently evil and therefore merited abolition were thoughts alien to Arab heads of state and their followers.'[886]

Then Gordon puts all these points together:

'It is this failure to have consigned slavery to moral oblivion that explains why it endured so long in the Arab world. The perennial character of this social institution ultimately rested on religiously-inspired values - a point that few Arabs were prepared to challenge. And because slavery was never questioned from a moral standpoint, it should be no surprise that it still persists in Mauritania and in the Sudan....

Slavery and slave-raiding, which never really died out in the Sudan, have reappeared on a large scale in the disaffected southern region of the country which has been fighting off and on for autonomy against the Muslim-dominated North. In 1987, the head of International Catholic Mission confirmed reports of widespread slave-raiding in the southern Sudan that was being carried out by armed Arab militias... According to this source, as well as accounts by journalists and scholars, hundreds if not thousands of people have been carried off by slave traffickers. The great majority of the victims are children between the ages of eight and fourteen who are forced to march from their native lands to the North where they are sold into slavery.... Can it be merely a coincidence that the prime minister of the Sudan, who is committed to a policy of imposing Islamic Shari'a law on the country, is Sadek al-Mahdi, whose great-grandfather defeated the British a century ago and revived the slave trade?

---

[884] Ibid; pp. ix-x.
[885] Ibid; p. x.
[886] Ibid.

To many Arabs, the issue of slavery is a source of discomfort. To speak out against it would be to impugn a tenet of Koranic law; to condone slavery would give offence to Africans whose ancestors and not-too-distant relatives in recent times fell victim to Arab slave traders and their agents. As a result, they instinctively keep silent on the subject, which to this day is a source of pain and humiliation for many Africans.'[887]

Gordon insists:

'IT IS A CURIOUS TWIST TO THE STUDY OF THE SLAVE TRADE that historians have conducted their inquiries into this nefarious traffic from the perspectives of the Americas and the sugar islands of the Caribbeans. Almost irresistibly, their attention has been drawn to the transatlantic trade which, from the middle of the fifteenth century down to the third quarter of the 1800s, brought an estimated ten million blacks across the Atlantic Ocean to work the plantations and mines of the New World. It was this traffic in blacks from Africa's West Coast, initiated by the Portuguese in 1441, that provided the labour that fuelled the rapid economic development of Brazil and the old American South; it made possible the growth of the plantations in Jamaica, Barbados, Hispaniola, St. Lucia, and the other islands in the Caribbean where sugar fortunes grew....

Yet, centuries before the first ship flying the flag of a European country slipped out from one of the numerous inlets along Africa's West Coast laden with human cargo, the peoples of North Africa, Arabia, and the Persian Gulf were forcibly transferring large numbers of blacks down the Nile to Egypt and across the network of the vast Saharan trade routes from West and Central Africa to the countries of the Maghreb. And decades after the last slave ship sailed westward to the Americas and the West Indies, where slavery had been abolished by the early 1870s, Arab dhows were furtively moving out of Zanzibar, Mombasa, and other East African ports, following the familiar Indian Ocean routes for the consignment of "ebony." The masters of these fast lateen-rigged ships, which were methodically packed in sardine-like fashion with men, women, and children, manoeuvred skilfully in evading the small force of British sloops charged with the impossible mission of interdicting this illicit traffic. The blacks caught up in this trade were fated to be sold in the slave marts of Arabia, the Persian Gulf, the Ottoman Empire, and India.

Relatively little has been written about this facet of the slave trade. Although the number of blacks who fell victim to Muslim slave traders can never be determined, there is little doubt that the figures ran to several millions over the centuries that the traffic was carried on....

So thoroughly were many parts of the region combed by Arab slavers that whole areas were depopulated. Africa was exporting its human capital through other routes as well...'[888]

Then, Gordon makes the following point:

---

[887] Ibid; pp. x-xi.
[888] Ibid; pp. 1-5.

'Focusing on the Muslim-dominated trade could do very little to show the Europeans and Americans in a bad light. Except in certain instances, as when French and Portuguese merchants acquired slaves from Arab traders for their sugar plantations in the Mascarene Islands and Brazil, European slave traders had little to do with their Arabian counterparts. The Arab slave traders operated within fairly well-established commercial circuits which were oriented mainly to supplying the demands of Muslim countries. It was this vast market that provided the underpinnings of the slave trade in West, Central, and East Africa.

Beginning in the nineteenth century, the European maritime nations, led by England and gradually joined by others, used their power to curtail and finally end the Muslim traffic in slaves. This laudable objective, which was later merged with narrow colonial ambitions, prompted these powers to suppress slavery itself in Africa. British diplomacy, often backed by naval power, contributed much to getting Muslim leaders in Oman, Persia, Zanzibar, and the Ottoman Empire to put an end to slavery in these lands. As shall be seen, it took England the better part of the nineteenth century to rid the Indian Ocean of the traffic in slaves....

In the light of this, writing about the Muslim role in the slave trade could scarcely evoke bad memories about a Western tie to this trade. The trade was essentially a Muslim enterprise: Arabs hunted for slaves in the vast spaces of Africa or acquired them from middlemen to sell in the markets of the Muslim world. The existence of slavery in Muslim society, and by implication, the traffic in slaves, moreover, found sanction in the Koran and in the Sharia, the body of Islamic law.'[889]

Gordon devotes a whole chapter (Two) to the role of Islam in promoting slavery. He contrasts Islam with Christianity, and holds:

'The weight of Islamic authority in a society where its writ ran far was sufficient to deaden any impulse to challenge slavery on religious grounds. Unlike Western societies, which in their opposition to slavery spawned anti-slavery movements whose numbers and enthusiasm often grew out of church groups, no such grass-roots organisations ever developed in Muslim societies. Muslim countries never knew of dissenting religious groups as the Methodists, Unitarians, and Quakers of eighteenth-century England who railed against the Church of England for finding virtue in slavery. In Muslim politics, the state unquestioningly accepted the teachings of Islam and applied them as law. And lest it be lost sight of, Islam, by sanctioning slavery, however mild a form it generally took, also extended legitimacy to the nefarious traffic in slaves.'[890]

Taking their cue from Gordon, Cox and Marks, tell us,[891]

> Slavery has been associated with some Islamic societies for at least a thousand years and continues to be so into the twenty first century.[892] The

---

[889] Ibid; pp. 7-9.
[890] Ibid; p. 21.
[891] C. Cox-J. Marks: *The West, Islam*; op cit; pp. 39-41.

case of Sudan is particularly well documented.[893] ... Moreover there is ample evidence of the existence of slavery and slave trades with Islam, with major growth taking place in the 18th and 19th centuries: 'The trans-Saharan slave trade increased in volume during the eighteenth and nineteenth centuries. Ottoman rulers in league with Muslim Bornu transported large numbers of slaves across the Sahara into the Ottoman Empire. Many eyewitness accounts talk of substantial loss of lives during the raids and journeys into servitude.[894]

There is some evidence that the scale of the intra-African slave trade is substantially greater in total than that of the Atlantic slave trade which peaked in the eighteenth century and was gradually abolished from the early nineteenth century onwards. Apart from the high loss of lives during the raids and journeys, conservative estimates suggest that between 11 and 14 million Africans were transported into Muslim lands.[895] Yet the number of studies which have been made of the intra-African slave trade is minute in comparison to the voluminous discussion of the Atlantic slave trade.[896] Where slavery has been abolished or diminished in Islamic societies this has almost always been at the instigation of or under pressure from colonial European powers:

'The anti-slavery measures of European colonial powers were generally viewed by Muslims not only as a threat to their very livelihood but also an affront to their religion... Muslims therefore resisted all abolition efforts and chattel slavery persists in Muslim countries today."[897]

.... Finally in discussing slavery it is worth remembering that: It was Europe.... that first decided to set the slaves free: at home, then in the Colonies, and finally in all the world. Western technology made slavery unnecessary; Western ideas made it intolerable.[898]

In January - February 2003, in a programme on the British Empire, the UK television channel, Channel 4,[899] again, insisted that it was Christian zeal that banned slavery and even returned slaves to Africa. Ignoring all evidence to the contrary,[900] and relying on the same source as Fisher above, that is Livingstone, the channel attributed the worst horrors of slave trading to Muslims.[901] Equally, the

---

[892] See: B. Lewis: *Race and Slavery in the Middle East, an Historical Enquiry;* (New York and Oxford University Press; 1990); S. Marmon ed., *Slavery in the Islamic Middle East;* Markus Wiener; (Princeton; 1999); P. Crone: *Slaves on Horses: The Evolution of the Islamic Polity;* (Cambridge University Press; 1980).
[893] C. Cox-J. Marks: *The West, Islam;* op cit; appendix.
[894] J. Azumah: Islam and Slavery; *Centre for Islamic Studies;* (London Bible College; 1999); p. 3. See also J. Azumah: *The Legacy of Arab Islam in Africa;* (Oneworld Publication; 2001).
[895] M. Gordon: *Slavery in the Arab World;* op cit; p. ix.
[896] H. Thomas: *The Slave Trade; The History of the Atlantic Slave Trade 1440-1870;* (Simon and Shuster; 1997), and sources cited herein.
[897] J. Azumah: Islam and Slavery; op cit; p. 5.
[898] B. Lewis: *Cultures in Conflict;* (Oxford University Press; 1995); p. 72.
[899] Seen on S4C; 18 February 2003; 12.10 am.
[900] See. R. B. Smith: *Mohammed;* op cit; pp. 350-2.
[901] Seen on S4C; 18 February 2003; 12.10 am.

BBC religious programme *Everyman* devoted a special programme to Christian missionaries freeing 'Black African slaves' from 'Muslim slave traders.'[902] In this programme, hundreds of 'African slaves' are shown sitting on the ground, under a tree, awaiting the arrival of the two Muslim slave traders to collect the payment of their ransom from the missionaries. Once the two men arrive, and once the payment is done, the two slave traders (bearing no weapons of any sort) give orders to the hundred or so slaves seated on the ground to go free to the great joy of their relatives and the missionaries. Then the two Muslim slave traders walk back north.[903] One would have thought they owned at least a camel to ride back to their Islamic haunts.

Films from Hollywood, scholarly books for children or college students, and the internet, all equally dwell on the Muslim slave trade of Africans and its horrors. In the film Ashanti, the Muslim is the vile, cruel, deceitful, cowardly slave trader. The hero, of course is the Western man. Black slaves in America, except in Tarentino's film (Jango Unchained), are, on the other hand, quite happy in their Christian households.

Now, the Facts

Without a doubt, there were Muslim slave traders, and surely many Muslims today still dream of having slaves that they could do whatever they like with, maybe even hang them if they spoiled the soup.
In Islam, whether in the Qur'an, as anyone can find, in the Tradition of the Prophet or in practice, reality contradicts the claims under the previous heading.
The Prophet is reported to have said:
    'The worst of men is the seller of men.'[904]
One of his first deeds was to free his slave Zeyd, who eventually died commanding a Muslim army. Abu Bakr, the closest companion to Mohammed, and the First caliph of Islam (632-634), in the early days of Islam devoted about all his wealth to buying the freedom of slaves from their Arab masters, especially the cruellest amongst them.[905]
Captives, if they became Muslims, were set free; and if they retained their own faith, they were, as Prophet Mohammed told the followers of Islam, nonetheless their brethren.[906] The master who treated them kindly would be acceptable to God; he

---

[902] BBC1 on 29 January 2001.
[903] Ibid.
[904] R.B. Smith: *Mohammed*; op cit; p. 330.
[905] M. Lings: *Muhammad, His Life Based on the Earliest Sources*; Islamic Texts Society; George Allen and Unwin; 1983; p. 79.
[906] R.B. Smith: *Mohammed*; op cit; p. 244.

who abused his power would be shut out of Paradise.[907] And the Muslim master who chastised his slave without a reason was bound to set him free.[908] As Segal points out:

> To a degree unmatched by the various states of Western Christendom, for all the conflict between Protestants and Catholic, the nature of society in Islam was informed by reference to the Divine will, as communicated by the Qur'an. And the Qur'an dealt in some detail with slaves. That pretensions to piety might co-exist with disregard for the spirit and even the letter of such details did not preclude their overall influence. Slaves were to be regarded and treated as people, not simply as possessions.[909]

Segal adds:

> The treatment of slaves in Islam was overall more benign, in part because the values and attitudes promoted by religion inhibited the very development of Western-style capitalism, with its subjugation of people to the priority of profit.... In short, far from pursuing the development of an economic system that promoted the depersonalisation of slave labour, Islamic influence was responsible for impeding it.[910]

It was also Islam, Rodinson points out, which became the defender of the oppressed people of Africa.[911] Also, in Blyden's words:

> The introduction of Islam into Central and Western Africa has been the most important, if not the sole, preservative against the desolation of the slave trade. Mohammedanism furnished a protection to the tribes who embraced it by effectually binding them together in one strong religious fraternity, and enabling them by their united effort to baffle the attempts of powerful pagan slave hunters. Enjoying this comparative immunity from sudden hostile incursions, industry was stimulated among them, industry diminished their poverty; and as they increased in worldly substance, they also increased in desire for knowledge. Gross superstition gradually disappeared from among them... they acquired loftier views, wider tastes, and those energetic habits which so pleasantly distinguished them from their pagan neighbours.[912]

Muslims surely, during conflict, in particular, took slaves; yet the crucial difference with Westerners was in the treatment of slaves. There is nothing (except in Western Christian writing, fiction and missionary witness accounts) in the whole history of Islam which compares to the Western inhumanity in the treatment of slaves, in plantations or in mines, making them toil to their death, or skinning or mutilating them, or burning them on stakes for dissent or for the crime of escape.[913] Islam

---

[907] Ibid.
[908] Ibid; p. 245.
[909] R. Segal: *Islam's Black Slaves;* (Atlantic Books; London; 2001); p. 5.
[910] Ibid; pp. 5; 6.
[911] Louis Massignon: l'Influence de l'Islam au Moyen Age sur la formation de l'essor des banques Juives; *Bulletin d'Etudes Orientales* (Institut Francais de Damas); vol 1; 1931; pp. 3-12; at p. 12.
[912] Blyden: Islam and Race Distinction, in N. Daniel: *Islam, Europe and Empire;* op cit; p. 313.
[913] See, for instance, R. Garaudy: *Comment l'Homme*; op cit.

never enslaved one hundred million Africans, nor did it ruin Africa.[914] The Atlantic Slave Trade between America, Europe and Africa did.[915]

More importantly, in Islam, the emancipated slave is actually, as well as potentially, equal to a free-born citizen. Throughout the Ottoman Empire, for instance, and at all periods in its history, slaves have risen repeatedly to the highest offices and have never been ashamed of their origins.[916] Sultans and venerated chiefs of Islam are born to female slaves, and they are very proud.[917] Captain Burton mentions that the Pasha of the Syrian caravan with which he travelled to Damascus had been the slave of a slave.[918] Sebuktegin, the father of Mahmud, the founder of the Ghaznavid dynasty (10th-11th centuries,) was a slave; so was Qutb-uddin, the conqueror and first king of Delhi, and the true founder, therefore, of Muslim India.[919] In fact a whole Turkish slave dynasty ruled India on behalf of Islam, and gave the country some of its finest hours.[920] Often, again, a great lord of Egypt raises, teaches and grooms a slave child, whom he marries later to his daughter, and gives him full rights; and we come across in Cairo stories of ministers, generals, and magistrates of the highest order who were originally purchased as young slaves.[921] A dynasty of slaves, the Mamluks, ruled Egypt from 1250 until 1798, and it is said that Christians from the Caucasus were pleased to be carried off as slaves to Egypt because each one felt that he might rise to be sultan.[922] Some Mamluk rulers such as Baybars (sultan 1260-1277) and Qala'un (sultan 1280-1291) occupy places of the first rank in Muslim history, which seems to follow a tradition centuries old. In the 9th century, Ibn Tulun, another slave of Turkish origin rose to the position of governor of Egypt. Many slaves of Slav origin were the highest serving ministers of the last Ummayad Caliph Marwan II in Damascus (744-50).[923] One of the most remarkable of Caliph Muawiya's lieutenants was Zayyad 'the son of his father' (of unknown father). He became governor of both Kufa and Basra.[924] It was that same Zayyad who took Bukhara for Islam.[925] Under the subsequent Abbasid dynasty, only three caliphs were born of free mothers, and all these belong to the eighth century.[926] In Andalusia, the Maghreb, and Sicily, many former slaves could be found in the army, administration, and arts.[927]

---

[914] Ibid; p. 275.
[915] E. Williams: *Capitalism and Slavery*; (North Carolina; 1944).
[916] R. B. Smith: *Mohammed;* op cit; p. 250.
[917] G. Le Bon: *La Civilisation des Arabes*, op cit; p. 293.
[918] Burton: Pilgrimage, I; p. 89; in R.B. Smith: *Mohammed;* p. 251; note 1.
[919] See Elphinstone's India; p. 320; 363; 370; in R. B. Smith: *Mohammed*: p. 251.
[920] I.H. Qureishi: Muslim India Before the Mughals, in *The Cambridge History of Islam*, edited by P.M. Holt, A.K.S. Lambton; B. Lewis; Cambridge University Press, 1970, vol 2A, pp. 3-34. A. Laljjrivastava: *The Sultanate of Delhi*; Shiva Lal Agarwala Publishers; Agra; 1950
[921] G. Le Bon: *La Civilisation des Arabes*, op cit; p. 293.
[922] J.J. Dollinger; p. 32; in R. B. Smith: *Mohammed;* op cit; p. 250.
[923] M. Esperonnier: Les Echanges commerciaux entre le Monde Musulman et les pays Slaves d'apres les sources Musulmanes medievales; pp. 17-27; *Cahiers de Civilisation Medievale;* vol 23; p. 26.
[924] J. Glubb: *A Short History*; op cit; p. 70
[925] Ibid.
[926] G.E Von Grunebaum: *Medieval Islam*, op cit; p. 202.
[927] M. Esperonnier: Les Echanges commerciaux; op cit; p. 26.

Finally, if Muslims had treated the Black Africans as badly as Western apologists state, one would ask then: what made and still makes these Africans cling to the faith of their oppressors when no Muslim army ever set foot on the Black African continent?

b. Slavery Under Western Christendom:

There is no need here to unearth the dark pages of the Western slave trade beyond few points to make the argument.

Firstly, in contrast to Islam, in Christendom, there is not one single example of any former slave, especially black, ever reaching any position of power or influence, or acquiring any sort of status. Only very recently do we begin to see some Black men and women attaining high positions. Muslim history, as shown above, is full of such examples of black people, or former slaves who reached high status, governorship, and even the sultanate and caliphate.

In relation to the attitude to slavery, it is first necessary to address the Western Christian 'intellectual' 'ideological' view of slavery. It is a Christian Saint, Thomas of Aquinas, who justified the ideology of slavery.[928] He was as charitable as a man can be, Sarton notes,

> Yet even the fact that a slave has an immortal soul did not alter in his eyes the essential nature of slavery: a slave was a piece of property like any other, which could not be alienated without the owner's consent.[929]

In the later Middle Ages, when the Christian West began to invade other continents and to subjugate and enslave their people en masse, thousands upon thousands of Native Americans were baptised, and then were sent to the consuming pestilence of the plantation and the mine.[930] Slavery, it was held, was only in the external way, but inside they were free men, because they were freed from paganism, although animals were treated better than humans.[931] The Church even endeavoured 'to salvage the soul of slaves, for eternity,' by slaying them en masse after converting them to Christianity.[932] Tens of millions of Native Americans were thus slain.[933]

Africa was to play a central role in the slave trade, and the Church was central to this trade. Bishop Barthlome da Las Casas (1474-1566), first priest to be ordained

---

[928] G. Sarton: *Introduction to the History of Science*; 3 vols; (The Carnegie Institute of Washington; 1927-48); vol II, p. 799.
[929] Ibid.
[930] W. Howitt: *Colonisation*; op cit; p. 120.
[931] BBC2 29 April 2000: Brazil an inconvenient history.
[932] Pedro de Leturia: Origen Historico del Patronato de Indias,' in Relaciones entre la Santa Sede e HispanoAmerica. Analecta Gregoriana, CI. (Roma, 1959), pp. 3-31, in D. M. Traboulay: *Columbus and Las Casas*; (University Press of America, New York, London, 1994); p. viii.
[933] See D.E. Stannard: *American Holocaust: The Conquest of the New World*; (New York; Oxford University Press; 1992).

in the New World (1512), exploited slave Indians at Hispaniola (Haiti),[934] and just like other religious humanists preached African slavery.[935] In memorials of 1516; 1518; and 1542, Las Casas recommended the use of African slaves to Espanola to reduce Native Indian suffering and also to solve the labour crisis.[936] It was obvious that Native Americans and African slaves suffered greatly, and death ravaged both peoples, yet the trade was also preached by other religious humanists.[937] Fellow Dominican, Pedro de Cordoba (1516), the Jeronymite friars (1518), the Franciscan Pedro Mexica (1518) all urged the introduction of African slavery.[938] As the Native Americans were cleared out, the Africans were made to toil.[939] Africa, 'the cradle of the accursed race of Ham,' was a reservoir which could be drawn on without qualms.[940] According to the current way of thinking,

> Noah's curse and the collective apostasy of Africans made it almost a duty for Europe to take slaves, since reduction to slavery was seen as a first and necessary stage in their conversion and ultimate salvation.[941]

Just as with Native Americans the Church sought to salvage the soul of Black Africans for eternity. We are assured by their own authors, notes Howitt, that the moment after they had baptised numbers of these creatures, they cut their throats that they might prevent all possibility of a relapse, and 'sent them straight to heaven.'[942] As Fontana outlines, in the century of mass slave trading, the 18th, enlightened Western views saw the slave trade with great favour. 'Whenever there is an effort to legitimise over-lordship,' says Fontana,

> There appear theories which demonstrate that those overlorded are inferior. What the Castilian theologians did for the subjection of the native Americans, the French philosophers of the eighteenth century did for the subjugation of the Black slaves. Voltaire insisted that the intelligence of the Black people 'is of a different kind from our understanding, it is very inferior.'[943] Montesquieu was still more direct. This man who wrote that 'slavery goes against the natural order according to which all men are born free and independent' went on to defend the enslavement of Negroes on the ground that their soul was corrupted by their colour.[944]
>
> The apparent illogicality of this has a key provided by a practical argument: Sugar would be excessively dear, were it not that the plant producing it is made to work by slave labour.[945]

---

[934] R. Garaudy: *Comment l'Homme;* op cit; p. 256.
[935] D.M. Traboulay: *Columbus and Las Casas*; op cit; p. 58.
[936] Ibid.
[937] Ibid.
[938] Ibid.
[939] R. Garaudy: *Comment l'Homme;* op cit; p. 257.
[940] P. Chaunu: *European;* op cit; p. 298.
[941] Ibid.
[942] W. Howitt: *Colonisation;* op cit; p. 120.
[943] Voltaire: *Essai sur les Moeurs et l'esprit des Nations*; Ch. 141.
[944] Montesquieu: *Mes Pensees*; 1935; and *De l'Esprit des lois*; XV; 5.
[945] J. Fontana: *The Distorted Past;* (Blackwell; Oxford; 1995); p. 123.

Setting aside the fact that countless millions of Africans were killed during capture and the hunt for slaves, the life and fate of African slaves was a succession of horrors. In the pursuit of the trade, Le Bon says, English skippers used to lure Africans by shows of friendship, then swooped on them, cut off their heads and exchanged them for a number of slaves with rival tribal leaders.[946] During ocean transportation, to maximise profit, Africans were stacked in the manner as shown in the often reproduced deck plan of the English slave-ship Brookes in 1783, where the slaves were stacked 'like books on a shelf'.[947] Death rates reached between 15 and 30 per hundred.[948] Once they reached lands of their destinations, the slaves were separated from their families. Hence the social fabric of their community was completely shattered. Then, they were made to toil in fields and mines, often to death. All slaves were locked in huts under such conditions that scores were found hanged in their wretched quarters.[949] African dissent was dealt with as described here by Gabriel Stedman, who went to Surinam in 1771 to help suppress one of many slave revolts there,[950] quoting a white colonist who described the torture-execution of a slave:

> Not long ago, this colonist told Stedman, "I saw a black man hanged alive by the ribs, between which with a knife was first made an incision, and then clinched an Iron hook with a chain. In this manner, he kept living three days, hanging with head and feet downwards and catching with his tongue the drops of water, it being the rainy season, that were flowing down his bloated breast, while the vultures were picking in the putrid wound."[951]

In the end, the African slave trade may have resulted in 10 million Africans shipped to America, but the counts tell of ten dead for one slave alive.[952] In total, it is a hundred million people killed as a result of the slave trade.[953]

As Armesto points out:

> Our traditional images of the horrors of the middle passage and the degradation of life in slave communities derive from slaves' memoirs and abolitionist tracts. Sceptics have wondered whether shippers can have been so careless of their cargo as to tolerate - and even invite - heavy losses of life en route; yet evidence such as the often reproduced deck plan of the slave-ship Brookes in 1783, where the slaves were stacked 'like books on a shelf,' or the tell tale case of the Liverpool captain in 1781 who had 130 slaves thrown overboard for the insurance confirm the horror stories of the slaves who survived. Some shippers had more rational policies for the protection of

---

[946] In G. Le Bon: *La Civilisation*; op cit; p. 468.
[947] F. Fernandez-Armesto: *Millennium;* A Touchstone Book; (Simon and Shuster; New York; 1995); p. 273. R. Garaudy: *Comment l'Homme*; op cit; p. 275.
[948] R. Garaudy: *Comment l'Homme*; op cit; p. 275.
[949] U. Bitterli: *Cultures in Conflict*; Polity Press; tr., from German; (Cambridge; 1989); p. 40.
[950] John Gabriel Stedman: *Narrative of a Five Years Expedition against the Revolted Negroes of Surinam;* (London; 1813).
[951] In T. Morganthau: Slavery: How It Built the New World; in *Newsweek*; Special Issue, Fall/Winter 1991, pp. 66-69.
[952] R. Garaudy: *Comment l'Homme;* op cit; p. 251.
[953] Ibid.

their investments, but the extent of both inhumanity and inefficiency in the trade are enough to shock moralists and pragmatists alike.[954]

If the history of the slave trade is to be further corrected, slavery, as Garaudy points out, was abolished in America neither by revolution nor by devout Christians.[955] White House papers also show that 'Honest' Lincoln did not start the war intending to free America's 3.5 million slaves.[956] By modern standards he was racist, claiming in private that black people were 'morally inferior.' He wanted to 'pack them all back to Africa where they will not cause us any more problems.'[957]

Behind the abolition of slavery was industrialisation, and the plantations becoming no longer profitable; the huge Black labour force now becoming a burden rather than the asset it had been in the 18th century. Williams shows the correlation between the fall of the contribution of slavery to the economy and the ease by which slavery was abolished.[958] Williams asserts that slavery was part of the capitalist system, which at some point in the 19th century lost its reason for existence; thus somehow dying on its own.[959] Before Williams, L.J. Ragatz[960] had reached the same conclusions.[961] Williams' demonstration constituted a stark reminder of reality and truth. Thus, it is not surprising that he has had to face intense criticism to our day.[962]

As for the notion that the West owes its wealth to the industrial revolution of the 18th –19th centuries, this is false. It was industrial exploitation of the Africans, which created Western wealth. 300,000 Africans were enslaved every year in the 18th century, the age of the supposed Industrial Revolution.[963] It ought to be known that the development of the plantation economies provided Europe with great quantities of tobacco, coffee, sugar and cotton at prices within the reach of ordinary consumers, which stimulated trade out of which modern economic growth has arisen.[964] Malachy Postlethwayt, the British mercantilist, wrote that the slave trade was the

> First principle and foundation of all the rest, the mainspring of the machine which sets every wheel in motion.[965]

Such were the huge profits from the trade, manufacturers, provisioners and sailors all benefited by the trade and petitioned for it to continue.[966]

---

[954] F. Fernandez-Armesto: *Millennium*; op cit; p. 273.
[955] R. Garaudy: *Comment l'Homme*; op cit; p. 277.
[956] Sunday Times March 18, 2001.
[957] Ibid.
[958] E. Williams: *Capitalism and Slavery*; (North Carolina; 1944).
[959] S. Drescher: Le Declin du systeme esclavagiste Britanique et l'abolition de la traite; in *Annales;* vol 31 (1976); pp. 414-35; p. 414.
[960] L. J. Ragatz: *The Fall of the Planter Class in the British West-Indies, 1763-1833*; (New York, 1928).
[961] S. Drescher: Le Declin du systeme esclavagiste Britanique; op cit; p. 414
[962] Ibid.
[963] R. Garaudy: *Comment l'Homme;* op cit; p. 275.
[964] J. Fontana: *The Distorted Past;* op cit; p. 123.
[965] M. Craton: *Sinews of Empire: A Short History of British Slavery;* Garden City; NY; (Doubleday. 1974); p. 120.
[966] E.R. Wolf: *Europe and the People Without History;* (University of California Press; Berkeley; 1982); p. 198.

As it enriched the West, the Atlantic slave trade resulted in the genocide of around 100 million Africans.[967] No re-writing of history can deny this fact.

Muslim 'Racists'

Under the large title stretching on two pages of the UK daily, the Independent:
'We're on the brink of a massive catastrophe, warns diplomat'
Then on page three of the same daily:
'They want to kill us because we are black.'[968]
Darfur has served to fuel the views of Muslim-Arab racism towards Black Africans.

Gordon, once more, tells us about 'Arab-Muslim racism':
> As white slaves became scarcer, however, they became a luxury in which only the wealthiest could indulge themselves. In time, the multiracial character of slavery in the Arab world virtually ceased to exist and became almost exclusively black. In this respect, it differed little from slavery in the New World.
>
> The association in the Arab mind of black people with slavery can be seen in the language itself... In time, the word *'abd* lost its exclusive meaning and came to mean a black person regardless whether he was slave or free. This semantic evolution of the word *'abd* from a social to ethnic designation undoubtedly derived from the popular image of the black person in Arab history as a slave.
>
> As long as slavery maintained a multiracial cast, Arab and Turkish slave owners favoured white slaves over blacks in so far as work assignments and what might be called career prospects were concerned. White slave girls were preferred as concubines over black girls; and among the latter, the fairer-complexioned Abyssinians were shown partiality over their dark-skinned African sisters.
>
> This order of racial preference is captured in a number of paintings of the *harem* by an assortment of Western artists who portray the white slave woman as the central figure in the secluded quarter.[969]

Gordon then adds:
> The negative attitudes displayed by Arabs towards blacks were rooted in feelings of racial prejudice and cultural superiority....
>
> It was the view of many Muslim scholars that the social behaviour and physical characteristics of people inhabiting lands of extreme temperatures were adversely affected by these climatic conditions.' (Gordon cites as

---
[967] R. Garaudy: *Comment l'Homme*; op cit; p. 275.
[968] *The Independent* 16 September 06; p. 3.
[969] M. Gordon: *Slavery in the Arab World*; op cit; pp. 98-9.

support for this assertion the ninth century Muslim scholar, Al-Jahiz,) who says:

"If the country is cold, they are undercooked in the womb; if the country is hot, they are burnt in the womb."[970]

Gordon concludes:

> Racist views expressed by Arab scholars tapped a deep root in public attitudes towards blacks. Indeed, given the widespread existence of slavery in the Arab world over so many centuries, it would have been surprising that such feelings did not exist.[971]

Also accusing Muslims of racism, but for the very opposite reasons from Gordon, Stoddard tells us:

> The European in the Orient is disliked not merely as a ruler and as a disturber, but also as a man of widely different race. This matter of race is very complicated but it cuts deep and is of a fundamental importance. Most of the peoples of the Near and Middle East belong to what is known as the 'brown' category of the human species.[972]

If we are to conclude from Gordon's and Stoddard's lines, on one hand Muslims hate those of dark skin (according to Gordon), then on the other they hate those of fair skin because they (the Muslims) are themselves of dark skin (according to Stoddard).

Never mind, here are the facts

a. Race under Islam:

As Segal notes, for much of Islamic history, there was no such virtually exclusive identification of slavery with blackness as came to exist in the Christian West.[973] He says:

> Such (Islamic) influence also successfully confronted the emergence of racism as a form of institutionalised discrimination, because the Qur'an expressly condemned racism along with tribalism and nationalism.[974]

As Lloyd writes:

> Any comparison between white slavery in the Regencies of Barbary and Negro slavery as it existed in the Americas is mistaken. The colour bar was a psychological factor of great importance in the treatment of Negro slaves. In Barbary there was no such prejudice, nor was there any racial distinction made in the multi-lingual slave population. There was, of course, a strong religious feeling against Christians, although there was a remarkable degree of tolerance of religious practices, ranging from extreme Protestant to

---

[970] Ibid; p. 100.
[971] Ibid; p. 102.
[972] L. Stoddard: *The New World of Islam;* op cit; p. 102.
[973] R. Segal: *Islam's Black Slaves*; op cit; p. 49.
[974] Ibid; pp. 5-6.

Orthodox Greek, shown in the building of chapels in the slave quarters and in the treatment of visiting priests. With the comparatively large number of renegades involved, there was ample opportunity to rise above slave status if apostasy was accepted. Who ever heard of a Negro slave owning a plantation as so many European slaves owned ships? Nor was slavery necessarily life-long, because there was always a chance of ransom or redemption. Indeed, as has already been remarked, slavery is not really the right word for the captives or unofficial prisoners of war who were held in Barbary.[975]

On Islam's view of races, it can safely be said that no faith can show an equal sense of brotherhood between diverse colours. It is worth quoting Malcolm X:

> The colour-blindness of the Muslim world's religious society and the colour blindness of the Muslim human society: these two influences had each been making a greater impact, and an increasing persuasion against my former way of thinking.

In Makkah there were 'no segregationists - no liberals'; indifference to colour was spontaneous, and for Malcolm X this was evidently a shattering experience:

> I shared true, brotherly love with many white-complexioned Muslims who never gave a thought to the race, or to the complexion, of another Muslim.[976]

The same observation had struck previous generations of Westerners. Lady A. Blunt, who in her trip to the Nedjed region (1878), stated that the governor of one of the largest cities of the region, Meskakeh, was 'A Negro completely black, with the repulsive features of the African.'[977] She added:

> It seemed to me absurd to see that Negro, who was still a slave, in the midst of a group of courtesans of the white race, because those Arabs, many of whom were of noble origins by blood, bent in front of him, ready to obey any of his glances, or to laugh at any of his poor jokes.[978]

This egalitarian attitude in Islamic society is not a recent manifestation by Muslims seeking to correct their dreadful past by pretending to over-accept the other, and end up at times creating ridiculous situations of excessive humanity. Instead, Islamic colour blindness went back to the early days of its history:

> Arab customs [wrote Rodinson] admitted and favoured the adoption by the clans of people of all sorts and all origins who thus became entirely Arabs. The flow of conversions slowly swelled and then became irresistible.[979]

Remarkably, Van Ess points out, Islamic countries have never had classes or a nobility in the Western sense.[980] The ideal of *limpieza de sangre* (Purity of Blood), so familiar to us from *Don Quixote*, did not survive the first century of Islamic history.

---

[975] C. Lloyd: *English Corsairs on the Barbary Coast*; op cit; p. 112.
[976] N. Daniel: *The Cultural Barrier*, op cit; p. 11.
[977] G. Le Bon: *La Civilisation des Arabes*, op cit; p. 31.
[978] Ibid.
[979] M Rodinson: *Mahomet*, (Le Seuil, Paris, 1961), in Y. Courbage, P. Fargues: *Chretiens*; op cit; p. 47.
[980] Joseph Van Ess: Islamic Perspectives; in H. Kung et al: *Christianity*; op cit; p. 80.

Islam is basically egalitarian.[981] In contrast to Roman and medieval law, Islamic law has no category of persons for whom separate regulations were in force.[982] Medieval Islamic society was relatively fluid. Under Muslim rule the offspring of a believer and a Christian captive was not just legitimate, but most of all was not stigmatised.[983]

Neither was a person stigmatised for their colour. To the contrary, whether in 10th century Morocco, or today, says Levi Provencal, there is no lack of coloured people in the ranks of aristocracy, or the bourgeoisie; the great merit of Muslim culture is that colour- prejudice has never existed, whether in the Middle Ages or today.[984] Van Ess insists that racial differences have never played the sort of role in Islam that they have in Christianity. Minor forms of discrimination erupted at times, but Islam has never known deliberate racism, which is one of the reasons, Van Ess identifies, why it succeeded in Africa more than Christianity.[985] Likewise Segal notes how, unlike in Christendom, slaves in Islam were not subject to special racial discrimination in law, and once freed, they enjoyed in law equal rights as citizens.[986]

> Travellers to the Spanish Peninsula [says Levi Provencal] without a doubt did not feel too much strangers in a milieu where Arabism was eminent, where oriental culture remained dominant, where the language of the Qur'an ruled over local dialects, but it was nonetheless striking to see side by side in the roads and in the Bazaars of towns and cities populations so little uniform: blond, brown, half-cast, whites and black, talking in Romanesque and in Arabic, living in such perfect symbiosis, together, alongside Christians and Jews, they, too, always loyal subjects of the regime.[987]

The monk Theodosius, in 883, acknowledged the grandeur of Palermo (in Sicily) (then under Muslim rule) describing it as

> Full of citizens and strangers, so that there seem to be collected there all the Saracen folk from East to West and from North to South ... Blended with the Sicilians, the Greeks, the Lombards and the Jews, there are Arabs, Berbers, Persians, Tartars, Negroes, some wrapped in long robes and turbans, some clad in skins and some half naked; faces oval, square, or round, of every complexion and profile, beards and hair of every variety of colour or cut.[988]

Even more, as Segal notes, there were black slaves in Islam who rose to positions of power without parallel among their counterparts in the West, even a few who became rulers.[989] Many of these have already been cited in the previous heading, and include many caliphs, generals, and regional governors. Amongst the many rulers of black origin that can be cited is Mulay Ismail, the second Alawid Sultan

---

[981] Ibid.
[982] Ibid.
[983] A. Lowe: *The Barrier and the Bridge*; (G. Bles; London; 1972); p. 79.
[984] E. Levi Provencal: *Histoire de l'Espagne Musulmane;* vol III; op cit; p.178
[985] Joseph van Ess: Islamic perspectives; op cit; p. 80.
[986] R. Segal: *Islam's Black Slaves*; op cit; p. 9.
[987] E. Levi Provencal: *Histoire de l'Espagne Musulmane*; op cit; p. 186.
[988] In C. Waern: *Medieval Sicily*; (Duckworth and Co; London; 1910); p. 19.
[989] R. Segal: Islam's Black Slaves; op cit; p. 9.

(1672-1727), who was himself the son of a black concubine.[990] The famed Almohad ruler, Abu Yusuf Ya'qub (r.1184-1199), likewise was the son of a black African woman, but who, from amongst his many half brothers, was chosen as the successor to his father due to his superior abilities.[991]

b. Race under Western Christendom:

Segal explains that whilst some Christians played a part in the abolition of slavery, it is doubtful they would have succeeded without support from industrial capitalists.

> The workshop of the world had outgrown the value of slave labour colonies.... By the time this combination of moral and economic campaigns captured the state, so that British financial, diplomatic, and naval power came to be deployed in their cause, the days of the Atlantic slave trade and then of slavery itself in the West were numbered.
>
> Yet racism vigorously survived the end of slavery. If old habits die hard, racism would already have been old enough to take an unconscionable time dying. But there were reasons why it thrived rather than declined. The colonial powers engaged in extending their rule across most of the world, found a pretext in the concept of the 'White man's burden,' with is corresponding presumption of the cultural and even biological inferiority of blacks and other colours.[992]

Identifying natives of Africa and America with wild animals to justify their subjugation was predominant amongst the early learned Western men such as Petrarch,[993] Lull,[994] or Zurara, who, for instance, holds that 'The Blacks, in the previous generation, seemed drawn from bestiality.'[995]

Le Canarien, the 15th century Catholic organ for The Canaries, tells us that

> 'The natives are miscreants and do not acknowledge their creator and live in part like beasts.'[996]

In modern 'Renaissance' writing, the Blacks were readily classified in a category not far removed from that of the apes, as 'Men made degenerate by sin.'[997] In part, this was because of the tradition that 'the sons of Ham were cursed with blackness,' as well as being condemned to slavery; in part through the mental associations evoked by:

---

[990] Ibid; p. 55.
[991] Al-Marrakushi: tr. into French: *Histoire des Almohades*, by E. Fagnan, Algiers, 1893, p. 189. See also Y. Bouabba: *Les Almohades*, SNED, Algiers, 1971.
[992] Ibid; p. 7.
[993] Petrarch: *De Vita Solitaria*; vi; 3rd ed., A. Altamura; (Naples; 1943); pp. 125-6.
[994] In F.F. Armesto: *Before Columbus*: op cit; pp. 233-4.
[995] G. Eannes de Zurara: *Cronica de Guine*; Chs 25-6; ed., T. De Sousa Soares; 2 vols; (Lisbon; 1978); vol I; chs 79-82; pp. 295-310.
[996] F. Fernandez Armesto: *Before Columbus*; op cit; p. 180.
[997] Ibid; p. 227.

A diabolical colour, generally preferred for the depiction of demons and the signifying of sin.[998]

Comparisons of African natives with animals also came readily to lay lips and pens, notes Armesto.[999]

Such comparisons would lead to and justify mass enslavement of Africans.[1000] At the height of the slave trade, in the 18th century, French philosophers justified the subjugation of the black slaves.[1001] To Voltaire

> The Negro race is a kind of men as different from ours as the race of bloodhounds differs from that of the greyhounds. It may be said that, unless their intelligence is of a different kind from our understanding, it is very inferior.[1002]

And to Montesquieu:

> Nobody can get used to the idea that God, a most wise being, could have placed a soul, especially a good soul, in an entirely black body.[1003]

Buffon concludes, that on account of the hostile environment in which they had developed, American natives were inferior to those of the Old World.[1004] Retzius' cephalic index which distinguishes between dolichocephalic and brachycephalic races, etc, justifies the claim that the various races had each a different origin and nature.[1005] The Blacks were in those times deemed to belong to

> The age of awakening consciousness, or nascent intelligence, a state of incipiency to moral and mental development.[1006]

Long concluded that the Negroes were of a totally different race 'that was nearer to the apes than to Man.'[1007] J.J Virey's *Histoire naturelle du genre humain*, published in 1802 sees the Celts as the most perfect species and compares the Negroes to apes.[1008] Cuvier, for his part, 'demonstrated' that the Negro was closer to the ape than to the European.[1009] James Cowles Prichard, dressed his racial theories in scientific garb, in his second work *The Natural History of Man* (1843), relying in large measure on Chateaubriand's description of Egypt. By measuring black men's skulls, Prichard sought to prove that the black man's brain was less advanced than the white man's, that

> He was caught in a state of primitiveness from which it was unlikely that he would ever emerge.[1010]

---

[998] Ibid.
[999] Ibid; pp. 240-1.
[1000] R. Garaudy: *Comment l'Homme;* op cit.
[1001] J. Fontana: *The Distorted Past;* op cit; p. 123.
[1002] Voltaire: *Essai sur les Moeurs et l'esprit des Nations;* Ch. 141.
[1003] Montesquieu: *Mes Pensees;* 1935; and *De l'Esprit des lois;* XV; 5.
[1004] Buffon: *Histoire Naturelle;* V; 'Varietes dans l'Espece Humaine; (Paris; 1769); pp. 285-6.
[1005] J. Fontana: *The Distorted Past;* op cit; p. 125.
[1006] J. Haller: *Outcasts from Evolution;* (Urbana; 1971); p. 51.
[1007] H. Long: *The History of Jamaica;* (London; 1774).
[1008] Quoted in A. Thomson: *Barbary and Enlightenment;* (Brill; Leiden; 1987); p. 72.
[1009] Ibid.
[1010] J. Cowles Prichard: *Researches into the Physical History of Mankind* (1813).

A view supported by Burton, who, too, considered the Black man the most inferior species of the human race.[1011] It is also amongst White American supremacists that one reads that:

> Negroes, having multiplied from a half to four millions in less than a century, were of necessity in their normal conditions in the South (of the USA); and it also shows, what the census returns show, that in 'freedom' they died out.... Furthermore it shows that amalgamation, as with varieties of our own race that come to us from the Old World, is impossible; and therefore human governments can not exist an hour anywhere where these widely different races are forced into legal equality...
>
> Every man and woman must accept the simple but stupendous truth of white supremacy and Negro subordination.[1012]

As Fontana points out,

> Those who claimed descent from the Franks made speeches with aristocratic tendencies like that of Gobineau, who declared that everything of any note in human history was the work of the Aryans, and that the decadence of societies came from the mingling of their blood with that of the inferior races.[1013]

As Kabbani writes:

> Travel writing of the Victorian period was linked to the nascent discipline of anthropology. Although anthropology was later to become a leveller of cultures and races, its beginnings often served to bolster the self-esteem of the European by convincing him that he was the culmination of excellence in the human species. Other races were his inferiors, lower down on the great scale of being (how low depending on how dark they were). And since they were lower down on that chimerical scale, they shared many qualities with animals, of which unbridled sexual ardour was one. It is illuminating to note how often the native is compared to an animal in this narrative. Iago's reference to Othello as a 'Barbary horse' is only a foreshadowing of the more opprobrious epithets that the Victorians were to coin.[1014]

This ideology stressing the inferiority of other races accounted for the extermination of native people in the Americas and Oceania. Stannard,[1015] Churchill Ward,[1016] and Howitt, in particular, have studied these matters.[1017]

Islam never had such a literature that justified such acts. Islam never had the equivalent of the Ku Klux Klan or Nazis parties. No Apartheid system was ever applied in Islam. Muslims never burnt a black man for his colour on a crescent shaped stake, and never has a black man been lynched by a Muslim mob. True,

---

[1011] R. Burton: *A Mission to Gelele, King of Dahomey*; (London, 1864); vol 2; p. 198.
[1012] J. Van Evrie: *White Supremacy and Negro Subordination;* Negro Universities Press; (New York; 1868); preface.
[1013] J. Fontana: *The Distorted Past;* op cit; p. 126.
[1014] R. Kabbani: *Imperial Fictions*; op cit; p. 8.
[1015] D.E. Stannard: *American Holocaust: The Conquest of the New World*; (New York; Oxford University Press; 1992).
[1016] W. Churchill: *A Little Matter of Genocide*; (City Lights Books; San Francisco; 1997).
[1017] W. Howitt: *Colonisation and Christianity*: (Longman; London; 1838).
D E. Stannard: "Genocide in The Americas" in *The Nation*, October 19, 1992; pp. 430-4.

Muslims have killed few Israelis, but Muslims never wiped out, or sought to wipe out the Jews. On the contrary, the Jews in many places have owed their survival thanks to Muslim protection, or more properly the protection afforded them by Islam.

Islam will not accept you if you are racist, and no Muslim needs to falsify his or her history to prove this.

Nine

'TURKISH BARBARISM' AND ITS EFFECTS

As the Ottomans began to decline, the Western depictions associated a new element to the old rhetoric of Turkish threat: the means and methods necessary for the destruction, i.e dismemberment, of the now lame foe. This and the ways to do it began to be expressed not long after the decline began to manifest itself in the late 17th century. The Frenchman, Lucinge, as here outlined by Cirakman:

> Firstly recommends to investigate the means that the Ottomans have practiced for their advancement and greatness. The second issue is "with what cunning and deceit they maintain what they have gotten" and the third one asks, "How we may be able to assail them and turn the chance of their victories and powers?" According to him, since the basic cause of Turkish greatness is the idleness of Christians, the war against the Turks must be offensive.
>
> However, the "empire of the Turk cannot receive any damage or alteration by outward causes, it is necessary that inward causes, either separate or mixed, effect it." So that it would be easier to defeat it by an open force. The inward and mixed causes are defined as the defects that might enable the enemy to introduce tumults into the empire. These include the hatred, contempt and disobedience of the emperor's officers and servants; the conflicts that may arise about the succession to the throne; disloyalty of the Janissaries might start to influence the government, or the possible rebellion and revolt of the people against their governors.....
>
> Lucinge offers to ruin the empire by conspiring against it abroad and at home...
>
> His (The Grand Turk) people must be provoked to rebellion, his great men and chief officers are to be gained.[1018]

The same strategy is advocated by his contemporary Knolles:

> With all their power and might, the Turks are not invincible. They have weaknesses. One of them is that it is not easy to keep obedience of so many distinct nations some of which he assumes are discontented.[1019]

The nation that was to spearhead the disintegration of the Ottoman realm was Greece, although others would also play their role. Eton notes how the solution to the miserable condition of the Greeks is very simple and profitable for Europe:

> Greece can no longer submit to the Turkish yoke; she pants for emancipation and already aspires to be ranked among the independent states of Europe.

[1018] R. de Lucinge: *The Beginning, Continuance and Decay of Estates;* tr. J. Finet; (London; 1606); in A. Cirakman: *From the Terror;* op cit; pp. 89-90.
[1019] R. Knolles: *The General Historie of the Turks....;* (London; 1687-1700); p. 990.

> The rise or rather the renovation of her power will form an important era for European politics.[1020]

He also says:

> The expulsion of the Turks from Europe and the reestablishment of the Greek Empire, is more to the advantage of Britain than even of Russia itself; that so far from being a usurpation, it is an act of justice; and that according to the laws of nations, the Turks have not, by length of possession, acquired a right to domain of the countries they conquered.[1021]

Craven, just like many others, throughout this same 18th century, could see the benefits of an alliance between Western Christian nations and Greece:

> Yes, I confess, I wish to see a colony of honest English families here; establishing manufactures such as England produces, and returning the produce of this country to ours: establishing a fair and free trade from hence, and teaching industry and honesty to the insidious but oppressed Greeks, in their islands -waking the indolent Turk from his gilded slumbers, and carrying fair liberty in her swelling sails.[1022]

Voltaire, in this century, acted as a leading, tireless voice, just as De la Croix, Byron, Chateaubriand and others were to do in the following century, urging such a dismemberment. Following the Russian victory over the Ottomans in September 1769, courtesy of French intrigues,[1023] Voltaire called the sovereigns of Europe to arms to march against the Ottomans 'for the glory of their crowns and the profit of their states.'[1024] To Catherine II of Russia (1726-1796) he suggested:

> Your majesty should be beating the Turks towards Yassi or elsewhere, were I Emperor of the Romans, Bosnia and Servia would soon see me, and afterwards I would come and beg a dinner of you at Sophia, or at Phillipopolis in Romania; after which we would partition in friendly fashion.[1025]

The only problem for Voltaire was that Frederick the Great, the Prussian Emperor, was totally opposed to the idea of such a partitioning.[1026]

As the Ottomans slumbered into greater decline, Voltaire's contemporary, Volney, held:

> The decree is gone forth, the day approaches when this colossal power shall be dashed to pieces and fall crushed by its own weight. Yes, I swear it by the ruin of so many empires destroyed: the empire of the crescent shall suffer the fate of the states whose scheme of government it copied. A foreign people shall chase the sultans from their metropolis; the throne of Orkhan shall be

---

[1020] W. Eton: *A Survey of the Turkish Empire;* (London; 1798); p. 334.
[1021] Ibid; p. viii.
[1022] E. Craven: *A Journey through the Crimea....;* (Dublin 1789); p. 249.
[1023] Beer; vol i., p. 256; in A. Sorel: *The Eastern;* op cit; p. 55.
[1024] Voltaire in A. Sorel: *The Eastern;* op cit; p. 55.
[1025] Voltaire to Catherine II, May 27, 1769.
[1026] In A. Sorel: *The Eastern,* op cit; p. 89.

overturned; the last shoot of his race shall be cut down and the hordes of Oguzians (the Turks by their pre-Ottoman designation), deprived of its head, shall be scattered.... Till there shall arise among the Arabs, the Armenians, or the Greeks, legislators who shall form new states.[1027]

The 19th century witnessed the grand disintegration of the Ottoman Empire, as the various Christian subjects, instigated and armed by France, Britain, and Russia, rose one after the other. The Serbs rebelled in 1806-7, a pig farmers' uprising, the leader also a pig farmer: Georges Petrovich (Georges the Black).[1028] The Serb rebellion had a patron: Russia, and the idea of Greater Serbia was now nurtured.[1029]

In February 1821, the Greeks of Morea went into rebellion, and in 1822 Greek independence was declared.[1030] Greece had rebelled with Franco-British assistance (with arms, finance and political support), and propaganda, too.[1031] Thomas Gordon, a soldier and author, published in 1832 the *History of the Greek Revolution*.[1032] He wrote while the events were still fresh in his mind, and noted how, in 1821, after the shipping of arms and gunpowder into the Peloponnese, at an agreed signal, the peasantry rose and massacred all the Turks - men, women and children- on whom they could lay hands.

'In the Morea [Peloponnese] shall not Turk be left,
Nor in the whole wide world.'

Thus ran the song, which from mouth to mouth, announced the beginning of a war of extermination of the Turks.[1033]

According to William St. Clair:

> The Turks of Greece left few traces. They disappeared suddenly and finally in the spring of 1821, un-mourned and unnoticed by the rest of the world...Upwards of 20,000 Turkish men, women and children were murdered by their Greek neighbours in a few weeks of slaughter... The men were killed at once, and the women and children divided out as slaves usually to be killed in their turn later. All over the Peloponnese roamed mobs of Greeks armed with clubs, scythes, and a few firearms, killing, plundering and burning. They were often led by Christian priests, who exhorted them to greater efforts in their holy work.[1034]

In 1827, the London treaty between France, Britain and Russia agreed to send a fleet to the Mediterranean to fight the Turks; and in the same year, the Ottoman navy was burnt at Navarino.[1035] Within a few years, the Ottomans found themselves

---

[1027] Volney: *Les Ruines*; (Paris; 1798-9); *The Ruins*; (London 1845); p. 22; in N. Daniel: *Islam; Europe;* op cit; p.72; and A. Cirakman: *From the Terror;* op cit; pp. 149-50.
[1028] E. Driault: *La Question;* op cit; p. 90.
[1029] Ibid.
[1030] H. Inalcik: Chronology of the Ottoman Empire; op cit; p. 101.
[1031] Details in E. Driault: *La Question;* op cit; and A. Sorel: *The Eastern;* op cit.
[1032] T. Gordon, *History of the Greek Revolution,* 2 vols; Edinburgh, William Blackwood, 1832.
[1033] See W. Alison Phillips, *The War of Greek Independence 1821 to 1833;* London: Smith Elder, 1897, p. 48.
[1034] William St. Clair, *That Greece Might Still Be Free - The Philhellenes in the War of Independence*, Oxford University Press; 1972 pp. 1-2.
[1035] H. Inalcik: Chronology of the Ottoman Empire; op cit; p. 101.

at war with Russia, facing a widespread rebellion in Montenegro (also with Russian support). Ali, the Pacha of Janina (who was supported by France), also rebelled, and in the process massacred Turks and their supporters.[1036] And so did Muhammad Ali of Egypt, whose army reached the southern parts of Turkey at a time when the Russian fleet was in the Bosphorous.[1037] France took advantage of all this to wrest Algeria from the Ottomans in 1830.

The acts on the ground, as now had become customary for centuries, were stimulated/justified by the usual rhetoric of Turkish barbarism. It came in all forms and from all quarters. Turkish 'barbarism' was immortalised by the French painter Delacroix in his 'Massacre at Chios,' where he painted the Turks slaying powerless Greek women, children and elderly. The philosopher Heine was of the opinion that the Turk bore

> A fanatical hatred' for people of different faiths whether Jews or Christians; for both creeds are hated by him, he looks upon them as dogs and gives them this honourable title as well.[1038]

At the outbreak of war between Russia and the Ottomans, he (Heine) celebrated the Russian Tsar Nicholas The First as avenger of the Greeks: 'The knight of Europe who protects Greek widows and orphans from the Asiatic barbarians.'[1039]

Whilst it was meritorious and acceptable for Christians to kill Muslims, alleged Turkish 'barbaric deeds' towards the Christians were used to call for tougher Western answers.[1040] The news of the 'atrocities' committed against fellow Christians reached the West, stirring a crusading hysteria. One of the leading campaigners was William Thomas Stead, a newspaper editor, who in an article in the *Northern Echo* in September 1876, declared that the crusades were 'no longer an enigma' to him and in January 1877, he compared himself directly with the preacher of the First Crusade:

> I wrote dozens of letters a day, exhorting and entreating and at last I raised the North. I felt that I was called to preach a new crusade. Not against Islam, which I reverenced, but against the Turks who disgraced humanity. I realised the feelings of Peter the Hermit. God was with me.[1041]

General Gordon (who was killed during the siege of Khartoum in the Sudan in January 1885) equally saw himself as a soldier fighting for the Christian cause and, in a letter dated January 1880, he declared:

> I will go to Rome and see the Pope and obtain a brief to mount a crusade and preach against these people (the Turks).[1042]

A contemporary Catholic pamphlet asked:

[1036] See E. Driault: *La Question*, 90 fwd.
[1037] H. Inalcik: Chronology of the Ottoman Empire; p. 101.
[1038] In P. Kappert: From Romanticisation; op cit; p. 39.
[1039] Ibid.
[1040] C. Grossir: *L'Islam des Romantiques*; (Maisonneuve; Larose; Paris, 1984); p. 103.
[1041] In E. Siberry: *The New Crusaders*; op cit; p. 84.
[1042] Ibid; p. 86.

> Why is there no Crusade against the Turks? There can be no moral crusade without an armed one… Why not exhort the native Christians to rebel?[1043]

The French 'philosopher,' St Simon, for whom Europe descended from Abel, whilst Africa and Asia from Cain, felt the duty to liberate Greece 'at the head of an army of New Crusaders.'[1044]

In the midst of the clamour the dismembering of the Ottoman realm proceeded. The great powers were involved in backing the Greek rebellion in Crete, in 1866, the Christian uprising in Bosnia in 1875, and rebellions by the Serbs and Montenegrins the same year. Tsar Alexander visited Europe to form an alliance against the Ottomans, with the partition of the Ottoman Empire on the agenda. To achieve such an aim, and rouse opinion, stories of Turkish 'barbaric deeds' towards Christians were spread widely, and led to calls for crusades against the Turks.[1045] In 1876 after the Ottomans suppressed a Bulgarian insurrection, and the news of the 'atrocities' committed against fellow Christians reached the West, the call for the anti Turkish crusade became more ardent.[1046]

In 1878, Ottoman territory was generously partitioned at the Berlin Congress, which proclaimed independence for Serbia, Montenegro and Romania from Turkey. The autonomy of Bulgaria was proclaimed; Russia took her territorial spoils: Batum, Kars, and Ardahan;[1047] France took her share, wresting Tunisia from the Ottomans in 1881. Britain had free hand in Egypt.

The role of the Arabs in the final break up of the Ottoman realm has now arrived. The Reverent John Dalton, the chaplain of the two sons of the Prince of Wales during their world cruise between 1879 and 1882, commenting on possible options for the future Christian governance of Palestine, held:

> Now the time cannot be far distant when once more Syria will be ruled by a Christian power. "The Franks are about to return" is the firm belief of both fellaheen and the Bedouin and such return, if it were under fair and reasonable arrangements, would be heartily welcomed by both, as deliverance from the yoke of the Turk.[1048]

In the view of Renan:

> Islam was in the hands of the Arabs, a refined and highly spiritual race, and the Persians, a race that leans strongly towards speculation; but it could not rule since the barbarians (Turks, Berbers) took over the lead of Islam. The Islamic world then entered a period of ignorant brutality, from which it

---
[1043] In N. Daniel: *Islam, Europe*; op cit; p. 345.
[1044] St Simon: Lettres; in N. Daniel: *Islam, Europe*; p. 229.
[1045] C. Grossir: *L'Islam des Romantiques*; (Maisonneuve; Larose; Paris, 1984); p. 103.
[1046] In E. Siberry: *The New Crusaders*; (Ashgate: Aldershot; 2000); p. 86.
[1047] H. Inalcik: Chronology of the Ottoman Empire; op cit; p. 103.
[1048] In E. Siberry: *The New Crusaders*; op cit; p. 66.

emerged only to fall into the mournful agony in which it is struggling at present.[1049]

Arab Christians played the leading role in awakening anti Ottoman feelings, Muslims would follow suite.

Sultan Abd al-Hamid (1876-1908) sought to halt the slide, but the situation by his time was that of utter collapse, Turkey's enemies from without, and above all from within, now out for the final kill. Armenian terror, in particular, with Western support, tore the country apart in the 1880s and 1890s, just at the time when Turkey faced problems in Bulgaria, whilst the British navy exerted more pressure in the Dardanelles.[1050] Russia was nurturing projects for the occupation of Istanbul (1895-6), whilst the Greeks were rising in Crete (1896), and the French attacked Mytelenes (1901).[1051]

The 'Revolution of the Young Turks' (1908-9) could hardly improve the situation as they were overtaken by external events. In 1911, in September, Italy declared war on Turkey. On October 13, 1911, the Italian commander of the invading force of Libya issued a proclamation to the 'population of Tripolitania and Cyrenaica' announcing that the Italians had come

> Not to subdue and render [the inhabitants] slaves, now under the bondage to the Turks, but to restore to them their rights, to punish the usurpers, to render them free and masters of their fate, and to protect them from these same usurpers, the Turks.[1052]

Eventually, the Italians wiped out about half the Libyan population.[1053]

In the Autumn of 1912 the Great Balkan War was declared against Turkey. In great secrecy, Bulgarians, Greeks, Montenegrins and Serbs, armed by France, and backed by Russia, embarked on their attempt to wrest from Turkey its last 'Christian' provinces, and to share the empire.[1054] Hundreds of thousands of Turks were mass slain, about a million fled to Turkey, and the remains of the former Ottoman European realm were shared out amongst the victors.[1055]

In the century of Ottoman decline, 1806-1912, rhetoric constantly stressed their barbaric status, yet, reality on the ground contradicts this. Every single Ottoman town or city that fell to Christian armies was followed by the wholesale massacre of its population.[1056] We set aside Greek and Serb deeds of the first half of the century. In the Russo-Turkish War of 1877-78, Russian and Bulgarian soldiers and militias

---

[1049] E. Renan: *Averroes et l'Averroisme*, 4th edition, (Calman Levy, 1882); p. iii.
[1050] See E. Driault: *La Question*; op cit. H. Inalcik: Chronology of the Ottoman Empire; op cit; p. 104.
[1051] Ibid.
[1052] F. Malgeri: *La Guerra Libica 1911-1912*, Rome, 1970, pp. 396-407.
[1053] See K. Holmboe: *Desert Encounter*, London, 1936. E.E. Evans Pritchard: *The Sanusi of Cyrenaica*, Oxford at the Clarendon Press, 1949. A. Del Boca: The Obligations of Italy towards Libya in R. Ben Ghiat and M. Fuller: *Italian Colonialism*, Palgrave, 2005, pp. 195-202.
[1054] R.C. Hall: *The Balkan Wars 1912-1913 - The Prelude to the First World War* (London: Routledge, 2000). S. Kocaba, Balkan Harbi-Son Haqli Seferi [The Balkan War-The Last Crusade] (Kayseri: Vatan Yayinlan, 2001).
[1055] Justin McCarthy: *Death and Exile*; The Darwin Press Inc; Princeton; New Jersey; p. 138 f.
[1056] S. Lane Poole: *Turkey;* Khayats; Beirut; 1966 ed; originally published in 1908.

killed 200,000–300,000 Muslims, and about one million people were displaced.[1057] After the war, more than half a million Muslim refugees were settled in the Ottoman Empire.[1058] In the meantime, Christian propaganda completely reshapes the truth:

> In 1870 the different nationalist groups joined in the new Bulgarian Revolutionary Central Committee and agreed that violence and revolution rather than negotiation should be used to gain independence. The new group was based mainly in Serbia.... The revolts now spread, leading to the massacre of hundreds of Muslims and the seizure of the main Ottoman forts in the Balkan passes nearby... Some massacre and counter-massacre between Muslim and Christian villages followed, with Ottoman regular forces striving to restore order and security for all. But now the forces of European propaganda went to work. While no more than 4,000 Bulgarian Christians had been killed (and considerably more Muslims), the British press trumpeted the charge of "Bulgarian horrors," claiming that thousands of defenseless Christian villagers had been slaughtered by fanatical Muslims. American missionaries estimated that as many as 15,000 Christians had been killed, and the Bulgars leaped ahead to estimates of from 30,000 to 100,000![1059]

In the wake of the Balkan Wars of 1912-1913, simultaneously, Greece, Serbia, Bulgaria and Montenegro attacked the Turks. The Turkish army, badly led, ill prepared, and surprised by the violence of the onslaught, retreated everywhere. Turkish towns and cities surrendered peacefully to militias, and the same eradication of Turks proceeded as before.[1060] Only the process differed. Mass burning was the method of execution chosen for the Muslim inhabitants of Rainovo, Kilkis, and Plantza.[1061] It applied to both civilians or wounded Turkish soldiers left behind.[1062] Turkish Muslims in Thrace were murdered in great numbers, which some observers put at more than 200,000 (a figure that included some Greeks murdered by Bulgarians as well).[1063] Serbian militias flogged the Muslim villagers of Drenova to death.[1064] The Greeks took Turks from all over the kaza of Pravista to the ravine of Kasrub, slaughtered them there like mere cattle, and left the bodies as witness to the deeds.[1065] Starvation and disease-the results of pillage, theft of land and crops, did their work.[1066] In Albania, many survived the massacres only to die a slow, more terrible death by starvation.[1067] Figures compiled from original sources

---

[1057] K. Karpat: *Ottoman Population 1830–1914: Demographic and Social Characteristics*, Madison 1985, pp. 49, 75.

[1058] J. McCarthy: *Death and Exile: The Ethnic Cleansing of Ottoman Muslims, 1821-1922*; The Darwin Press; New Jersey; 1995, p. 90.

[1059] E. and S. Shaw: *History of the Ottoman Empire and Modern Turkey*, Cambridge University Press, 1976, vol 2; p. 162.

[1060] See the contemporary works full of witness statements: Ernst Jäckh; *Deutschland im Orient nach dem Balkan-Krieg;* Chapter 7: Deutsche und französische Augenzeugen von christlichen Massakers. (Die Balkangreuel des 30 jährigen Krieges); Martin Mörikes Verlag, Munich, 1913; pp. 83-98. P. Loti: *Turquie Agonisante*; Calman Levy; Paris; 1913. See also Justin McCarthy: *Death and Exile*.

[1061] Based on report of father Gustav Michel as did Consul Lamb. *The Crimes of Bulgaria*, Washington, 1914; pp. 12-15.

[1062] F.O.195-2438, no 6650; Lamb to Lowther, Salonica 3 December 1912.

[1063] Based on the report of Rene Puaux of the Paris *Temps;* corroborated by various contemporary sources.

[1064] FO. 371-1762, no 55161; Greig to Crackanthrope, Monastir, 19 November 1913.

[1065] The Report of the Carnegie Commission of Investigation; pp. 282-3.

[1066] Justin McCarthy: *Death and Exile*; op cit; p. 141.

[1067] F.O. 371-1842, No 36364, Durham to Nevison, Scutari, 28 July 1931.

by Western witnesses confirm the figure of millions of Turks slain and forced into permanent exile.[1068]

Left: Turks massacred during the Balkan Wars 1912-1913

Right: Prayers for Turks drowned en masse during Balkan Wars of 1912-1913.

Turks fleeing East.

[1068] J. McCarthy: *Death and Exile*; see also E. Jaeckh; P. Lotti: *Turquie agonisante*; and official documents and archives.

In the wake of the First World War, in November 1914, the Sultan of Turkey, pressed by the three individuals in power then (Enver, Tala'at, and Cemal) in his capacity of Caliph, declared a jihad or holy war, calling upon all the Muslims in the world to fight against France, Britain and Russia. To Britain in India and Egypt, and to France in North Africa, a universal rising of Muslims would have been embarrassing to the extreme.[1069] Just then, the Turkish-German alliance was rocked by a vast Russian offensive in the Caucasus and Armenia, and the Sharif of Makkah rose against the Turks. 'The Arabs refused obedience to the usurper from Constantinople,' the Frenchman Driault said triumphantly.[1070]

Just a year after the end of the First World War, the French and British, who had come to free the Arabs from the Turkish 'despot,' instead divided Arab lands between themselves. This was justified on the grounds that the Arabs needed the enlightened hand of the French and British, as expressed by Driault:

> Some will say that the Arab civilisation seeks to be reborn after six centuries of Turkish darkness. From Egypt to Syria and Mesopotamia and the Arab states try to come back to life, and bear with difficulty the European tutorship, which however is indispensable for their political and economic re-organisation.[1071]

Thus, by 1918, nearly ten centuries after the first crusade, the Holy Land was in the hands of the Christians again, and Ottoman power was finished. Driault brings down the curtain:

> The European soil was emptying rapidly of Muslims; the roads of Asia are covered with their miserable exodus; they covered in the opposite way, pain in their soul, the traces of their ancestors, who long ago, under Bayazid, the 'Lightning', and under Muhammed II the conqueror, had run triumphantly, from the far East to the Adriatic. What happened to the house of Othman? Has it provoked the disgrace of the heavens? Isn't this punishment for having listened to the infidel traitors? And if the hand of God has withdrawn from it, was it necessary to leave supreme power? Is it still capable of leading the destinies of Islam?[1072]

> It is not too early to see the end of Turkish Islam. The Great War has dealt a mortal blow to the sick man... and the event of 1453 is now entirely paid for.... The Sultan keeps Constantinople because of an irony of fate, and because there is difficulty in knowing to whom it should be granted... The sultan will not keep the Dardanelles, nor the guardianship of the Bosphorus, of which he has been a 'bad door-keeper.[1073]

[1069] J. Glubb: *A Short History;* op cit; p. 273.
[1070] E. Driault: *La Question d'Orient depuis ses origines jusqu'a la paix de Sevres;* Librairie Felix Alcan; 8th ed; 1920; p. 431.
[1071] Ibid; p. 440.
[1072] Ibid; p. 345.
[1073] Ibid; pp. 440-1.

Following the war, Western nations embarked on the project for the dismemberment of what's left of Turkey (ie Turkey as we know it today). Again in order to justify the deed, Turkish barbarism and incapacity to rule became focus of rhetoric, which we have looked at in great detail in our books on the Turks. Keeping it brief, here, according to one, the Turks:

> Were from the black day they entered Europe, the one great anti-human specimen of humanity.[1074]

Driault, the leading French advocate for the removal of Turkey:

> In every closer contact with the Christians, it only raised in them (the Turks) fanaticism and accentuated their Asiatic character, and so they come forth as even more strange and barbaric, and could hardly comprehend Europe's revolutionary ideas. The Turk has remained the stubborn, fearless Muslim of the past; and his hatred of the Christian has remained extreme and expressed itself in lust for blood; and to the sight of his enemy's progress, he replies with abominable massacres.[1075]

Viscount Bryce held:

> No one who has studied the history of the Near East for the last five centuries will be surprised that the Allied Powers have declared their purpose to put an end to the rule of the Turk in Europe, and still less will he dissent from their determination to deliver the Christian population of what is called the Turkish Empire, whether in Asia or in Europe, from a Government which during those five centuries has done nothing but oppress them. These changes are indeed long overdue. They ought to have come more than a century ago, because it had then already become manifest that the Turk was hopelessly unfit to govern, with any approach to justice, subject races of a different religion. The Turk has never been of any use for any purpose except fighting. He cannot administer, though in his earlier days he had the sense to employ intelligent Christian administrators. He cannot secure justice. As a governing power, he has always shown himself incapable, corrupt and cruel. He has always destroyed; he has never created…
>
> As a famous English historian wrote, the Turks are nothing but a robber band, encamped in the countries they have desolated. As Edmund Burke wrote, the Turks are savages, with whom no civilised Christian nation ought to form any alliance.
>
> Turkish rule ought to be ended in Europe, because, even in that small part of it which the Sultan still holds, it is an alien power, which has in that region been, and is now, oppressing or massacring, slaughtering or driving from their homes, the Christian population of Greek or Bulgarian stock. It ought to be turned out of the western coast regions of Asia Minor for a like reason. The people there are largely, perhaps mostly, Greek speaking Christians. So

---

[1074] In N. Daniel: *Islam; Europe*; op cit; p. 378.
[1075] Driault: *La Question*; p. 402.

ought it to be turned out of Constantinople, a city of incomparable commercial and political importance, with the guardianship of which it is unfit to be trusted. So ought it to be turned out of Armenia and Cilicia, and Syria, where within the last two years it has been destroying its Christian subjects, the most peaceful and industrious and intelligent part of the population.

If a Turkish Sultanate is to be left in being at all, it may, with least injury to the world, be suffered to exist in Central and Northern Asia Minor, where the population is mainly Mussulman, and there are comparatively few Christians and those only in the cities to suffer from its misgovernment.[1076]

Mandelstam, also a contemporary held, as summed up here,[1077]

There is absolutely no question that the Ottoman realm be allowed to survive, including under the Allies' tutelage; this tutelage that has allowed this state to murder its Armenian subjects by cheating its European tutors. This tutelage has proved itself bankrupt. With the Turks the most extreme policies have to be applied and consecrated, and their consecration is nothing other than the utter destruction of the Ottoman state. Our entire work has worked towards this conclusion.[1078]

Driault, again:

Other nations such as Hungary have reformed themselves and joined the club of the civilised, but they are Christians; however, the Turks have remained Muslim, and therefore have refused to amalgamate with European culture, the Koran only inspiring them with contempt for others and hatred. In every closer contact with the Christians, it only raised in them fanaticism and accentuated their Asiatic character, and so they come forth as even more strange and barbaric, and could hardly comprehend Europe's revolutionary ideas. The Turk has remained the stubborn, fearless Muslim of the past; and his hatred of the Christian has remained extreme and expressed itself in lust for blood; and to the sight of his enemy's progress, he replies with abominable massacres. The Turk has been cheating Europe in regard to his true aims... Europe, tired of being duped, but also afraid of a dismemberment that might draw it into chaos, decided to reform the empire by force, even under the threat of the gun, a strong use of cautery, but the powers have never agreed on this cautery...[1079]

We have not refrained in this book from defining the Eastern Question by the retreat of Turkish Islam in front of the push of Christian nations: there is no other way of understanding the scale and historical greatness of this. The solution is the end of Turkey.[1080]

[1076] Viscount Bryce: Preface, in A.J. Toynbee: *The Murderous Tyranny of the Turks*;.
[1077] A. Mandelstam: *The Sort de l'Empire Ottoman*; Lausanne, Imprimeries Reunies; 1917; p. 573, and throughout.
[1078] Ibid; p. 577
[1079] E. Driault: *La Question d'Orient depuis ses origines jusqu'a la paix de Sevres*; Librairie Felix Alcan; 8th ed; 1920; pp. I-IV and p. 402.
[1080] Ibid; pp. 461-462.

Consequently, just before the infamous Congress of Sevres, in 1920, plans were made for Turkey to be reduced to a Bantustan somewhere in Anatolia, with a 5,000 or so police force, without an army, and also with over 80% of its population disposed off, and 85% of its territory shared out amongst the deserving (France, Britain, Italy, Greece, and Armenia.)[1081] The Turks put up a tough resistance, and against all the odds saved their land.[1082]

Turkey, eventually survived under a new status, no longer the upholder of the Caliphate, but a strongly secularised nation. As for the Arabs, when at last they realised Western duplicity, they rose against it, and were bombed and gassed in the tens of thousands into submission.[1083]

[1081] For the best source on the events of the time, see the contemporary magazine of the New York Times: *Current History*. It contains all details as they happened then. For the above figures, see *Current History*, vol 12; Apr-Sep 1920; Dismemberment of the Turkish Empire. Terms of the Final Peace Treaty of the World War — Effects on the Map of Asia Minor p. 446.

[1082] For details see this author's *Long War* and *Decisive Victories*, both at MSBN Books, 2018.

[1083] T.E. Lawrence; on BBC2: Saturday 6 and 13 December 2003; 8.10 p.m.

Ten

THE CIVILISING MISSION IN THE LANDS OF ISLAM

Marmier, in 1847, wrote on the French colonisation of Algeria:
> There was nothing to regret in having added to the annals of France: A magnificent providential mission, a mission of order and peace, in parts of the world that in the past enriched themselves through pillaging, and which took great pride in inflicting cruelties; a civilising mission amongst peoples with lively minds, but who needed only guidance; a religious mission on soil, which our faith has soaked with the blood of our martyrs.[1084]

The Civilising Mission Outlined:

Just prior to the French occupation of Morocco (in 1912), a vast literature depicted the retarding influence of Islam on the country, and insisted on the need for France to intervene there, and bring back the country into the realm of modernity and progress.[1085] For the French historian, Moulieras, the Moroccans are intolerant fanatics, just like their co-religionists; traitors, and incapable of forming stable government owing to their hostility to authority.[1086] Authority, if it exists amongst them, is despotism, because it is 'a theocracy, the sultan being emperor and pope at once.'[1087] The French review, *Bulletin*, dredged up many stories in the 1890s about the violence in Morocco proving that, truly, the 'Moors' were uncivilised, in need of French guidance.'[1088] Robert de Caix, a journalist, took every opportunity to show Morocco as inhabited by barbarians 'eager for rape and pillage.'[1089] De Caix argued strongly that 'The time had come for France to restore order in the Western Maghrib.'[1090]

France was to bring order and civilisation, the Moroccans having failed due to their attachment to Islam.[1091] It was Islam, in the view of the French, which had banned science, and was the source of backwardness, fanaticism, chaos, and fatalism.[1092] Therefore, they claimed, it was the duty of France to bring back civilisation, which these parts had been lacking through their Islamic history.[1093] The London Times,

---

[1084] In A. Daniel: *Islam, Europe,* op cit; p. 332.
[1085] Well outlined by both M. Garcia-Arenal: Historiens de l'Espagne, historiens du Maghreb au 19em siècle; Comparaison des stereotypes; *Annales;* vol 54; 1999; pp. 687-703. And J.J. Cook: The Maghrib through French Eyes; 1880-1929; in *Through Foreign Eyes;* edited by A.A. Heggoy (University Press of America; 1982), pp. 57-92.
[1086] A. Moulieras: *Le Maroc Inconnu* (Paris; 1895), pp. 21-3.
[1087] Seconzac: *Au Coeur de l'Atlas;* (Paris; 1910); p. 258, in M. Garcia Arenal: Historiens; op cit; p. 691.
[1088] J.J. Cook: The Maghrib; op cit; p. 76.
[1089] Ibid; p. 83.
[1090] *Bulletin*: Pays Independant: Maroc; XIV 1; (January 1904); p. 23.
[1091] A. Moulieras: *Le Maroc Inconnu;* op cit; p. 23.
[1092] M. Garcia Arenal: Historiens; op cit; p. 691.
[1093] A. Dariac in his preface to J. du Tallis; *Le Nouveau Maroc*; (Paris; 1923).

just as the French media, such as Le Matin and other journals, emphasised the incapacity of the sultan as an effective leader. Most of the stories simply reflected the French position that 'Until the French flag flew over Morocco, there would be no peace or progress in the land.'[1094]

The bombardment of the press overrode the protest against expansionism into Morocco.[1095] As the French were beginning to occupy Morocco in 1912, most French papers hailed this as 'The final culmination of a drive to bring modernity and peace to a bloody land.'[1096]

This was the culmination of the same impressions that eventually had the same effect. 18th century-early 19th century observers shared the same views.

Saint Sauveur noted how

> Superstition and despotism will shortly have transformed this breeding ground of fine men into a desert. The Qur'an and the cudgel do not suffice to make heads of families happy in a promising, but poorly cultivated, region.[1097]

The same for Abbé Vincent Mignot:

> Their Prophet's solemn promise that all those who die fighting the infidels will be admitted to paradise regardless of any crimes they may have committed.[1098]

Rozet writes of Turkish rule in Algeria:

> As excessively despotic and the Dey as a 'Despote sanguinaire' (Bloody Despot); he exercised arbitrarily the right of life and death over his subjects until he was unavoidably murdered in one of the many revolts by the army (an undisciplined, rag tag armed gang,) during which blood flowed.[1099]

For Chevallier D'Arvieux:

> This is more or less what I could say about this unpleasant country, which is only peopled by the dregs of the provinces of the Ottoman Empire, and which we can consider without fear of errors as the most unworthy rabble in Africa and as a lair of thieves, which I shall never regret having left.[1100]

Other travellers and men of letters shared the prognosis. They, Kabbani notes, travelled for their country, as it were:

> They were the seeing eye and the recounting voice. They often had financial backing from officialdom, since their travelogues ultimately served to forge the imperial representation of the world. The traveller was now Pilgrim and Hero and Christian Soldier.[1101]

[1094] Published accounts in *The London Times*; 19 June 1905; p. 6; 22 June 1905; p. 5; 26 June 1905; p. 4; 28 June 1905; p. 5.
[1095] J.J. Cook: The Maghrib through French Eyes; op cit; p. 85.
[1096] Ibid; p. 83.
[1097] Saint Sauveur in L. Valensi: *North Africa*; op cit; p. xxi.
[1098] Abbe Vincent Mignot: *Histoire de l'Empire Ottoman depuis son origine....*; (Paris; 1771), in A. Gunny: Images; op cit; pp. 172-3.
[1099] M.P. Rozet: Alger; in *Algerie par Capitaines du genie Rozet et Carette*; (F. Hoefer; Paris; 1846); p. 14.
[1100] Chevallier d'Arvieux: *Memoires*; R.P. Labat; 6 Vols; (Paris; 1735); vol V; pp. 288-9.
[1101] R. Kabbani: Imperial Fictions; op cit; pp. 1-8.

The Civilising Mission in the Lands of Islam

One such traveller, Lane,[1102] although claiming his judgements were unemotional, unerring, highly specialised, and all-encompassing, as he himself says, 'What I have principally aimed at in this work is correctness,'[1103] still found the Orientals 'Indolent, superstitious, sensually over-indulgent and religiously fanatical.'[1104]

He observes about the Egyptians that they are marked by

> Quickness of apprehension, a ready wit, and a retentive memory. Unfortunately [he writes] their mental energy is lessened by their religion, laws, government and climate.[1105]

He insists on Egyptian ignorance, and offers an apologia for the nation's shortcomings:

> Such being the state of science among the modern Egyptians, the reader will not be surprised at finding the present chapter on science followed by a long account of their superstitions; a knowledge of which is necessary to enable him to understand their character, and to make due allowance for many of its faults.[1106]

This nation, with the character of its inhabitants so 'heavily plagued by faults, had only one hope for improvement - the enlightenment that could be brought to it through contact with the West':

> We may hope for, and, indeed, reasonably expect, a very great improvement in the intellectual and moral state of this people, in consequence of the introduction of European sciences, by which Mohammad 'Alee, in some degree, made amends for his oppressive sway.[1107]

Lane's optimism, however, is short-lived: 'It is not probable that this hope will soon be realised to any considerable extent.'[1108]

Doughty, a geologist/traveller, who went across the desert of Arabia in order to find 'the bare face of the world as it was when it began,' records his impressions.[1109] The attachment to Islam of the people repulses him: 'Perilous every bond which can unite many of the human millions, for living and dying.'[1110] He portrayed the Arabs as superstitious beings who live in filth while cloaked in holiness. One much-quoted phrase sums up his mental picture of the Arabs: 'The Semites are like to a man sitting in a cloaca to the eyes, and whose brows touch heaven.'[1111]

He goes on:

> The contagion of the Arab's religion has spread nearly as far as the pestilence: a battle gained and it had overflowed Europe. The nations of

---

[1102] E.W. Lane: *Manners and Customs of the Modern Egyptians*; (London; 1836).
[1103] In N. Daniel: *Islam, Europe,* op cit; p. 52.
[1104] E.W. Lane: Manners; in R. Kabbani: *Imperial Fictions*; op cit; pp. 38-9.
[1105] E.W. Lane: *Manners;* vol 1; pp. 377 ff.
[1106] Ibid; p. 221.
[1107] Ibid.
[1108] Ibid.
[1109] C.M. Doughty: *Arabia Deserta*, edition; 2 vols; (London J. Cape; 1936). (First published by Cambridge University Press, 1888); See R. Bevis 'Spiritual Geology: C.M. Doughty and the land of the Arabs,' *Victorian Studies*, 16 (1972-3); pp. 163-81.
[1110] Doughty: *Arabia Deserta;* vol 1: p. 141.
[1111] Ibid; p. 95.

Islam, of a barbarous fox-like understanding, and persuaded in their religion that knowledge is only in the Koran, cannot now come upon any way that's good.[1112]

And so to the normal conclusion: that it might be possible to redeem Muslims if they were governed by Christians who would convert 'those who are now scarcely superior to the brute creation into good men and industrious citizens.'[1113]

Eliot Warburton, in *The Crescent and the Cross*,[1114] holds that Britain may well have the responsibility to enter this section of the world (the Middle East):

> To vindicate the Cross where her best and bravest blood was shed six hundred years ago, to bring civilisation and morality to these degenerate peoples.[1115]

Bayard Taylor, in his work *Lands of the Saracens*, says:

> What a paradise might be made of this country, were it in better hands! or more directly: Give Palestine into Christian hands, and it will again flow with milk and honey.[1116]

A contemporary, Shaler, insists:

> True civilisation could only come about by a transfer of responsibility into the hands of Christian nations who would favour agriculture, industry and commerce and thus civilise the region. The 'primitive' was incapable of progressing by its own unaided efforts.[1117]

For Renan, speaking at the height of the colonial era, towards the end of the 19th century:

> It is the Aryan spirit, which has created everything: political life in the real sense, art, literature - the Semitic peoples have nothing of it, apart from some poetry - above all science and philosophy.... The Semitic spirit has produced monotheism... closing the human brain to every subtle idea, to every fine sentiment, to all rational research. The future of humanity therefore lies with the peoples of Europe. But there is a necessary condition for this to happen: the destruction of the Semitic element in civilisation, and of the theocratic power of Islam.[1118]

Just as Christianity explained the moral and material superiority of European society, Islam, Cromer affirmed, helped to account for the backwardness of the East. Islam was a religion of appeal to primitive peoples, and in Christian charity, Muslims ought to be led.[1119] Likewise, writing in the missionary organ, the Moslem World, W.G. Mombasa held:

[1112] Ibid; p. 142.
[1113] F. Pananti: *Narrative*; op cit; p. 416.
[1114] E. Warburton: *The Crescent and the Cross;* (New York; Wiley and Putnam; 1845); I; p. 65 f.
[1115] Ibid; I; p. 242.
[1116] Bayard Taylor: *Lands of the Saracens*; New York; Putnam; 1855; p. 129.
[1117] W. Shaller: *Sketches of Algiers*; Boston; 1826; p. 56.
[1118] E. Renan: De la Part des peuples semitiques dans l'histoire de la civilisation' in *Oeuvres completes*, (Paris, Calmann-Levy, 1947), vol II; pp. 332-3.
[1119] Cromer: *Modern Egypt*; (New York; 1916); ii; p. 134.

> It behoves each Christian man and woman in this 20th century to do something definite 'to stem the tide of Muslim advance,' for the adoption of the faith of Islam by the pagan people is in no sense whatever a stepping stone towards, or preparation for, Christianity, but exactly the reverse. Notwithstanding its fair show of outward observance and its severe legal enactments, there is something in Islam which strikes at the very root of morals, poisons domestic life, and disorganises society. Freedom of judgment is crushed, and a barrier has been raised not merely against the advances of Christianity, but against the progress of civilisation as well.[1120]

So, concludes Kabbani:

> If it could be suggested that Eastern peoples were slothful, preoccupied with sex, violent, and incapable of self-government, then the imperialist would feel himself justified in stepping in and ruling. Political domination and economic exploitation needed the cosmetic cant of *mission civilisatrice* to seem fully commendatory. For the ideology of empire was hardly ever a brute jingoism; rather, it made subtle use of reason and recruited science and history to serve its ends. The image of the European coloniser had to remain an honourable one: he did not come as exploiter, but as enlightener. He was not seeking mere profit, but was fulfilling his duty to his Maker and his sovereign, whilst aiding those less fortunate to rise toward his lofty level. This was the white man's burden, that reputable colonial *malaise* that sanctioned the subjugating of entire continents.[1121]

Loot in the Name of the Lord and Civilisation:

In his travels through Egypt and Syria, in the last decades of the 18th century, the Frenchman, Volney, dwelt on the 'despotism' of the Mamluks and Turks.[1122] He spoke of the mistreatment of the Christians done in a 'thousand manners.'[1123] Volney devoted almost the whole of his book to Mamluk corruption, cruelty, anarchic rule, and despotism. He also informs the reader in great confidence that

> In Egypt riotous and rebellious spirits, which indicate a simmering fire under cover (are) waiting to explode if kindled by hands that can stir it.[1124]

Likewise, the French merchants established in Egypt, despite having been granted considerable privileges by the Mamluks, in the early 1790s, sent written requests for French military intervention 'to protect them from Mamluk despotism and tyranny.' One request was sent to the Chamber of Marseilles, the other to the Constituted Assembly. In the first they speak of French men 'shaking under the yoke

---

[1120] W.G. Mombasa: Islam is not a stepping stone towards Christianity; *The Moslem World*; vol 1; pp. 365-72; at p. 372.
[1121] R. Kabbani: *Imperial Fictions*; op cit; pp. 1-8.
[1122] C. Chasseboeuf (Volney): *Voyage;* op cit; at p 373.
[1123] Ibid.
[1124] Ibid.

of despotism, forced to trade under ruinous conditions, and leading a precarious existence.'[1125]

In 1794, another request went:
> We need urgent succour, because our predicaments are at their worst.... French people suffer under tyranny and call on their country to come to their rescue.[1126]

In response, the French army, led by Napoleon (Bonaparte), invaded Egypt in July 1798 so as to remove the Mamluk 'tyrants.' On entering Egypt, the French presented their aims to the Egyptians as follows:
> For very long, the Beys who now rule Egypt have insulted the French nation, and have heaped insults on its tradesmen. Now has arrived the hour of punishment. For very long, this collection of slaves (the Mamluks), purchased from Georgia and the Caucasus has inflicted its tyranny upon the most beautiful part of the world, but God, on Whom all depends, has ordered that their reign ends.... People of Egypt, I (Napoleon speaking) have come to restore your rights, punish the usurpers; and more than the Mamluks I only have respect for God, his Prophet and the Qur'an.[1127]

In truth, the real reasons for the French occupation of Egypt had nothing to do with the French claims, but had long been established already. France realised the strategic significance and commercial potential of Egypt, and for a very long time French statesmen had been considering many schemes for the conquest and occupation of the country.[1128] In 1686, Father Jean Coppin published a book '*Le Bouclier de l'Europe ou la Guerre Sainte*' (The Shield of Europe, or Holy War) in which the dismantlement of the Ottoman realm was envisaged, and in which Egypt was attributed to France.[1129] On top of its strategic position, the French hoped to occupy Egypt permanently and to profit from its agriculture and trade under the guise of 'liberating' the Egyptians from Mamluk rule.[1130] Complaints, or calls for intervention, by French merchants were only to serve as pretext for Bonaparte's expedition.[1131]

In the short time they stayed in Egypt, roughly two years, besides hanging Egyptian religious figures, the French slew Egyptians en masse, in places burning whole populations in their homes.[1132] They also looted the Egyptian countryside, and taxed the Egyptians into ruin.[1133]

[1125] G. Hanotaux: *Histoire de la Nation Egyptienne*; (vol 5 by H. Deherain.) (Paris; Librarie Plon; 1931); p. 208.
[1126] Ibid; p. 209.
[1127] Ibid; p. 254. For more on this proclamation, and the first seven months of French presence in Egypt, see Al-Jabarti: *Al-Jabarti's chronicle of the first seven months of the French occupation of Egypt*. Ed and tr., by S. Moreh; (Leiden, 1975).
[1128] P.M. Holt: *Egypt and the Fertile Crescent: 1522-1922*. Cornell Paperbacks; (Ithaca; New York; 1966); p. 155.
[1129] G. Hanotaux/H. Deherain: *Histoire*; op cit; p. 202.
[1130] P.M. Holt: *Egypt*; op cit; p.156.
[1131] Ibid; p. 155.
[1132] G. Hanotaux/ H. Deherain: *Histoire*; op cit; p. 387.
[1133] Al-Jabarti: *Al-Jabarti*, op cit; pp. 67-8.

The central French aim was also to advance on the Holy Land from Egypt, somehow renewing with the Crusade tradition interrupted centuries earlier. They launched a bloody campaign, where, in places such as Jaffa, French troops butchered both garrison and population of the city.[1134] Failing in their siege of Acre, and weakened by a much fiercer resistance than they first anticipated on the part of the Mamluks reinforced by Muslim volunteers (Mekkans, Moroccans, Algerians and Tunisians), and the outbreak of the plague, which considerably depleted their numbers, the French retreated from Egypt two years after the campaign began.[1135]

Following the French failure, nearly a century later, the British entered the country for noble aims, too, such as to resolve the Egyptian debt situation, and, of course, to fight 'Muslim fanaticism'. Lord Cromer, who was to the British Commissioner, but de facto ruler of Egypt,[1136] expresses such aims:

> Let us, in Christian charity, make every possible allowance for the moral and intellectual shortcomings of the Egyptians, and do whatever can be done to rectify them.[1137]

In truth the British aims were the same as the French, one of them being to assert Western Christian rule. British intervention, according to Morley, meant

> Egypt will be wrested from Muslim fanaticism, from military revolution, and he commented that France would benefit, for 'Muslim agitation' might otherwise spread to Tunis and Algiers.[1138]

Returning the favour, the Frenchman, Emile de Lavelaye, assured the British that in Egypt they had a tacit mandate from Europe.[1139]

Sir A.C. Lyall of the British Foreign Office recalled the ancient expulsion of Christian power from Egypt and concluded:

> Moslems can hardly complain if Christianity and civilisation are now taking their revenge.[1140]

Egypt was looted by the imperial powers, helped by the governments put in place and also officials, largely Christian Copts and other Muslim collaborators. Ismail Pasha, the Khedive, was put in control of the country in 1863 by Western powers.[1141] Over and above the millions wasted in entertainments, in largesse, in the erection of numerous palaces, he threw away millions on diverse failed schemes.[1142] To finance these, he borrowed heavily; a long series of loans negotiated by major banking firms.[1143] A brief scrutiny of some such loans shows

---

[1134] Officer Malus detailed account of the massacre of the population in G. Hanotaux/Deherain: *Histoire*; op cit; pp. 406-7.
[1135] See G. Hanotaux/Deherain: *Histoire*, vol 5; op cit.
[1136] Ibid; pp. 60-1.
[1137] Lord Cromer: *Modern Egypt;* (London; 1908); 2 vols; vol 2; p. 538.
[1138] Viscount J. Morley: Egyptian Policy; a Retrospect; in *Fortnightly Review*; 1 July and 1 August issues; 1882; in N. Daniel: *Islam, Europe and Empire*; op cit; p. 399.
[1139] E. De Lavelaye: Egypt for the Egyptians; in the *Fortnightly Review;* 1 December 1882.
[1140] Sir A.C. Lyall: Foreign Office /633/ 12; pp. 37-40.
[1141] Viscount Milner: *England in Egypt;* (Edward Arnold; London; 1907); p. 176.
[1142] Ibid; p. 177.
[1143] M. Morsy: *North Africa*; op cit; p. 173.

how the ruling elites borrowed in the name of the state, at extravagant rates, under conditions which ended in bankrupting their country.[1144] When the Egyptian patriots, led by Arabi, sought to alter this reality by mounting an uprising, they were bombarded into submission in 1882; Western control was re-established.[1145] The loot of the country under the same Western-controlled Egyptian elites proceeded. Writing in 1884, Le Bon said:

> The Egyptian peasants are going to be just like the Hindu, and find themselves caught in unforgiving claws; formidable and quiet, which crush silently until nothing is left to extract. From the figures published by M. Van den Berg in 1878, out of a total of 1.4 bn French Francs, totalling from five loans, the European financiers have retained (in all sorts of forms) the amount of 522 millions; 875 millions have reached the Egyptian government; that latter had already paid, and long ago, the whole amount of the loans it has contracted just by paying interests on such debt.[1146]

The looting of Egypt proceeded under the watchful Western eyes, the staggering amounts taken out of the country in the 20th century recently revealed by a former Egyptian politician in the know.[1147]

Muslims' barbarism was sufficient reason to loot their land. MacKenzie,[1148] like Le Bon,[1149] a century before him, noted that in the process of European imperialist domination of Islamic countries, whole chunks of Islamic culture were removed. Several artists were members of official diplomatic, scientific and military expeditions, even present at acts of imperial violence.[1150] MacKenzie notes how:

> Some extolled the virtues of French rule in North Africa and bought property there to capitalise upon it themselves. Many, however, went further in the looting of antiquities of all sorts, robbing tombs, buildings etc, and in this respect, just as Nochlin put it, some of the artists distinguished between visual beauty and moral quality; the moral superiority of the West, able to preserve while the East destroyed, justifying such plunder.[1151]

The Ottoman Turks were also deemed too barbaric to hold on to any form of possession. Nothing belonged to the Turks except mosques. It was held, for instance, that the castle on the Island of Candia that was built by the Venetians, was now 'ruined at the hands of the Turks... 'for it is usual with the Turks to let their fortifications and public buildings run to decay.[1152] As long as such treasures stayed

---

[1144] J.C.B. Richmond: *Egypt 1798-1952*; (Methuen & Co Ltd; London; 1977); pp. 100-1.
[1145] Ibid; pp. 129-31.
[1146] Note in G. Le Bon: *La Civilisation;* op cit; p. 463.
[1147] M. Haykal: Haykal; *Al-Jazeera*-25 August 05; 21-22 pm; seen by this author.
[1148] J. M. MacKenzie: *Orientalism, History, Theory and the Arts*; (Manchester University Press; 1995); p. 53.
[1149] G. Le Bon: *La Civilisation;* op cit; p. 466 ff.
[1150] J. MacKenzie: *Orientalism;* op cit; p. 53.
[1151] Nochlin in J. M. Mac Kenzie: *Orientalism;* p. 53
[1152] C. Thompson: *Travels through Turkey in Asia...*; (London; 1754); vol 2; p. 277.

in Ottoman lands, they were bound to decay.[1153] Craven points out that the Turks not only build their houses on ruins but also do not let travellers take anything away.[1154] Chandler proposes the idea that people in the Levant trade should apply:

> To persons concerned for permission to remove these antiquities. If not, the Turks should be 'Secretly persuaded with all available gold in order to rescue these valuable treasures from barbarism.' According to him, these relics were suffered to lie neglected, exposed in the open air, whereas they should be under the safe custody of (Western) museums.[1155]

As far as Turkish attitudes are concerned, they don't even care to look at these treasures:

> The attention and knowledge of our guests (Turks) was wholly confined to agriculture, their stocks and herds. They called the ruin of the temple an old castle, and we informed from their answers to our inquiries about it that the magnificence of the building had never excited in them one reflection, or indeed attracted their observation even for a moment.[1156]

Throughout the nineteenth century, most of the antiquities would be removed by permission (or otherwise) to European museums.[1157] We learn from the travels of Edward Brown that there was already a profitable enterprise among many European adventurers who, like him, travelled through the empire in order to collect (or rather steal) valuable and ancient materials. This is in accord with the prevailing tendency, the Europeans feeling justified to plunder what they believed was theirs by right (but was also quite lucrative), as Brown himself states:

> Our friends proposed that we should make the tour of a part of the Ottoman Empire, beginning with Egypt, in order to collect Medals, Stones, Manuscripts, and other curiosities for which there never was so great a demand as at present through all Europe, particularly in Italy, France and England where for genuine relics of antiquity no price whatsoever is held to be extravagant.[1158]

Algeria: Slay, Loot, and Whatever in the Name of the Lord and Civilisation:

Hain, of the *Société Coloniale de l'Etat d'Alger* (Colonial Society of Algiers), in a pamphlet entitled *A la Nation Sur Alger*, explains:

> It is ridiculous to think of civilising the inhabitants of the conquered territory, for they are incapable of any improvement; they must be cleared off the land to make the way for French colonists. ... Every Arab is a criminal; criminal by

---

[1153] A. Cirakman: *From the Terror*; op cit; p. 168.
[1154] E. Craven: *A Journey through Crimea;* (London; 1789); pp. 333-4.
[1155] R. Chandler: *Travels in Asia Minor*; (Dublin; 1775); p. 38.
[1156] Ibid; p. 153.
[1157] A. Cirakman: *From the Terror*; op cit; p. 169.
[1158] E. Brown: *The Travels of Edward Brown;* (London; 1753); vol 1; p. 207.

> birth; criminal in essence; criminal by vocation. They delight in causing suffering.[1159]

To him, only extermination would be good enough for them.[1160]

Algeria was meant to become a second America; a land for European settlers, without the barbaric Natives. In order to justify the extermination of the Algerians, like that of the Indians in North America by, the colons held that

> There was a constant threat from an uprising, but in this case it was not Sioux or Cheyenne Indians, but Algerian Muslims.[1161]

The French justified their mass extermination of millions of Algerians,[1162] and in doing so, they resorted to the same depictions of Natives as barbarians.[1163]

Volney, in his *Considerations sur la Guerre des Turcs,* wrote of the Turks' fanaticism, ignorance and violent prejudices, and their 'spreading of the plague':

> It is these barbarians who brought this scourge; it is they, who, by their stupid fanaticism, keep alive the disease by spreading its germs. If just for this reason could perish their rule. May other people establish themselves in their place, and that the sea and the land were freed of their enslavement.[1164]

Pananti who had resided in the country early in the 19th century, says:

> These degraded people... monsters who vie with each other in the deepest hatred and bitterest hostility towards Christianity and civilisation.[1165]

> There is something harsh and ominous in their physiognomy, extremely repulsive to the European. Their countenance is never enlivened by a noble thought or a generous sentiment, theirs is the smile of death. They are perfidious, debauched, avaricious and so on.[1166]

For Pelissier, the only hope of Muslim regeneration was that there should cease to be Muslim governments.[1167] Pelissier even believed that if the Turkish sultan adopted the religion of 'the majority of his European subjects, 'it would have startling results.'[1168]

For J. Grey Jackson:

> The only solution is conquest, and the conquerors should then set up a firm government to quell the inhabitants' religious prejudices, until they are reconciled to a rational government, mild compared to the present despotism. The only reason for hostility on the part of the inhabitants is to be their religious fanaticism.[1169]

[1159] V.A. Hain: *A La Nation. Sur Alger*; (Paris; 1832); pp. 31; 58; 78; 94.
[1160] In A. Thomson: *Barbary and Enlightenment:* (Brill; Leiden; 1987); p. 101.
[1161] J.J. Cook: The Maghrib; op cit; p. 63.
[1162] M. Morsy: *North Africa*; op cit; p. 9.
[1163] A.A. Heggoy: *Through Foreign Eyes;* (University Press of America; 1982); Introduction; p. 3.
[1164] Volney: *Oeuvres Completes*; (Paris; 1864); p. 765.
[1165] F. Pananti: *Narrative of a Residence in Algiers*; tr., E. Blaquiere: (London; 1818); p. 416.
[1166] F. Pananti: *Narrative of a residence in Algiers*; tr., E. Blaquiere: (London; 1818); pp. 192-7.
[1167] N. Daniel: *Islam, Europe and Empire*; op cit; p. 331.
[1168] Ibid.
[1169] J. Grey Jackson: *An Account of Timbuctu and Hausa*; (London; 1820); p. 463.

For Jackson, this conquest might not be welcomed by those who are supposed to be liberated, but once their fanaticism and bigotry are overcome, they would realise how much their situation had improved.[1170]

Algeria also needed to be conquered so as to remove 'Muslim piracy which infested the Mediterranean.'[1171] The view that the Barbary corsairs were slaying countless thousands of Christians was a powerful call for action against the 'nest of pirates' (Algeria).[1172] The appeal made in 1858 by Monsegnor Pavy, Bishop of Algiers, for the erection of the Cathedral de Notre Dame d'Afrique in Algiers dwelt on the horrors of 'la piraterie Musulmane' (Muslim piracy). Monsegnor Pavy insisted that the conquest of 1830 of Algeria had brought 'these horrors to an end.'[1173] In 1884, Sir Lambert Playfair, once a consul at Algiers, wrote a book entitled: *The Scourge of Christendom*, which shows the conventional view of the previous three centuries, of 'Barbary Corsairs' capturing Christian vessels and enslaving their seamen.'[1174]

Of course Barbary piracy, as demonstrated by Fisher, most particularly, was one of the greatest myths of modern history to justify the colonisation of Algeria and North Africa.[1175] This was a pattern established long before, the Portuguese conquest of Ceuta in 1415, for instance, was blamed on Muslim piracy, and similar justifications were used for Spanish attacks on Mers el-Kebir and Oran early in the following century.[1176] Algeria, moreover, had no fleet left in the 19th century to justify the argument of piracy, this fleet having terminated its life in the 18th century.[1177] When William Shaler, the new American ambassador arrived in Algiers, in 1815, all he could see of the Algerian fleet were four frigates, five corvettes, one brig, and a galley, a total of eleven vessels.[1178] These were to suffer final annihilation by Lord Exmouth's bombardment of Algiers in 1816.[1179] There were barely any Christian captives, either. In 1830, when the French took Algiers, the number of Christian captives in the city was a mere hundred.[1180]

Still, it was under such noble premise, of seeking to remove Islamic piracy that the French invasion in 1830 took place. Barbour notes how:

> In reality there is little doubt that the basic motive of the French Government was its desire to restore the tottering credit of the regime by a military

---

[1170] J. Grey Jackson: *An Account*; pp. 457-63; in A. Thomson: *Barbary and Enlightenment:* (Brill; Leiden; 1987); p. 131.
[1171] P. Earle: *Corsairs of Malta and Barbary;* op cit; p. 10.
[1172] A. Thomson: *Barbary;* op cit; p. 128.
[1173] In *Revue Africaine*; vol 2 (1858); pp. 337-52.
[1174] C. Lloyd: *English Corsairs on the Barbary Coast;* op cit; p. 18.
[1175] G. Fisher: *Barbary Legend;* op cit; L. Valensi: *North Africa;* op cit;
[1176] G. Fisher: *Barbary Legend*; p. 24.
[1177] See for instance:
L. Valensi: *Le Maghreb Avant la Prise d'Alger*; (Paris; 1969). J. Mathiex: Trafic et prix de l'Homme en Mediterranee au 17 et 18 Siecles; ANNALES: Economies, Societes, Civilisations: vol 9; pp. 157-64. F. Braudel: *Civilisation Materielle*; 15-18em siecle; vol 3; (Paris; 1979).
[1178] A. Hollingsworth Miller: One man's View: William Shaler and Algiers; in *Through Foreign Eyes;* (ed., A.A. Heggoy), op cit; pp. 7-55; at p. 18.
[1179] C. Lloyd: *English Corsairs on the Barbary Coast*, op cit; pp. 163-4.
[1180] N. Barbour: *A Survey;* op cit; p. 36.

success; and to win for the Restoration Government the credit which Napoleon had lost by the evacuation of Egypt.[1181]

The expedition had been accompanied by propaganda to the effect that the French were coming to liberate the Algerians from their Turkish tyrants:

> We French, your friends [said one document], are leaving for Algiers. We are going to drive out your tyrants, the Turks who persecute you, who steal your goods, and never cease menacing your lives . . . our presence on your territory is not to make war on you but only on the person of your Pasha. Abandon your Pasha; follow our advice; it is good advice and can only make you happy.[1182]

The real aims of the French invasion, however, became apparent soon after their entry into Algeria. One of them was to bring back Christianity to 'a former Christian land.' General De Bourmont said to his soldiers, 'You have renewed the crusades.'[1183] 'Our war in Africa is a continuation of the Crusades,' said Minister Poujoulat to General Bugeaud in 1844.[1184] A crusading mind dressed in a modern form, to reform the Algerian personality, here expressed by Antoine Salles about Cardinal Lavigerie:

> He sought for Algeria to escape the yoke of Islam, which for centuries, suffocated its rise and prosperity, but on condition that it placed itself under the protection of France once its freedom was secured. This is a remarkable programme to turn Christian and to turn French this land which was according to the Cardinal an extension of France.[1185]

To the Algerians, Christianity was on offer but at a price. The country's treasure-chests were ransacked as soon as the French took the country.[1186] Dey Husseyn, ruling on behalf of the Ottoman Sultan, left Algiers but not before he granted access to the Treasury, which was estimated then at 50 millions Francs (worth billions today).[1187] The treasury was delivered to the French in exchange for they not blasting the city to rubbles.[1188] In the city itself, following occupation, soldiers and officers fought amongst each other in the narrow streets of the Kasbah over the loot from private households; crowds of them filling the streets, overloaded with silks, women clothes, luxury footwear with golden decorations, their pockets overflowing with jewellery of all sorts, precious objects soon to be peddled in the streets of Paris.[1189] The superior officers who were quartered in the public buildings of the

---

[1181] *A Spedizion d'Arge*; (Genoa; 1834).
[1182] Baudicourt: *La Guerre et le Gouvernement de l'Algerie*; (Paris; 1853); p. 160.
[1183] A. Surre-Garcia: l'Image du sarrasin dans les mentalites de la litterature Occitanes: *De Toulouse a Tripoli*, Colloque held between 6 and 8 December, 1995, University of Toulouse; (AMAM, Toulouse, 1997); pp. 181-9; p. 186.
[1184] Ibid.
[1185] A. Salles: *Le Cardinal Lavigerie et l'Influence Francaise en Afrique*; Lyon; 1893; in N. Daniel: *Islam; Europe*; op cit; p. 332.
[1186] J. Fontana: *The Distorted Past*, op cit; p. 137.
[1187] P. Gaffarel: *Lectures Geographiques et Historiques sur l'Algerie*; op cit; p. 42.
[1188] M.A. Nettement: *Histoire de la Conquete d'Alger*; op cit; pp. 443-4.
[1189] H. Alleg et al: *La Guerre d'Algerie*, op cit, p. 34.

city stole all precious collections and treasures of the country.[1190] The splendid vases, the rich arms, buried in the vaults of the Kasbah, were stolen; and the rich plate, of considerable artistic value, was melted and coined.[1191]

Land and real estate were the main assets. Immediately after the capture of Algiers, 'a flight of human vultures swooped on the country,' says Ageron, trafficking in real estate in the cities, grabbing land and cutting down the woods.[1192] The Sahel or coastal hills of the promontory on which Algiers stands, had been full of estates and country houses whose owners had been chased away through violence of war, intimidation, or were simply slain; as these properties became vacant they were offered to dubious European purchasers.[1193] Marshal Clauzel, an ardent 'colonist,' acquired many large properties at low prices, and set out to make the plain of the Mitidja the 'dump for Europe's beggars'.[1194] Cheap passages brought poor immigrants from Spain, the Balearic Islands, Malta and Italy; Parisian labourers and German and Swiss emigrants were brought in as an official measure.[1195] A policy of systematic expropriation began to confine the Native tribes to ever smaller areas of their traditional territory.[1196] Their most fertile lands were taken away for the purposes of colonisation.[1197] In the 1860s, 4 million hectares of arable land were appropriated by the so-called Senatus Consultus of 1863, a piece of legislation that individualised tribal lands before these passed from powerless Muslim individuals to European hands.[1198] In the end, Algerians became destitute beggars in heir own country, exposed to recurrent epidemics and famines.

The overall French aim was 'to drive away the mass of savages (the Algerians) to make room for better men.'[1199] North Africa in general, Algeria in particular, was seen as a land where the value of French life would be preserved by a colon (European settler) majority since the Muslim 'was a hostile element, a roadblock to progress.'[1200] According to Etienne, the powerful and influential deputy of Oran (1881-1921), Muslims had to stand aside to make way for the inevitable march of progress and technology in Algeria.[1201] For Marmier, Algeria was a land for a new France, to grow what the old France lacked, house the surplus population, expand industry and shipping, with 'no room for inferior natives.'[1202]

The story of the French presence in Algeria was also a story of devastation, it is needless for us to dwell upon here, but such a story is found in great details in the

---

[1190] M. Wagner: *The Tricolor on the Atlas*, op cit, p. 233.
[1191] Ibid.
[1192] C.R. Ageron: *Modern Algeria;* op cit; p. 24.
[1193] Ibid; pp. 24-5.
[1194] Ibid; p. 25.
[1195] Ibid.
[1196] C.R. Ageron: *Modern Algeria*, op cit, p. 25.
[1197] J.M. Abun-Nasr: *A History of the Maghrib*, op cit, p. 249.
[1198] For good detail, see D. Sari, *La Dépossession des Fellahs 1830-1962*. Algiers, SNED. 1978.
[1199] V.A. Hain: *A La Nation. Sur Alger*; (Paris; 1832).
[1200] J.J. Cook: The Maghrib through French Eyes; 1880-1929; in *Through Foreign Eyes;* op cit; pp. 57-92; at p. 58.
[1201] Ibid; at p. 77.
[1202] X. Marmier: *Lettres sur l'Algerie*; (Paris; 1847).

memoirs of French high officers or those Europeans marching with the French army.[1203] In words, towns, hamlets, crops, and livestock, orchards and whatever the tribes possessed were either systematically looted or destroyed. A total of 18 million sheep, and 3.5 million cattle and one million camels were killed between 1830 and 1845.[1204] Hundreds of thousands of people were killed either in combat or in the wake of conflict in the form of reprisals.[1205]

> Soldiers [said General Bugeaud in 1841] you have often beaten the Arabs. You will beat them again, but to rout them is a small thing; they must be subdued.

To the civilians he added:

> The Arabs must be reduced to submission so that only the French flag stands up on this African soil.[1206]

A French army report from an operation in the Kabyle region says:

> Our soldiers returning from the expedition were themselves ashamed.... About 18,000 trees had been cut down; houses had been burnt; women, children, and old men had been killed. The unfortunate women particularly excited cupidity by the habit of wearing silver ear rings, leg rings, and arm rings. These rings have no catches like French bracelets. Fastened in youth to the limbs of girls they cannot be removed when they are grown up. To get them off, our soldiers used to cut off their limbs and leave them alive in this mutilated condition.[1207]

Every Arab, every Kabyle was treated as a belligerent; his cattle and his crops, his house and his tent, his wife and his child, were fair game for the invading armies.[1208]

The total death toll resulting from the French civilising Mission remains unknown to this day. We can only note that, between November 1867 and June 1868, alone, 300,000 died.[1209] Some sources say that the Algerian population fell from 10 million in 1830 to 2.1 million in 1872.[1210] Others speak of the more realistic figure of

---

[1203] Dawson Borrer: Narrative of a campaign against the Kabailes of Algeria; Spottiswoode and Shaw, London, 1848.
General Boyer to Minister of War, Oran, 25 April 1832, no. 2984, AHG: H-13.
G. Esquer: Correspondence du general Voirol; Voirol au MG., 14 September 1833; Paris, 1924.
G. Esquer: *Correspondence du Duc de Rovigo*, 1831-1833; t1. Algiers, 1914; T2. Algiers, 1920; T3: Algiers, 1921; t.4 Algiers, 1924. T.1; p. 43; 1st January 1832.
Le Comte d'Herisson: *La Chasse a l'Homme, Guerre d'Algerie*; Paul Ollendorff; Paris; 1891.
Count H. Ideville: Memoirs of Marshal Bugeaud from his Private Correspondence and Original Documents; 2 vols; edited from French by
Clemens Lamping: The French in Algiers. Soldiers of the Foreign Legion; Prisoners of Abd el Kader; tr. from German and French by Lady Duff Gordon, London; 1855.
Colonel L. Francois de Montagnac: *Lettres d'un Soldat*; Paris; 1885.
A. Rastoul: Le Marechal Randon; D'apres ses Memoirs et Documents Inedits; Firmin Didot; Paris; 1890.
St Arnaud: Lettres de St Arnaud; 2 vols; Michel Levy; Paris; 1855.
[1204] N. Abdi quoted in Louis Blin: *l'Algerie du Sahara au Sahel*, (l'Harmattan, Paris, 1990); p. 68.
[1205] H Alleg et al: *La Guerre d'Algerie*; op cit; vol 1; p. 77 ff.
[1206] Rousset: La Conquete de l'Algerie; (1889); in N. Barbour: *A Survey*; op cit; p. 43.
[1207] Baudicourt: *La Guerre et le gouvernement de l'Algerie*; op cit; p. 372.
[1208] W. Blunt: *Desert Hawk*; Methuen & Co. Ltd; London; 1947; p. 167.
[1209] A.G. Slama: La Guerre d'Algerie, (Decouvertes, Paris, 1996); p. 18. See also D. Sari: La Depossession des Fellahs 1830-1962; Algiers; SNED; 1978. C. Ageron: *Histoire*; op cit; p. 37 ff.
[1210] Louis Blin: *l'Algerie du Sahara*; op cit, p. 68.

between eight to ten million Algerians losing their lives to the various uprisings, epidemics, hunger and disease between 1830 and 1962.[1211] One of the apologists of the French colonisation, Dr Bodichon, had held:

> It matters little that France in her political conduct goes beyond the limits of common morality at times; the essential thing is that she establishes a lasting colony and that, later, she brings European civilisation to these barbaric countries. When a project which is to the advantage of all humanity is to be carried out, the shortest path is the best. Now, it is certain that the shortest path is terror. Without violating the laws of morality, or international jurisprudence, we can fight our African enemies by powder and fire, joined by famine, internal division, war between Arabs and Kabyles, between the tribes of the Tell and those of the Sahara, by brandy, corruption and disorganisation. That is the easiest thing in the world to do.[1212]

[1211] Lacheraf, in L. Blin: *l'Algerie;* op cit; note 3, p. 112.
[1212] Cited in C.H. Favrod: *Le FLN et l'Algerie;* (Paris; Plon; 1962); p. 31.

TRIPLE EXÉCUTION A SÉTIF

Mission Civilisatrice a la Francaise in Algeria

Eleven

FROM BOSNIA TO IRAQ

In the 1990s, in Western magazines, media, academic writing, and fiction, the fiend was still the Muslim, even if on the same page, reports of mass slaying of Muslims in Bosnia, and mass rape of their women were evident. The Serb and Croat scholars and media were well aware of this, when prior to, and during the mass killing and mass rape of Muslims, they bombarded opinion with the view that the cleansing of Bosnian Muslims in 1992-5 was a preventive measure to save Western civilisation from Muslim fanaticism and barbarism.[1213] Prior to, and during this genocide, Serb and Croat academics insisted on the dangers Islam represents. Academics such as Popovic who lectured in Paris wrote to inform the educated public about Islam, seeing in it 'a totalitarian system, one whose totalitarianism far exceeds that which a well-intentioned and informed Western mind could comprehend or imagine.'[1214] Another, Jetvic, warned of this:

> Islam clearly prescribes that its faithful must bring a victim to Allah. That animal victim is a ram which is slaughtered ritually, so that its blood gushes out all over. If the members of the Islamic civilisation become used from their childhood to seeing how a lamb which is everyone's favourite animal is slaughtered, then it is clear that a person who partakes in the Islamic worldview becomes clearly accustomed to the shedding of blood in a very brutal fashion. It is not a great step to go from killing animals to killing human beings.[1215]

Dabic, another intellectual, warned that in Great Britain, Italy and France, this Muslim threat was shared by all.[1216] N. Todorov, for his part, considered the Muslims in Bosnia as motivated by their 'Islamic way of life,' which is alien to European civilisation, warranting its removal.[1217]

The need to eliminate such a totalitarian, strange, and would-be murderous foe, alien to modern Western civilisation, was achieved through mass rape and mass slaughter of a quarter of a million people between 1992 and 1995. Sharing in the Serb and Croat fear of this Islamic infection, the West, with rare exceptions, stood by and watched as the Muslims were systematically exterminated and mass raped. On top of the mass slain, mass rape, and multiple cruelties, which we avoid dwelling into as we are tired of that by now,

---

[1213] See N. Cigar: Serbia's Orientalists and Islam: Making a genocide intellectually respectable; in *Islamic Quarterly* Vol 38 (1994); pp. 147-170; at p. 151
[1214] Ibid.
[1215] Miroljub Jetvic in Javnost, quoted in Ljudi I vreme (People and Time), *Vreme*; Belgrade; 15 November 1993; p. 55, in N. Cigar: Serbia's Orientalists; op cit; p. 153.
[1216] Interview with Vojin Dabic: Polumesec muci zapad (The Crescent worries the West), *Evropske Novosti (New Europe)*, 14 April 1993, p. 18.
[1217] N. Cigar: Serbia's Orientalists; op cit; p. 151.

> The war, [as Murtaza Hussain correctly observes] attempted to not just wipe out Bosnia's Muslims as a people, but to erase evidence that they had even existed. Historic mosques were dynamited and the rubble carted to garbage dumps. The places where they stood, including in Rogatica, were grassed over or turned into storage yards.[1218]

Blame has been focused for one reason or another on the Serbs, and somehow the Catholic Croats have been left barely touched, and yet their role in causing the disintegration of ex Yugoslavia and the start of the war was, without a doubt, essential. Their provocation and aggression against the Serbs, besides their past crimes against the Serbs, surely ignited and amplified the latter's criminal tendencies and actions.

The Croats were also and more importantly full partners in the crime against Muslims of Bosnia, if not playing the leading role in stirring it. Franjo Tudjman, the Croat president, throughout the 1992-5 war, made his preoccupations quite clear in his book *Wastelands of Historical Reality*, published in 1990. In this book he suggests that

> Jews are genocidal by nature', and that their problems are of their own making. Had they heeded what he calls the 'traffic signs', the Holocaust would never have occurred.[1219]

Tudjman's main preoccupation, though, were the Bosnian Muslims. Claiming to be acting on the behest of Western powers, he spoke of the 'contamination by the Orient, and asserted that, 'Croatia accepts the task of Europeanising the Bosnian Muslims.'[1220] The Croats' aim was the creation of a Catholic *cordon sanitaire* against Islam.[1221] The Croat defence minister, Gojko Susak, claimed in front of an Israeli audience that about '110,000 Bosnian Muslims studying in Cairo', in order to create 'a fundamentalist state in the heart of Europe.'[1222]

Croat crimes against Muslims are chilling, but, thanks to the Catholic Church excellence at burnishing its image, you can hardly find any trace of them today except in the odd work or film,[1223] although for those who followed events in the 1990s, they much surpassed those of the Serbs and by a long distance. They killed, they raped, they mass tortured, they demolished anything that bore a Muslim mark, from mosques to the famed Mostar Bridge. Particularly recurrent was their policy of

---

[1218] Murtaza Hussain: The Intercept: From al Paso to Saravejo, How White Nationalists have been Inspired by the Genocide of Muslims in Bosnia. September 1, 2019
https://theintercept.com/2019/09/01/bosnian-genocide-mass-shootings/
[1219] Michael Sells, *The Bridge Betrayed: Religion and genocide in Bosnia* (Berkeley: University of California Press, 1996, 95.
[1220] A. H. Murad: The Churches and the Bosnian War,
http://masud.co.uk/ISLAM/ahm/the_churches_and_the_bosnian_war.htm
[1221] A. H. Murad: The Churches and the Bosnian War,
http://masud.co.uk/ISLAM/ahm/the_churches_and_the_bosnian_war.htm
[1222] Cigar, 124; Sells, 119.
[1223] Such as the excellent Peter Kosminsky's *Warriors*, 1999; series for British Television.

constructing 'blood shrines', which took the form of Christian shrines or crucifixes constructed on the site of demolished mosques.[1224]

The Serbs and Croats are, however, hardly alone. Any nation, any group with power seeking the mass extermination of its burdensome Muslims, or its burdensome Islamic elements (in the case of a Muslim country) resorts to the same technique of demonising them before and whilst unleashing mass killing on them, with such mass killing presented as a means for protecting the land. In fact any force seeking to remove its Muslims/Islamic elements joins the Great War on Terror, the master key to all doors that can justify anything, from military interventions, to the most intrusive surveillance, to mass arrests, torture, disappearances, and mass murder. This also follows a most basic and yet highly effective method. Pseudo-Islamic terror groups are set up by some secret services. They create outrages, which both give practical instances of terror, and which justify 'Counter-Terror Measures.' In the cycle of 'terror and counter terror,' Muslim elites are physically eliminated; those amongst such elites with intellectual and religious standing are murdered by the 'terrorists' (who accuse them of being moderate or traitors), whilst young Muslim activists are killed as terrorists.[1225]

De Zayas gives us this instance and its lesson:

> 'If I say: 'yesterday a man killed another,' it would be assumed that this man, the murderer, could have acted differently, but this is a matter for justice to decide. However, if I say, 'a Norman man beheaded a young, pregnant woman, and showed delight at such killing,' or 'This morning, an Andalusian Muslim murdered an innocent French girl under the horrified eyes of her mother,' everyone would agree that all Normans, or Andalusians, are dreadful people, and that as a matter of emergency, it is necessary to take decisive measures against them. This is precisely what happened in Spain, as extracted from a note sent to the King of Spain, Philippe III, by a certain Martin Gonzales de Cellorigo Oquende, solicitor for the Inquisition of Valladolid. In seeking to demonstrate that the Muslims were murderers of the worst kind, he cited a horrific case:
>
> Andre Alonso, a good Christian, was taking five mules loaded with merchandise on the road of Valladolid to Burgos. He was attacked, robbed, decapitated, and his remains put in a bag. His head was never found, nor were ever recovered his mules, or merchandise. As at the time no corpse could be identified, that body could have been that of any person. The murderers were never found, but this hardly restrained our Inquisitor from using this incident and inflammatory rhetoric much reminiscent of today's

---

[1224] www.haverford.edu/relg/sells/stolac/bloodshrines.htm

[1225] This technique worked to near perfection in many countries throughout the 1990s and after. By the time the technique was applied in Iraq in the years 200s, it had reached its summit of perfection. On 14 November 06, for instance, supposedly in tit for tat measures, the whole Sunni staff of a ministry was abducted en masse by state special forces (or terrorists dressed as such, for in these situations confusion has its place, too) and taken to an undeclared destination. The fate of those abducted like this is to end up with mutilated bodies, dumped in rubbish tips. See also The Times online - January 10, 2005.

media: this crime could only have been the work of the Moors, barbaric murderers infesting the highways; proof that it is necessary to put an end to their killings of the Followers of Truth (i.e. the Christians); these Moors giving free rein to their murderous deeds.'

This technique (of using one horrific crime, committed (or not) by Muslims, and to generalise it to the whole community, to justify harsh measures against them,) De Zayas concludes, is of course aged today, but 'it still serves its purpose.'[1226]

Back to Bosnia to take note with Murtaza Hussain:
> The Balkans are often condescendingly stereotyped as a backward region stuck in the grip of old prejudices. In reality, Serbs, Croats, and Muslims had lived together as compatriots in the former Yugoslavia for a long time before violent demagogues came to power; it took years of effort during the late 1980s and early 1990s for ultranationalist leaders to drum up the level of fear and hatred necessary for war to start. Before it fell apart, the former Yugoslavia was a relatively modern place, with a highly educated elite in its cities and a solid professional class.[1227]
> When Yugoslavia began to violently be carved into competing ethno-states, there remained many people, including Serbs, Croats, Muslims, and Slovenes, who refused to go along with the new sectarian reality. Some of them, in fact, continued to call themselves Yugoslavs: citizens of a multicultural society that would soon cease to exist. What many who remembered the time before the war will tell you is that they never imagined that such a thing could happen in their country. Yugoslavia was a modern country that, by most appearances, had left the past behind. In 1984, the city of Sarajevo was the home of the Winter Olympics. Less than a decade later, it was under the worst military siege Europe had witnessed since Stalingrad.[1228]

Indeed, what is haven of tolerance today might become hell any time in the future. Hence this book in large measure

The Churches, both Catholic and Orthodox, played a leading role in the Muslim tragedy. The only difference between their crimes is that today we are glutted with facts and details about the Orthodox Church crimes but hardly if at all hear of anything of the Catholic side. We need not dwell on such crimes by the Church, although we make the effort to cut them to the bare minimum just for the sake of highlighting the role of such institution. As Sell writes

---

[1226] R. de Zayas: *Les Morisques et le racisme d'etat*; (Les Voies du Sud; Paris, 1992); pp. 282-3.
[1227] Murtaza Hussain: The Intercept: From al Paso to Saravejo, How White Nationalists have been Inspired by the Genocide of Muslims in Bosnia. September 1, 2019
https://theintercept.com/2019/09/01/bosnian-genocide-mass-shootings/
[1228] Murtaza Hussain: The Intercept: From al Paso to Saravejo, How White Nationalists have been Inspired by the Genocide of Muslims in Bosnia. September 1, 2019
https://theintercept.com/2019/09/01/bosnian-genocide-mass-shootings/

> The violence in Bosnia was a religious genocide in several senses: the people destroyed were chosen on the basis of their religious identity; those carrying out the killings acted with the blessing and support of Christian church leaders; the violence was grounded in a religious mythology that characterized the targeted people as race traitors and the extermination of them as a sacred act.[1229]

Serb Orthodox soldiers forced Bosnian Muslim and Catholic Croat prisoners to sing Christian folks songs; and soldiers also sang them as they slit the throats of their captives; and crucifixes dangled from the necks of soldiers who raped Muslim women in the Srebrenica prison camp.[1230] The 44th Patriarch of the Serbian Orthodox Church, His Holiness the Archbishop of Pe´c, Metropolitan of Belgrade and Karlovc, Serbian Patriarch Pavle (known more commonly as Patriarch Pavle), branded Muslims as evil.

> Evil always attacks, and good must defend itself.... Cain always tries to kill Abel, and Abel has to defend himself. Defending oneself against attacks by wrongdoers, defending one's life, life and the peace of one's nearest and dearest against the criminals.[1231]

The Church further condoned violence through official publications and speeches supporting the nationalist government and antipathies toward Muslims (including an admonishment of Serb pacifism), providing concrete assistance through logistical and moral support, even at times leading cleansing activities.[1232] In 1992, the local church in Brˇcko, a town in northern Bosnia acted as a base for killing, body disposal, and concentration camp operations, all overseen by the self-proclaimed "Serb Adolf", Goran Jelisi.[1233] Church officials also blessed weapons and forces, conducted formal rituals in recognition of the successful ethnic cleansing of towns, and supplied chaplains to and fostered the morale of the Bosnian Serb Army, and spearheading cleansing operations.[1234]

The same on the Croat side. In 2005, Carla del Ponte, the chief war crimes prosecutor in the Hague, insisted that:

> The leading Croat war crimes suspect, General Ante Gotovina, was being sheltered in a Catholic monastery. 'The Catholic Church is protecting him,' she concluded, adding that 'I have taken this up with the Vatican and the Vatican totally refuses to cooperate with us.'[1235]

[1229] Michael Sells: *The Bridge Betrayed: religion and genocide in Bosnia*, 144.
[1230] K.E. Temoney: Religion and Genocide Nexuses: Bosnia as Case Study, in Religions 2017, 8, 112; doi:10.3390/rel8060112, p.7
[1231] K.E. Temoney: Religion and Genocide Nexuses: Bosnia as Case Study, in Religions 2017, 8, 112; doi:10.3390/rel8060112, p. 13.
[1232] K.E. Temoney: Religion and Genocide Nexuses: Bosnia as Case Study, in Religions 2017, 8, 112; doi:10.3390/rel8060112, p.7
[1233] M. Sells: Kosovo Mythology and the Bosnian Genocide. In God's Name: Genocide and Religion in the Twentieth Century. Edited by Omer Bartov and Phyllis Mack. New York and Oxford: Berghahn Books, 2001, p. 188.
[1234] K.E. Temoney: Religion and Genocide Nexuses: Bosnia as Case Study, in Religions 2017, 8, 112; doi:10.3390/rel8060112, p. 14-15.
[1235] news.bbc.co.uk/1/hi/world/europe/4263426.stm

More generally, she complained that 'the Church, on all sides, is adding legitimacy to visions of history which are twisted in accordance with nationalist biases'.[1236]

Abd al Hakim Murad makes the pertinent point:

> The reality, which was frequently one of militant Christian extremism, was never, to my knowledge, frankly discussed. The war was, we were told, a contest between 'ethnic factions'; and the fact that its protagonists were divided primarily by religion, and shared a race and a language, was deemed insignificant. Anti-Muslim prejudice was no doubt at work here: one may assume that if the Serbs and Catholics had been Muslims, and their victims Christians, then the Western mind would immediately have characterised the war as a case of violent Muslims murdering secular, integrated, democratic Christians. Since in Bosnia the favoured stereotypes were reversed, the memory has largely been dismissed, censored and forgotten as an annoying anomaly.[1237]

We always hear of Muslim fighters/terrorists joining in the wars against Christians, but we hardly if ever, hear of Christian volunteers, or Nazis, joining the Christian side. In the Civil war in Lebanon, a large contingent of Catholics, Frenchmen, in particular, fought on the side of the Christian Maronites in the 1970s,[1238] and participated in the massacres of Palestinians. In Bosnia, whilst we hear a lot of the volunteers who fought on the Serb side, and the Muslim 'terrorists' who fought on the Muslim side, the latter subsequently hounded by the various secret agencies, we know little, if at all, of the even greater support given to the Croat side by such volunteers, generally with full local Catholic Church assistance. The Croat side attracted many neo-Nazis from across the continent during this period, which happened

> Thanks in no small part to the decision by the national government in Zagreb to reprise as national markers the World War II-era symbols of the Independent State of Croatia, a fascist puppet regime of the Third Reich.[1239]

Arklov, for example, was a Liberian-Swedish neo-Nazi who joined the Croatian Defense Forces, and who victims say conducted brutal tortures in Croat-run concentration camps in Herzegovina. He was arrested and convicted for war crimes by the Bosnian government but was released a year after, returning to Sweden, where he was acquitted of the crimes for lack of evidence.[1240]

[1236] www.un.org/icty/pressreal/2005/p1001-e.htm
[1237] A. H. Murad: The Churches and the Bosnian War, http://masud.co.uk/ISLAM/ahm/the_churches_and_the_bosnian_war.htm
[1238] See Emmanuel Albach: Un Volontaire au Liban, 1976-2016, https://www.youtube.com/watch?v=UXC8p7a34L4
Jean Ives Camus: The French National Front and Lebanon, The progressive Post https://progressivepost.eu/spotlights/french-national-front-lebanon
[1239] A. Ibrahim, Hikmet karcic: The Balkan wars Created a Generation of Christian Terrorists, May 24, 2019; https://foreignpolicy.com/2019/05/24/the-balkan-wars-created-a-generation-of-christian-terrorists/
[1240] A. Ibrahim, Hikmet karcic The Balkan wars Created a Generation of Christian Terrorists, May 24, 2019; https://foreignpolicy.com/2019/05/24/the-balkan-wars-created-a-generation-of-christian-terrorists/

We take particular note of some facts which have remained consistent throughout history, whether in the wake of the eradication of Muslims in Sicily or Spain, or the colonial wars, or the American invasion of Iraq, in words any onslaught on Islam: the particular focus by the slayers on Muslim elites. As noted by Murtaza Hussain:

> But what made the killings effective beyond their numbers was their terrifying nature. Intellectuals, politicians, religious leaders, and others somehow esteemed in their community were murdered in horrible public spectacles. The net effect seemed calculated to destroy the Muslims' ability to regenerate themselves as a community. With their leaders murdered in terrifying ways, the morale of their people would be broken.[1241]

But here, as noted by Buchenau, where the most important fact resides:

> The Serbian Orthodox Church and the Catholic Church enjoy an enormous prestige in 'their' respective societies. If a certain version of history is spread from the pulpit, it easily acquires a dignity it has not had before transforming it into sacred history. The myth of Serbs and Croats as centuries-long victims needs constant renewal, if it is to survive. For so far [sic], the Churches have provided solid fuel for its survival.[1242]

Vile narrative of history is the demon this author fights, and inept Muslims hardly see it, with rare exceptions as in these extracts:

> There are wars that happen where people are taken somewhere, lined up against a wall, and shot," Sabanija said as we drove slowly through the sunlit streets of his hometown. "This was different. There was so much cruelty and even enjoyment; they invented new ways of killing people in this war. All that hatred, we never saw it! These people were our friends and our neighbors. Suddenly, they turned and told us that we were enemies. Why? 'Because of history.' [1243]

Indeed, we are back to the main and central element of this work, that in narrative Muslims and Islam are the culprits, regardless of what happens and has always happened on the ground as we saw through this work. The other side, the Christian, of course, as white as an angel, and since the birth of times. And it is working wonders in Bosnia, as we can read through these extracts:

> In the ethnically cleansed areas of Bosnia, where the genocide occurred, today the perpetrators seem to have narrowed their responses to either

---

[1241] Murtaza Hussain: The Intercept: From al Paso to Saravejo, How White Nationalists have been Inspired by the Genocide of Muslims in Bosnia. September 1, 2019
https://theintercept.com/2019/09/01/bosnian-genocide-mass-shootings/
[1242] K. Buchenau: The Churches and the Hague Tribunal: A Serbian Orthodox and a Croat Catholic Perspective. Forschungsplattform Südosteuropa, 2009 at http://www.google.com/url?sa=t&rct=j&q=&esrc=s&source=web&cd=1&cad=rja&sqi=2&ved=0CDUQFjAA&url=http%3A%2F%2Ffpsoe.de%2Ffileadmin%2F2FPDFs_Beitraege%2FFPSOE_Buchenau_Churches_and_ICTY.pdf&ei=fABlUY31N4XWygGSvIDoCw&usg=AFQjCNGJscQAzOk0lTDfeQ4jAiRvZqDFww&sig2=ul_eTDPONUzp-k1nKAi68w&bvm=bv.44990110,d.aWc
[1243] Murtaza Hussain: The Intercept: From al Paso to Saravejo, How White Nationalists have been Inspired by the Genocide of Muslims in Bosnia. September 1, 2019
https://theintercept.com/2019/09/01/bosnian-genocide-mass-shootings/

ignoring what happened or celebrating it. In addition to the memorial on the hill above Višegrad, in the town center a bronze statue stands in honor of local military veterans, several of whom have been convicted of war crimes at The Hague. Aside from a few small plaques put up by victims' groups in neighborhoods where mass killings happened, there is no recognition of the massacres — and those plaques have been placed on the upper floors of buildings to keep them out of reach after repeated vandalism. A few years ago, the local municipality even sandblasted the word "genocide" off a memorial stone erected by victims' families in the town's Muslim graveyard. When I visited that cemetery this summer, the word had still been obliterated from the monument — though someone had defiantly written it back in with black marker.[1244]

Iraq 2003-

At the height of the American led invasion of Iraq, early in the Summer of 2006, next to the report on the American massacre of Iraqis in Haditha, the British daily newspaper *The Guardian*, had the following report, titled: ***'21 Shias and Kurds taken off bus and shot at fake checkpoint.'***

This article went on to say:

> A group of students on their way to end-of-year exams were among 21 people massacred by gunmen at a bogus checkpoint in Iraq's restive Diyala province yesterday in one of the most shocking sectarian attacks in the country in recent weeks.
>
> The 12 students who were studying at al-Yarmouk University of Baquba, 40 miles north of Baghdad, were among passengers who were hauled by the gunmen from their convoy of three minibuses early yesterday morning.
>
> According to local police the passengers were separated on the side of the road into Sunni Arabs and non Sunni Arabs. The non-Sunnis, including 19 Shia Turkomen and two Kurds, were then shot. Some tried to escape but were gunned down.
>
> The dead also include several elderly men, police said. One person was wounded. Four Sunni Arab passengers who survived the ordeal were later helping police with their enquiries.
>
> The attack came a day after the police discovered seven heads in banana boxes by the roadside in Baquba, a mixed Sunni-Shia town that has seen an upsurge in violence. Another head, that of a local Sunni cleric, was perched on top of the boxes. A note with the heads said:

[1244] Murtaza Hussain: The Intercept: From al Paso to Saravejo, How White Nationalists have been Inspired by the Genocide of Muslims in Bosnia. September 1, 2019
https://theintercept.com/2019/09/01/bosnian-genocide-mass-shootings/

> 'This is the fate of every traitor. Hell will be his final destination.'
> Police believe the seven beheaded men were Sunni cousins who worked together driving lorries for foreign contractors...
> In other weekend violence, 33 people died in Basra when a suicide bomber attacked a busy local market...
> Tensions in the port city worsened yesterday when Sunni religious groups in the city accused the Shia-dominated security forces of killing 12 unarmed worshippers in a mosque in revenge for the bombing,...[1245]

This article dwarfed into insignificance the report by its side of American atrocities committed on Iraqis, bringing into focus the barbaric side of the Muslims instead. This article, of course, failed to say that for centuries Sunnis and Shias have lived side by side, inter-marrying, and never inflicted on each other such atrocities. The report failed to say that Sunnis and Shias, instead, and in equal measure, have suffered the worst atrocities at the hands of the Westernised/Western backed secular and other elites which have been ruling the Arab world to this day (despite the fleeting hope given by the so-called Arab Spring of 2011-2012, before things returned to business as usual, or in fact worse than usual. May the days of Mubarak return in Egypt). This article highlights the quite effective Western practice of showing alternate sympathies to one ethnic/sectarian/tribal/ side of the Muslim world, and then to another, before thrashing both, beginning with the strongest.

The article above, most of all, failed to raise one crucial question: who really was behind such killings, which were so very well organised and expertly carried out, with their authors never being caught. This article, like all other media reports that covered the horrors of Iraq, often with great delight at the news of Shia killing Sunnis and vice versa,[1246] failed to ask the question, how could such killings take place in front of units of the army itself, killings witnessed by soldiers who refused to intervene, as reported by the Western media themselves.[1247] These expert killings require considerable logistical capabilities and demand much better-organised, managed and structured groups, with the power to mount operations much beyond the capability of the ordinary insurgency which relied mainly on roadside bombs. How could it be possible other than for state sponsored death squads to pick people, take them across towns and cities, torture them to death, behead them, and then dump their corpses in waste dumps, in banana boxes or wherever.[1248] The responsibility of the dark agencies in these massacres and in acting as the death squads (and bombers when convenient), was further highlighted in mid November 2006 when a mass kidnapping took place.[1249]

[1245] *The Guardian*, 5 June 06, p. 15.

[1246] A Western journalist working for one of the biggest news agencies in Iraq reported with unparalleled enthusiasm the supposedly tit-for tat killings amongst Sunnis and Shias on 23 November 06 (seen by this author).

[1247] The Independent 25 November 06; p. 32.

[1248] See The Independent 22 September pp. 1-2 for brief summary of this report, a report the Independent journalists sought to dilute by adding their own interpretations of events.

[1249] All media reported this incident which occurred on 14 November 06.

The killings in Iraq have served the aim of removing the unwanted, to decapitate opposition to occupation, and to divide the country, and from there the rest of the Muslim land, into sectarian Bantustans, literally tearing each other apart. Here mission accomplished, indeed: Sunnis and Shias hatred for each other and slaughtering each other are at their optimum as they had never been in history.

More importantly, the report above is one of the hundreds that have come from Iraq, one among thousands of similar reports, which in recent decades have surfaced from the Muslim world, are all aimed at maintaining an image, a thousand year old, an image that serves a multiplicity of purposes as we see throughout this work: Islamic barbarism.

Let's have two extracts from the equally liberal and Muslim loving *The Independent*. In the first report, it says:

> As Islamic militancy increases, women find it more dangerous not to wear a veil in Sunni and Shia neighbourhoods. One was warned not to drive a car. Others were told to cover their faces and to stop using mobile phones. Threats against women who do not accept this second-class status have escalated in the last two months. It has also become dangerous for men to wear shorts or jeans in public, or for children to play outside wearing shorts.[1250]

Four days later,[1251] the same daily on the sad plight of an Iraqi woman:

> Her husband was dragged from his car by insurgents, tortured, mutilated and murdered-his body left at the road side.... He was a rare man in Iraq. He treated her like an equal...
>
> With the re-introduction of Islamic tradition of passing a man's wealth to surviving male members of his family, she could have been left penniless. Even in her own home she must always wear black and knows she will suffer the wrath of militants if she disobeys. The few hours a week she emerges are to teach but she has been told she must give up her job.

Firstly, it never occurred to *The Independent* journalist or to many others telling us the most fantastic tales about Islamic terror, that in the chaos of Iraq, or Syria, or in many parts of the Muslim world, in fact, anyone can issue any order to kill, kidnap, maim, and commit the most atrocious that the dark side of humans can devise. How can one in countries where chaos rules, where the law has no place, where human life is utterly meaningless, where anyone who puts his or her nose in such murky businesses ends up chopped off to pieces; how can one, indeed, be certain anyone is who they claim. Any bearded, or cagouled, thug, could be either a blinded fanatic, a fanatic or not, under the orders of someone in an office far in a civilised land, or he could simply be a champion criminal and atheist, or maybe not Muslim at all. And none, at the risk of their own life (and dreadfully painful last moments of it), is allowed to find who this fiend truly is.

[1250] P. Cockburn: Leaked memo reveals plight of Iraqis; *The Independent*; 20 June 06; p. 2.
[1251] T. Judd: A Woman without a man is like a tree without water; in *The Independent* Saturday 24 June; 06; p. 23.

Secondly, it would not occur to these journalists that these stories are meant to discredit Islam whether in Iraq or Syria, or anywhere else there is conflict of the sort, and anywhere states and powerful organisations and interests are engaged in removing Islamic opposition, or just seeking to undermine Islam. Such states/organisations commit the worst of deeds such as the senseless, barbaric slaughter of hostages or prisoners, always decent, innocent, figures, and then let 'the Islamic militants' claim such acts.

Thirdly, it would never occur to journalists and others that what they say about Islamic crimes run in contradiction with everything else we hear. In Iraq, for instance, Western journalists could not tell us what's going on there because they could not leave the Green Zone (*The Guardian* March 12, 07; p. 3 of Media Section.) So how could the *Independent* journalists relate the stories above with confidence from behind the walls of the Green Zone, and from even further distances? It is the same in Syria and any other zone of violence, for none of the assertions or claims of whatever deed can be verified as to who truly are the authors of such deeds.

Finally, in respect to Iraq, in particular, so little has been said, most particularly of the flattening of whole towns and cities beyond the view of cameras, the countless disappearances, and the mass extra-judicial killings perpetrated in secret places, the works of the secret death squads masquerading as Shia and Sunni extremist groups. These questions raise one fundamental problem we started with this chapter: in rhetoric: the Muslim is the beast, but on the ground, strewn is his mangled body, together with that of his family at times, unless, of course, these Islamists do it to themselves or each other. Anyway, the usual good critical sense of the Westerners, who go to extremes to find every detail that could deny, for instance, Islamic accomplishments in sciences and civilisation, suddenly this same inquisitive, good sense deserts them in these situations, and with rare exceptions, they become impotent, utter cretins in fact.

But let's tell you more on the Iraqi masquerade in the language of journalists and other commentators, but a tragedy for Muslims. It, of course, began with the West fostering the demonic figure of Saddam Hussein, whom they had themselves helped to reach and stay in power. Then they used his crimes against his people and his neighbours, which they themselves supported by every means, to enhance his barbaric image. Then, to justify invasion, they created the usual threat of Iraq armed with weapons of mass destruction. They unleashed a terrible onslaught on Iraq in 2003, which they disguised behind the usual noble rhetoric of 'Operation freedom, democracy, rebuilding of Iraq,' and similar empty expressions used for centuries in relation to the Muslim world. In truth, all that we saw and still see in Iraq has been the killing of hundreds of thousands of its population, and the wiping out of many of its cities and villages, besides the looting of its oil wealth.[1252]

[1252] See article by K. Mahdi: Iraqis will never accept this sellout to the oil corporations; *The Guardian;* 16 January 2007; p. 28.

In order to justify some 'radical' policies, such as the destruction of Felloujah, the hub of resistance to the invaders, there, by some miracle, emerged the greatest modern terrorist of all: Abu Musa'ab al-Zarqawi, precisely in the city of Felloujah. So it was flattened in November 2004 with an unknown number of casualties to this day. Al Zarqawi, of course, thanks to his superhuman powers, common to all 'Muslim terrorists,' fled the city but only to reappear whenever and wherever a bombardment of a town or a city was needed. After him, we had another convenient 'terrorist,' Al Baghdadi, who seems to have the life of ten cats, dead at least fifty times, and reborn at least another fifty, and surely will live until another equally un-dead terrorist will appear. Terror by these and others was, and still is, used to justify the mass arrests, disappearances, torture, extra judicial liquidations (the same as happened in many countries in previous decades), besides explaining bombings of civilian targets, killings of leading and intellectual figures, assassination of decent military officers, and the mass killings by death squads (also as happened in many countries).

But here comes the most vile of all institutions, the UN, to tell us who and what are the sources of the mayhem, not a mention, not a word blaming the invasion, rather as we see in these extracts from its report dated 14 September 2006: **IRAQ NOW ONE OF MOST VIOLENT CONFLICT AREAS IN WORLD, CHALLENGES FACING PEOPLE NEVER MORE DAUNTING, SPECIAL REPRESENTATIVE TELLS SECURITY COUNCIL**[1253]

> Despite the significant achievements in the political transition process, meeting the benchmarks endorsed by the Council in resolution 1546 (2004) has not translated into an improved security and human rights situation, the report states. This remains a major challenge. Insurgent, militia and terrorist attacks, as well as gross violations of human rights, including killings, kidnappings and torture, continued unabated in many parts of the country. Iraq today has become one of the most violent conflict areas in the world.
> Over the past three years, the Iraqi people have made many sacrifices to support their country's political transition, the report says. Through their active participation in two elections, the constitutional process and the constitutional referendum, they have demonstrated their commitment to a peaceful, democratic and prosperous Iraq, despite the very tight transitional timetable and challenging security environment. The Iraqi people now have every right to expect their elected leaders -- first and foremost their constitutionally-elected Government -- to do everything possible to deliver tangible improvements in their day-to-day lives
> JOHN BOLTON (United States), reporting on behalf of the 29 countries making up the Multinational Force, said the most recent reporting period coincided with the first 90 days of a democratically elected, representative

---

[1253] At https://www.un.org/press/en/2006/sc8829.doc.htm

unity Government -- a substantial break from Iraq's past. In early June, the formation of a national unity Government had been completed with the appointments of the Ministers of Interior, Defence and State for National Security Affairs. On 25 June, Prime Minister Al-Maliki had presented a "National Reconciliation and Dialogue Project" to the Council of Representatives. That Project sought to reconcile past inequities and rally Iraqis around the principle of equality without sectarian divisions. It looked to establish the basis for national unity through the democratic process and create the conditions for Iraq to assume a leading regional and international role. Most of the 24 Council Committees had formed and named chairs, and was making progress on key legislation required to implement the provisions of the Iraqi Constitution.

In late July, the Iraqi Government and the United Nations, with the strong support of the United States, the United Kingdom and other donors had launched the International Compact with Iraq. The Compact would, over the next five years, bring together the international community and multilateral organizations to help Iraq achieve its vision of a united, federal and democratic country, at peace with its neighbours and itself, and economically self-sufficient and prosperous.

Since July 2003, there had been significant successes in the development of legitimate political, economic and governmental institutions in Iraq, he said. The unfolding of the democratic electoral process had been a crucial success in building the foundations of a new free and democratic Iraq. Despite those achievements, obstacles remained. Setbacks in the level and nature of violence in Iraq continued to create significant challenges to stability, reconstruction and transition. Sectarian tensions purposely incited by insurgents and extremists had increased over the last quarter, resulting in increased killings, kidnappings, attacks on civilians and increasing numbers of internally displaced persons. Extremists were increasingly interlocked in retaliatory violence and seeking to expand their existing areas of influence. The sustained level of ethno-sectarian violence was one of the most significant threats to security and stability in Iraq.

Nonetheless, the Iraqi people continued to reject violence overwhelmingly as a means to drive political change, he said. The international community remained steadfast with the Iraqi people in their determined drive for a secure, stable and democratic country.

On the security situation, he noted that insurgents, extremists and terrorists remained capable and intent on carrying out attacks against Iraqi civilian officials and security forces, with a goal of destabilizing the legitimately elected Iraq Government and denying the Iraq people the democracy and promise of a better future that they had chosen through free and fair elections.[1254]

John Bolton, one of the artisans of the war, together with Tony Blair, to this very moment sees nothing wrong in the invasion, rather the opposite. He states:
> Our broad international coalition accomplished its military mission with low casualties and great speed, sending an unmistakable signal of power and determination throughout the Middle East and around the world. Despite all the criticism of what happened after Saddam's defeat, these facts are indisputable.
> Nonetheless, relentless hostility by the war's opponents now threaten to overwhelm, in the public mind, the clear merits of eliminating Iraq's Ba'athist dictatorship. Leaving the critics unanswered, combined with the utterly erroneous policy conclusions they have derived, will only lead to more serious problems down the road. Let us consider a few of the prevailing myths...[1255]

He devotes plenty of attention to debunking such myths, and we are not interested.

Tony Blair, perhaps the person responsible for the Iraq tragedy more than any other, for he legitimised more than the rest, still has no regrets:
> I don't think this struggle was in vain in the end [Blair said in an interview on BBC Radio 4.' I sincerely believe that we would be in a worse position if we hadn't acted in that way. It's not simply because of the hundreds of thousands of people that were victims of Saddam before he was deposed. If he'd been left in power, he would have gone back to his programs again.[1256]

Of course Blair does not speak of the hundreds of thousands and possibly a million by now people who have paid the ultimate price besides the horrors and destruction. Even worse, he, just like all Westerners, avoids mentioning the worst monster the Iraq war has unleashed, that has already claimed millions inside and outside Iraq, and will claim millions more, Sectarianism, and Blair and other Westerners were aware of what they were doing. The war was neither started to remove Saddam, or build, or free Iraq, neither was it started for oil. Only idiots believe in these things. The war was started in order to ignite the Sectarian monster, just as all the policies in the region since the First World War, to this moment. And in the following we see how Western opinion makers try to deviate or divert the issue, never blaming the invasion for the unleashing of the monster. Instead they blame the victims, as they always do, whether in regard to the killings

---

[1254] At https://www.un.org/press/en/2006/sc8829.doc.htm
[1255] J. Bolton: Overthrowing Saddam Hussein was the Right Move for the US and its Allies; in The Guardian, Tuesday, 26 February, 2013 at https://www.theguardian.com/commentisfree/2013/feb/26/iraq-war-was-justified
accessed 10 January 2020
[1256] Zoya Sheftalovitch" Tony Blair: I regret Mistakes but the Iraq War was justified on 7 July 2016, at https://www.politico.eu/article/tony-blair-i-regret-mistakes-but-iraq-war-was-justified/
accessed 10 January 2020

in the Balkans in the 1990s, or the Native Indians centuries earlier in the Americas (on their innate barbarism,) or the centuries of 'hatred between Berbers and Arabs, Arabs and Turks, and Sunnis and Shias.' They never remember that the Sunnis and Shias never inflicted on each other what Protestants and Catholics did to each other, forgetting, most of all, that it would take a firework to explode in a Protestant or Catholic Church anywhere for the episodes of 1618-1648 to return, for Sectarianism only needs to be tickled a little to wake up in anger spouting fire from all corners.

But let's just cite a couple of these wonderful men of intellect and lovers of justice and goodness, and all that is wonderful on this turd filled earth, explaining to us the genesis of the Sunni-Shia Hatred, and the particularly evil role of the Sunnis in this:

Patrick Cockburn again:

> I was in Iraq in April 1991 when government security forces crushed the Shia uprising against Saddam Hussein's regime, killing tens of thousands and burying their bodies in pits. I had been expelled from Iraq to Jordan at the start of the rebellion in March and then, to my surprise, allowed to return, because Saddam wanted to prove to the world that he was back in control.
>
> Coalition forces stood aside as Saddam's tanks, with helicopters overhead, smashed their way into Shia cities like Karbala, Najaf and Basra, and then began their mass executions.
>
> Three decades later, the US and its allies are still making the same mistake, treating the millions of Shia in Iraq, Lebanon, Syria, Bahrain, Yemen and Afghanistan as if they were Iranian agents.
>
> Down the centuries, the Shia have been one of the most savagely persecuted religious minorities; they fear today that in the wake of the assassination of Qassem Soleimani, they are once again being demonised, as Donald Trump denounces all who oppose the US in the Middle East as Iranian proxies.
>
> One of the most significant developments in the Middle East since 1945 has been the rise of the previously marginalised and impoverished Shia communities in many – though not all – of the region's countries, above all Lebanon and Iraq, the latter becoming the first Shia-ruled state in the Arab world since Saladin overthrew the Fatimid dynasty in Egypt in 1171.
>
> Yet American and British politicians too often treat the rise of the Shia as if this was purely the outcome of unjustifiable Iranian interference. Western leaders find it convenient to adopt the anti-Shia propaganda line pumped out by Sunni states like Saudi Arabia, which persecutes its own Shia minority, and Bahrain, which has an even more oppressed Shia majority.
>
> In both countries, Shia demanding civil rights are punished as terrorists and alleged proxies of Iran. Often, the Sunni authorities are convinced by their own propaganda: when the Bahraini government, backed by Saudi troops, crushed the Arab Spring protests on the island in 2011, Shia

doctors in a nearby hospital were tortured to make them admit that they were receiving orders from Iran.[1257]

Michael Axworthy wrote the piece, "Sunni vs Shia: the roots of Islam's civil war". Amongst others, he informs us:

> More than 85 per cent of the world's Muslims are Sunni, and historically many have distrusted and disliked Shias.
>
> There is nothing on the Iranian or Shia side to compare with the damage done by the extreme Wahhabi world-view that led to the attacks of 11 September 2001, the atrocities of IS in Iraq and Syria and its outrages in Paris, Nice, London and Manchester. However paranoid the Saudis are, and whatever the degree to which they believe their own propaganda about Iran, they know the greatest threat to their retention of power in Saudi Arabia is from home-grown Wahhabi extremists.
>
> Most Islamic terrorism in the last 20 years, overwhelmingly, has been carried out by Sunni extremists, not Shias or Iranians.
>
> Even Hezbollah has reduced its violent activity towards Israel, as it tries to present itself as a Lebanese political party rather than a paramilitary group. The reality is that most Islamic terrorism internationally is associated with Sunni militant groups.[1258]

Of course it is not just the media, but also the influential and gentle figures such as Obama, who in 2013, claimed in his State of the Union address that unrest in the Middle East was "rooted in conflicts that date back millennia."

This is the same Obama who was neither harsh on the coup perpetrators whether in Egypt in 2013, nor those of Turkey in 2016, rather... but let's leave what we don't know in the realm of what we don't know.

[1257] Patrick Cockburn: The West is still Buying Nonsense Claims about Iran's regional Influence, Friday 10 January, 2020, https://www.independent.co.uk/voices/iran-iraq-middle-east-crisis-shia-proxy-influence-a9278696.html accessed 10 January 2020

[1258] Michael Axworthy "Sunni vs Shia: the roots of Islam's civil war", The New Statesman, 29 August 2017, at https://www.newstatesman.com/world/middle-east/2017/08/sunni-vs-shia-roots-islam-s-civil-war; accessed 10 January 2020. See also his article in the *Guardian* 28 January 2015: Is it time to make Iran our friend and Saudi Arabia our enemy?

Twelve

THE LATEST: THE 2016 COUP IN TURKEY

What part did Western countries play in the coup on 15 July, 2016, is impossible for this author, a mere mortal, to know. Allah, secret agencies, and a couple of people themselves involved surely know. For this author, therefore, to accuse any country would be completely barmy on his part. But, like everything else, give it some time, and we will know.

We can at this stage, of course, venture to say that no coup takes place unless the Western masters are first notified, and they say 'go ahead, mate.' The reason for the notification and seeking approval is simple: no coup plotter likes to find himself later in the Hague, especially after tens of thousands of people had been slain, and especially if some of the wrong people, i.e friends or allies, also fall victims to the coup. So, whilst this author cannot say a word on whether the West played any concrete part in the carrying out of the coup, he can, however, give details on the part the West played in justifying the coup before, during, and after.

a. Before the coup.

First released 24 March 16:
By Michael Rubin: Will There Be a Coup Against Erdogan in Turkey?
http://europe.newsweek.com/will-there-be-coup-against-erdogan-turkey-439181
This article First appeared on the American Enterprise Institute Site:

'The situation in Turkey is bad and getting worse. It's not just the deterioration in security amidst a wave of terrorism. Public debt might be stable, but private debt is out of control, the tourism sector is in free fall, and the decline in the currency has impacted every citizen's buying power.

There is a broad sense, election results notwithstanding, that President Recep Tayyip Erdogan is out of control. He is imprisoning opponents, seizing newspapers left and right and building palaces at the rate of a mad sultan or aspiring caliph. In recent weeks, he has once again threatened to dissolve the constitutional court. Corruption is rife. His son Bilal reportedly fled to Italy on a forged Saudi diplomatic passport as the Italian police closed in on him in an alleged money laundering scandal.

His outbursts are raising eyebrows both in Turkey and abroad. Even members of his ruling party whisper about his increasing paranoia which, according to some

Turkish officials, has gotten so bad that he seeks to install anti-aircraft missiles at his palace to prevent airborne men-in-black from targeting him in a snatch-and-grab operation.

Turks—and the Turkish military—increasingly recognize that Erdogan is taking Turkey to the precipice. By first bestowing legitimacy upon imprisoned Kurdish leader Abdullah Öcalan with renewed negotiations and then precipitating renewed conflict, he has taken Turkey down a path in which there is no chance of victory and a high chance of *de facto* partition.

After all, if civil war renews as in the 1980s and early 1990s, Turkey's Kurds will be hard-pressed to settle for anything less, all the more so given the precedent now established by their brethren in Iraq and Syria.

Erdogan long ago sought to kneecap the Turkish military. For the first decade of his rule, both the U.S. government and European Union cheered him on. But that was before even Erdogan's most ardent foreign apologists recognized the depth of his descent into madness and autocracy.

So if the Turkish military moves to oust Erdogan and place his inner circle behind bars, could they get away with it?

In the realm of analysis rather than advocacy, the answer is yes. At this point in election season, it is doubtful that the Obama administration would do more than castigate any coup leaders, especially if they immediately laid out a clear path to the restoration of democracy.

Nor would Erdogan engender the type of sympathy that Egyptian President Muhammad Morsi did. When Morsi was ousted, his commitment to democracy was still subject to debate.

That debate is now moot when it comes to the Turkish strongman. Neither the Republican nor Democratic front-runners would put U.S. prestige on the line to seek a return to the status quo ante. They might offer lip service against a coup, but they would work with the new regime.

Coup leaders might moot European and American human rights and civil society criticism and that of journalists by immediately freeing all detained journalists and academics and by returning seized newspapers and television stations to their rightful owners.

Turkey's NATO membership is no deterrent to action: Neither Turkey nor Greece lost their NATO membership after previous coups. Should a new leadership engage sincerely with Turkey's Kurds, Kurds might come onboard.

Neither European nor American public opinion would likely be sympathetic to the execution of Erdogan, his son and son-in-law, or key aides like Egemen Bağış and Cüneyd Zapsu, although they would accept a trial for corruption and long incarceration. Erdoğan might hope friends would rally to his side, but most of his friends—both internationally and inside Turkey—are attracted to his power. Once out of his palace, he may find himself very much alone, a shriveled and confused figure like Saddam Hussein at his own trial.

I make no predictions, but given rising discord in Turkey as well as the likelihood that the Turkish military would suffer no significant consequence should it imitate Abdel Fattah el-Sisi's game plan in Egypt, no one should be surprised if Turkey's rocky politics soon get rockier.

Michael Rubin is a resident scholar at the American Enterprise Institute. A former Pentagon official, his major research areas are the Middle East, Turkey, Iran and diplomacy.

****

By Peter Korzun
Article dated: 19 May 2016 In Strategic Culture Foundation Online Journal
Title: Turkey: On the Brink of Military Coup?

'The situation in Turkey keeps getting worse. Private debt is out of control, the tourism sector is in free fall and the decline in the currency has impacted every citizen's buying power. Because of increasing pressures on the central bank and political storms, Turkey's annual growth rate has already slowed.

The 2013 Gezi protests and corruption charges against the government, the 2014 presidential election and two general elections in 2015 have put the Turkish economy under stress. Turkey's annual growth rate, which for 50 years had averaged 4.5%, remained at an average 3% in the past four years. Economists are warning that delays in structural reforms and Erdogan's economic views could push the growth rate even lower, triggering a crisis.

Kamil Yilmaz, a professor of economics at Koc University, says «*Turkey has slowed down because it could not implement structural reforms. Because of the political developments of the past three years, investment have all but come to a halt. Further slowing of the economy is inevitable under these conditions*».

President Recep Tayyip Erdogan seems to be out of control. He is cracking down on opposition, imprisoning opponents and seizing media outlets. Not once the Turkish leader has threatened to dissolve the constitutional court. It is taking place at the time the security problems have deteriorated amidst a wave of terrorism.

The events make the Turkish military emerge on political landscape again after many years of marginalization during «Sultan» Erdogan's rule. The divisions between the Turkish military and Erdogan have a long history, but today it is amplified by tumultuous events in and outside the country. For instance, the plans to create a buffer zone in Northern Syria and send the Turkish troops to Syria and Iraq are opposed by military brass.

It makes spring to mind the decision of Egyptian military to take the reins in the country when US President Obama supported the takeover of Egypt by the Muslim Brotherhood. The military challenged the United States and took power to prevent the worst from happening. In the 1990s the military saved Algeria from collapse.

The current President of Turkey has never trusted the military viewing it as a challenge to his insatiable imperial ambitions. Despite that, the outbreak of war in Syria and the ongoing operations against the Kurdistan Workers' Party (PKK) in the southeastern part of the country make the President reconcile with the role of the military re-emerging as an influential force.

Michael Rubin, a resident scholar at the American Enterprise Unit and a former Pentagon official, predicts an imminent military coup in Turkey. According to the expert, *«Turks – and the Turkish military – increasingly recognize that Erdogan is taking Turkey to the precipice»*. Rubin believes that *«he* [Erdogan] *has taken Turkey down a path in which there is no chance of victory and a high chance of de facto partition»*. According to him, *«If the Turkish military moves to oust Erdogan and place his inner circle behind bars, could they get away with it? In the realm of analysis rather than advocacy, the answer is yes»*. Rubin writes, it is doubtful that the Obama administration would do more than castigate any coup leaders, especially if they immediately laid out a clear path to the restoration of democracy. Neither Turkey nor Greece lost their NATO membership after coups.

The Turkish military has long seen itself as the «guardian of Turkish democracy», which it defines as the staunchly secular state created by Mustafa Kemal Ataturk, the founder of the modern Turkish republic. It directly intervened three times (1960, 1971 and 1980) in Turkish politics. In 1997 the military carried out what some scholars describe as a «postmodern coup». Back then the military issued a series of «recommendations», which the government had no choice but to accept.

The Ergenekon trials, a series of high-profile court hearings, took place in 2008-2011. 275 people, including military officers, journalists and opposition lawmakers, all alleged members of ERGENEKON, a supposed secularist clandestine organization, were accused of plotting against the Turkish government. The trials resulted in lengthy prison sentences for the majority of the accused. In 2010 Turkish police arrested hundreds of current and former military officials accused of plotting to overthrow Mr Erdogan's government. Hundreds were sent to jail, but the cases eventually crumbled.

The «palace coup – 2016» took place just a few days ago. After losing a power struggle with Mr Erdogan, Prime Minister Ahmet Davutoglu decided to step down after an extraordinary party meeting on May 22 and not run for the office again. Critics of Mr Erdogan called it a «palace coup» that would let the president consolidate power.

«The restoration of the Turkish army's influence has resurrected concerns all the way up to the presidential palace that generals might try to topple Mr Erdogan, a polarizing figure whose extensive crackdown on domestic dissent has triggered alarm in Western capitals, according to people familiar with the matter», writes Dion Nissenbaum, a US national security expert based in Washington, in his article published by *The Wall Street Journal*.

Turkey is at a crossroads. The time is right for changes. One way or another the movement down the slippery slope should be stopped. Turkish people have a very simple choice: either to replace insanity with intelligence and wisdom on the way to peace and prosperity, or continue on the present downward course under the smoldering ashes of civil war and destruction. With Mr Erdogan in power the country seems to have no future.

****

b. During coup in chronological order:

German news anchor in Turkey celebrates success of coup.

Tim Robins of the BBC yells that Erdogan has fled the country

No condemnations of the coup from anyone except the former British ambassador to Turkey who was livid at the whole enterprise, 'disaster,' he said 'will follow, whether the coup succeeded or failed.' He was the only voice in the West against the coup.

"Moscow is most concerned at the latest events in Turkey," the foreign ministry said in a statement. Moscow confirmed its "readiness to work constructively with the legally elected leadership."

On Saturday, July 16 at 12:14 a.m. (Turkish local time), U.S. Secretary of State John Kerry issued the statement following: "I hope there will be stability and peace and continuity within Turkey, but I have nothing to add with respect to what has transpired at this moment."

The UN Secretary-General underscores "that military interference in the affairs of any state is unacceptable. It will be crucial to quickly and peacefully affirm civilian rule and constitutional order in accordance with principles of democracy."

Turks standing to the coup in their hundreds of thousands; first coup perpetrators being arrested and shown on Western television screens.

Afterwards Erdogan addressed coup plotters: Not to obey orders

Once more pictures of police and special forces taking army coup members prisoners in large numbers shown on television screens. Reports of helicopter of coup plotters downed.

Condemnation of coup by American administration. The following statement was issued at 2:13 a.m. (Turkish local time):

"The President and Secretary agreed that all parties in Turkey should support the democratically elected government of Turkey, show restraint, and avoid any violence or bloodshed.'

Turkish scholar working in American university livid at Obama's administration denouncing the coup before it was over, for there was plenty more, he kept claiming.

****

M. Rubin: Why the coup in Turkey could mean hope (written straight after the beginning of the coup but read/accessed later). 15 July 16:
'The Turkish military has staged a coup. Bridges are closed in Istanbul. There is gunfire in Ankara. The Turkish General Staff says that it is in control, although the intelligence service disputes this.
Turkey is no stranger to coups. Historically, the Turkish military has been the guarantor of Turkey's Constitution. In 1960, it overthrew Prime Minister Adnan Menderes after he sought to consolidate control and erode separation of mosque and state.
In 1971 and again in 1980, it intervened as chaos and political violence threatened to consume the country. In 1997, the military forced Turkey's first Islamist government to step aside.
While any coup is tragic, in Turkey there is hope: The military has never tried to retain power; rather, it has always assumed a caretaker role, seeking to repair the constitutional checks and balances in order to return Turkey to democracy.
There are other reasons for hope. It'll likely be a day or two before we see if the coup holds, but Recep Tayyip Erdoğan, the prime minister-turned-president now apparently overthrown, was an autocrat. He flirted with support for terrorists groups like Hamas, the al-Qaeda-linked Nusra Front and even the Islamic State.
Some regimes believe flirtation with radical Islamists might fulfill short-term policy ends, but in the long-term there is always a heavy price. The past year's attacks in Ankara and Istanbul may have convinced Turks outside Erdoğan's inner circle that their reckoning was near.
Erdoğan ruled through the Justice and Development Party (AKP), a party that started out promising not only religious tolerance but also technocratic expertise.
It increasingly delivered the opposite. In the first nine years of AKP rule, for example, the murder rate of women skyrocketed 1,400 percent as Islamists conducted honor crimes with impunity.
The good news is that, with the exception of Mustafa Kemal Atatürk's secular political movement, no Turkish party has ever survived the death of its charismatic leader.
Erdoğan's removal might open space for both religious conservatives and liberals to again compete in the marketplace of ideas.

That said, Turkey's future is far from assured. Over his 13 years in power, Erdoğan has transformed the bureaucracy.

He has changed education to brainwash a generation of students. He has allowed Islamist students to leapfrog over secular requirements to enter top universities.

He has inserted party cadre into every government bureaucracy. He and his family have seized newspapers and TV stations and used them to broadcast nonstop streams of anti-American and anti-Semitic conspiracies.

Undoing this will be no easy feat, especially since half of Turkey's population supports Erdoğan blindly.

There also needs to be serious soul-searching within the Turkish military. How did it manage to misread Turkish society for so long? Career officers lived and socialized with other officers; they lost touch with Turkey at large.

Should the Turkish military engage in a violent purge, the reverberations may last generations. Nor does the coup resolve real ethnic problems between Kurds and Turks.

Absent real reform, the coup won't resolve the Kurdish insurgency Turkey now faces. Nor is the opposition a panacea. Party leaders act as mini-dictators within their own parties. Few are charismatic.

Turkey has no obvious savior. Get ready for a rocky ride.

Michael Rubin is a resident scholar at the American Enterprise Institute

****

c. After the coup:

The UK daily The Independent, on the same day 16 July:
'Astonishing pictures show violent clashes as mobs attack soldiers attempting to overthrow Erdogan.'

Robert Fisk of the same Independent: same day 16 July, writes:
'Recep Erdogan had it coming. The Turkish army was never going to remain compliant while the man who would recreate the Ottoman Empire turned his neighbours into enemies and his country into a mockery of itself.

Instability is now contagious as corruption in the region, especially among its potentates and dictators, a class of autocrat of which Erdogan has been a member ever since he changed the constitution for his own benefit and restarted his wicked conflict with the Kurds.

Needless to say, Washington's first reaction was instructive. Turks must support their democratically elected government.

The real question will be the degree to which is his momentary success will embolden Erdogan to undertake more trials, imprison more journalists, close down more newspapers, kill more Kurds, and, for that matter, go on denying the 1915 Armenian genocide.'

Ralph Peters: Turkey's last hope dies; 16 July, 2016; Fox News:
Friday night's failed coup was Turkey's last hope to stop the Islamization of its government and the degradation of its society. Reflexively, Western leaders rushed to condemn a coup attempt they refused to understand. Their reward will be a toxic Islamist regime at the gates of Europe.

Our leaders no longer do their basic homework. The media relies on experts-by-Wikipedia. Except for PC platitudes, our schools ignore the world beyond our shores. Deluged with unreliable information, citizens succumb to the new superstitions of the digital age.

So a great country is destroyed by Islamist hardliners before our eyes—and our president praises its "democracy."

That tragically failed coup was a forlorn hope, not an attempt to take over a country. Turkey is not a banana republic in which the military grasps the reins for its own profit. For almost a century, the Turkish armed forces have been the guardians of the country's secular constitution. Most recently, coups in 1960, 1971 and 1980 (with "non-coup" pressure in 1997) saw the military intervene to prevent the country's collapse.

Each time, the military returned the government to civilian rule as soon as that proved practical. My own first experience of Turkey came just before the 1980 coup. Turkey was broke and broken. The economy was in such a shambles that you could not buy a cup of Turkish coffee in Istanbul. I walked because taxis and public transportation had no fuel. Murderous political violence raged. Reluctantly, the generals stepped in and saved their country.

Friday night, mid-grade officers led a desperate effort to rescue their country again. They failed. The West cheered. Soon enough, we'll mourn.

The coup leaders made disastrous mistakes, the worst of which was to imagine that the absence of President Erdogan from Ankara, the capital, presented the perfect opportunity. Wrong. In a coup, the key is to seize the leaders you mean to overthrow (as well as control of the media). Instead of fleeing into exile, Erdogan was able to return in triumph.

So who is the man our own president rushed to support because he was "democratically elected?" Recep Tayyip Erdogan is openly Islamist and affiliated with the Muslim Brotherhood, which President Obama appears to believe represents the best hope for the Middle East. But the difference between ISIS, Al Qaeda and the Muslim Brotherhood isn't one of purpose, but merely of manners: Muslim Brothers wash the blood off their hands before they sit down to dinner with their dupes.

With barely a murmured "Tut-tut!" from Western leaders, Erdogan has dismantled Turkey's secular constitution (which the military is duty-bound to protect). His "democracy" resembles Putin's, not ours. Key opposition figures have been driven into exile or banned. Opposition parties have been suppressed. Recent elections have not been held so much as staged. And Erdogan has torn the fresh scab from the Kurdish wound, fostering civil war in Turkey's southeast for his own political advantage.

Erdogan has packed Turkey's courts with Islamists. He appointed pliant, pro-Islamist generals and admirals, while staging show trials of those of whom he wished to rid the country. He has de facto, if not yet de jure, curtailed women's freedoms. He dissolved the wall between mosque and state (Friday night, he used mosques' loudspeakers to call his supporters into the streets). Not least, he had long allowed foreign fighters to transit Turkey to join ISIS and has aggressively backed other extremists whom he believed he could manage.

And his diplomatic extortion racket has degraded our own military efforts against ISIS.

That's the man President Obama supports.

And the leaders of the ill-fated coup? What did they stand for? Mustafa Kemal Ataturk's legacy and a secular constitution. One of the great men of the last century, Ataturk (an innovative general by background) pulled Turkey from the wreckage of World War One, abolished the caliphate, suppressed fanatical religious orders, gave women legal rights and social protections, banned the veil, promoted secular education for all citizens of Turkey, strongly advocated Westernization and modernization...and promoted a democratic future.

The officers who led the collapsed coup stood for all those things. President Obama and Secretary of State Kerry opposed them.

By Saturday morning, it was clear that the mullahs and mobs behind Erdogan had won. Erdogan will use the coup as an excuse to accelerate the Islamization of his country and to lead Turkey deeper into the darkness engulfing the Muslim world. His vision is one of a neo-Ottoman megalomaniac.

NATO, which operates by consensus, will find itself embracing a poisonous snake. New crises will reawaken old fears in southeastern Europe, which western European states will dismiss condescendingly, further crippling the badly limping European Union. Syria will continue to bleed. And educated, secular Turks will find themselves in a situation like unto that of German liberals in the 1930s. We may see new and unexpected wars.

A desperate, ill-planned coup has failed in Turkey. Here comes the darkness.

Fox News Strategic Analyst Ralph Peters is a retired U.S. Army officer and former enlisted man. He is the author of prize-winning fiction and non-fiction books on the Civil War and the military.

******

Turkey's sad death signals more chaos in the Middle East
By John Bolton, 17 July 2016:
'The failed coup d'état by elements of Turkey's military signals more repression and chaos in the Middle East.

We still lack important information on what motivated the attempt to overthrow President Recep Tayyip Erdogan, its timing and how and why it collapsed so quickly. Nonetheless, we confidently predict Turkey will suffer several major domestic consequences, in turn causing significant international ripples.

Most importantly, Erdogan's relentless pursuit of an increasingly radical Islamicization of Turkey will proceed largely unfettered. And no significant institutional or political opposition inside Turkey now stands athwart his penchant for authoritarianism.

The triumph of Erdogan's government means he has swept the board clear of any real impediments to implementing his radical policies. Both as prime minister and now as president, Erdogan has focused single-mindedly on an Islamicist attack on Turkey's secular constitution, and the very foundations of a modern Turkey, rising from the ashes of the Ottoman Empire after World War I, envisioned by Mustafa Kemal.

Turkey's military, following the pattern laid down by Kemal (known widely as "Ataturk," meaning "father of the Turks"), was intended to be the guardian of the new, Europe-oriented nation-state he strove to create.

For years, Erdogan has replaced high-ranking, secular military officers with loyal Islamicists in a blatant effort to bend the military away from its secular vocation, toward endorsing or at least accepting a re-established state Islam, harking back to the deceased Ottoman caliphate.

Erdogan's success at stuffing the military's top officer corps with Islamicists and political loyalists likely explains why Turkey's military wasn't fully behind the coup attempt. Indeed, as seemed clear even in the revolt's early hours, it appeared more an act of desperation, a last gasp by the military's pro-secular elements, rather than a concerted effort by a united military establishment.

Erdogan's increasingly dictatorial approach to governance has in recent years become ever clearer internationally, epitomized by his arrests and harassment of both foreign and domestic journalists he deemed critical of his regime. In earlier days, serving as mayor of Istanbul, he said publicly: "Democracy is like a street car. You ride it to the stop you want, and then you get off." Friday's coup attempt may well be precisely the stop Erdogan was waiting for.

When he says the coup plotters "will pay a heavy price," he isn't kidding. And he will not stop with the coup's central figures.

Obviously, any military coup in a theoretically democratic state is illegal (at least until it succeeds), but we can expect Erdogan's crackdown to be relentless and thorough.

Conveniently, Erdogan has been hard at work for years packing the Turkish judiciary with Islamicists and political supporters. As with his "cleansing" of the military's officer corps, Erdogan's placement and promotion of loyalists within the judiciary will now pay important benefits as hundreds, maybe even thousands of "coup plotters," accomplices and mere political opponents of Erdogan face the consequences of failure.

Erdogan will also have a free hand in dealing with Kurdish political and military opposition efforts, particularly those pursuing an independent Kurdistan.

Internationally, Erdogan will obviously be strengthened significantly, at least once Turkey settles back down. It comes as no surprise that Iran was among the first governments to congratulate Erdogan on retaining power. His victory is a significant blow to the West and to the NATO alliance, with every indication that Turkey will turn increasingly rapidly away from Western values and America in particular, Obama's personal friendship with Erdogan notwithstanding. And despite Erdogan's recent reconciliation with Israel, there should be no celebrations in Jerusalem.

The lamps have been going out all over the Middle East for years. Many more went out this weekend in Turkey. Whether we will see them relit in our lifetime remains unknown.

John Bolton, now at the American Enterprise Institute, was the US ambassador to the United Nations from August 2005 to December 2006.

****

European Union
E.U. Officials Urge Erdogan to Show Restraint After Coup Attempt in Turkey
By James Kanter JULY 18, 2016, BRUSSELS

'European Union foreign ministers appealed on Monday to President Recep Tayyip Erdogan of Turkey to use restraint after he successfully put down an uprising against his leadership over the weekend.

Mr. Erdogan has shown an increasingly authoritarian bent, and his government Has detained nearly 6,000 military personnel since an attempted coup on Friday night amid signs that he is using the moment to widen a crackdown on perceived enemies.

Even before the failed coup and the hard-line response, Mr. Erdogan has represented a quandary for the European Union ministers, who are holding a scheduled meeting in Brussels that includes breakfast with John Kerry, the United States secretary of state.

But the scale of the crackdown in the wake of the attempted coup in Turkey has rattled European leaders. Alongside the members of the military, the Turkish government also dismissed thousands of judges, who seemingly played no role in the military revolt.

Johannes Hahn, the European commissioner for regional affairs, suggested on Monday that Mr. Erdogan was putting in place plans that had been drawn up ahead of the unrest.

The arrests showed "at least that something has been prepared" because "lists are available already," said Mr. Hahn, apparently referring to lists of people who have been subject to reprisals.'

****

NATO, US, EU warn Turkey on coup crackdown
Danny Kemp and Dave Clark, AFP Mon 18 Jul
Brussels (AFP):

'The United States, the European Union and NATO on Monday warned Turkey to respect the rule of law after President Recep Tayyip Erdogan's government launched a massive crackdown following the failed coup.

Germany and the EU also said any move by Turkey, a key Western ally, to reinstate the death penalty for the plotters of the uprising would derail Ankara's long-stalled EU membership bid.

US Secretary of State John Kerry and EU foreign policy chief Federica Mogherini said in Brussels that Friday's attempted putsch was "no excuse" for excessive action, as Turkish authorities said they had arrested over 7,500 people.

"We will certainly support bringing the perpetrators of the coup to justice but we also caution against a reach that goes well beyond that," Kerry told a press conference with Mogherini.

The EU and US "urge the government of Turkey to uphold the highest standards of respect for the nation's democratic institutions and the rule of law", he added.

Kerry said that NATO, the western military alliance of which Turkey is a key member, would "measure very carefully what is happening" with respect to democracy.

NATO chief Jens Stoltenberg later said he had spoken to Erdogan to say that "valued" ally Turkey must stick to the same standards as the other 27 members.

"Being part of a unique community of values, it is essential for Turkey, like all other allies, to ensure full respect for democracy and its institutions, the constitutional order, the rule of law and fundamental freedoms," Stoltenberg said in a statement.

Earlier, Mogherini said, as EU foreign ministers met, that the "rule of law has to be protected in the country, there is no excuse for any steps that take the country away from that."

The EU commissioner dealing with Turkey's long-stalled bid for membership of the bloc said it appeared that the government had already prepared a list before the coup of people to be rounded up.

"I mean, (that) the lists are available already after the event indicates that this was prepared and at a certain moment should be used," enlargement commissioner Johannes Hahn told reporters.

- 'Revolting' -

German Chancellor Angela Merkel's spokesman denounced "revolting scenes of caprice and revenge against soldiers on the streets" after disturbing pictures emerged of the treatment of some detained suspects.

After Erdogan said Sunday that Turkey would consider a return of capital punishment, spokesman Steffen Seibert said such a move "would mean the end of EU membership talks".

Mogherini was quick to echo the German position: "Let me be very clear... no country can become an EU state if it introduces the death penalty," she said.

Turkey has called on Washington to hand over exiled Muslim cleric Fethullah Gulen, Erdogan's chief foe, over the failed coup, but Kerry said Ankara must produce proof.

He said he had told Turkey's foreign minister "to make certain that in whatever portfolio and request they send us, they send us evidence, not allegations".

Turkey's attempts to join the 28-nation European Union have been hobbled in recent years by concern over the increasingly authoritarian Erdogan's record on human rights and press freedom.

But the EU agreed to speed up its membership bid and give visa-free travel to Turks as part of a migrant crisis deal in which Ankara agreed to take back people landing in the Greek islands.

French Foreign Minister Jean-Marc Ayrault said that "the rule of law must prevail".

Belgian Foreign Minister Didier Reynders also urged restraint, saying: "It's normal to punish those involved in the coup, but it's (also) normal to ask for respect for the rule of law."

****

Alon Ben Meir: Senior Fellow, Center for Global Affairs, NYU:c Turkey's Elected Dictator; 07/20/2016 04:37 pm 16:37:26

'Even before the failed military coup, Turkey's President Erdogan governed like a dictator who had the last word on all state matters. The botched coup was nothing but, as he put it, "a gift from God" to purge what is left of Turkey's democracy and cleanse the army and judiciary in order to ensure the total subordination of all institutions to his whims.

For Erdogan, being elected was akin to being granted a license to trample and dismantle all democratic tenets to consolidate his powers and promote his Islamic agenda.

As a shrewd and highly skilled politician, Erdogan painted the coup as an assault on democracy, which was supported by a chorus of Western powers, knowing full well that Turkey under Erdogan is anything but a democracy.

In fact, one of the main reasons behind the coup was to stop Erdogan from completely destroying Turkey's remaining secular and democratic pillars, which were established by Turkey's founder Mustafa Kemal Ataturk in 1923.

Ataturk sought to establish a Western-style secular democracy and made the military the custodian of Turkey's constitution. The armed forces exercised that prerogative four times before to prevent the country from sliding into disorder.

The first coup, in 1960, led to the overthrow and execution of Prime Minister Adnan Menderes due to his increasing Islamization of the country; the fourth coup in 1997 ended with the forced resignation and banishment from politics of Prime Minister Necmettin Erbakan, also because of his degradation of secular principles of the country.

While affecting regime change through a military coup is certainly not the preferred method, given how Erdogan gradually and successfully pillaged the country of all its democratic substance, a segment of the military felt it had little choice but to stage a coup to change the perilous path that Erdogan is pursuing.

Turkey's role in hosting nearly 2.5 million Syrian refugees and its ability to either stem the flow, or open up the gates to allow refugees to flood European cities further strengthened Erdogan's hand.

He successfully exploited the EU's deep concerns over the refugee crisis by making a deal that provides Turkey several major benefits that outweighed its obligations.

Although thus far the EU resisted Erdogan's threat to cancel the deal if it were to renege on its agreement on visa-free entry due to his post-coup threat to restore the death penalty, Erdogan remained defiant, believing that he can bully the West with impunity.

Moreover, Erdogan presumed Turkey's significant role in fighting ISIS and his consent to allow the US Air Force to use Turkey's Incirlik Air Base to strike ISIS targets gave him increased leverage against the US, which further muted any criticism for his continuing gross violation of human rights.

Those who had hopes that Erdogan might just take heed of the coup and show some restraint in dealing with those suspected of being involved in it had those hopes quickly dashed.

He wasted no time in initiating a massive witch-hunt—nearly 9,500 are currently facing legal proceedings, and around 50,000 soldiers, judges, civil servants, and teachers have been suspended or detained. Hundreds if not thousands will languish in jail under emergency laws that permit indefinite administrative detention without formal charges.

More ominously, Erdogan 'raided' higher learning institutions by barring all academics from any foreign travel even for scholarly purposes, while the state education council demanded the resignation of over 1,500 university deans.

The vast number of people rounded up so quickly raises suspicions that these individuals had already been blacklisted; Erdogan was able to do so with a nearly 200,000-strong internal police force and intelligence units, who are extremely loyal to him.

Leave it now to Erdogan, who has emerged stronger than before the coup, to further intensify his brutal war against the Kurdistan Workers' Party (PKK) and the Syrian Kurds, who are the US's allies no less, and continue to refuse to resume negotiations with Turkey's significant Kurdish community.

Perhaps the time has come for the EU and the US to reassess their relations with Turkey and stop enabling Erdogan to exercise free reign, when in fact his behavior has a direct and indirect impact on Western interests, both domestically and in the Middle East.

The US cannot afford any member of NATO to squash all democratic rules with no consequences. Moreover, Erdogan has demonstrated time and again a lack of loyalty and commitment as a NATO member.

Turkey should be put on notice, as Secretary of State John Kerry recently stated that NATO has a "requirement with respect to democracy... Obviously, a lot of people have been arrested very quickly." He grimly added, "Hopefully we can work in a constructive way to prevent backsliding."

Moreover, Erdogan should be warned that Turkey's prospect of becoming an EU member will be a thing of the past if he continues to grossly undermine the principles of democratic governance, including the complete subordination of the judiciary to his political agenda.

In that regard, Erdogan must understand that there will be serious consequences if he does not end his assault against the Syrian Kurds under the pretext of fighting terrorism (he conveniently accuses their military wing, the PYD, of working in conjunction with the PKK).

Whereas Erdogan viewed the failed coup as a God-sent opportunity to wipe out whoever is perceived to be his enemy, the US and the EU must use this occasion to put Erdogan on notice that history has shown time and again that totalitarian regimes come to a bitter end, and that he too will not be spared his day in court.

****

The BBC seeking people affected not by coup but crackdown
Link: http://www.bbc.co.uk/news/world-europe-36843180
Retrieved 23 July 15.42

Are you in Turkey? Have you lost your job or been affected in some way by the crackdown? You can email haveyoursay@bbc.co.uk with your experiences.
- ▪ Whatsapp: +44 7525 900971
- ▪ Tweet: **@BBC_HaveYourSay**
- ▪ Send an SMS or MMS to 61124 or +44 7624 800 100

Or use the form below
Top of Form
Your contact detailsName Your E-mail address (required) Town & Country Your telephone number Comments (required)

If you are happy to be contacted by a BBC journalist please leave a telephone number that we can contact you on. In some cases a selection of your comments will be published, displaying your name as you provide it and location, unless you state otherwise. Your contact details will never be published. When sending us pictures, video or eyewitness accounts at no time should you endanger yourself or others, take any unnecessary risks or infringe any laws. Please ensure you have read the terms and conditions.

Terms and conditions

****

d. Had the coup succeeded:

-By the end of 2016, over 50,000 would be dead.
-Tens of thousands would be locked up in stadiums, warehouses, open fields, and factories.
-'A blurred leaked recording would show Erdogan, members of his family, and his aides summarily tried and executed.'
-The waterways of the Bosphorous and Marmara Sea would be daily flowing with tens, at times hundreds, of corpses of unidentified persons.
-The EU, NATO and the UN would be 'welcoming the announcement by the new authorities that a return to democracy will be implemented as soon as the situation allows, within the next few years.'
-By now, tens of thousands would have already been disappeared.
-The EU, NATO, and UN 'call on all parties to show restraint.'
-The IMF would be considering to reply favourably to a loan worth $22 billions to Turkey to help alleviate the economic crisis.
-The Western media would be full of reports of incidents of 'Islamist depravity and savagery' (as those from Iraq described earlier).
-Amnesty International would be calling 'on the reopening of all newspapers shut under Erdogan, and enquiries into the excesses of his government.'
-Wikileaks would be full of reports 'of cases of corruption under Erdogan.'
-The Turkish countryside would be full, daily, of corpses strewn all over. The corpses show signs of torture and severe mutilations. The authors of these outrages have not been identified, but 'could be elements from the previous regime or Islamists.'
-Hundreds of thousands of emigrants would be on their way into Europe.
-And occasionally, a slight excess on the part of the new government, 'which promises to enquire into the matter.'

Years later:
'As the situation in Turkey could no longer be brought under any control, a new partitioning of the country would have to be implemented. To this effect an international committee has been appointed..........'
The EU will be inviting some of the newly formed republics to become part of the Union.

Then, years later in Western historical narrative:
Of course what has been cited above never happened. You will read, instead:
'Following many years of dictatorship under Erdogan, a salvation coup by patriotic officers brought his dictatorship down, and ushered a new era of freedom, justice and progress. There were few excesses, but the whole venture in the end breathed a

new climate of optimism and democracy in the region. It was a great victory against the fanaticism of Islam.'

Ah, yes, and this is precisely what will be taught in Muslim schools, colleges, and universities (a few exceptions aside).

CONCLUDING WORDS/QUOTES

'I fear you, therefore you are guilty,' says Fuchs.[1259]
'The Islamist frightens, the others have, thus, the right and the possibility to reduce him into a non being.'[1260]

The projection of evil onto marginal or powerless groups has always been a convenient method of producing scapegoats Kabbani explains.[1261] Medieval Europe, for example, tried Jews for a medley of mythic crimes: poisoning wells, killing children for their blood, crucifying victims, and eating them too.[1262] By the same token, women were associated with the devil, and seen as enemies of the Church and civilisation.[1263] This went to justify the witch-hunts that tried women for sexual rapaciousness, cannibalism, consorting with evil spirits, and being generally intractable and capricious.[1264] In colonial America, there was a systematic attempt to portray the Indian as 'an abductor of women, a killer of children, and a collector of scalps, as an apology for White brutality against him.'[1265]
Muslims therefore belong to a select club, but to their misfortune, whilst the other groups are either largely extinct (Native Indians), or have become untouchable thanks to their formidable powers today (Jews and women,) Muslims are still there available for culling. So, somehow, they are the only group who, from the medieval period till our day in 2020, are being slain en masse, and will remain so for a long while to come because, indeed, the same ingredients produce the same results.

Blanks and Frassetto note how:
> During the Middle Ages, Islamic civilisation was so far ahead of its Christian rival, offering enticing advances in architecture, law, literature, philosophy, and indeed in most areas of cultural activity. It was therefore from a position of military and perhaps, more importantly, cultural weakness that Christian Europe developed negative images, some of which survive to the present day. In part, this hostility was the result of continued political and military conflict, but it likewise ensued from a Western sense of cultural inferiority.[1266]

Tolan also says:

[1259] E. Fuchs, Comment cela est-il possible? In 'La Torture, le corps et la parole' *Actes du IIIe Colloque Interuniversitaire*, Fribourg 1985, Editions Universitaires Fribourg, 1985.
[1260] E. Fuchs, Comment cela est-il possible?
[1261] R. Kabbani: *Imperial Fictions*; op cit; pp. 1-8.
[1262] W. Arens: *The Man Eating Myth*, Oxford University Press; 1979; p. 95.
[1263] *Women and Colonisation: Anthropological Perspectives*; Mona Etienne and E. Leacock eds; (New York; 1980); p. 175.
[1264] See A. Mac Farlane: *Witchcraft in Tudor and Stuart England*; (London; 1970).
[1265] L. K. Barnett: *The Ignoble Savage: American Literary Racism; 1790-1890;* (Connecticut; 1975); p. 5.
[1266] D.R. Blanks-M. Frassetto: Introduction; in *Western Perceptions*; (Blanks and Frassetto ed); p. 3.

> Both as a rival religion and as a rival civilization, Islam was tremendously successful. It was hence appealing, intriguing, and frightening. The attraction of Muslim learning, Muslim culture, and Muslim sophistication was extremely strong... But the more Christians were attracted to Islam, the stronger others felt the need to condemn it - for it was this attraction, more than the might of Muslim armies, that was most threatening to Christendom.[1267]

Likewise, today, Islam does frighten the West. Lueg says:

> The Enlightenment and the related separation of religion and state count among the most important aspects of Western superiority. In our eyes whoever fails to fulfil this separation is immature and bound by religion. We believe we have displaced religion from the public arena into the private one, and have thereby somehow overcome it. Islam nonetheless terrifies us as a *religion* - and it is precisely through this religious element, to which we restrict our perception, that the rift between the Orient and the Occident is made even deeper. Anything we hear from the Islamic world, we assume to be stated from an inferior position, and in a religious context, i.e. that of Islam. We do not try to understand Islam as a religion, but instead often reject it on principle. I am not defending Islam or any other faith, but one cannot help noticing what terror a religion manages to spread in a supposedly secular society. The reactions to Islamic movements are anything but rational and enlightened. Yet much of the Western media set much store by factual and objective reporting.[1268]

Lueg adds:

> Human rights, which received world-wide recognition through the United Nations Universal Declaration of Human Rights, are often cited as a 'Western product' and another symbol of Occidental superiority. Islam, by contrast, is portrayed as being hostile to human rights, as an ideological structure which is virtually antithetical to the Western understanding of human rights.
>
> The actual situation of human rights and democracy in most Islamic countries is certainly shocking. In many of these countries torture is commonplace, and press censorship, the death penalty and, above all, unequal treatment of men and women are to be found everywhere. These are all totally unacceptable conditions, which must be denounced constantly until the conditions of the people improve. Yet we must nonetheless ask who or what is responsible for these catastrophic conditions. The Western media again often make Islam out to be the main evil, and they love to divert our attention to the belief of 'Islamic zealots', namely that 'human rights are an imported Western body of thought' and are therefore to be rejected.[1269]

[1267] J.V. Tolan ed: *Medieval Christian Perceptions of Islam*; (Routledge; London; 1996); preface; pp. xix-xx.
[1268] A. Lueg: The Perception of Islam; op cit; pp. 21-2.
[1269] A. Lueg: The Perception of Islam; op cit; p. 22.

Since the Bolshevik revolution in 1917, and during the whole era of communism, down to the late 1980s, Islam had a sort of reprieve from the usual onslaught. Muslims served the good cause by dying in Vietnam, Korea, Monte Casino, and a couple more places. However, once communism fell in the late 1980s, it was back to business as usual. Samuel Huntington, in his now famed Clash of Civilisation calls for both political and military reawakening of the West:

> To check the military expansion of both Confucian and Islamic states, to stop the reduction of the military capacity of the West, and to maintain the military capacity of the West vis à vis Asia... The West must keep enough military and economic power to protect its interests vis à vis non-Western civilisations.[1270]

General Helmut Willman, chief of the Euro-corps, asserted that it was absolutely clear that the axis of threat against Europe has moved to the south.[1271] Thus, the rising call today is 'For a crusade against the Green peril, the new universal enemy.'[1272]

As Hippler and Lueg note:

> The idea of an Islamic threat is nothing new. It has deep historical roots that date back as far as the Crusades..... As a result of the end of the Cold War, the perceived Islamic threat has, however, acquired a particularly explosive power in the 1990s. We no longer have the Soviet Union or communism to serve as enemies justifying expensive and extensive military apparatuses.[1273]

But the main reason for hating Islam remains one and the same as outlined by some good scholars. Geanakoplos observes:

> For centuries before the advent of Muhammad in the sixth century, the primitive Bedouin tribes of Arabia had pursued their uneventful lives, interrupted at times perhaps to serve as minor allies to the Persian or Byzantines in their struggle with one another. Why this people, originating in the Arabian peninsula - unorganised, disunited, and backward - would one day be able to overthrow the great Persian empire and wrest from Byzantium some of its choicest provinces is one of the great questions of medieval history.[1274]

Sarton:

> Illiterate Bedouins, but they were absolutely unified and exalted by an ardent faith. In this, again, the Prophet was completely vindicated.[1275]

[1270] *Foreign Affairs*, vol. 72, No. 5, 1993.
[1271] *El Pais*, 7 July 1994.
[1272] M. Aguirre, director of studies at the Centro de Investigaciones para la paz (CIP), Madrid; and vice director at the Transnational Institute, Amsterdam.
[1273] J Hippler and A. Lueg: Introduction; in *The Next Threat*; op cit; p. 5.
[1274] D. J. Geanakoplos: *Medieval Western Civilisation, and the Byzantine and Islamic Worlds*, (D.C. Heath and Company, Toronto, 1979); p. 146.
[1275] G. Sarton: *The Incubation of Western Culture in the Middle East*, A George C. Keiser Foundation Lecture, March 29, 1950; (Washington DC 1951); p. 26.

And when, as in Spain, the Muslims were slaughtering each other in the messy times of the early 11th century, and were threatened by Christian extinction, only Islam 'had become the main cohesive force binding the Moriscos culturally, after their leaders had failed them politically,' Monroe says.[1276]

Gibbon also notes:

> The Arabs and Saracens who spread their conquests from India to Spain had languished in poverty and contempt till Mahomet breathed into those savage bodies the soul of enthusiasm.[1277]

Simultaneously, Gibbon warns that although 'the menace of Islam was only a memory that might serve to warn Europe not to indulge too freely in the prospect of endless security' because of the present weakness of the foe:

> This apparent security should not tempt us to forget that new enemies, and unknown dangers, may possibly arise from some obscure people, scarcely visible in the map of the world.[1278]

The philosopher Heine also understood this, when he reflected:

> The genius of the Arabs had never died completely but had fallen asleep in the quiet life of the Bedouin. Perhaps the Arabs are only awaiting the right call in order to storm out as before from their sultry wastelands, refreshed by sleep.[1279]

Thus, as Esposito notes:

> There is an easy path and a hard one. The easy path is to view Islam and Islamic revivalism as a threat - to posit a global Pan-Islamic threat, monolithic in nature, a historic enemy whose faith and agenda are diametrically opposed to the West. This attitude leads to support for secular regimes at almost any cost rather than risking an Islamic-oriented government in power.[1280]

And as Jameelah sums up:

> Islam is the only serious rival that Western civilisation has ever encountered in its history... The West hates and fears Islam because it challenges the very existence of everything it stands for. Although today the Muslims are unorganised, backward and impotent, politically, economically and militarily, the West has nothing to fear from actual power which is non-existent but is mortally afraid of our (Muslim) potential power.[1281]

[1276] J.T. Monroe: The Hispanic-Arabic World: in Jose Rubia Barcia: *Americo Castro, and the Meaning of Spanish Civilisation*. (University of California Press, Berkeley, 1976), pp. 69-90; at p. 86.
[1277] E. Gibbon: History of the Decline and fall of the Roman Empire; quoted in R.W. Southern: *Western Views of Islam in the Middle Ages*; (Harvard University Press; 1962); p. 13.
[1278] Ibid.
[1279] In P. Kappert: From Romanticisation; op cit; p. 39.
[1280] J. Esposito: *The Islamic Threat;* op cit; p. 169.
[1281] M. Jameelah: *Islam and Orientalism*; M.Y Khan and Sons; Lahore; 1990; p. 136.

Select Bibliography

-C.R. Ageron: *Modern Algeria*, tr., by M. Brett, Hurst and Company, London, 1990.
-H Alleg; J. de Bonis, H.J. Douzon, J. Freire, P. Haudiquet: *La Guerre d'Algerie*, 3 vols; Temps Actuels, Paris, 1981.
-F F Armesto: *Before Columbus*: Macmillan Education; London, 1987.
-T. Arnold: *The Preaching of Islam*; M. Ashraf Publishers; Lahore; 1979.
-T. Arnold and A Guillaume ed: *The Legacy of Islam;* 1st edition Oxford; 1931.
-A.S. Atiya: *Crusade, Commerce and Culture*; Oxford University Press; London; 1962.
-C. Bennett: *Victorian Images of Islam*; Grey Seal; London; 1992.
-D.R. Blanks, and M. Frassetto ed: *Western Views of Islam in Medieval and Early Modern Europe;* St. Martin's Press; New York; 1999.
-C. Bouamrane-L. Gardet: *Panorama de la Pensee Islamique*, Sindbad; Paris, 1984.
-Denise Brahimi: *Opinions et Regards des Europeens sur le Maghreb aux 17em et 18em siecles*; SNED; Algiers; 1978.
-H. Bresc: *Politique et Societe en Sicile; XII-XV em siecle*; Variorum; Aldershot; 1990.
-C. Chasseboeuf (Volney): *Voyage en Egypte et en Syrie;* Paris, Mouton and Co; 1959 ed.
-S. Chew: *The Crescent and the Rose;* New York; 1974.
-W. Churchill: *A Little Matter of Genocide*; City Lights Books; San Francisco; 1997.
-N. Cigar: Serbia's Orientalists and Islam: Making a genocide intellectually respectable; in *Islamic Quarterly;* 38 (1994); pp. 147-70.
-A. Cirakman: *From the Terror of the World to the Sick man of Europe;* Peter Lang Publishing; New York; 2002.
-J.J. Cook: The Maghrib through French Eyes; 1880-1929; in *Through Foreign Eyes;* edited by A.A. Heggoy; University Press of America; 1982; pp. 57-92.
-Y. Courbage, P. Fargues: *Chretiens et Juifs dans l'Islam Arabe et Turc*, Payot, Paris, 1997.
-G.W. Cox: *The Crusades*; Longmans; London; 1874.
-N. Daniel: *The Cultural Barrier*, Edinburgh University Press, 1975.
-N. Daniel: *The Arabs and Medieval Europe*; Longman Librarie du Liban; 1975.
-N. Daniel: *Islam, Europe and Empire*, Edinburgh University Press, 1966.
-N. Daniel: *Islam and the West*; Oneworld; Oxford; 1993.
-J. Davenport: *An Apology for Mohammed and the Koran*; J. Davy and Sons; London; 1869.
-R De Zayas: *Les Morisques et le racisme d'etat*; Les Voies du Sud; Paris, 1992.
-*De Toulouse a Tripoli*, Colloque held between 6 and 8 December, 1995, University of Toulouse; AMAM, Toulouse, 1997.
-J.W. Draper: *A History of the Intellectual Development of Europe*; vol I; Revised edition; George Bell and Sons, London, 1875.
-J.W. Draper: *History of the Conflict Between Religion and Sciences;* Henry S. King and Co; London; 1875.
-J. Esposito: *The Islamic Threat; Myth or Reality?* Oxford University Press; 1992.
-I.R. al-Faruqi and L.L al-Faruqi: *The Cultural Atlas of Islam;* Mc Millan Publishing Company New York, 1986.
-R. Finucane: *Soldiers of the Faith*; J.M. Dent and Sons Ltd; London, 1983.
-G. Fisher: *The Barbary Legend*; Oxford; 1957.

-R. Garaudy: *Comment l'Homme devint Humain,* Editions J.A, 1978.
-R. Garaudy: *Appel aux vivants*, Le Seuil, Paris, 1979.
-M. Garcia-Arenal: Historiens de l'Espagne, Historiens du Maghreb au 19em siecle. Comparaison des stereotypes, in *ANNALES: Economies, Societes, Civilisations*: 54 (1999): pp. 687-703.
-S.D. Goitein: *A Mediterranean Society*, 5 vols, Berkeley; 1967-90.
-V.P. Goss ed: *The Meeting of Two Worlds*; Medieval Institute Publications, Michigan, 1986.
-C. Grossir: *L'Islam des Romantiques*; Maisonneuve; Larose; Paris, 1984.
-A. Gunny: *Images of Islam in Eighteenth Century Writing*; Grey Seal, London, 1996.
-G. Hanotaux: *Histoire de la Nation Egyptienne*; (vol 5 by H. Deherain.) Paris; Librarie Plon; 1931.
-W. Howitt: *Colonisation and Christianity*: Longman; London; 1838.
-T.B. Irving: Dates, Names and Places: The End of Islamic Spain; in *Revue d'Histoire Maghrebine;* No 61-62; 1991; pp. 77-93.
-Al-Jabarti: *Al-Jabarti's Chronicle of the First Seven Months of the French Occupation of Egypt.* Ed and tr. by S. Moreh; Leiden, 1975.
-Ernst Jäckh; *Deutschland im Orient nach dem Balkan-Krieg;* Chapter 7: Deutsche und französische Augenzeugen von christlichen Massakers. (Die Balkangreuel des 30 jährigen Krieges); Martin Mörikes Verlag, Munich, 1913; pp. 83-98.
-E. Jäckh: *The Rising Crescent* (New York, 1944).
-M. Jameelah: *Islam and Orientalism;* M.Y.Khan and Sons; Lahore; 1990.
-Ibn Jubayr: *The Travels of Ibn Jubayr*; tr. R.J.C. Broadhurst; London; 1952.
-C. A. Julien: *Histoire de l'Algerie Contemporaine,* 1827-1871: Presses Universitaires de France, 1964.
-R. Kabbani: *Imperial Fictions;* Pandora; London; 1994.
-B.Z. Kedar: *Crusade and Mission;* Princeton University Press; 1988.
-S. Lane-Poole: *The Moors in Spain;* Fisher Unwin; London; 1888.
-S. Lane Poole: *Turkey;* Khayats; Beirut; 1966 ed; originally published in 1908.
-H.C. Lea: *A History of the Inquisition in Spain;* 4 vols; The Macmillan Company, New York, 1907; vol 3.
-H.C. Lea: *The Moriscos of Spain;* Burt Franklin; New York; 1968 reprint.
-G. Le Bon: *La Civilisation des Arabes*; IMAG; Syracuse; Italie; 1884.
-P.T. Levin: 'From Saracen Scourge to Terrible Turks; Medieval, Renaissance and Enlightenment Images of the Other in the Narrative Construction of Europe;' A Dissertation Presented to the Faculty of the Graduate School of University of Southern California, in Partial Fulfillment of the Requirements for the Degree Doctor of Philosophy (International Relations;) August, 2007.
-Z. Lockman: *Contending Visions of the Middle East*; Cambridge University Press; 2004.
-P. Loti: *Turquie Agonisante*; Calman Levy; Paris; 1913.
-E. Lourie: Anatomy of Ambivalence; Muslims under the crown of Aragon in the late thirteenth century; in E. Lourie: *Crusade and Colonisation; Muslims, Christians and Jews in Medieval Aragon*; Variorum; Aldershot; 1990; pp. 1-75.
-A. Lueg: The Perception of Islam in Western Debate; in *The Next Threat*; edited by J. Hippler and A. Lueg; Pluto Press; London; 1995; pp. 7-31
-J. McCarthy: *Death and Exile: The Ethnic Cleansing of Ottoman Muslims, 1821-1922*; The Darwin Press; New Jersey; 1995.

-N. Matar: Introduction; in *Piracy, Slavery, and Redemption*; edited by D.J. Vitkus; Columbia University Press; New York; 2001.

-J. Mathiex: Trafic et prix de l'Homme en Mediterranee aux 17 et 18 Siecles; *ANNALES: Economies, Societes, Civilisations*: 9; pp. 157-64.

-M.R. Menocal: *The Arabic Role in Medieval Literary History*, University of Pennsylvania Press, Philadelphia, 1987.

-D. Metlitzki: *The Matter of Araby in Medieval England*, Yale University Press, 1977.

-M. Morsy: *North Africa 1800-1900*; Longman; London; 1984.

-D.C. Munro: The Western attitude toward Islam during the period of the Crusades; *Speculum* Vol 6 No 4, pp. 329-43.

-A. H. Murad: The Churches and the Bosnian War,
 http://masud.co.uk/ISLAM/ahm/the_churches_and_the_bosnian_war.htm

-Murtaza Hussain: The Intercept: From al Paso to Saravejo, How White Nationalists have been Inspired by the Genocide of Muslims in Bosnia. September 1, 2019
 https://theintercept.com/2019/09/01/bosnian-genocide-mass-shootings/

-Baron G. D'Ohsson: *Histoire des Mongols,* 4 vols; Les Freres Van Cleef; la Haye and Amsterdam; 1834.

-Z. Oldenbourg: *The Crusades*; tr., from the French by A. Carter; Weinfeld and Nicolson; London; 1965.

-D.A. Pailin: *Attitudes to Other Religions;* Manchester University Press, 1984.

-K.M. Panikkar: *Asia and Western Domination*; George Allen and Unwin Ltd; London; 1953.

-P. Pelliot: *Mongols and Popes; 13th and 14th Centuries;* Paris; 1922.

-*The Meaning of the Glorious Qur'an*; an explanatory translation by M.M. Pickthall; Taha Publishers; London; first printed 1930.

-M. Rodinson: *Europe and the Mystique of Islam*; tr., R. Veinus; I.B. Tauris and Co Ltd; London; 1988.

-M. Rodinson; *Islam and Capitalism;* tr., by R. Pearce; Allen Lane; London; 1974.

-B. Rosenfeld and E. Ihsanoglu: *Mathematicians, Astronomers and Other Scholars of Islamic Civilisation*; Research Centre for Islamic History, Art and Culture; Istanbul; 2003.

-S. Runciman: *A History of the Crusades*, Cambridge University Press, 1962.

-E. W. Said: *Orientalism;* London, 1978.

-J. Salt: *The Unmaking of the Middle East;* University of California Press, 2008.

-Z. Sardar; M-W. Davies: *Distorted Imagination*; Grey Seal Books; London, 1990.

-Z. Sardar ed: *The Touch of Midas; Science, Values and Environment in Islam and the West,* Manchester University Press, 1984.

-G. Sarton: *Introduction to the History of Science*; 3 vols; The Carnegie Institute of Washington; 1927-48.

-J.J. Saunders ed., *The Muslim World on the Eve of Europe's Expansion*; Prentice Hall Inc; New Jersey; 1966.

-R. Schwoebel: *The Shadow of the Crescent: The Renaissance Image of the Turk*; Nieuwkoop; 1967.

-K.I Semaan ed: *Islam and the Medieval West.* State University of New York Press/Albany.1980.

-E. Siberry: *The New Crusaders*; Ashgate: Aldershot; 2000.

-R.B. Smith: *Mohammed and Mohammedanism*; 1874; London.

-R.W. Southern: *Western Views of Islam in the Middle Ages*, Harvard University Press, 1978.

-D. E. Stannard: *American Holocaust; The Conquest of the New World;* Oxford University Press; 1992.
-D E. Stannard: "Genocide in The Americas" in *The Nation*, (October 19, 1992 pp. 430-434); article available on the internet.
-J.W. Sweetman: *Islam and Christian Theology*; Lutterworth Press; London; 1955; vol I; Part II.
-J. Sweetman: *The Oriental Obsession*: Cambridge University Press, 1987.
-A. Thomson: *Barbary and Enlightenment:* Brill; Leiden; 1987.
-A. Thomson and M.A Rahim: *Islam in al-Andalus*; part two; Taha Publishers; London; 1996.
-A. Tibawi: English Speaking Orientalists; in *Islamic Quarterly*; vol 8; pp. 25-45.
-J.V. Tolan ed., *Medieval Christian Perceptions of Islam*; Routledge; London; 1996.
-David. M. Traboulay: *Columbus and Las Casas*; University Press of America, New York, London, 1994.
-L. Valensi: *Le Maghreb avant la Prise d'Alger;* Paris; 1969.
-L. Valensi: *North Africa Before the French Conquest; 1790-1830*; tr. by K.J. Perkins; Africana Publishing Company; London; 1977.
-W.M. Watt: *Muslim Christian Encounters*; Routledge; London; 1991.
-E. Williams: *Capitalism and Slavery*; North Carolina; 1944.
-E.R. Wolf: *Europe and the People Without History*; University of California Press; Berkeley; 1982.

Printed in Great Britain
by Amazon